THE ZULU WAR
AND THE
80th REGIMENT OF FOOT

Robert Hope

Published by

CHURNET VALLEY BOOKS

43 Bath Street
Leek
Staffordshire
01538 399033

ISBN 1897949 24 3

Printed in Great Britain by the Ipswich Book Company, Suffolk

Colours of the 80th Regiment carried throughout the Sekukuni and Zulu Wars 1878-79
Artist Geoff Bell

To the Soldiers
Past, Present and Future
and their Families

Lord Chelmsford

King Cetshwayo

CONTENTS

10. Analysis Report on the 80th Regiment of Foot
General Information
Rank and File, Places of Birth - Counties
Rank and File, Places of Enlistment
Year and Month of Attestation 1854-1878 1)Non commissioned Officers. 2) Privates. 3) Rank and File.
Rank and File, Trades and Occupations
Epilogue The Costs of War
Casualties of the 80th Regiment of Foot
Supplementary List of Officers, Non-commissioned Officers and Men who died 1877-1880
Appendix Members of the 1st Squadron Mounted Infantry
Bibliography

Maps, Plates, Sketches and Photographs

FOREWORD
by Colonel H.C.B. Cook O.B.E., Late South Staffords

Robert Hope is to be congratulated for producing the full record of the services of the Eightieth Regiment of Foot in the Zulu War and elsewhere in South Africa during the period. Whenever people nowadays think of this contest they tend to remember only the disaster to the Twenty-Fourth Foot at Isandhlwana and the subsequent defence of Rorkes Drift and to forget the final victory at Ulundi, when the Eightieth formed most of the front of the British square and by its controlled volleys was largely responsible for smashing the Zulu attack before their 'Impi' could come to close quarters. Very few people will remember that the Eightieth itself had suffered a miniature Isandhlwana when a detachment was surprised and overwhelmed at the Intombi River.

The Intombi Drift must loom large in any account of the Regiment's activities and it received much publicity at the time. One contemporary book containing portraits of the 'Heroes of the Zulu War' included Captain Moriarty, who commanded the troops involved, among the column commanders and other leading soldiers. Actually the blame for the disaster must rest upon Moriarty, for any officer who allows his men to be surprised and virtually massacred while still in their tents in hostile country can hardly escape responsibility; but the story that he was killed in his night-shirt while urging his men to fight on appealed to Victorian sentimentality. A modern critic may well wonder why in the circumstances he was in his night-shirt and why some of those who escaped across the river were stark naked. However the whole sorry episode was largely retrieved by the gallantry of Colour Sergeant Booth and his small party in covering the withdrawal of the survivors. Booth was awarded a well deserved Victoria Cross, the second to a member of the Eightieth during the campaign.

The sad sequel to the disaster concerned the officer present, Lieutenant Harward, who commanded the small body on the near bank. Unlike Moriarty he had stood his men to at the first sign of danger and it was their steady covering fire that enabled at least a few of the main party to get away. As the Zulus swarmed round, Harward decided it was essential to get help from the Regiment, situated about five miles away, and as he was, he claimed, the only one who could ride, mounted his horse, left Booth in charge and galloped off for assistance. He was subsequently court marshalled for 'shamefully abandoning his men in the face of the enemy'. The court accepted his explanation and he was acquitted, but his career was in ruins and he had to resign his commission. His name is not inscribed with the other officers of the Eightieth who fought in Zululand on the 'Ulundi Vase' kept in the officer's mess.

One disadvantage from which the Eightieth suffered in South Africa was that it was always having to find numerous detachments. Indeed it is recorded that when it was about to leave South Africa for home in 1880, it was the first time it had been concentrated since it had sent off a large detachment from Hong Kong to take part in a punitive expedition to Perak in Malaya in 1875. During its whole time in South Africa it was continually on the move and usually under field conditions, although the only actual operations in which it was involved were those against the Swazi chief Sekukuni. Whenever it found itself in or near a town, it nearly always received messages from the civil authorities congratulating it on its good behaviour. Its final service, was when just after it had left Pretoria on the first stage of its journey home, it was suddenly diverted to Potchefstroom, where a number of potentially hostile Boers had gathered. The Boer leader was arrested and the threatening assembly dispersed without any bloodshed. This action probably postponed the outbreak of the First Boer War for a year and once again the local authorities testified to the excellent conduct of the troops. This good reputation of the Eightieth was to be kept down the years. When in 1945, as the 2nd South Staffords, it took part in the liberation of Norway, after having, as part of the 1st Airborne Division distinguished itself at Arnhem by being the only British Battalion to win two Victoria Crosses in the same battle during the 1939-45 War and was about to return to the UK, the Commanding Officer received a letter from his Brigadier saying: "I have heard through entirely reliable Civil Affairs sources that the inhabitants of Eidsvoll were much impressed by the discipline and behaviour of your Battalion while it was quartered there. Before the war they had Norwegians and during the war Germans; yet they consider that your Battalion set by far the highest standard of all.

Apart from the sixty men lost at the Intombi Drift, the Eightieth only had nine killed in action during the Zulu War and seven of these were with the mounted infantry detachment at Isandhlwana; but it had over twice as many who died from other causes. People looking back at these Colonial campaigns often note just the battle casualties and forget the horrendous total of the others. In 1852-3 the Eightieth had fought in the Second Burma War, for which its Colours were emblazoned with the Campaign Honour 'Pegu', and during the eighteen months it was in the country it had only ten men killed in action, but lost over three hundred and fifty officers and men, mainly from disease!

At a time when few English regiments were at all strongly linked with the areas they were supposed to represent, the Eightieth always had a strong Staffordshire connection. Its subsidiary title of the 'Staffordshire Volunteers' arose from the fact that it had been originally raised in 1793 mainly from volunteers from the Staffordshire Militia. The list of casualties in the Zulu War shows that twenty-five percent of its men came from Staffordshire and another twenty-five percent from adjacent Midland counties. This proportion continued down the years. I still have details of my machine gun platoon in the 2nd South Staffords in Bangalore in 1934 and they show fifty percent Staffordshire and twenty-five percent other Midlanders.

The outstanding character in the Eightieth in South Africa was its Commanding Officer, Charles Tucker. He went on to command a division in the South African War and was finally G.O.C. in C. Scottish Command, a rather unusual job for an Englishman. In 1911 he became Colonel of the South Staffordshire Regiment and he continued to be so until he died, well into his nineties in 1935, there being no age limit for the appointment at that time. To the end he retained the liveliest interest in his Regiment and although latterly living in the South of France seldom missed an important function. There are numerous stories about him. As the British square was about to advance at Ulundi, he saw one of his company on his knees and his stentorian voice shouted: 'Captain .... this is no time to hedge your bets with the Almighty. Your place is leading your Company'. When the Eightieth arrived in Dublin on its return from South Africa its uniforms were in a very tattered state and a staff officer came aboard to suggest that its landing should be prosponed for a day so that some fresh issues could be made to smarten it up. Tucker blasted the wretched officer off the ship with the comments; 'My Eightieth may be a bared arsed lot, but most of them have not slept in a proper bed for months and they are bloody well going to do so tonight'. So the scruffy looking Eightieth did march through to the cheers of admiring crowds. Tucker was well known throughout the Army for his strong and often lurid language. At a much later date, after he had become Colonel of the South Staffordshire Regiment he visited Lichfield Cathedral to see the Zulu War Memorial and found that some assegais which had adorned it had been removed, as the then Dean felt that weapons of war were unsuitable in a church. He summoned the Dean and in no uncertain terms told him what he thought of him and his opinions. As the party left the Cathedral the Verger remarked to the Depot Commander: 'I think perhaps we should have the sacred edifice re-consecrated'.

The Eightieth continued to have a somewhat tribal feeling for long after it became the 2nd Battalion, South Staffordshire Regiment in 1881. To its officers and men it was always the Eightieth. When I was commissioned in 1932, I was, in conformity with the rules at that time attached for my first year to the 1st Battalion at Lichfield and was duly, 'dined in'. When I arrived in India I found a formal invitation to dine with the officers of His Majesty's Eightieth Foot. Being a fairly honest chap I felt I should point out that I had already been, 'dined in' to the Regiment. I was told firmly; 'You may have been, 'dined in', but now you have the honour to be a member of the Eightieth'.

PREFACE

British armies have taken part in many theatres of war throughout the world in conflicts ranging from small colonial wars to those of world war status. The 80th Regiment of Foot came into existence during 1793, and from that point in time has been employed both at home and abroad in many parts of the world.

In May 1876, the first detachment of the 80th Regiment, consisting of three hundred men under the command of Lieutenant-Colonel Twenlow, arrived in South Africa. The Regiment were to remain there until May 1880 and were to be engaged during 1879 in the war against the Zulu Nation. The British and Colonial forces invaded Zululand in January 1879, anticipating an easy victory, but during the engagements against the Zulus, the British and their Colonial allies received a number of serious set-backs and despite being seen as a small Colonial war, apparently of little consequence, few campaigns have attracted so much controversy. When the Zulu War is mentioned, Isandhlwana, the major disaster which took place on January 22nd 1879, is the first to come to mind. In this battle, the British and Colonial forces were attacked and a thousand of their number slaughtered. The heroic defence of the Army's hospital and stores at Rorke's Drift is also famously remembered.

Following the defeat at Isandhlwana, a second disaster occurred on March 12th 1879 at the Intombi River and this involved a detachment of Company strength from the 80th Regiment of Foot. Initially the 80th were stationed at Luneburg to protect the border and to keep an eye on the Transvaal Boers. However, during the latter part of the war, for the second invasion of Zululand, the 80th formed part of the 'Flying Column' which was under the command of Colonel Wood VC CB and the Regiment had the distinction of being in the vanguard of the force which took part in the final battle of the Zulu War at Ulundi on July 4th 1879.

The Victoria Cross, Britain's highest award for bravery, was awarded no fewer than twenty-three times for actions during the Zulu War. Of these, two were awarded to members of the 80th Regiment of Foot.

The contents of this book are meant as a guide to the involvement of the 80th Regiment of Foot in South Africa around 1879. It is also hoped that it will give a brief insight into the men of the 80th Regiment of Foot, who they were and what they were like. The information relates to those soldiers listed on the medal list for the South Africa Medal whose entitlement is described under General Order No.103 dated August 1st 1880, a total of seven hundred and fifty names. A further one hundred and seventy-one medals were conferred to soldiers of the 80th under General Order No.134 dated October 1880. Reference is also made to the South Africa Medal list compiled by D.R.Forsyth, through which a further two hundred and ninety named recipients belonging to the 80th have been identified. In all, a grand total of one thousand, two hundred and eleven medals were awarded to members of the 80th Regiment of Foot.

The book does not try to describe the soldier's life in detail, the hardships, joys and grief, the ability to withstand fatigue and sickness, the endurance and stamina required in a foreign clime. However, it is hoped that it will, in some small way, illustrate the type of man that filled the ranks of a typical British army regiment of the time and also prove useful for future research and study.

ACKNOWLEDGEMENTS

First and foremost I must thank Linda my wife and Jonathan my son for their unlimited forbearance, listening, supporting and accompanying me in what must have appeared at times an unquenchable thirst for knowledge with visits to museums, libraries, churches, graveyards, etc, in my quest.

I am indebted to the generous help of the staff of the Staffordshire Regiment's Regimental Museum at Whittington Barracks near Lichfield. They have given freely of their time and the use of their priceless and valuable records. Special mention must be made of the Regimental Secretary, Major E.Green and of Major R.D.W.McLean, (retired Regimental Secretary, and Major M.K.Beedle MBE, who have always been at hand to offer help and advice.

Without the help of the well-established institutions such as the Public Records Office at Kew, London and the National Army Museum, Chelsea, it would have proved difficult to obtain and collect the necessary information. I would like to acknowledge the help and assistance given by the staff of these establishments. Thanks also to the South African Library, Cape Town, South Africa.

I must also mention the many friends, colleagues and family who have shown an interest, given their reassurance and advocated that the book should be completed; too many to mention by name.

I also acknowledge all those nameless people far and wide who have given me help - the museum attendant or serving soldier, vicar or verger, church flower arranger or grave digger, the local historian or policeman; I thank them all for their help.

Thanks to Harry and Samuel Wassall, grandsons, and Stephen Wassall, great grandson of Samuel Wassall VC for their help in the research of the man who was awarded the first of the Zulu War Victoria Crosses, and to Victor Charles Booth and Barry Booth who helped in compiling the information on their grandfather and great grandfather, Anthony Booth VC. Also for Angela Cobbin's help in obtaining information about William Ingram Cobbin MRCS.

It has previously been mentioned that I have had the freedom of the Regimental records at Whittington Barracks. It is with the Staffordshire Regiment's kind permission that some of the Regiment's time in South Africa has been reproduced direct from the 80th Regiment's Regimental Digest. The Museum have given their kind permission for the photographs of South Africa to be reproduced.

The photographs of St.Michael's Chapel and memorials within Lichfield Cathedral are reproduced by kind permission of the Dean and Chapter of Lichfield Cathedral.

Chapter 1
A BRIEF HISTORY OF THE REGIMENT

The Staffordshire Regiment, (The Prince of Wales's)
During the year 1993, the Staffordshire Regiment, 'The Prince of Wales's', so very nearly disappeared like so many distinguished Regiments destined to be only names on a bookshelf or in a museum. But the Government of the day suddenly changed their mind and reprieved this threat of extinction. The soldiers who serve in the Regiment may be soldiers of the Queen, but above all they are members of the 'Staffords'. It was a relief for the Regiment, for its members past and present and for their families and for all the friends of the Regiment, that the Staffordshire Regiment was allowed to survive and remain a 'living history' as opposed to a dead one.

The Staffordshire Regiment has evolved from the various amalgamations of four regiments, the 38th, 80th, 64th and the 98th Regiments of Foot. Throughout the histories of these four distinguished regiments, they have undergone numerous restructurings including name changes. The history of the Regiment can be traced back as far as 1705, when Colonel Luke Lillingston raised a regiment at Lichfield in the County of Staffordshire on March 25th of that year. The original headquarters and place for enlistment was the 'Kings Head' in Bird Street. The building is still in existence as a public house to this day. From 1705 to 1707, the Regiment was based in Ireland. From 1707 to 1764, it was posted abroad to Antigua with detachments in Montserrat and St.Kitts. The 38th Regiment of Foot was formed in 1751 from Lillingston's Regiment and during 1781, it was given the title of the '1st Staffordshire' Regiment.

In 1793, Henry William Lord Paget raised a Regiment of Foot which was to be known as the 80th Regiment of Foot 'Staffordshire Volunteers'. Lord Paget later rose to the rank of Field Marshall and became the Marquis of Anglesey KG, GCB. The 80th Regiment was at first based at Chatham in Kent and was then posted to Guernsey in 1794.

During the year 1758 the 64th Regiment of Foot was formed, but the origins of this particular regiment go back further to 1756, when the 2nd Battalion the 11th Regiment of Foot (North Devonshire) was formed and stationed in Southampton. The first Colonel was the Hon. John Barrington. In 1782 the 64th Regiment was given the title of the '2nd Staffordshire'.

The 98th Regiment of Foot was formed in 1824 and first based at Chichester in Sussex. Major-General Henry Conran was its first Colonel, with Colonel Mildmay Fane its Lieutenant-Colonel and Commanding Officer. The Regiment's first appointment abroad was in Cape Town for six years between 1824-1830. In 1876 the 98th was given the title of the 'Prince of Wales's Regiment.

In 1881, the 38th Regiment of Foot, '1st Staffordshire' and the 80th Regiment of Foot,'Staffordshire Volunteers' were amalgamated to form 'The South Staffordshire Regiment', and became the 1st and 2nd Battalions respectively. During the same year, the 64th Regiment '2nd Staffordshire' and the 98th Regiment 'Prince of Wales's were also merged to form 'the 'North Staffordshire Regiment', again the Regiments becoming the 1st and 2nd Battalions respectively. In 1920 the North Staffordshire Regiment regained the title of 'the Prince of Wales's.

Due to the restructuring of the British Army in 1948, both the South Staffordshire and North Staffordshire Regiments lost a Battalion each, the South Staffordshire's losing its 1st Battalion and the North Staffordshire its 2nd Battalion. Then in 1959 the South Staffordshire and North Staffordshire Regiments were finally amalgamated to form the Staffordshire Regiment, 'The Prince of Wales's Regiment.

Throughout its long history, the Regiment has visited many parts of the world and taken part in many wars and campaigns. It has won many battle honours and its members many campaign medals and gallantry awards. These antecedent regiments and the Staffordshire Regiment have between them been credited with no less than two hundred and five battle honours, the first being 'Guadaloupe' in 1759, the last two being 'Wadi al Batin' and 'Gulf 1991', for actions during the Gulf War. The

Regiment saw its peak numbers during the First World War when the North and South Staffordshire Regiments raised a total of thirty five battalions between them. During World War II, a total of seventeen battalions were to serve King and Country. So far thirteen members of the Regiment have been awarded the Victoria Cross, Britain's highest award for gallantry. The first was gained during the Indian Muntiny at Cawnpore in 1857 and the last two for bravery during the Battle at Arnhem in Holland 1944 - the South Staffordshire Regiment has the unique distinction of being the only Regiment during the whole of the Second World War to win two Victoria Crosses in the same battle.

There is no doubt that the soldiers of today, like those of yesteryear, will agree that their actions and spirit are not given solely for their Sovereign and Country, but also for their fellow comrades and for their Regiment - the Staffordshire Regiment.

THE COLOURS

In ages past, in the midst of battle, the rallying point was the flag or flags of the regiment. This flag is known as the 'Colours'. Each regiment or battalion has two 'Colours', one referred to as the Queen's or King's 'Colours', the other the Regimental 'Colours'. For the purposes of this book the former will be referred to as the Sovereign's 'Colours'.

The present Sovereigns's 'Colours' are that of the Union flag with the name of the Regiment in the circle, the badge depicted inside the circle with the crown above. On these 'Colours' are displayed thirty-four selected Battle Honours gained by the Regiment in the two world wars as follows:-

MONS	CAMBRAI 1917, 1918	CAEN	ROME
MARNE 1914	ST QUENTIN CANAL	DYLE	SICILY 1943
LOOS	SARI BAIR	NORTH WEST EUROPE 1940, 1944	NORTH AFRICA 1940, 1943
ARMENTIERES 1914	VITTORIO VENETO	FALAISE	AISNE 1914, 1918
YPRES 1914, 1917, 1918	YPRES-COMINES CANAL	NOYERS	MARRADI
MESSINES 1917, 1918	NW FRONTIERS INDIA 1915	LANDING AT SICILY	ANZIO
SOMME 1916, 1918	KUT AL AMARA 1917	MEDJEZ PLAIN	BURMA 1943, 1944
ARRAS 1917, 1918	BRIEUX BRIDGEHEAD	ARNHEM 1944	CHINDITS 1944
SELLE			

The Sovereign's 'Colours' represent the British Crown and its armed forces. The present Regimental 'Colours' are yellow with the badge encircled with the title of the Regiment embroidered on a crimson background. On the bottom corner nearest to the stave is emblazoned the Spinx superscribed 'Egypt' and on the outer bottom corner the China Dragon. The fringes of the 'Colours' are of yellow and black which is unique in as much it represents two regiments. The Regimental 'Colours' are embellished with a further thirty-eight battle honours, as follows:

GUADALOUPE 1759	NIVE	PEGU	CENTRAL INDIA
MARTINIQUE 1762	VITTORIA	ALMA	SOUTH AFRICA 1878-1879
MONTE VIDEO	ST SEBASTIAN	BUSHIRE	HAFIR
ST LUCIA 1803	MOODKEE	SEVASTOPOL	KIRBEKAN
SURINAM	PENINSULA	RESHIRE	NILE 1884-1885
CORUNNA	AVA	LUCKNOW	AFGHANISTAN 1919
ROLICA	PUNJAUB	KOOSH-AB	SOUTH AFRICA 1900-1902
VIMIERA	FEROZESHAH	PERSIA	MARTINIQUE 1794
SALAMANCA	SOBRAON	EGYPT 1882	
BUSACO	INKERMAN		
BADAJOZ			

Both the Sovereign's and Regimental 'Colours' are of great significance to the Regiment and in the past many men have been killed or severely wounded defending them. One can still see, within the walls of Lichfield Cathedral and the Garrison Church of St.George's, many old and former 'Colours' which have been laid to rest. They may be tattered, torn and faded - even threadbare - but they still hold the memories of days long past, of the men who fought and served with the Regiment, of the battles they fought in and the battle honours they bravely gained.

The Ulundi Vase.

Part of the Regimental Silver

St. Michael's Chapel. Dedicated to the Staffordshire Regiment 31st January 1959.

Lichfield Cathedral.

THE REGIMENTAL TREE

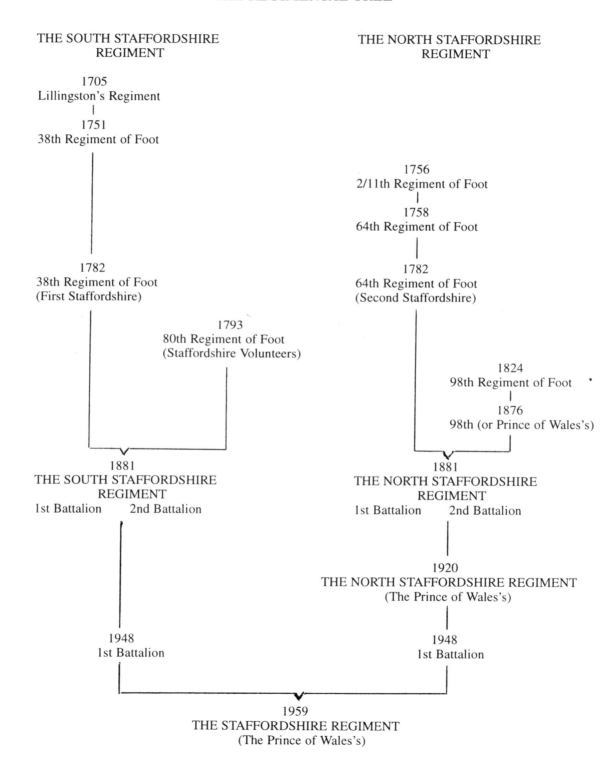

THE SOUTH STAFFORDSHIRE
REGIMENT

1705
Lillingston's Regiment

1751
38th Regiment of Foot

THE NORTH STAFFORDSHIRE
REGIMENT

1756
2/11th Regiment of Foot

1758
64th Regiment of Foot

1782
38th Regiment of Foot
(First Staffordshire)

1782
64th Regiment of Foot
(Second Staffordshire)

1793
80th Regiment of Foot
(Staffordshire Volunteers)

1824
98th Regiment of Foot

1876
98th (or Prince of Wales's)

1881
THE SOUTH STAFFORDSHIRE
REGIMENT
1st Battalion   2nd Battalion

1881
THE NORTH STAFFORDSHIRE
REGIMENT
1st Battalion   2nd Battalion

1920
THE NORTH STAFFORDSHIRE REGIMENT
(The Prince of Wales's)

1948
1st Battalion

1948
1st Battalion

1959
THE STAFFORDSHIRE REGIMENT
(The Prince of Wales's)

The Former Colours of the Staffordshire Regiment in Lichfield Cathedral

The 80th Regiment of Foot (Staffordshire Volunteers)

The 80th Regiment of Foot was formed in 1793. Henry William Lord Paget, later the Marquis of Anglesey KG GCB, was responsible for raising the Regiment. He came from a military family and eventually rose to the rank of Field Marshall.

The recruitment area for the 80th was primarily in the County of Staffordshire although the Regiment was at first based in Chatham in Kent. Many of the Regiment's first recruits came from the vast estates owned by Henry Paget's father which were situated in the centre of Staffordshire, and the Regiment was given the title of the 'Staffordshire Volunteers'. Foot regiments of the day wore red tunic uniforms. To distinguish the regiments from each other, they had differing coloured 'facings' - collars and cuffs. The colour designated to the 80th Regiment of Foot was yellow.

The Regiment first saw active service on the continent of Europe in Holland during 1794, under the command of the Duke of York. In its relatively short history of some eighty-eight years, two members of the Regiment were awarded the Victoria Cross, both for brave deeds during the Zulu War of 1879. Private Samuel Wassall gained the award at Isandhlwana on January 22nd 1879 and Colour Sergeant Anthony Booth was awarded the VC for his part in the battle at the Intombi River on March 12th 1879.

The 80th Regiment of Foot (Staffordshire Volunteers) served in many parts of the world and for its participation in a number of battles and campaigns was awarded a total of seven battle honours - Egypt with the Sphinx, Moodkee, Ferozeshah, Sabraon, Pegu, Central India and South Africa 1878/79.

During the Napoleonic Wars when the French General and Emperor endeavoured to conquer Europe and beyond, Napoleon's forces entered the continent of Africa, his route to India. The French fleet suffered a major defeat at the Battle of the Nile at the hands of Nelson and consequently they had a major force land-locked in Egypt. Britain and her allies sent armies from England, the Mediterranean, the Cape of Good Hope and India to fight this French army and the 80th Regiment was part of this, coming from India. They suffered greatly on their journey both from and then back again to India. They had to travel via the Red Sea and across the desert to the Nile and in the end unfortunately arrived too late to take part in the fighting! However, both the British and Indian Governments were so impressed by the 80th's performance, the Regiment received the battle honour 'The Sphinx superscribed Egypt' and the British Government issued the 'Military General Service Medal' (1793-1814) to its troops. A total of twenty-nine bars were issued, the first being 'Egypt' ('March 2nd - September 2nd 1801').

During Britain's rule of India there were many wars and campaigns. During the First Sikh War in India, the 80th were to gain a further three battle honours. The Sikh army, with 60,000 European trained soldiers, 200 guns and support from numerous irregular forces, became increasingly dominant in state affairs. The British and Indian Governments had only 35,000 men and one hundred guns to oppose them, deployed at Ferozepur, Ludhiana, Ambala and Meerut. The invading army crossed the Sutlej into British Territory on December 11th 1845.

At Moodkee on December 18th 1845 a force of between 15,000 and 25,000 Sikhs was met by 12,000 men of the British and Indian Army under the command of General Sir Hugh Gough. The battle commenced with artillery and the cavalry held the Sikh's cavalry at bay. The British regiments facing the worst of the fighting eventually drove the Sikhs from the field of battle. It was calculated that the Sikh forces had lost seventeen of their forty guns and a great many lives. The British and Indian casualties amounted to 870 killed or wounded and of these twenty-four belonged to the 80th, one officer and nineteen men being wounded and four killed. A total of 824 soldiers from the 80th took part in the Battle at Moodkee.

Following the victory at Moodkee, General Sir Hugh Gough moved to confront the main Sikh forces, approximately 50,000 strong, with British and Indian forces which had been reinforced and now totalled 18,000 soldiers. The battle at Ferozeshah commenced late in the afternoon of December 21st and continued the next day. Gough's forces eventually cleared the Sikh's encampment but then had to oppose a further 35,000 fresh troops. Their leader Tej Singh eventually withdrew. The total Sikh losses were estimated to be 10,000 casualties and seventy-four guns captured; the British and Indian losses were in the region of 2,800 killed and wounded. A total of 817 soldiers from the 80th Regiment of Foot took part in this battle, one hundred and twenty became casualties, four officers were killed and four wounded, thirty-nine men were killed and seventy-three wounded.

The final battle took place on February 10th 1846 at Sobraon, a British and Indian force of 20,000 facing 35,000 Sikhs. The battle commenced with artillery followed by attacks involving infantry; the Sikhs' fortifications were finally breached and they were driven across the Sutlej River, suffering 10,000 casualties with a loss of sixty-seven guns. General Sir Hugh Gough's forces sustained 2,385 killed and wounded. Eight hundred and sixteen men of the 80th took part, four officers were wounded, thirteen men killed and seventy-four wounded. For this campaign, the 'Sutlej Campaign Medal' (December 18th 1845 - February 22nd 1846) was issued. There were three bars issued to this Medal: 'Ferozeshuhur 1845', 'Aliwal 1846' and 'Sobraon 1846'.

Six years later, during the Second Burma War, the 80th won a further battle honour, 'Pegu'. At the conclusion of the First Burma War, the King of Ava signed the Treaty of Yendaboo on February 24th 1826 which allowed trading facilities at the port of Rangoon. When trading ships including British warships were increasingly attacked, on April 2nd 1852 war was declared again. The 80th Regiment was part of an expeditionary force sent on March 28th 1852 under the command of Major General Godwin. Although the Province of Pegu was annexed on December 20th 1852, the war was not concluded until June 30th 1853, following the capture of Donubyu. The 'Indian General Service Medal' (1854-1895) was issued. The Medal was to have twenty-nine bars, the first being 'Pegu' (March 28th 1852-June 30th 1853) which was authorised on December 22nd 1853. A total number of 460 members of Her Majesty's 80th Regiment of Foot took part in this war and were awarded the medal with the 'bar'. The 80th Regiment suffered five officers killed and four wounded, and four men killed and forty wounded.

During the Indian Mutiny the 80th gained its penultimate battle honour. They arrived at Calcutta during February 1858 and took part in the closing stages of the mutiny, making endless marches in minor punitive expeditions, a hazardous type of warfare lasting some twelve months for which the battle honour 'Central India' was awarded. A total of 153 members of the Regiment were awarded the bar 'Central India' to the Indian Mutiny Medal for being part of the forces under the command of Major General Sir Hugh Rose and Major General Whitlock between January and June 1858. A total of 811 members of the Regiment were issued with the 'Indian Mutiny Medal' (1857-1858), the majority with no bar.

The final battle honour awarded to the Regiment was gained for their services in South Africa during the years 1878 and 1879. The Regiment took part in various operations against Sekukuni during 1878 until the suppression of this Basuto tribe was suspended for varying reasons. Later the same year, one of these reasons, the expected war against the Zulu Nation, commenced when the British and Colonial combined forces invaded Zululand on January 11th 1879, and effectively ended when the Zulu leader, Chief Cetshwayo was captured on August 28th 1879. The final battle took place at Ulundi on July 4th 1879.

Members of the Regiment took part in the victories and some of the reverses of this small war. British and Colonial casualty returns for the war show that the number killed and wounded were 1,987, inclusive of the native returns which were never complete. The 80th suffered a total of seventy-seven casualties. At the conclusion of the Zulu War, the Regiment again embarked on the task of defeating Sekukuni. Following a number of minor confrontations, on November 28th 1879 the British and Colonial forces attacked and took the Sekukuni Town stronghold. At this final battle a total of 256 were killed and wounded, but a wounded private was the only casualty belonging to the 80th.

During the year of 1881, the 80th Regiment of Foot (Staffordshire Volunteers) ceased to exist as an independent regiment, amalgamating with the 38th Regiment of Foot (1st Staffordshire) to form a new regiment, the South Staffordshire Regiment.

The 80th Regiment of Foot

Marches:	(Quick) Come Lasses and Lads (Traditional)
	(Slow) In the Garb of Old Gaul (Reid)
Nick-names:	The Staffordshire Knots
	The Pump and Tortoise Brigade

The Staffordshire Regiment (The Prince of Wales's)

Marches:	(Quick) The Staffordshire Regiment (Traditional)
	(Slow) God Bless the Prince of Wales (Richards)

Postings: The 80th Regiment of Foot -

1793-1794	Chatham
1794	Guernsey
1794-1795	Campaign in the Low Counties
1795	Isle Dieu Expedition
1796-1797	Cape Town
1797-1801	Trincomalee, Ceylon
1801-1802	Egypt, Det. Malabar Coast Southern India
1802-1803	Madras, Det. Poonamalee
1803-1804	Operations in Southern Mahratta Country
1804-1807	Cannanore, Southern India
1805	Operations against Nairs of Wynaud
1807-1809	Seringapatam, Southern India
1809-1811	Cannanore, Southern India
1811-1813	Seringapatam, Southern India
1813-1817	Quilon, Southern India
1817-1818	Chatham
1818	Colchester, Det.
1818-1819	Hull, Det.
1819	Glasgow, Det.
1819-1820	Aberdeen, Det.
1820	Edinburgh, Det.
1821	Gibraltar
1822-1828	Malta
1828-1830	Corfu, Ionian Is.
1830-1831	Cephalonia, Ionian Is. Dets.
1831-1832	Lancashire and Cheshire
1832	Dublin
1832-1833	Belfast, Det.
1833-1834	Naas, County Kildare, Dets.
1834	Lancashire and Cheshire
1834-1835	Salford
1835	Liverpool, Dets.
1835-1836	Chatham
1836-1837	Sydney N.S.W. (Convict escort duty to Australia)
1837-1841	Windsor N.S.W. Dets. incl. Norfolk Is.
1840-1844	Det. in New Zealand
1841-1845	Parramatta, N.S.W. Dets.
1845	Agra, United Provinces
1845-1846	1st Sikh War
1846-1847	Lahore, Punjab
1847	Meerut, U.P.
1847-1852	Dinapore, Bihar
1852-1853	2nd Burmese War
1853-1854	Calcutta
1854-1855	Fort George, Scotland
1855	Portsmouth
1855-1856	Aldershot
1856-1857	Fort Beaufort, Cape Colony. Dets.
1858-1859	Indian Mutiny
1859	Cawnpore, U.P.

1860-1861	Saugor, Central Provinces
1862-1864	Jhansi,U.P. Dets.Gwalior & Seepree, Central India
1864-1865	Dum Dum, Bengal
1865	Bhutan Field Force
1866-1867	Devonport
1867	Portland, Det. Weymouth
1867-1868	Aldershot
1868-1869	Fleetwood, Dets. Leeds & Liverpool
1869-1870	Birr. County Tipperary Dets.
1870-1872	Belfast, Dets.
1872	Singapore, Dets. Penang & Malacca
1872-1876	Hong Kong
1875-1876	Det. Perak Operations
1876-1877	Singapore
1877	King William's Town, Cape Colony
1877-1878	Pietermaritzburg, Natal. Det. Newcastle
1878-1879	Zulu War
1880-1881	Dublin

1881 Amalgamation   Formation of the South Staffordshire Regiment

1881-1883	Tralee, County Kerry
1883-1844	Lichfield, Det. Weedon
1884-1886	Manchester, Det. Weedon
1886-1888	Plymouth
1888-1889	Devonport
1889-1891	Curragh, County Kildare
1891-1893	Aldershot
1893-1895	Cairo
1895-1897	Southern India, Det. Cannanore
1895-1898	Dets. Calicut & Malapuram Southern India
1897-1900	Thayetmyo, Burma. Det. Meiktila
1900-1902	Amballa & Subathu, Punjab
1902-1904	Agra
1904-1907	Allahabad U.P. Det. Benares
1907-1911	Pretoria, Transvaal
1911-1913	Lichfield
1911-1914	Aldershot
1914-1918	France and Flanders
1918-1919	Duren, Germany
1919	Liverpool
1919-1920	Lichfield
1920-1922	Cork
1922-1923	Irvinestown, County Fermanagh
1923-1926	Plymouth
1926	Hamilton Dets. Glasgow and elsewhere
1926-1928	Shorncliffe
1928-1929	Malta
1929-1930	Palestine
1930-1932	Cairo
1932-1936	Bangalore, Southern India
1936-1939	Cawnpore U.P.
1936-1938	Det. Benares
1939-1940	Nowshera N.W.F.P.
1940-1943	United Kingdom
1943	Sicily, Italy
1943-1944	United Kingdom (1944 - Arnhem)
1944-1945	United Kingdom
1945	Norway
1946	Schoningen, Germany
1946-1948	Marienthal, Germany
1948	Sudbury, Derbyshire

1948 Reorganisation The South Staffordshire Regiment loses one of its battalions. The 1st Battalion (38th Regiment of Foot) and the 2nd Battalion (80th Regiment of Foot) combine to form the single 1st Battalion.

1948	Sudbury, Derbyshire
1948-1949	Lichfield
1949-1951	Hong Kong
1951-1952	Ballykinler
1952-1954	Minden, Germany
1954-1955	Tel-el-Kebir, Egypt
1955-1957	Nicosia, Cyprus
1957-1959	Luneberg, Germany

1959 Amalgamation The South and North Staffordshire Regiments are amalgamated to form the Staffordshire Regiment (The Prince of Wales's)

1959	Minden
1959-1960	Lichfield
1960-1961	Kenya
1961-1962	Colchester
1962-1964	Kenya (including Uganda Mutinies)
1964-1968	Dover (Det. British Honduras Aug. 1965 - Feb. 1967)
1968-1970	Berlin
1971	Bahrain and Sharjah
1971-1973	Dover (Armagh Sept. 1972 - Jan. 1973)
1973-1977	Osnabruck (Londonderry 1974, Belfast 1976)
1977-1979	Colchester Det. Belize July 1977 - Jan. 1978
1979-1981	Londonderry
1981-1983	Gibraltar
1983-1986	Colchester (South Armagh Feb. - July 1984)
1986-1990	Fallingbostel
1990-1991	Saudi Arabia - Iraq - Kuwait (Gulf War)
1991-1994	Chester
1994-1996	Ballykinler
1996-	Ternhill, Shropshire - Hong Kong Sept.'96- Feb.'97

Commanding Officers of the 80th Regiment of Foot - Staffordshire Volunteers

1793-1795	Lieutenant-Colonel Lord Henry William Paget
1795	Lieutenant-Colonel Forbes Champagnee
1795-1801	Lieutenant-Colonel Josiah Champagnee
1801	Lieutenant-Colonel William Ramsay
1801-1803	Lieutenant-Colonel William Harness
1803-1804	Major John White
1804-1810	Lieutenant-Colonel Benjamin Forbes
1810-1815	Lieutenant-Colonel John White
1815-1817	Lieutenant-Colonel James Sturt
1817-1822	Lieutenant-Colonel James Cookson
1822-1837	Lieutenant-Colonel George Deane Pitt
1837-1845	Lieutenant-Colonel Narborough Baker
1845-1850	Lieutenant-Colonel Thomas Bunbury, C.B.
1850-1852	Lieutenant-Colonel Charles Lewis
1852-1858	Lieutenant-Colonel George Hutchinson
1858-1864	Lieutenant-Colonel Samuel Tolfrey Christie, C.B.
1864-1866	Lieutenant-Colonel Robert Hawkes
1866-1872	Lieutenant-Colonel Robert Prescott Harrison
1872-1877	Lieutenant-Colonel Hamilton Charles Smith
1877	Lieutenant-Colonel George Hamilton Twenlow
1877-1879	Lieutenant-Colonel Charles Frederick Amiel
1879-1884	Lieutenant-Colonel Charles Tucker, C.B.
1884-1887	Lieutenant-Colonel Charles Augustus Fitzgerald Creagh
1887-1891	Lieutenant-Colonel James Webber Smith
1891-1895	Lieutenant-Colonel John Edward Hale Prior

1895-1899	Lieutenant-Colonel William Moore
1899-1903	Lieutenant-Colonel Newton Seymore Allen
1903-1907	Lieutenant-Colonel Edward Kaye Daubeney, D.S.O.
1907-1911	Lieutenant-Colonel Ivone Kirkpatrick
1911-1915	Lieutenant-Colonel Charles Steer Davidson
1915	A/Lieutenant-Colonel Lionel Boyd Boyd-Moss
1915-1916	A/Lieutenant-Colonel Rosslewin Westropp Morgan, D.S.O.
1916-1917	A/Lieutenant-Colonel George Dawes, D.S.O., M.C.
1917-1918	A/Lieutenant-Colonel Clifton Edward Rawdon Grant Alban, D.S.O.
1918	A/Lieutenant-Colonel R. Orme, M.C.
1918-1919	A/Lieutenant-Colonel William John Jervoise Collas, D.S.O.
1919	A/Lieutenant-Colonel G.A. Yool, D.S.O.
1919-1921	Lieutenant-Colonel Alfred Henry Cotes James, D.S.O., M.V.O.
1921-1925	Lieutenant-Colonel Morris Benjamin Savage, C.B.E., D.S.O.
1925-1927	Lieutenant-Colonel Percy Ryan Conway Commings, C.M.G., D.S.O.
1927-1931	Lieutenant-Colonel Walter William Roche
1931-1934	Lieutenant-Colonel Guy de Courcy Glover, D.S.O., M.C.
1934-1935	Lieutenant-Colonel Percy Frederick Keene
1936-1939	Lieutenant-Colonel George Dawes, D.S.O., M.C.
1939-1941	Lieutenant-Colonel William Charles Green, M.C.
1941-1942	T/Lieutenant-Colonel Andrew Daniel Clinch
1942-1943	T/Lieutenant-Colonel Osmond Luxmore Jones
1943-1944	T/Lieutenant-Colonel William Derek Hessin McCardie
1944-1945	T/Lieutenant-Colonel Hugh Christopher Bolt Cook
1945-1948	T/Lieutenant-Colonel Dennis Bruce Pike

The South Staffordshire Regiment 1st Battalion (38th/80th)

1948	T/Lieutenant-Colonel Dennis Bruce Pike
1948-1951	Lieutenant-Colonel Frederick Lawrence Martin, D.S.O.
1951-1954	Lieutenant-Colonel Ronald Degg, D.S.O.
1954-1957	Lieutenant-Colonel John C. Commings, O.B.E.
1957-1959	Lieutenant-Colonel Michael Ward Brennan

The Staffordshire Regiment - The Prince of Wales's 1st Battalion (amalgamation)

1959	Lieutenant-Colonel Robert George Levett
1959-1961	Lieutenant-Colonel Robert Louis Hargroves
1961-1964	Lieutenant-Colonel Kenneth Mark Stuckey, M.B.E.
1964-1966	Lieutenant-Colonel Ralph Stewart Stewart-Wilson, M.C.
1966-1969	Lieutenant-Colonel Anthony Michael Cranstoun
1969-1971	Lieutenant-Colonel Derek Boorman
1971-1974	Lieutenant-Colonel John Gilbert Levey
1974-1976	Lieutenant-Colonel Malcolm Hugh McLarney, O.B.E.
1976-1979	Lieutenant-Colonel Michael John Hague
1979-1982	Lieutenant-Colonel John Robert Collins, O.B.E.
1982-1984	Lieutenant-Colonel Ian Lennox Freer, O.B.E.
1984-1988	Lieutenant-Colonel Timothy Richard Cottis, M.B.E.
1988-1989	Lieutenant-Colonel Nigel Hugh Christie Brown
1989-1991	Lieutenant-Colonel Charles Thomas Rodgers
1991-1994	Lieutenant-Colonel Nigel Stephen Alderman
1994-1996	Lieutenant-Colonel Simon James Knapper, M.B.E., M.C.
1996	Lieutenant-Colonel James Kenneth Tanner BA

N.B. The Officers listed above held the Ranks and Awards indicated at the time of being the Officer Commanding the Regiment. However for the majority, they were to be further promoted and honoured throughout their military careers.

Chapter **2**
THE ZULU WAR 1879

Brief history of the Zulu War

Military history is normally written by the victors and consequently may be somewhat biased! When the Dutch were defeated by the French in 1794, the Cape and its various harbours became available to French ships. To eliminate the threat of these French men-of-war controlling the seas in the area,the British set forth and seized the Cape in 1795. The Cape was handed back to the Dutch following the Peace Treaty of Amiens in 1801 but they were again to lose it to the British in 1806 during the Napoleonic War. The British then chose to remain there indefinitely to keep a base for their ships en route to India and the Far East

Of the tribes in Southern Africa, the Zulus were the strongest. They were a self-sufficient nation rearing cattle and cultivating the fertile river valleys. Zululand extended from the Pongola River in the North to the Tugela River in the South and from the coast in the east to the Drakensberg Mountains in the West. The Father of the Zulus was Shaka who was born about 1787 and assassinated in 1828. He ascended the throne of his tribe in 1816 and at that time had approximately four hundred warriors but by 1817 he had quadrupled his forces. At the time of his death he could call upon some thirty thousand warriors.

The Dutch, namely the Boers, shunning British domination, started to leave the area around the Cape to enter the interior looking for fresh land and self-rule. Good fertile land became in great demand and the black population although vastly outnumbering the whites, had to compete for it. As a result, the Zulu Nation was slowly being squeezed out by the British in the south, by the Portuguese in the north and the Dutch Boers coming from the west - the Transvaal and Orange Free State.

In the 1870s diamonds were discovered in South Africa. Many of the minerals were found on the surface, but many more were buried below the surface. Prospectors rushed to the area but the riches needed black labour - preferably cheap - to mine them. The principle political figures in South Africa who were to influence the events leading up to, and the implementation of the Zulu War were Sir Bartle Freer, Governor of Cape Colony and High Commissioner for Native Affairs in South Africa and Sir Theophilus Shepstone, Secretary for Native Affairs in Natal and Administrator of the Transvaal from 1877. Their Military Commander was Frederic Augustus Thesiger, Lieutenant-General Commanding British Forces in South Africa (who in 1878 inherited his father's title and became the 2nd Baron Chelmsford, Lord Chelmsford).

Whether or not the threat the Zulu Nation posed to the British was real or imagined, the facts were that the Zulu culture was based around military training and military institution and fifty thousand warriors could be called upon. Sir Bartle Freer felt that if the Zulus could be conquered, other tribes in Africa would be subdued and other states and areas subsequently would soon become part of the British Empire. Freer wanted a war with the Zulus, although his own Government in England did not. Taking advantage of the great distance from Britain and the length of time needed for communication, he eventually forced a war on the Zulus. A tract of land was in dispute and a court of inquiry was called which met at Rorke's Drift on March 7th 1878, but to his great annoyance, it was confirmed that the land belonged to the Zulus.

Another opportunity to challenge the Zulus came later in the year when two married Zulu women ran away and crossed the river Tugela into Natal. Some Zulu warriors followed them, eventually captured them and took them back to Zululand where they were executed. Sir Theophilus Shepstone demanded that the warriors be handed over to the Natal Police. The demands were not met - this was the excuse Sir Bartle Freer wanted. On December 11th 1878, on the banks of the River Tugela, an ultimatum was handed to King Cetshwayo's representatives, consisting of ten demands, the first four relating to the border incident. These had to be complied with inside twenty days:

1) Sihayo's brother and three sons were to be surrendered for trial by Natal Courts
2) A fine of five hundred head of cattle was to be paid for Mehlokazulu's outrages and for Cetshwayo's delay in acceding to Natal's previous request for surrender
3) A further fine of one hundred head of cattle was to be paid for the offence committed against a surveyor named Smith and a trader called Deighton
4) Mbilini and others to be named later, were to surrender for trial by the Transvaal Courts

The last six demands which had a time limit of thirty days were the most difficult for the Zulu King to fulfil, for in essence they were directed at the Zulu's traditions and their way of life and required them to submit to foreign rule - British rule!

5) The observance of the Zulu King's promises he made at his Coronation
6) A British Diplomatic resident to be stationed in Zululand to enforce these provisions
7) The Zulu Army to be disbanded
8) Young warriors to be free to marry
9) Missionaries to be allowed into Zululand to carry on with preaching
10) The Zulu Nation would not be able to declare war or implement any form of retribution including expulsion etc., without the consent of the British Resident or National Council

History shows that the ultimatum was such as to be impossible to comply with. War was inevitable but it was to be a war without any clear authority or justification and this war against the Zulus was against the desires of Her Majesty's Government in England.

The Zulu War started on January 11th and 12th 1879 when three columns of British and Colonial troops invaded Zululand. Their main tasks were to defeat the Zulu Army, destroy the Zulu King's principle residence, Ulundi, and to capture Cetshwayo the Zulu King. The British Military leaders believed the conflict would be over in six weeks! However, the Zulu warriors were to prove no pushover, even though they were armed only with spears and shields and a few obsolete rifles. The war effectively ended when the Zulu Army was defeated at Ulundi.

Lord Chelmsford at the onset of war had at his command seventeen thousand men consisting of five thousand regular infantry and fifteen hundred regular and irregular mounted infantry/calvalry, with the remainder made up of Native troops. Following the disaster at Isandhlwana and to ensure that Britain's might triumphed, reinforcements were hurried out from home to increase the British forces to thirty-four thousand men. Although they were still greatly outnumbered, they were confident of victory because of their modern weapons of war.

The first major battle took place at Inyezance on January 22nd when Colonel Pearson's No.1 Column was attacked by six thousand Zulus and the attack successfully repulsed. But this small and previously insignificant colonial war hit the headlines when the Zulus attacked and took the British base camp at Isandhlwana on January 22nd, a day in which over a thousand British and Colonial soldiers were slaughtered by a so-called army of savages, armed only with spears and shields. British honour was restored later that day when the hospital and stores at Rorke's Drift were successfully held by only one hundred and thirty-nine men against four thousand Zulus.

A further two reverses were to take place, one on March 12th when a Company of the 80th Regiment was attacked and many were killed at Myer's Drift on the Intombi River. The second when nearly two hundred men were killed in the disastrous action on the Hlobane Mountain on March 28th. But the battle which did most damage to the Zulus took place on March 29th at Kambula, when a force of twenty thousand warriors was chased off the battlefield. During the second invasion of Zululand on April 2nd, Lord Chelmsford's forces were attacked by twelve thousand Zulus at Gingindhlovu and were again driven off.

One of the most dramatic events that occurred during the war was at the Ityotosi River on June 1st when a European dynasty was brought to an abrupt end with the death of the Prince Imperial, Louis Napoleon (see page 176).

The final major battle against the Zulus was on July 4th at Ulundi when a force of twenty thousand Zulus was defeated and Ulundi and other kraals burnt to the ground.

On August 15th, the principle chiefs of the Zulus surrendered to Sir Garnet Wolseley and on August 28th, Cetshwayo the Zulu King was captured. On September 1st, the chiefs accepted the terms and conditions for settlement and the next day the British and Colonial troops started to withdraw from Zululand.

Battles and Events of the Zulu War

1 SEPTEMBER 1873
Cetshwayo was crowned King of the Zulus and was to rule until 1879 when he was deposed by the British. Cetshwayo was briefly restored 1883-1884.
11 DECEMBER 1878
On the banks of the lower Tugela River British representatives presented an **ultimatum** to Cetshwayo's emmissaries.
11/12 JANUARY 1879
The ultimatum expired and because of the non-compliance of the Zulus, the British Army invaded Zululand.
12 JANUARY 1879
The first of the Zulu kraals was attacked. Sihayo's kraal was to suffer the fate of many, when it was attacked by Colonel Glyn's No.3 Column.
22 JANUARY 1879
The first major battle of the campaign took place when Colonel Pearson's No.1 Column was attacked at Inyezane. The column successfully drove off a Zulu Impi of between four and six thousand warriors.
Lord Chelmsford divided his forces, leaving a part of his No.3 Column encamped at **Isandhlwana**. The camp was attacked and destroyed by a force of twenty thousand warriors - the British and Colonial forces suffered the worst defeat of the campaign when a thousand plus of their men were massacred
22/23 JANUARY 1879
Following the victory at Isandhlwana, part of the Zulu Impi broke away and marched to attack the post at **Rorke's Drift**. One hundred and thirty-nine men successfully defended the hospital and stores against four thousand Zulus. In this one single action eleven of its defenders were awarded the Victoria Cross.
23 JANUARY 1879
Lord Chelmsford and the remnants of No.3 Column retraced their steps and regrouped at Rorke's Drift.
29 JANUARY 1879
Colonel Pearson and No.1 Column remained at Eshowe and decided to hold their ground, consequently the Zulus lay siege to their fortified position.
12 MARCH 1879
The British suffered a second defeat when a detachment of one hundred and six men belonging to the 80th Regiment of Foot were attacked and many of them massacred at **Myer's Drift** on the **Intombi River**.
16 MARCH 1879
Uhamu, the half-brother of King Cetshwayo, defected to the British.
28 MARCH 1879
Brevet Colonel Wood's No.4 column instructed to carry out diversions to attract the Zulus away from Lord Chelmsford who marched to relieve the besieged troops at Eshowe. Some of Colonel Wood's forces whilst attacking a stronghold on Hlobane mountain suffered a defeat with many losses.
29 MARCH 1879
The first major victory against the Zulus was gained when a force consisting of twenty thousand warriors was defeated at **Kambula**. This was the battle in which the Zulus realised that they had little chance of beating an army whose men were issued with modern rifles and the latest weapons of war.
2 APRIL 1879
Lord Chelmsford's relieving column attacked at **Gingindhlovu** by twelve thousand Zulus. The British and Colonial forces successfully defended their positions and drove off the Zulus.
3 APRIL 1879
The besieged encampment held by Colonel Pearson and men of No.1 column was relieved by Lord Chelmsford.
29 MAY 1879
The second invasion of Zululand commenced.
1 JUNE 1879
At a place near the Ityotosi River, as the result of an ambush, the Prince Imperial (Louis Napoleon) whilst on patrol was killed.
17 JUNE 1879
Following a reorganisation of the British and Colonial forces, Lord Chelmsford with the 2nd Division and the Flying Column regrouped and prepared to march to Ulundi.

19 JUNE 1879
The 1st Division moved across the Tugela River into Zululand
2 JULY 1879
Cetshwayo attempted for the last time to sue for peace.
4 JULY 1879
The final major battle took place at **Ulundi** in which the Zulu army was finally defeated. The Zulu King knowing his army was defeated became a fugitive.
15 AUGUST 1879
The principle chiefs of the Zulu nation surrendered to Sir Garnet Wolseley.
28 AUGUST 1879
The fugitive king, Cetshwayo after numerous searches was eventually captured at the Kraal of Umhlungulu, in the remote Ngome forest located north of the Black Umfolozi River.
1 SEPTEMBER 1879
The Chiefs of the Zulus accepted the terms and conditions for settlement.
2 SEPTEMBER 1879
The British and Colonial Forces withdrew their forces from Zululand.

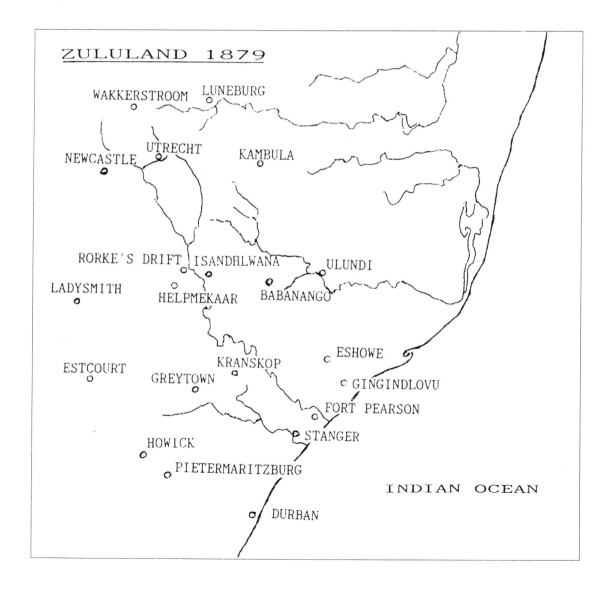

Chapter 3
THE PLAN OF CONQUEST

Zululand in 1879

The Zulu Nation was a totally independent country, self-sufficient and in military terms the most powerful of all the black tribes. The Zulu Nation therefore posed a threat, real or imagined. In 1879 there were no roads in Zululand only a series of native and trader mud-holed tracks which meandered from one kraal to another. No maps existed and the only information available was provided by traders or such others who had ventured into the interior.

The frontiers of Zululand which would have to be defended in time of war were approximately two hundred miles long. The greater part of the Transvaal border was open land, but beyond the Buffalo and Tugela Rivers the land was broken and mountainous and in some areas covered by forests. Zululand was a country of vast green downlands and red soil, studded with prominent rocky topped hills and threaded with twisting water courses. These vast grasslands proved difficult to negotiate, the ground being broken by boulders, thorn-scrub, ant hills, water courses and gullies.

The climate in Zululand varied from the coastal region to the interior. Near to the coast it was unfavourable to health, malaria and other diseases detrimental to man and his animals were rife. Approximately five miles from the coast the conditions improved and were agreeable to both animals and man. There were two seasons, a wet and a dry season. The rainfall from April to September on average was only 178mm to 203mm (7"-8"). From October to March approximately 711mm to 914mm (28"-36") of rain fell. During 1879 it was recorded that the range of the barometer varied very little over twelve months, approximately 12mm(0.5"). A noticeable atmospheric highest per day was reached at around 10.00am with a lowest at 2.00pm. The cold season, was from May to August, temperatures ranging from -2C to 21C.

The Plans and Objectives

The British representatives, Sir Bartle Freer, Sir Theophilus Shepstone and others, thought that the best thing for South Africa was to put an end to the fragmented politics and subject the African people to a form of indirect rule. This would allow organisation of labour, migration control and the efficient development of the new mineral discoveries. A decision was made to conquer the Zulus and the Honourable Frederic Augustus Thesiger, Lieutenant-General Commanding British Forces in South Africa 1878-79, devised a plan of conquest, the objects being:-

1. To defeat the Zulu army
2. To destroy the Zulu King's principal residence, Ulundi
3. To capture the Zulu King, Cetshwayo

The Zulu armies were highly mobile, they had no transport vehicles and carried on their person all they required. After a few days campaigning, they to lived off the land. The mobility of the Zulu army was therefore achieved at the expense of its supply of provisions. Lord Chelmsford estimated that the campaign would last six weeks or at the most two months. Because of the mobility of the Zulu forces it was decided not to invade Zululand in one single column because it was anticipated that the Zulus would not attempt to attack the column but might try to sweep round it and attack Natal.

The date of the invasion was set for January 1879 - harvest time in Zululand when food would be in short supply and the harvest would have to be gathered in - or the Zulu nation would starve. The Zulus could not afford a lengthy war and their border stretched for approximately two hundred miles and was therefore impossible to guard and defend against attack. During the dry season the rivers which bordered Zululand were easy passable; however when the rains came they could only be crossed in flat iron-bottomed ponts. At these crossing points a watch could be maintained, thus restricting the risk of the Zulus crossing the border undetected.

The British and Colonial forces were distributed into five columns. Columns 1, 2 and 4 were to invade Zululand at three different points on the border, reducing the risk of an out-flanking movement by the Zulus. Column 2 was to be held in reserve and Column 5 was to be positioned on the Northern borders to keep surveillance.

No.1 Column, Eastern (or Right), would cross the the border at Fort Pearson at the lower drift of the Tugela River. No.3 Column, Central, would cross into Zululand at Rorke's Drift. No.4 Column, Northern (Left), would cross the disputed territories around the headwaters of the Blood River. The intention was for these three columns to proceed to Ulundi, some seventy miles from each of the points of invasion, destroy it and capture King Cetshwayo. It was hoped that one of the columns would be attacked by the Zulu army and be so convincingly defeated that Cetshwayo would immediately sue for peace. With every day that passed during the invasion, each of the columns as they proceeded to Ulundi would get closer and more able to march to each others aid in the event of attack. The British forces being a modern army with modern weapons would, without doubt, defeat a foe armed only with spears and shields and antiquated rifles! No.2 Column was to be kept in reserve at the middle drift of the Tugela River below Kranz Kop. No.5 Column was to be based at Luneburg to protect the border and to keep an eye on the Transvaal Boers.

At the onset of war, in January 1879, Lord Chelmsford had approximately 17,000 men. At the various depots there was adequate ammunition and food stores to keep the columns supplied and the army on the move. The military establishment had the use of 977 waggons and 123 two-wheeled carts, 5955 oxen, 803 horses and 713 mules. The soldiers were equipped with some of the most modern weapons available.

Distribution of Columns (The First Invasion) South Africa 11th January 1879
General Commanding Lieutenant General Lord Chelmsford KCB.
No.1 Column Eastern (Right) Colonel Commanding, Colonel Charles Pearson, 3rd Foot. Totalling 4750 men
No.3 Column Central Commanding Brev. Colonel Richard Glyn, C.B, 24th Foot. Totalling 4709 men
No.4 Column Northern (Left) Commanding Brev.Col.Evelyn Wood, VC CB. 90th Foot. Totalling 2278 men
No.2 Column Reserve Commanding Lt. Colonel Anthony Durnford, R.E. Staff. Totalling 3871 men
No.5 Column Colonel Commanding Colonel Hugh Rowlands, VC., C.B. Staff. Totalling 1565 men

No.5 Column in detail
COLONEL COMMANDING Colonel Hugh Rowlands, VC., CB.
STAFF OFFICERS   Principal Staff Officer, Captain Harvey, 71st Foot
                          District Adjutant, Lieutenant Potts, 80th Foot
                          Senior Commissariat Officer, Asst. Commissary-General Phillips
                          Commissary of Ordanance, Commissary Wyon
                          Sub District Paymaster, Asst. Paymaster-Burgers
                          Senior Medical Officer, Surgeon Major Johnson
TROOPS
        80th Regiment of Foot   Schutte's Corps   Eckersley's Contingent   Raaff's Corps
            Ferreira's Horse   Border Horse   Transvaal Rangers   Cape Mounted Rifles
ARTILLERY   1 Krupp gun 2 No. 6-prs, Armstrong

Lines of Communication
No.1 Column Eastern (Right) The column obtained supplies from Stanger and Durban, crossing the border at Fort Pearson at the lower drift of the Tugela River. The route for the column would then be towards Eshowe.
No.3 Column Central The lines of supplies were Helpmakaar, Greytown, Ladysmith, Pietermaritzburg and Durban. The column would then cross into Zululand via Rorkes Drift.
No.4 Column Northern (Left) The assembly point was at Balte Spruit. The column drew supplies from Newcastle and Utrecht whilst advancing to Conference Hill and then onto Bemba's Kop.
No.2 Column Reserve In reserve at the middle drift of the Tugela River below Kranz Kop.
No.5 Column Located at Luneburg in the Transvaal, to protect the border and to keep eye on the Transvaal Boers.
The three invading columns used 4895 oxen, 185 horses and 311 mules to pull 645 waggons and 111 carts.

South Africa May 1879 Second Invasion

Following the disaster at Isandhlwana on January 22nd 1879, in which half of No.3 Column were destroyed, Lord Chelmsford with Brevet Colonel R.Glyn C.B. and the remnants of the column, retraced their steps, licked their wounds and regrouped on the border of Zululand. Colonel Pearson with No.1 Column was besieged at a place called Eshowe. Brevet Colonel E.Woods V.C., C.B. with No.4 Column was instructed to carry out a 'holding' position and act on his own initiative until such times as reinforcements arrived. After obtaining reinforcements, on 29th May 1879 Lord Chelmsford proceeded to carry out the Second Invasion of Zululand.

Distribution of Troops (The Second Invasion) 29th May 1879
General Commanding Lieutenant General Lord Chelmsford KCB

1st DIVISION
Major General Commanding Major General Henry Hope Crealock C.B.

1st Brigade Colonel Charles Pearson 3rd Foot. 2/3rd Regiment of Foot 8 Companies, 88th Regiment of Foot 6 Companies, 99th Regiment of Foot 8 Companies

2nd Brigade Lt.Colonel Charles Mansfield Clark 57th Foot, 57th Regiment of Foot 8 Companies, 3rd/60th Rifles 7 Companies, 91st Regiment of Foot 8 Companies, Divisional Troops Naval Brigade (inc 3 guns) 795 men, 4th Battalion N.N.C. 789 men, 5th Battalion N.N.C. 1107 men, John Dunn's Scouts 112 men, Mounted Troops 564 men, M/6 Royal Artillery (6-7 prs) 160 men, 8/7 Royal Artillery (2-7 prs) 50 men, 11/7 Royal Artillery (2-7 prs) 25 men, O/6 Royal Artillery Amn. Col. 75 men, 30th Company Royal Engineers 85

2nd DIVISION
Major General Commanding Major General Edward Newdigate

1st Brigade Colonel Richard Glyn C.B. 24th Foot. 2/21st Regiment of Foot 6 Companies. 58th Regiment of Foot 6 Companies

2nd Brigade Colonel William Pole Collingwood 1/24th Regiment of Foot 7 Companies. 94th Regiment of Foot 6 Companies. Divisional Troops N/5 Royal Artillery (6-7 prs) 150 men, N/6 Royal Artillery (6-9 prs) 150 men, O/6 Royal Artillery Amn. Col. 68 men, 2nd Company Royal Engineers 55 men, Mounted Troops 210 men, 2nd Battalion N.N.C. 900 men, Army Service Corps 150 men Army Medical Department 46 men.

The Cavalry Brigade (attached to the 2nd Division) Major General Commanding Major General Frederick Marshall. 1st Dragoon Guards 634 men, 545 horses, 17th Lancers 613 men, 583 horses, Natives attached 108 men, 110 horses.

FLYING COLUMN
Brigadier General Commanding Colonel Evelyn Wood V.C. C.B. 1/13th Regiment of Foot 617 Men, 80th Regiment of Foot 373 men, 90th Regiment of Foot 654 men, 11/7 Royal Artillery (4-7prs) 81 men, 10/7 Royal Artillery Gattlings 64 men, 5th Company Royal Engineers 82 men, Mounted Infantry 95 men, Frontier Light Horse 209 men, Transvaal Rangers 77 men, Baker's Light Horse 202 men, Natal Native Horse 117 men, Natal Native Pioneers 104 men, Natal Light Horse 84 men, Wood's Irregulars 485 men.

Lines of Communication.

GARRISON-POST
Durban, Stanger, Lower Tugela Forts, Pietermaritzburg, Greytown, Krantz Kop near Middledrift, Dundee, Helpmaaker, Rorke's Drift, Ladysmith, Utrecht, Newcastle, Balte, Spruit, Luneburg, Conference Hill

Field of soldiers on parade.

Chief Ncwadi and Headmen. Typical Zulu warriors.
(Note the dress, shields and epecially the assegai held by the chief).

Chapter 4
THE OPPONENTS

The British Army

Viscount Edward Cardwell was born in 1813 and died in 1886. From 1868 to 1874 he was Secretary of State for War and he is best known for his work in implementing reforms to the British Army. These incorporated a short service agreement consisting of six years with the colours and six years in the reserve. There was to be no more purchasing of commissions with the nobility buying the privilege for themselves or their offspring as soon as they were born. The "Cardwell" reforms were being implemented by the British army in the 1870s and were still being carried out during 1879.

Organisation

The army establishment was organised into sixty-nine administrative Brigade Districts each one relating to an existing county, the depot of the regiment being associated to that area. The regiment comprised of two regular battalions of the line, combined with several battalions of Militia and Volunteers, these being based territorially in the county. Recruitment and training was based in the region. During 1879, 82 battalions were abroad and 59 were at their home depots. Each battalion consisted of 8 companies lettered A to H each of which contained about 100 men.

Uniforms

Rank and file infantrymen on campaign were issued with a uniform consisting of a single breasted red tunic and blue trousers. They were also issued with a cork sun helmet covered with white canvas and with a regimental badge fitted at the front. This canvas material was darkened sometimes whilst in the field. The uniform issued was replaced only when in 'a state beyond repair'. One could imagine the uniforms soon becoming stained with sweat, dust and mud, and ripped, torn and patched - so different to the smart appearance of the parade ground!

Buttons, badges and facing differentiated between the regiments. The 80th Regiment had yellow coloured facings (pointed tabs on their uniform collar and cuffs), to distinguish them from other regiments in the field. Officers' uniforms were comparable although the Royal Artillery, Royal Engineers and Staff Officers often wore dark blue patrol jackets in the field.

Armaments

The British Army infantrymen were issued with a standard infantry 1875 Henry-Martini mark II rifle, the original being designed in 1871. This weighed 4 kilograms (9 lbs) and was 1.25 metres (4' 1½") in length. It fired a .45 calibre single shot and was a breach loading rifle with an effective range of 900 metres and capable of being fired at the estimated rate of 40 rounds every three minutes. The rifle was fitted with a rectangular bayonet approximately .55m in length, often known as a "lunger" which was of standard issue from 1876. Sergeants and above were issued with an 1871 pattern sword bayonet for their rifles. The only problems with the Martini-Henry rifle were that it had a ferocious recoil and that, when it became hot, cartridge cases became jammed in the breach and were difficult to extract. Officers normally carried a sword and a double-action .45 revolver, usually an Adams or a Webly. Regular cavalry from 1877 were issued with a Martini-Henry carbine, although they still retained either the sword or a lance for the charge.

Colonial Troops

Irregular or Colonial cavalry normally had use of a Snider or Swinburn-Henry carbine, both rifled breach loaders. Of the Natal Native Contingent at the beginning of the war, only one in ten was trusted with a firearm, usually an obsolete muzzel-loader - the remaining troops carried traditional weapons only.

Artillery

The British artillery used rifled muzzel loading steel guns which could fire a 7-pounder shell. These guns weighed 406 kilogrammes (8 cwt) and had a maximum range range of 2860 metres for explosive shells. During the latter stages of the war, 9 pounders with a range of 3230 metres were sometimes used. Rocket projectiles were also used; they had explosive heads and were known as 'Hale' rockets. 9 pounder rockets were fired from V-shaped launching-troughs and the 24-pounder type were launched from tubes. In 1871 the Gatling Gun (designed by Richard Jordan Gatling 1818-1903) was brought into service. This could fire 400-600 rounds per minute from ten rifled .45 calibre barrels which were rotated by manually operating a cranked mechanism. The barrels were gravity fed from a revolving upright case holding 40 cartridges. The Gatling Gun was highly effective up to 1100 metres although at times it was prone to jamming.

Naval Establishment

Her Majesty's forces in South Africa during the campaign also contained men from the Royal Navy and Royal Marines belonging to Her Majesty's ships, 'Active', 'Boadicea', 'Shah' and 'Tenedos', which swelled the ranks by nearly 900 men. Part of the duties of the naval detachment were to man the river crossings and operate the ferry ponts but other men of the Royal Navy and Royal Marines, complete with their own 7 and 9 pounder guns, rockets and Gatling guns, were attached to the various artillery batteries.

The Zulu Nation

During 1816 Shaka succeeded to the throne of a small Bantu clan known as Zulus. Under him they began a conquest of the neighbouring tribes. The Zulus, from a regular armed force of around 400 men, were transformed into a military machine, which ensured victory with ferocious savagery. In 1817 they had quadrupled their territories conquering all in their path and killing all those unwilling to serve the Zulu Kingdom. By 1824 the area controlled by the Zulus stretched from the Pongola River into Central Natal and from the coast of Africa to the Drackensberg Mountains. Shaka died in 1828, murdered by his half brothers, Dingane and Mhlangana. By this time the Zulu army amounted to some 30,000 men who could be called upon at any time to bear arms.

During 1879, the Zulu Nation under the Kingship of Cetshwayo, caused consternation in the heart of the British Government, controlling as it did at the time all the might of the British Empire. The Zulu Chiefs taking on and out manoeuvering the British Generals and beating an army equipped with the most modern accoutrements of war was an embarrassment to say the least.

Organisation

On the 1st September 1873, Cetshwayo was crowned King of the Zulus. He continued the traditions implemented by the great King Shaka and the structure of the army remained an integral part of the nation. The Zulus were self sufficient, maintaining a good agricultural system, rearing cattle and farming the river valleys. The men were organised into regiments, serving the King by means of herding his cattle, working the land and policing his subjects, eg collecting fines or destroying kraals of disobedient subjects. Women formed the majority of the Zulu workforce, tending the crops which fed their menfolk and the King's army.

Boys between the ages of fourteen and eighteen years would serve as 'cadets' for a period of two to three years, herding cattle, working in the fields and practising military skills. At the age of seventeen or eighteen these cadets would report to the military kraals to offer their services to the King. During 1879 there were twenty-seven military bases, some thirteen located on the Mahlabathini Plains, the remainder distributed throughout the Zulu Kingdom. These bases represented the King and served as mobilization points in times of war. Cetshwayo in the late 1870s could call upon approximately 50,000 warriors, the strength of the Zulu army consisting of 33 regiments, each containing between 500 and 6000 men and residing in special military kraals. Eighteen of the regiments consisted of unmarried men. who were not allowed to marry until the King gave his consent, and then when his permission was given, it was to the whole regiment.

Uniforms

Zulu warriors wore the minimum of clothing, fur and hide tail strips held around the waist with string, and a strip of cowhide hung loosely at the back with the addition of fur, hide and feather bracelets around their necks, arms and lower legs to enhance their appearance of ferocity and also to identify regiments. Married men also had a fibre head ring woven into their hair.

Armaments

The arms of the Zulu army were shields and stabbing spears known as assegai. A bludgeoning weapon called a knobkerry was also used. This knobkerry (iWisa) was a heavy wooden stick with a burled end. They had some guns although the majority were ancient obsolete muzzle loading type. After the Zulu victory at Isandhlwana, nearly a 1000 modern Martini-Henry rifles were captured, but for the want of expertise the Zulu army did not take advantage of these - likewise with the canon they captured.

The Zulu warrior normally carried a number of assegai (umKonto), the most common being the 'iklwa', a short stabbing weapon with a short blade (ukuDla) 18 ins in length and $1\frac{3}{4}$ins wide, with the blade fitted to a wooden shaft 30 ins in length. Another stabbing spear used was the 'uNtlekwane', of similar size but with a 12 inch by $1\frac{1}{4}$ inch blade. Three types of throwing spears were also carried. These were called, 'isiJula', isiPapa' and the 'iNgcula'. Each had a long shaft (3ft 6 ins), the 'isiJula' with a 7 inch blade, the 'isiPapa' with a blade the same length but wider and the 'iNgcula', with a blade of 9 inch by 1 inch with a neck of 9 inches.

In close combat the Zulu's defensive armament was the shield which was made from stiffened cowhide and was oval in shape. The fabric was attached to a pole by using strips of hide threaded through a series of slotted holes. The head of the pole had a crest of fur and on the inside of the pole a leather thong was attached. The shield came in two sizes, the 'war' shield known as the 'isiHlangu' introduced by Shaka was 30 inches wide and between 54 inches and 72 inches high. Cetshwayo introduced a smaller version 24 inches wide and 48 inches high which was called 'umBumuluso'. The age and experience of each regiment was depicted by the colouring of their shields, black for the young Regiments, increasing in whiteness as age and experience increased.

Supplies

The structure of the Zulu army was such that it had no real supply or ordnance problems. From the time of Shaka, the army could travel fast, lightly clad, over long distances and still be able to fight a battle at the end of the journey. At the start of any campaign, the Zulu forces moved out as one body. Young boys and girls would follow carrying the warriors baggage and food but because of the difficulty of the young keeping up with their elders, the army would split up into various columns and move independently prior to reforming before the fight. This enabled the independent columns to forage off the land and obtain food from the neighbouring kraals. The Zulu army was a disciplined army that could run some fifty miles in a day before fighting a battle and they were to prove by the end of the Zulu War that they were a brave race and a fighting force to be reckoned with.

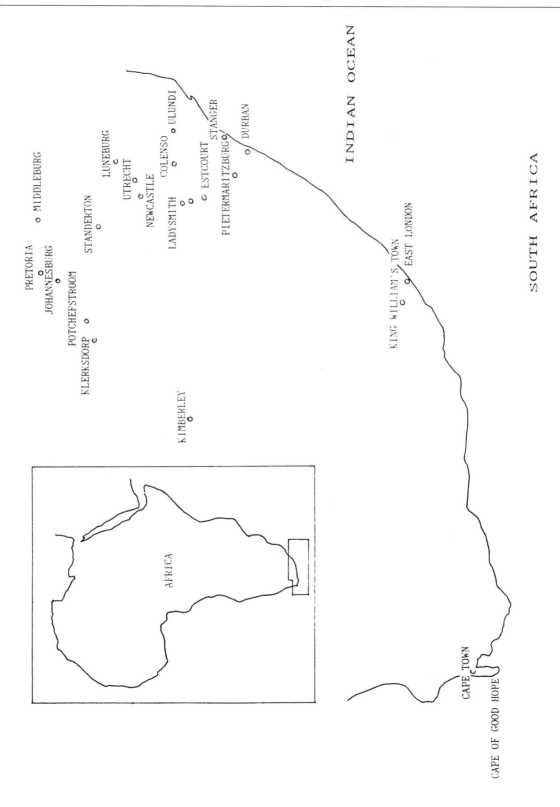

Chapter 5
IN SOUTH AFRICA - THE JOURNAL
The 80th Regiment of Foot (Staffordshire Volunteers) in South Africa up to and including 1880

14th MAY 1876 The first detachment of the 80th Regiment of Foot set sail from Hong Kong for South Africa on board the ship *'Orontes'* The party consisted of 300 officers and men under the command of Lt.Colonel Twenlow.

MAY 1876 Of all the Regiments who would be fighting the Zulus, the 80th had the longest experience of the Zulu borderland. Three hundred soldiers of the 80th Regiment were stationed at Newcastle South.Africa as early as May 1876.

29th JANUARY 1877 Another three hundred Officers and men under the command of Lt.Colonel Amiel set sail for Mauritius on board the ship H.M.S. *'Orontes'*, captained by Captain Seymour RN.

13th FEBRUARY 1877 Whilst at sea a case of measles occurred amongst the soldiers' children of the 1st Battalion 10th Regiment, on passage to England.

15th FEBRUARY 1877 Another case of measles discovered on board.

16th FEBRUARY 1877 H.M.S. *'Orontes'* arrived at Port Louis Mauritius, but owing to the outbreak of disease, passage would not be granted by the Health Officer of the port. The detachment was not therefore permitted to land and Captain Seymour RN was directed to take his ship into the quarantine harbour and there to await orders. Coals were taken on board and provisions. Subsequent orders were received to convey the 80th to Natal.

20th FEBRUARY 1877 Captain Seymour and his ship sailed for Natal.

28th FEBRUARY 1877 H.M.S. *'Orontes'* arrived on the coast of Africa. More cases of measles occurred during the passage. At Durban, the arrival of the ship was telegraphed to the Commandant of Natal at Pietermaritzburg, but not being expected, orders were received to proceed to East London for instructions.

1st MARCH 1877 The ship sailed for East London.

2nd MARCH 1877 The *'Orontes'* arrived at the port at East London and reported arrival by telegraph to Headquarters in Cape Town.

4th MARCH 1877 Orders received to return to Natal and land the detachment in quarantine. Captain Seymour steamed for Durban!

6th MARCH 1877 Second arrival at Durban. Due to the lack of harbour facilities and bad weather no troops could be landed.

8th MARCH 1877 Captain R.W.Stone with "A" Company put ashore and quartered in a narrow strip of beach on the 'bluff' and placed in strict quarantine. It was intended to land the whole detachment but the 'bar' suddenly became very rough and made it impossible to disembark further. On the quarantine ground the space for tents was so limited that at high water the tide reached the doors. The officers were partly put up in the lazaretto or in tents. The detachment remained here in quarantine for fourteen days.

10th MARCH 1877 The remaining two companies on board the *'Orontes'* were disembarked. In consequence of their children having measles, nine non-commissioned officers and men and ten wives with fourteen children were not allowed to land but were taken onto Cape Town and landed there. There appears to be little records kept during this time regarding the provision for families.

11th MARCH 1877 Captain White RN and Headquarter staff set sail from Singapore for East London, South Africa, on board the ship R.M.S. *'Himalaya'*.

25th MARCH 1877 Captain Stone and his men having satisfied quarantine regulations moved across the bay to the town side and proceeded by rail to encamp near the fort, a small earthworks enclosing a barracks capable of accommodating forty men.

14th MAY 1877 The remaining force under Lieutenant Colonel Amiel were relieved by a detachment of 30 men of the 2nd Battalion Buffs Regiment (under Lieutenant N.N.Davis) and proceeded to Newcastle via Pietermaritzburg taking eighteen days to cover 140 miles.

18th MAY 1877 The detachment reached Fort Napier and encamped outside the fort.

21st MAY 1877 The detachment resumed its march for Newcastle at 6.00am. Nothing of importance occurred by the way and the men were reported to be in excellent spirits and health.

2nd JUNE 1877 The detachment reached Newcastle and encamped on a flat at the west end of the village. The arrival here of the detachment was intended as a supporting movement to the troops in advance, the 1st Battalion 13th Light Infantry and 1/2 Battery Royal Artillery, for the annexation of the Transvaal. A detachment of mounted infantry was also encamped here. Under instructions from His Excellency Lt.General Sir

A.Cunynghame K.C.B commanding the troops in South Africa, two mountable guns were handed over to the detachment, with an instructure in order that two-thirds of the men might be fully drilled to their use.

23rd JULY 1877 Lieutenant T.J.Chamberlain joined the detachment, having arrived from Hong Kong.

31st JULY 1877 A working party of 100 men under the command of Lt..Anderson was detailed to begin throwing up a defensive work on a spur of the bluff at the north-west of Newcastle about one mile away. Lieutenant W.T.Anderson acted as Assistant Field Engineer. Working parties were also engaged in the construction of mud huts for shelter for the officers and men.

3rd AUGUST 1877 Lieutenant H.H.Harward joined the regiment from England.

6th AUGUST 1877 Headquarter staff had been stationed at King William's Town until 6th August 1877.

7th AUGUST 1877 Headquarter staff embark and sail on the H.M.S. 'Orontes'.

11th AUGUST 1877 H.M.S. 'Orontes' arrived at Durban.

13th AUGUST 1877 Headquarter staff departed from Durban for Pietermaritzburg.

15th AUGUST 1877 On the departure of Headquarters for Pietermaritzburg from Durban, Lieutenant J.O.Sherrard, 1 Sergeant, 3 Corporals and 28 men were left in detachment at that station.

19th AUGUST 1877 The officers and men reached Pietermaritzburg under the command of Lieutenant Colonel Amiel. Other officers included in the party were as follows:- Captain R.W.Stone, Captain D.B.Moriarty, Lieutenant A.W.Hast (acting Pay-master), Sub.Lieutenant T.E.Griffin (acting Adjutant).

21st AUGUST 1877 Thirty-one short service non-commisioned officers and men proceeded to Piertermaritzburg under the charge of Lieutenant Chamberlain for the purpose of returning to England to be transferred to the 1st Class Army Reserve.

22nd AUGUST 1877 Lt.Colonel Amiel reached Pietermaritzburg to assume command of the Headquarter staff. He was succeeded in the command of the detachment at Newcastle by Major Henry Rowland.

29th AUGUST 1877 Lieutenant T.J.Chamberlain arrived from Newcastle with the non-commissioned officers and men.

8th SEPTEMBER 1877 Lieutenant A.B.Horsbrugh and 30 men leave to join the detachment at Newcastle.

17th SEPTEMBER 1877 Lieutenant A.B.Horsbrugh and his command reach Newcastle.

20th SEPTEMBER 1877 Major Henry Rowland leaves Headquarters to take over command at Newcastle.

22nd SEPTEMBER 1877 Major Rowland arrives at Newcastle and assumes command.

29th & 30th OCTOBER 1877 The annual inspection of the Regiment was made by the Honourable Commandant of Natal, Colonel C.K.Pearson, Buffs.

8th NOVEMBER 1877 Lt.Colonel George Hamilton Twenlow died at King William's Town aged 51 years. Major and Brevet Lt.Colonel C.F.Amiel succeeded to command. Captain and Brevet Major C.Tucker promoted to Major and Lt.W.T.Anderson became a Captain.

17th NOVEMBER 1877 Major Henry Rowland died at Newcastle aged 44. Captain and Brev.Major C.J.R. Tyler obtained his Majority in succession and Lieutenant J.E.H. Prior his Captaincy.

22nd NOVEMBER 1877 Major C. Tucker proceeds to take over the command of the Newcastle detachment.

24th NOVEMBER 1877 Major C.Tucker took over the command of the Newcastle detachment.

25th NOVEMBER 1877 Captain and Brevet Major C.A.F.Creagh arrived from the depot companies.

1st DECEMBER 1877 Lieutenant L.C.Potts joined the Regiment from England. Affairs in Zululand critical. Theophilus Shepstone K.C.M.G., Administrator of the Transvaal requested that the Lieutenant Governor of Natal, Sir Henry Bulwer K.C.M.G., send a force of 200 men to Utrecht as a precautionary measure.

7th DECEMBER 1877 Major Charles Tucker with 200 officers and men left Newcastle for Utrecht at twenty four hours notice. The force included two mountain guns. The officers who accompanied Major Tucker were as follows:- Captain D.B.Moriarty "E" Company, Captain W.T.Anderton "D" Company, Lieutenant A.W.Hast, Lieutenant A.B.Horsbrugh, Sub.Lieutenant T.E.Griffin. Captain & Brigade Major R.W.Stone remained at Newcastle with "A" Company. Lt.Hast assigned the responsibility of the mountain gun detachment comprising twenty-five men of the 80th Regiment of Foot.

8th DECEMBER 1877 The officers and men of Major Tucker's force arrived at Utrecht and made camp. At this time His Excellency the Administrator was residing at Utrecht and consequently a portion of mounted troops were also here to act as an escort.

12th DECEMBER 1877 At Utrecht there was a stone settlers laager. An adjoining military earthwork fort was started by men of the 80th Regiment of Foot.

12th JANUARY 1878 "H" Company under the command of 2nd Lieutenant A.H.Lindop consisting of 5 sergeants, 4 corporals, 2 drummers and 85 privates left Lydenburg to increase Brev. Major Creagh's command at Derby on the Zulu border.

16th FEBRUARY 1878 The military earthwork fort at Utrecht completed. Water becoming very scarce at Utrecht, several wells were sunk by the troops and water procured.

23rd FEBRUARY 1878 Brev. Major Creagh left Derby.

3rd MARCH 1878 Due to the disturbed state in the Transvaal, "C", "B" and "F" Companies left Pietermaritzburg for Utrecht, Lt.Colonel Twenlow in command of the force consisting of 260 officers and men - Captain W.Howard "F" Company, Captain A.Saunders "B" Company, Lieutenant T.J.Chamberlain, Lieutenant W.Moore, Lieutenant H.H.Harward "C" Company, 15 sergeants, 15 corporals, 5 drummers, 220 privates. This force reached Howick about 40 miles distance but were recalled as three Companies of the 90th Light Infantry were ordered to proceed instead.

4th MARCH 1878 The command of Troops in South Africa was handed over by General Sir A.Cunynghame to Lt.General the Honourable F.A.Thesiger (later Lord Chelmsford) at King William's Town. The Imperial troops consisted of two Batteries Royal Artillery (N/5 and N/117), the 7th Company of Royal Engineers and the 1/24th, 88th and the 90th Regiment of Foot in the Cape Colony. The 2/3rd with the 80th Regiment of Foot being in Natal and the 1/13th in the Transvaal. This amounted to 5000 Imperial troops.

12th APRIL 1878 The Annexation of the Transvaal took place.

10th MAY 1878 2nd Lieutenant J.E.Griffin appointed Adjutant.

17th MAY 1878 Two 2nd Lieutenants joined the Regiment from England on appointment, F.W.Lyons and T.A.Porter.

3rd JUNE 1878 Distribution of Troops - Pietermaritzburg:

Fort Napier: 2 Field Officers 3 Captains 8 Subalterns 1 Staff 31 Sergeants 13 Buglers 547 Rank & File 5 Horses.

Durban: 1 Subaltern 2 Sergeants 33 Rank & File.

Newcastle: 1 Captain 1 Subaltern 6 Sergeants 2 Buglers 53 Rank & File.

Sent to Transvaal: 1 Field Officer 2 Captains 2 Subalterns 8 Sergeants 1 Bugler 172 Rank & File.

Kokstaladt: 1 Sergeant.

8th JUNE 1878 Distribution of Troops, Transvaal Pretoria:

Utrecht: 1 Field Officer 2 Captains 2 Subalterns 8 Sergeants 1 Bugler 172 Rank & File 2 Horses 2 Guns 39,000 Small Arms Ammunition 2 Mountain Guns 12 Mules.

2nd JULY 1878 2nd Lieutenant H.A.Raitt joined the Regiment from England on appointment.

24th JULY 1878 Lieutenant J.O.Sherrard with 1 sergeant, 2 corporals and 23 privates left Durban for Newcastle.

25th JULY 1878 Quartermaster J.Belt left behind ill at Weston Mooi River, unfit to travel with the Column. He is later taken to Pietermaritzburg.

26th JULY 1878 Headquarter staff left Pietermaritzburg for Utrecht. The force consisted of the following officers and men:- Major C.J.R.Tyler, Captain and Brev. Major C.A.F.Creagh "H" Company, Captain W.Howard "F" Company, Captain C.E.W.Roworth "G" Company, Captain A.Saunders "B" Company, Lieutenant H.J.Johnson, Lieutenant W.Moore, Lieutenant H.H.Harward "C" Company Lieutenant H.C.Savage, 2nd Lieutenant T.E.Griffin (Adjutant), Quarter Master J.Belt, Civil Surgeon W.I.Cobbin, 32 sergeants, 23 corporals, 12 drummers, 457 privates. Lieutenant Chamberlain remained behind in charge of a detail consisting of 1 sergeant and 34 privates including the soldiers' families.

5th AUGUST 1878 Quartermaster J.Belt died at Pietermaritzburg aged 45 years. He is buried in the Military cemetery at Fort Napier, Pietermaritzburg.

7th AUGUST 1878 The Regiment reached Newcastle and orders were received to send out three detachments with all possible speed to relieve the 1/13 Light Infantry from Garrison duty, to enable them to take to the field against Sekukuni, the Kaffir Chief. Sekukuni's territory was in the North Eastern portion of the Zulu mountains. Detachments sent out on the 12th and 13th August.

12th AUGUST 1878 "B" Company under the command of Captain A.Saunders and Lieutenant W.Moore, with 3 sergeants, 3 corporals, 2 drummers and 71 privates stationed at Stanterton. Lieutenant Moore acting as Commissariat Officer there.

13th AUGUST 1878 "F" Company under the command of Captain W.Howard, 2nd Lt.H.A.Raitt with 3 sergeants, 5 corporals, 2 drummers and 88 privates to Middlesburg. Brev. Major C.A.F.Creagh accompanied by Captain C.E.W.Rowarth, Lts H.H.Howard and H.C.Savage and 2nd Leiutenant F.W.Lyons with "G" and "H" Companies consisting of 8 sergeants, 9 corporals, 3 drummers and 176 privates to Lydenburg. Headquarters to march to Pretoria with the least possible delay, to be followed by the Utrecht and Newcastle detachments. All the troops, Imperial and Colonial in the Transvaal District placed under the command of Colonel H.Rowlands VC, CB.

Interior view of the fort at Utrecht.
(Local History Museum Durban)

Exterior view of the fort at Utrecht.

14th AUGUST 1878 Lieutenant J.O.Sherrard's force joined Headquarters at Newcastle.

16th AUGUST 1878 Colonel C.F.Amiel too ill to travel. Headquarters under the command of Major C.J.R.Tyler, accompanied by Lieutenant Sherrard and 2nd Lts T.E.Griffin and T.A.Porter, with Civil Surgeon Cobbin and 18 sergeants, 6 corporals, 4 drummers and 84 privates leave Newcastle with six Mill waggons and march to Pretoria. Lieutenant A.B.Horsbrugh and 10 men follow the convoy of ox waggons.

18th AUGUST 1878 Lieutenant A.W.Hast is directed to hand over to Lieutenant Nicholson R.A. command of the mountain gun detachment which he had commanded for some time. Lt.Hast is conveyed probation of "H" Company. The Lieutenant General Commanding the forces in South Africa pleased with the satisfactory manner in which Lt.Hast had performed his duties with the gun detachment.

25th AUGUST 1878 A farewell address from the inhabitants of Utrecht received by Major C.Tucker setting forth the good behaviour and kindly feelings towards the civil population by the the men of the Detachments. A detachment of 182 officers and men left Utrecht for Pretoria under the command of Major C.Tucker, consisting of the following:- Captain D.B.Moriarty, Captain W.T.Anderson, Lieutenant L.C.Potts, Lieutenant A.W.Hast, 7 sergeants, 9 corporals, 1 drummer and 160 privates.

27th AUGUST 1878 Major C.J.R.Tyler and Headquarters reached Pretoria.

29th AUGUST 1878 Major C.J.R.Tyler remained at Pretoria being in command from the 29th August 1878, with Lieutenant L.C.Potts as District Adjutant.

4th SEPTEMBER 1878 Lieutenant A.B.Horsbrugh and his command reached Pretoria.

9th SEPTEMBER 1878 Major Tucker with his force of 182 men of all ranks arrived at Pretoria and took command.

10th SEPTEMBER 1878 Lt.Nicholson RA. and the mountain gun detachment consisting of 20 men marched from Pretoria and accompanied the column commanded by Major Russell 12th Lancers commanding 1st Squadron Mounted Infantry.

11th SEPTEMBER 1878 Captain Roworth with 50 non-commissioned Officers and men proceeded to Kruger's Post. Lieutenant Harward with 50 non-commissioned officers and men went to MacDonald's Farm.

14th SEPTEMBER 1878 Captain D.B.Moriarty and "E" Company consisting of Lieutenants Hast and Horsbrugh including 4 sergeants, 4 corporals, 1 drummer and 85 privates leave Pretoria for Lydenburg. They are stopped next day and their destination changed to Fort Weeber. The force is increased by 26 men.

17th SEPTEMBER 1878 Captain D.B.Moriarty and "E" Company recommence the march to Fort Weeber.

18th SEPTEMBER 1878 Lieutenant H.H.Harward with a force of 50 non-commissioned officers and men left MacDonald's Farm and proceeded to Labuseogues Farm, these movements of the 11th and 18th were intended to preserve the lines of communication between Fort Burgher and Lydenburg.

20th SEPTEMBER 1878 Captain and Brev .Major Creagh appointed Acting Staff Officer to the Lydenburg District.

24th SEPTEMBER 1878 Major Tucker and Lieutenant Sherrard with 30 non-commissioned officers and men of "C" Company proceeded to Fort Weeber. Major Tucker is assigned the command of the Left attack against Sekukuni. Lieutenant J.O.Sherrard is appointed Adjutant.

27th SEPTEMBER 1878 2nd Lieutenant F.M.H.Marshall joins the Regiment from England on his first appointment. He proceeds from Newcastle with a force of 1 lance-sergeant and 20 privates to Lydenburg. Lieutenant H.J.Johnson with "A" Company consisting of 3 sergeants, 4 corporals, 2 drummers and 49 privates left Newcastle for Lydenburg.

28th SEPTEMBER 1878 Captain J.E.H Prior with two 2nd Lieutenants A.H.Lindop and E.K.Daubeney and a force consisting of 1 sergeant and 59 privates arrived at Durban from the Depot.

30th SEPTEMBER 1878 Captain Moriarty and Lieutenant Horsbrugh with 100 non-commissioned officers and men march from Fort Weeber for Fort Oliphant.

1st OCTOBER 1878 Captain Moriarty's force arrive at Fort Oliphant.

3rd & 4th OCTOBER 1878 The mountain gun detachment are engaged with the enemy in supporting movements and repelling attacks.

5th OCTOBER 1878 Lieutenant H.C.Savage with a detachment of 19 men escort a convoy containing a supply of ammunition from Lydenburg to Fort Burgher. The mountain gun detachment are again engaged with the enemy either in supporting movements or repelling attacks.

6th OCTOBER 1878 The mountain gun detachment are engaged with the enemy again.

7th OCTOBER 1878 2nd Lieutenant F.W.Lyons with an escort of 19 men are employed on escort duty conveying ammunition from Lydenburg to Fort Burgher.

9th OCTOBER 1878 Lieutenant H.J.Johnson arrives with "A" Company at Pretoria.

15th OCTOBER 1878 "A" Company and Lieutenant Johnson leave Pretoria for Fort Weeber. The Company is made up of 4 sergeants, 3 corporals, 1 drummer and 60 privates. 2nd Lieutenant Marshall with an escort of 21 men arrive at Lydenburg. He immediately proceeds to Labuseoques Farm with a force consisting of 47 non-commissioned officers and men. He is to replace Lt.Harward, who is ordered to go to Speckboom Drift with his detactment of 50 men.

18th OCTOBER 1878 Lieutenant Savage and 2nd Lieutenant Lyons each with an equal force of 19 men return to Lydenburg.

23rd OCTOBER 1878 Captain Moriarty and Lieutenant Horsbrugh with 99 men of "E" Company, march from Fort Oliphant for Pretoria Flats.

24th OCTOBER 1878 Lieutenant Harward takes a party of men including some volunteers on patrol and succeeds in destroying a quantity of mealie belonging to the enemy. Lieutenant Harward had been reinforced by 2nd Lieutenant Lyons and 34 non-commissioned officers and men. Lieutenant S.W.Cameron and 2nd Lieutenant Daubeney arrive at Pretoria.

25th OCTOBER 1878 Lieutenant Cameron's force proceeds to join Headquarter Staff at Fort Weeber.

27th OCTOBER 1878 Lieutenant Johnson in command of "A" Company, consisting of 46 non-commissioned officers and men, accompanied by Civil Surgeon Nardop moves from Fort Weeber to Fort Morlock. The mountain gun detachment are engaged with the enemy again.

31st OCTOBER 1878 2nd Lieutenant B.W.R.Ussher joins the Regiment at Pretoria on first appointment.

13th NOVEMBER 1878 The District Order is issued as follows:-
The following distribution of the Companies in the right and left attack are directed to be carried out: Right column under the command of Brev. Major Creagh, at Lydenburg one Company "H", at Krugers Post one Company "G" and at the Bieg, one Company "A". The left advance under the command of Major Tucker at Fort Weeber, one Company "C", at Middleburg one Company "F" and at Whitport one Company "E".

15th NOVEMBER 1878 "E" Company with Captain Moriarty, Lieutenant Horsbrugh and 82 non-commissioned officers and men are directed to march to Whitport, a station on the road to Fort Weeber and Middleburg.

16th NOVEMBER 1878 "A" Company returns to Fort Weeber.

18th NOVEMBER 1878 "A" Company marches to Lydenburg.

26th NOVEMBER 1878 By instructions from Army Headquarters, the detachments at Krugers Post and the Bieg directed to concentrate at Lydenburg and the detachment at Fort Weeber to march to Middleburg on being relieved by Raaff's Volunteers.

27th NOVEMBER 1878 The second part of the above Order of Distribution cancelled and the company of the 80th Regiment at Fort Weeber and Whitport are ordered to concentrate at Middleburg. Major Tucker takes command of the Regiment.

3rd DECEMBER 1878 Lieutenant H.H.Harward and 2nd Lieutenant F.W.Lyons with 5 sergeants, 5 corporals and 70 privates move to Lydenburg from the fort on the Burg to join Brev. Major Creagh's force.

4th DECEMBER 1878 Captain C.E.W.Roworth with 2 sergeants, 2 corporals, 1 drummer and 45 privates join Brev. Major Creagh's force from Kruger's Post.

9th DECEMBER 1878 Captain J.E.H.Prior proceeds to Newcastle from Pretoria for service with the Frontier Light Horse, under command of Major Redvers Buller CB for impending war with the Zulus.

17th DECEMBER 1878 Major Tucker, Lieutenants J.C.Sherrard and A.W.Hast and Headquarter staff at Fort Weeber consisting of 3 sergeants, 4 corporals, 3 drummers and 72 privates, march for Middleburg.

22nd DECEMBER 1878 Major Tucker's force arrives at Middleburg.

31st DECEMBER 1878 Major C.Tucker proceeds to Middleburg from Lydenburg in accordance with orders received from Colonel Rowlands, Commandant, to assume command of the troops there. "C" and "E" Companies under the Command of Brev. Major Creagh march from Middleburg to Derby, New Scotland so to relieve the Detachment of the 1/13 Light Infantry who proceed to Utrecht to take part in any operation against the Zulu King. The officers accompanying Brev. Major Creagh being Captain D.B.Moriarty, Lieutenants J.O.Sherrard, T.J.Chamberlain, A.W.Hast and 2nd Lieutenant B.W.R.Ussher. The strength of the two Companies is 7 sergeants, 7 corporals, 3 drummers and 37 privates.

1st JANUARY 1879 "B" Company under the command of Captain A.Saunders accompanied by Lieutenant W. Moore with 2 sergeants, 2 corporals and 69 privates march for Pretoria. "H" Company with 5 sergeants, 4 corporals, 2 drummers and 85 privates under the command of 2nd Lieutenant A.H.Lindop leave Lydenburg to increase the strength of Brev. Major Creagh's force on the Zulu border at Derby. Lieutenant J.O.Sherrard is appointed as the Commissariat Officer to the troops under the command of Colonel Rowlands VC CB.

8th JANUARY 1879 Captain A.Saunders and "B" Company arrive at Pretoria.

11th JANUARY 1879 The British Army invades Zululand at three points on the border. At the start of the war the 80th Regiment of Foot located at Luneburg and assigned to No.5 Column under the command of Colonel H. Rowlands. It is intended that they keep out of the invasion force so as to guard the Zulu border against Zulu attacks as well as keeping an eye on the Transvaal Boers. Colonel Rowlands has a force of some 1565 men consisting mainly of the 80th Regiment of Foot.

11th JANUARY 1879

No.5 COLUMN:

Commanding Officer	Colonel H.Rowlands VC CB;
Staff Officers	
Principal Staff Officer	Capt.Harvey 71st Foot;
District Adjutant	Lieutenant L.C.Potts 80th Foot;
Senior Commissariat Officer	Asst.Commissary-General Phillips;
Commissary of Ordnance	Commissary Wyon;
Sub District Paymaster	Asst Paymaster Burgers;
Senior Medical Officer	Surgeon Major Johnson;
Corps	Officer Commanding (Colonel H.Rowlands)
80th Regiment of Foot	Major C Tucker;
Schutte's Corps	Captain Schutte;
Eckersley's Tranvaal Native Contingent	Captain Eckersley;
Raaff's Corps	Captain Raaff;
Ferreira's Horse	Captain Ferreira;
Border Horse	Lt.Colonel Weatherley;
Transvaal Rangers	
Cape Mounted Rifles	

Artillery One Krupp gun
Two 6 pounder Armstrong guns.

Strength
15 Staff and Departments
834 Infantry
553 Cavalry
338 Native Contingent
25 Conductors, drivers and Foreloopers
17 Waggons, 2 Carts, 150 Oxen, 10 Horses, 12 Mules.

14th JANUARY 1879 Lieutenant W.Moore is appointed as District Adjutant at Pretoria. Lieutenant L.C.Potts is ordered to proceed to Derby to take over the command of "H" Company.

17th JANUARY 1879 Lieutenant Potts with a force of 2 sergeants, 2 corporals and 31 privates march from Pretoria for Middleburg and upon joining "H" Company he takes over command.

22nd JANUARY 1879 Captain W.T.Anderson in command of "D" Company accompanied by 2nd Lieutenant E.K Daubeney, 2 sergeants, 2 corporals, 2 drummers and 64 privates march from Pretoria for Derby to increase the force there. The troops at Derby stationed as part of No.5 Column in readiness for action against the Zulus. The Regiment suffers its first casualties of the war. Seven of its members attached to the 1st Mounted Infantry are killed when the camp belonging to No.3 Central Column is destroyed by the Zulus at Isandhlwana (refer to the list of Casualties). The first act of bravery resulting in the award of the Victoria Cross occurs - Private Samuel Wassall of the 80th Regiment of Foot. Private Wassall, attached to the Mounted Infantry Section, No.3 Central Column, saves a comrade from drowning whilst under enemy fire and retreating from the stricken camp at Isandlhwana.

26th JANUARY 1879 "A" Company under the command of Lieutenant H.H.Harward, 3 sergeants, 1 corporal, 1 drummer and 65 privates, proceed from Lydenburg to Derby to increase strength at that place.

31st JANUARY 1879 2nd Lieutenant A.H.Lindop is appointed Ordnance Officer to the Transvaal Column. Lieutenants L.C.Potts and A.W.Hast, 1 sergeant and 31 privates arrive at Derby from Middleburg in charge of two mountain (Armstrong) guns. Lieutenant A.W.Hast with 1 sergeant and 24 privates are detailed to form the gun detachment to the two 6 pounder Armstrong guns. The officer, non-commissioned officers and men have their pay made up to the Royal Artillery rates.

31st JANUARY 1879 By Clause 198 of the Army Orders 1878, the establishment of the 80th Regiment of Foot for 1879 is fixed as follows:-

1 Colonel; 1 Lt. Colonel; 2 Majors; 8 Captains; 8 Lieutenants; 8 2nd Lieutenants; 1 Adjutant; 1 Quarter-Master; 30 Officers; 1 Sergeant Major; 1 Quarter Master Sergeant; 1 Bandmaster; 1 Drum Major; 1 Paymaster Sergeant;

Mounted Infantry Circa 1879

1 Armourer Sergeant; 1 Orderly Room Clerk; 8 Colour-Sergeants; 1 Sergeant Pioneer; 1 Sergeant Cook; 1 Sergeant Instructor of Musketry; 32 Sergeants; 50 Non-Commissioned Officers; 16 Drummers; 40 Corporals; 760 Privates; 816 Rank and File. Total of all Ranks: 896

OFFICERS OF THE 80th REGIMENT OF FOOT

Colonel H. Rowlands VC CB.		1 Lt.Colonel	C.F.Amiel
2 Majors	C.Tucker; C.J.R.Tyler	Brevet Major C.A.F.Creagh "H" Company	
8 Captains	W.T.Anderson "D" Company; W.Howard "F" Company; D.B.Moriarty "E" Company J.E.H.Prior (Frontier Light Horse); C.E.W.Roworth "G" Company; A.Saunders "B" Company; R.W.Stone "A" Company.		
8 Lieutenants	T.J.Chamberlain; H.H.Harward "C" (later "A") Company; A.W.Hast "E" Company A.B.Horsbrugh "E" Company; H.J.Johnson "A" Company; W.Moore "B" Company; L.C.Potts "H" Company; H.C.Savage; J.O.Sherrard; S.W.Cameron		
8 2nd Lieutenants	E.K.Daubeney "D" Company; T.E.Griffin; A.H. Lindop "H" Company F.W.Lyons; F.M.H.Marshall; T.A.Porter; H.A.Raitt; B.W.R.Ussher		

5th FEBRUARY 1879 Captain W.T.Anderson with 2nd Lieutenant E.K.Daubeney and 71 non-commissioned officers and men of "D" Company arrive at Derby. Major C.Tucker with Lieutenant H.J.Johnson leave Lydenburg for Derby to take over command of the Regiment.

6th FEBRUARY 1879 "A" Company under the command of Lieutenant H.H.Harward comprising of 70 non-commissioned officers and men arrive at Derby from Lydenburg.

9th FEBRUARY 1879 Major C.Tucker arrives at Derby accompanied by one soldier servant, to take over command of the Regiment. Five Companies of the 80th Regiment of Foot take over the responsibilities of the Luneburg Laager.

14th FEBRUARY 1879 At Luneburg the total strength of the military force under the command of Major Tucker is as follows:-

Brev. Major C.A.F.Creagh;
Captains D.B.Moriarty; W.T.Anderson;
Lieutenants T.J.Chamberlain; H.H.Harward; A.W.Hast; H.J.Johnson; L.C.Potts; J.O.Sherrard;
2nd Lieutenant E.K.Daubeney; A.H.Lindop; B.W.R.Ussher;
18 Sergeants; 16 Corporals; 6 Drummers; 397 Privates.
2 6-pounder Armstrong mountain guns under the command of Lieutenant A.W.Hast.

The force march for Lydenburg in the Pongola District, N.W. of Zululand, the border of which is disputed territory.

19th FEBRUARY 1879 Major C. Tucker and his force arrive at Luneburg.

28th FEBRUARY 1879 Brev. Major Creagh leaves Luneburg to take over command of the troops in the Lydenburg District.

1st MARCH 1879 Major C.Tucker orders out "D" Company to meet a convoy of eighteen waggons at Derby and escort it into Luneburg.

3rd MARCH 1879 Brev. Major Creagh arrives at Pretoria.

5th MARCH 1879 "D" Company is required for other duties and is therefore recalled.

7th MARCH 1879 Captain D.B.Moriarty is ordered to provide the escort in place of "D" Company. Captain Moriarty's command is of company strength, two Lieutenants, 1 Civil Surgeon and 103 non-commissioned officers and men. Within a couple of hours, the escort meets part of the waggon convoy at Myer's Drift on the Intombi River and makes camp.

8th MARCH 1879 Captain Moriarty sets off north in search of the remaining part of the convoy. Brev. Major Creagh leaves Pretoria for Lydenburg accompanied by his soldier servant Private J.Linnett.

9th MARCH 1879 Captain Moriarty's command and the convoy reassemble at Myer's Drift.

10th MARCH 1879 Adverse weather conditions. Captain Moriarty's command remains at Myer's Drift.

11th MARCH 1879 Major C.Tucker with Lieutenant H.H.Harward arrives at Myer's Drift in the afternoon to establish the cause for the delay of the convoy. Later that same day Major Tucker returns to Luneburg with Lieutenant H.J.Johnson and 2nd Lieutenant A.H.Lindop, the two original Lieutenants appointed for escort duty. Lieutenant H.H.Harward remains with Captain Moriarty.

12th MARCH 1879 Captain D.B.Moriarty commanding a detachment of Company strength is attacked at Myer's Drift on the banks of the Intombi River by Mbilini's irregulars.

British casualties: Killed 1 officer, 60 non-commissioned officers and men, 1 civil surgeon, 2 white waggon conductors, 15 black drivers. Wounded 1 man. (refer to list of casualties)

Zulu Casualties: 25 Casualties were found on the banks of the Intombi River. It is estimated by the British that Zulu losses were as high as 200. At this engagement the second Victoria Cross is earned by a member of the 80th Regiment of Foot, for gallant conduct in front of the enemy. Sergeant Booth in rallying a few men and keeping control although heavily outnumbered manages to retreat for some three miles until help arrives. It is reported that,

"Had it not been for the coolness displayed by this non-commissioned Officer, not one man would have survived". (For a more detailed report refer to the Intombi River-Drift Incident - Chapter 7)

19th MARCH 1879 The following letter was received at Pretoria from Major C.Tucker, dated, Luneburg 12th March 1879, from Officer Commanding 80th Regiment of Foot to Officer Commanding Detachment 80th Regiment of Foot, Pretoria. (Transcript from Vol.1, Regimental Digest 2nd Battalion Staffordshire Regiment)

"I have to inform you that an escort of the 80th Regiment under the command of Captain D.B.Moriarty accompanied by Lieutenant Harward was attacked on the Intombi River Drift on the morning of the 12th March instant. The escort left here on the 7th last to meet the waggons coming from Derby, but owing to the late heavy rains were unable to cross the river, part of the escort 1 Subaltern 1 Sergeant 33 rank and file were encamped on the Luneburg side of the river and the remainder 1 Captain 1 Sergeant 4 Corporals and 64 rank and file with Civil Surgeon Cobbin were in a laager, constructed of waggons on the Northern side. At about 4.40am, an impi of Zulus estimated at from 4000 to 9000 attacked the camp. It had been raining heavily during the night and when the rains ceased shortly before daylight a fog settled down. The attack was made from the North side and owing to the nature of the ground near the river the approach of the enemy was not observed by the sentry outfit, they were on them. Resistance on that side was useless and Captain Moriarty and Doctor Cobbin and a great number of men were killed on the spot. Some swam across the river and were covered by the party under Lieutenant Harward who kept up a heavy fire until the enemy were climbing up the bank close to them. They then retired towards Luneburg pressed by the Zulus for nearly three miles. Forty-four succeeded in reaching Luneburg including Lieutenant Harward, and of the remainder, 39 were found dead on the ground and were buried, the others are still missing. I enclose a list of killed and missing. All of the cattle belonging to the waggons were driven away and the contents were either taken or scattered about. The bodies of Captain Moriarty and Doctor Cobbin have been brought into Luneburg for internment. The small party on the Luneburg side of the river behaved exceedingly well, only for well sustained fire, I doubt if any would have escaped.

Signed C. Tucker Major Commanding 80th Regiment of Foot

The following letter was received by Major Tucker, the Detachment Officer Commanding 80th Regiment of Foot at Pretoria. The letter was sent by Colonel Glyn CB 24th Regiment of Foot Commanding 3rd Column Zululand.

"In the name of all ranks of both battalions of the 24th Regiment, I beg most sincerely to thank you and the Officers and men of the 80th Regiment for the sympathy with us in our heavy losses. We all appreciate most thoroughly the kind feelings which you have shown in subscribing so handsomely to the widows and families of our poor fellows who fell on the 22nd instant. I also thank you for the kind way in which you elude in the defence of Rorke's Drift.

Signed R. Glyn Colonel Commanding 3rd Column Helpmaaker 7th March 1879"

27th MARCH 1879 "D" and "H" Companies march from Lydenburg for Utrecht. The Officers were Captain W.T.Anderson, Lieutenants L.C.Potts and H.H.Harward with 2nd Lieutenants A.H.Lindop and E.K.Daubeney. Strength, 6 sergeants, 8 corporals, 2 drummers and 148 privates.

28th MARCH 1879 Lieutenant H.J.Johnson was gazetted Captain vis Captain J.E.H.Prior being seconded for special services at the Cape of Good Hope.

29th MARCH 1879 The mountain gun detachment attached to Colonel Wood's Column were hotly engaged in the attacks made upon the camp at Kambula by over 20,000 Zulus. They are reported to have behaved well and done good service as gunners in this action. During this engagement, Lance Sergeant T.Brown in charge was severely wounded in the head. Colonel Wood VC,CB in Column Orders, thanked soldiers of all ranks for their behaviour before the enemy, by which complete victory was gained.

30th MARCH 1879 "D" and "H" Companies arrive at Utrecht from Luneburg.

3rd APRIL 1879 2nd Lieutenant G.A.Williams joins the Regiment at Pretoria on his first appointment.

5th APRIL 1879 Captain J.E.H.Prior (attached to the Frontier Light Horse) takes out a mounted patrol from Luneburg. Whilst on patrol near to the Intombi River, in the Pongola valley, native kaffirs inform him that a party of Zulus are sweeping horses and cattle out of a nearby valley. The patrol immediately gives chase and upon making contact, the raiders, release their loot and run. Captain Prior chases after two of the raiders and opens fire, bringing one down, and mortally wounding him, this being Tshekwane a son of Chief Sihayo. The other Zulu is also hit but escapes. The Zulu who escapes, it is later learnt is Mbilini, who led the Zulu attack on Captain Moriarty's command at Myer's Drift on the Intombi River. From intelligence sources Mbilini reaches his cave, but on the way to the Hlobane Mountains dies.

8th APRIL 1879 "H" Company under the command of Lieutenant L.C.Potts accompanied by 2nd Lieutenant A.H.Lindop with 4 sergeants, 6 corporals, 1 drummer and 78 privates march from Utrecht for Balte Spruit arriving on the same day.

9th APRIL 1879 Major C.Tucker Commanding 80th Regiment, "A","C" and "E" Companies with Captain J.E.H.Prior, Lieutenants H.J.Johnson, J.O.Sherrard, T.J.Chamberlain, A.W.Hast and 2nd Lieutenant B.W.R.Ussher including 10 sergeants, 9 corporals, 3 drummers and 189 privates march from Luneburg for Utrecht.

11th APRIL 1879 Major C.Tucker with "A", "C" and "E" Companies arrives at Utrecht.

18th APRIL 1879 Major Tucker accompanied by Captain J.E.H.Prior with Lieutenants' H.J.Johnson, J.O.Sherrard, T.J.Chamberlain, A.W.Hast and 2nd Lieutenant B.W.R.Ussher with "A", "C" and "E" Companies march for Balte Spruit. "A", "C" and "E" Companies consisting of 10 sergeants, 8 corporals, 3 drummers and 183 privates. "D" Company remain at Utrecht.

22nd APRIL 1879 Major C.Tucker in command of "C" and "H" Companies including Lieutenants' J.O.Sherrard, L.C.Potts, T.J.Chamberlain and 2nd Lieutenant B.W.R.Ussher, 5 sergeants, 9 corporals, 2 drummers and 131 privates proceed from Balte Spruit to Doornburg to collect fuel for General Wood's column.

26th APRIL 1879 Major C.Tucker in command of three Companies ordered to cut wood for fuel at Doornburg. At the northerly point they construct an earthen fort.

28th APRIL 1879 The Adjutant General produces the following returns on the recommendations of His Royal Highness the Field Marshal Commanding in Chief. The Secretary of State for War decides that the drafts shall be sent to the Cape to replace casualties sustained in the present conflict:-

    2nd Battalion 3rd Regiment of Foot 1 Officer 1 Capt. 2 Sgts. 86 Rank & File
    2nd Battalion 21st Regiment of Foot 1 Capt. 2 Sgts. 41 Rank & File
    90th Regiment of Foot 1 Subaltern 1 Sgt. 31 Rank & file
    91st Regiment of Foot 1 Subaltern 1 Sgt. 48 Rank & File
    1st Battalion 13th Regiment of Foot 1 Capt. 58 Rank & File
    24th Regiment of Foot 2 Subalterns 1 Sgt. 51 Rank & File
    57th Regiment of Foot 1 Capt. 1 Sulaltern 2 Sgts. 2 Trumpeters/Drummers 113 Rank & File
    58th Regiment of Foot 1 Capt. 1 Trumpeter/Drummer 43 Rank & File
    3rd Batt. 60th Regiment of Foot 1 Capt 1 Subaltern 2 Sgts 2 Trumpeters/Drummers 96 Rank & File
    75th Regiment of Foot 2 Rank & File
    80th Regiment of Foot 1 Capt. 1 Subaltern 3 Sgts. 2 Trumpeters/Drummers 146 Rank & File
    88th Regiment of Foot 1 Capt. 1 Subaltern 2 Sgts. 1 Trumpeter/Drummer 113 Rank & File
    Royal Engineers 1 Sgt. Ordance Branch, Army Service Corps. 1 Staff Sgt. 1 Sgt. 4 Rank & File
    Army Hospital Corps. 1 Sgt. 3 Rank & File Army Medical Corps. 5 Staff.

The Adjutant General's report also contained the following statement indicating articles of necessities for six months supply issued to the troops marked for the Cape in February 1879, the 80th Regiment of Foot:

50 Kit bags	250 Pairs of braces	50 Bugles	150 Blacking brushes
200 Brass brushes	125 Clothes brushes	150 Polishing brushes	200 Combs
430 Forage caps (Sergeants plus Rank & File)	600 Table Knives		600 Forks
300 Spoons	300 Mess tins	25 Holdalls	50 Pairs of mitts
600 Flannel shirts	1750 Pairs of worsted socks		200 Razors and cases
5000 Pieces of soap	100 Sponges	250 Towels	

1st MAY 1879 Captain W.T.Anderson and 2nd Lieutenant E.K.Daubeney with "D" Company, 2 sergeants, 4 corporals, 1 drummer and 60 privates leave Utrecht and march for Balte Spruit arriving the same day. H.M.S. 'Orontes' with 2 officers and 151 non-commissioned officers and men of the 80th Regiment on board leave Portsmouth on voyage to South Africa.

3rd MAY 1879 Lieutenant H.J.Johnson with "A" Company reinforce Major Tucker's force at Doornburg.

10th MAY 1879 "D" Company arrives at Doornburg.

15th MAY 1879 2 sergeants, Drum Major O.O'Day, 4 drummers and 3 privates leave Pretoria to join their respective Companies in the field in Zululand. 1 sergeant, 5 corporals, 1 drummer and 59 privates, all time expired or invalids, march to Durban for passage to England. Lieutenant W.Moore in command of these details with instructions to rejoin his regiment after reaching Pietermaritzburg and handing over his charge.

17th MAY 1879 The five Companies "A", "C", "D", "E" and "H" are at Doornburg.

18th MAY 1879 The mountain gun train rejoins the Regiment for duty.

26th MAY 1879 The following order published by Colonel Hugh Rowlands on relinquishing the Command of the Transvaal Column, Pretoria 26th March 1879.

"District Orders. By Col. Rowlands V.C., C.B. on leaving the command of the Transvaal to take up a Command with the army operations in Zululand, desires to thank all Officers commanding Companies and Heads of Departments for their support and assistance which they have given him. He desires particularly to record the zeal and judgement with which the Officers Commanding the principal stations, Major C.J.R.Tyler, Brevet. Major C.A.F.Creagh, Captain W.Howard 80th Regiment and Brevet. Major F.W.Carrington 24th Regiment of Foot, have invariably carried on their duties during the period of continued disturbance on the Northern frontier of the Transvaal.

By Order Signed C.L.Harvey. Captain Staff Officer"

27th MAY 1879 Major C.Tucker with five Companies of the 80th Regiment leaves Doornburg and marches to join General Wood's Column via Conference Hill, to take part in the second invasion of Zululand. Force includes a battery of gatling guns,18 sergeants, 20 corporals, 5 drummers and 328 privates. The officers: Captains W.T.Anderton, J.E.H.Prior, Lieutenants H.J.Johnson, J.O.Sherrard, L.C.Potts, T.J.Chamberlain, A.W.Hast, 2nd Lieutenants A.H.Lindop, E.K.Daubeney, B.W.R.Ussher, and Lieutenant Tovry of the Queens Tower Hamlets Militia attached to the 80th Regiment.

Colonel W.O.Lanyon CB, CMG. Administrator of the Transvaal takes up appointment of Commandant Transvaal.

28th MAY 1879 Major C.Tucker with five Companies of the 80th Regiment join General Wood's Column at his encampment located between Mundla and Incanda Hills.

29th MAY 1879 The second invasion of Zululand commences.

30th MAY 1879 H.M.S. *'Orontes'* with Brevet Major J.L.Bradshaw and Lieutenant C.C.Cole and 3 sergeants, 3 corporals, 2 drummers and 143 privates arrives at Cape Town.

1st JUNE 1879 Major C.Tucker's force marches from Mundla and camps near the Itelzi.

2nd/3rd JUNE 1879 The five Companies with Major Tucker arrive at the Ityotyosi River near its junction with the Tombokala and encamp at Nondwine.

4th JUNE 1879 Brevet Major J.L.Bradshaw and Lieutenant C.C.Cole with 3 sergeants, 3 corporals, 2 drummers and 143 privates are landed at Durban.

5th/6th JUNE 1879 Major C.Tucker and his command encamp at Machonchlabi.

6th JUNE 1879 By Gazette 6th June 1879, the promotion of Captain H.J.Johnson was ante-dated to the 13th March 1879 vis when Captain Moriarty was killed in action. Lieutenant J.O.Sherrard promoted Captain vis 28th March 1879 and Lieutenant C.C.Cole vis Brevet -Major S.G. Huskinsson promoted Major half pay 17th May 1879. Brevet Major S.G.Huskinsson arrives in South Africa from Hong Kong in compliance with instructions, from Horse Guards, directing him to rejoin his regiment for duty. He did not however join his promotion to half pay having been notified before he could do so.

7th JUNE 1879 Major Tucker and the five Companies marched to Fort Newdigate on the Nondweni River.

8th JUNE 1879 Major Tucker and his men march to Koppie Allein and camped.

8th/12th JUNE 1879 Encamped at Koppie Allein.

13th JUNE 1879 Major Tucker and his command reaches Isipezi Hill and encamps. Brevet Major J.L.Bradshaw and force leaves Durban and marches to join Headquarters.

14th JUNE 1879 Major Tucker leaves the Isipezi River for Fort Newdigate.

15th JUNE 1879 Major Tucker and his force of five Companies reach Fort Newdigate.

17th JUNE 1879 Major Tucker with his men leave Fort Newdigate for Fort Marshall and after marching some distant encamp on the Upoki River. The London Gazette publishes the award of the Victoria Cross to Private Samuel Wassall.

18th JUNE 1879 The five Companies with Major Tucker arrive at Fort Marshall.

19th JUNE 1879 The Companies leave Fort Marshall and march to Ibabanango Spruit.

20th JUNE 1879 The Companies continue their march and reach Itala Ridge.

21st JUNE 1879 After encamping at Itala Ridge, Major Tucker and his men march to the Umhlatoosi River.

22nd JUNE 1879 Major Tucker with his five Companies arrive at Fort Evelyn.

24th JUNE 1879 Major Tucker and his command leave Fort Evelyn and reach Taikals Ridge.

The 80th Regiment
on the move.

The Monument to the Fallen
80th Regiment of Foot. Intombi River
(looking South East).

25th JUNE 1879 March to Lundhla and camp. A strong reconnaissance of mounted men and Royal Artillery destroy three military Kraals, these being Ochlambedhla, Usixepi and Dugaiza.

27th-30th JUNE 1879 March for and reach top of Entonjaneni Hill and remain until the 30th instant.

30th JUNE 1879 Leave Entonjaneni Hill and march for Fort Victoria.

1st JULY 1879 Reach the right hand bank of the White Umvolosi River and encamp.

2nd JULY 1879 A draft of 105 men arrive at Durban under the command of Captain M.S.Crofton of the 38th Regiment of Foot (1st Staffordshire).

3rd JULY 1879 The 2nd Division spends the day making a defensive laager.

4th JULY 1879 Lord Chelmsford and part of his forces cross the White Umvolosi River and proceed to Ulundi. The British forces consist of the 2nd Division (132 officers 1752 white troops and 540 black troops) and the Flying Column (122 officers 2159 white troops and 465 black troops). Eleven officers and 357 non-commissioned officers and men of the 80th Regiment of Foot formed part of this force. The invading force is formed into a "hollow rectangle", the 80th Regiment of Foot forming the leading side with a pair of gatling guns in its centre manned by the 10th Battery 7th Royal Artillery. The Zulus, having been provoked by mounted troops attack the British square between 8.45 am and 9 am. At 9.35 am approximately, Lord Chelmsford orders the mounted troops to pursue the retreating Zulus.

The British casualties are as follows:- 3 officers killed, 10 men killed, 69 men wounded. Of the casualties 2 men killed and 5 men wounded belonged to the 80th Regiment of Foot, (refer to casualty list). The Zulu casualties are as follows:- 950 to 1500, it is estimated that probably half of these were accounted for by the mounted troops. After the Battle of Ulundi the destruction of Ondine, Nodwenga, Undalbakaounbe, Kwa Bulawayo, Duikasgi, Umlambougheuya and other military kraals takes place. Lord Chelmsford and his forces then return to their camp on the banks of the White Umvolosi River.

5th JULY 1879 Major C.Tucker with members of the 80th Regiment leave the White Umvolosi River and march for Fort Victoria. "F" Company under the command of Captain W.Howard proceed from Middleburg to Fort Weeber.

6th JULY 1879 Reach Fort Victoria. The following General Order was published on the 6th July 1879 General Order No.124:

"The Lt. General Commanding desires to place on record his hearty appreciation of the gallantry and steadfast displayed by all ranks of the force under the command during the battle of Ulundi. The fine discipline of all the Corps was beyond all praise and mainly contributed to the defeat of the enemy being so rapidly accomplished. That defeat was made complete by the gallant charge of the 3rd squadron of the 17th Lancers and by the effective pursuit of the Mounted Corps of the flying Column. The Lt. General desires special to notice the fine behaviour of the Native Horse who both at the beginning and end of the fight fully sustained the reputation they already established. The Lt. General has had much pleasure in bringing to the notice of the Secretary of State for War the excellent behaviour of the troops and he feels sure that the good service they have rendered will be fully appreciated. The two Companies being about to separate, Lt.General begs to tender his best thanks to Major General Newdigate and to Brigadier General E.Wood VC.,CB for the assistance rendered him during the recent operations
By Order Signed G. Pomeroy - Colley Brig. General Chief of Staff"*

7th JULY 1879 Leave Fort Victoria and marched for Entonjaneui Hill.

8th JULY 1879 Reach Entonjaneui Hill and halt there. Brigadier General E.Wood VC,CB holds parade of the Flying Column and reads out the order previously recorded and afterwards thanks the non-commissioned officers and men in his own name, saying they had rendered all his work a pleasure to him more than duty.

9th JULY 1879 Five Companies of the 80th Regiment march two miles from Entonjaneui Hill in the direction of Kwamagwasa and encamp. The draft under the command of Brevet Major Bradshaw receive orders to join the Headquarters in Zululand. In the London Gazette, Major Charles Tucker succeeded to the Lieutenant Colonelcy vice Lieutenant Colonel C. F.Amiel retired on full pay 9th July 1879. Captain and Brevet Major Charles Augustus Fitzgerald Creagh becoming Major and Lieutenant Lipton Cummings-Potts Captain in succession.

10th JULY 1879 The five Companies march a further ten miles and then encamp.

11th/12th JULY 1879 The force continues its march and reaches the deserted Kwamagwasa Mission Station and halt there for two days.

12th JULY 1879 The following dispatch was received from Major C.Tucker commanding the Regiment. White Umvolosi River Zululand Detachment 4th July 1879 7pm. Officer Commanding 80th Regiment Pretoria.

"Ulundi burnt this day. Heavy engagement with Zulus this morning, 80th post of honour in front. Troops fought in immense square cavalry in centre, the western Umvolosi River was crossed at 6 am. by the 80th, other Regiments in rear when opposite the military kraal uNodwenga, Zulus appeared in large numbers from adjacent hills completely surrounded us. Artillery opened fire at 8-40 am. the regiment of Zulus engaged by the 80th from the King's kraal direct which was about two miles from us. After forty-five minutes heavy firing Zulus became demoralised, Cavalry then pursued them and at 9-25 am. the whole of our troops ceased firing. After a short rest we marched on to the King's Kraal which was burnt. Other large military kraals were also burnt, the following are casualties of the 80th :- 1630 Sgt H. Watts "H" Company Killed, 1892 Pvt J. Floyd "H" Company Killed, 1249 Sgt J. O'Neill "D" Company severely wounded, 19/636 Crp A. Beecroft "H" Company severely wounded 1616 Pvt M. Duffy "A" Company Slightly wounded, 1213 Pvt W. Lunt "E" Company severely wounded, 19/669 Pvt R. Tully "D" Company severely wounded, 7 P.M. Inst. Returned without exception of above all correct our men behaved splendidly Signed C. Tucker Major." At Ulundi Lt. Gen. Lord Chelmsford K.C.B. commanded in person the troops present. In addition to the 80th Regiment were the 17th Lancers, Frontier Light Horse, Imperial Mounted Infantry, 1/13 and the 90th Light Infantry and a portion of the following Regiments:- 21st, 58th and 94th., two Companies of Royal Engineers, two gatling guns and eight Armstrong guns with Royal Artillery.

13th JULY 1879 The five Companies leave Kwamagwasa and march for St.Paul's Mission. After completing seven miles the force encamps.

14th JULY 1879 After completing a further seven miles the force encamps.

15th JULY 1879 The five Companies continues march and reach St.Paul's Mission Station. "F" Company with Captain W. Howard arrive at Fort Weeber.

16th JULY 1879 His Excellency Sir Garnet Wolseley G.C.M.G., K.C.B. inspects the Flying Column.

17th JULY 1879 The following order was published by the General Commanding the forces with reference to the victory at Ulundi. To Headquarters, Inspector General, lines of communication and base Pietermaritzburg 17th July 1879.

"General Orders by General Sir Garnet Wolseley G.C.M.G., K.C.B. Commanding the forces in South Africa Camp near Fort Crealock Zululand 16th July 1879 The General Commanding congratulates Lt. General Lord Chelmsford K.C.B. and the Officers and men serving under his command upon the brilliant success achieved by them upon the 4th instant at Ulundi where they defeated with severe loss the Zulu army led by the King in person. The General Commanding learnt with great satisfaction from Lt. General Lord Chelmsford the admirable behaviour of the troops under his command and hoped that their gallant conduct will have made the action at Ulundi decisive of the fate of the campaign. By Order Signed Henry Brackenbury Lt. Colonel Military Secretary for the Chief of Staff". Lt. Gen. Lord Chelmsford K.C.B left for England and Brig.Gen. E. Wood V.C.,C.B. published the following Order. *"St. Paul's 17th July 1879 Column Orders 3 "The Brigadier proposes to leave for Pietermaritzburg tomorrow in saying goodbye to soldiers of all ranks, Staff, Departmental and Regimental he wished to express his warmest gratitude for the support he is invariably received. The Brigadier General has gained a commendation of his superiors for the successful operation of the Flying Column he feels that credit has been obtained by the courage and untiring devotion to duty of his fellow soldiers and he will never forget his comrades of the Flying Column. By Order Signed F.Clery Major Staff Officer"*

Colonel Harrison Royal Engineers succeeded Brigadier General E. Wood V.C, C.B. in command of the Flying Column.

22nd JULY 1879 The 2nd Division march to a new camp site approximately two miles down the Upoko and remain there till it is broken up.

26th JULY 1879 Part of the 2nd Division leaves and marches for Fort Newdigate.

30th JULY 1879 In General Orders No.23 dated 30th July 1879 it was notified that the Queen had been graciously pleased to signify her intentions to confer the decoration of the Victoria Cross upon Private S.Wassall of the 80th Regiment attached to the Imperial Mounted Infantry for his gallant conduct in having at imminent risk of his own life saved that of Private Westwood of the same Regiment on the 22nd January 1879 when the camp at Isandhlwana was taken by the enemy. Private Wassall retreated towards the Buffalo River in which he saw a comrade struggling and apparently drowning. He rode to the bank dismounted his horse on the Zulu side rescued the man from the stream and again mounted his horse dragging Private Westwood across the river under heavy shower of bullets.

31st JULY 1879 The Flying Column under the Command of Colonel Harrison is broken up. Five Companies under the Command of Major C.Tucker march from St.Paul's for Ulundi and cover six miles towards

Kwamagwasa. 83 time expired and reserved men having been handed over to the 1/13th Regiment of Foot proceed to England.

1st AUGUST 1879 The Regiment march a further seven miles and halt.

2nd AUGUST 1879 The Regiment remain encamped.

3rd AUGUST 1879 The march is resumed and the Regiment reach Kwamagwasa.

4th AUGUST 1879 The Regiment leave Kwamagwasa and march for Entonjaneni. Eight miles is completed and a halt is called. Brev. Major C.A.F.Creagh takes over command of the Colonial Mounted Volunteers, Derby, New Scotland.

5th AUGUST 1879 The Regiment remains encamped.

6th AUGUST 1879 The march is resumed and six miles is completed.

7th AUGUST 1879 The Regimet breaks camp and marches beyond the Entonjaneni by about five miles towards Fort Victoria. The draft under the command of Brev. Major Bradshaw joins the Regiment here.

8th AUGUST 1879 Regiment encamps at Fort Victoria. In General Orders 2nd Lieutenants A.H.Lindop and F.W.Lyons were gazetted as Lieutenants, via J.O.Sherrard and C.C.Cole being promoted to Captains.

10th AUGUST 1879 Regiment leaves Fort Victoria and reaches the White Umvolosi River.

11th AUGUST 1879 Headquarters crosses from the right bank of the White Umvolosi River and camps two miles north west of the ruins of Ondine kraal near to the camp of Gen. Sir Garnet Wolseley on the Hammer Alabetine Plains, Ulundi.

13th AUGUST 1879 Lieutenant Randall and W.Johnson on mar Militia were appointed 2nd Lieutenant in succession to Lieutenant H.J. Johnson promotion. Gentleman Cadet Mark Averum Kerr was promoted to 2nd Lieutenant in succession to F.W.Lyons being promoted.

16th AUGUST 1879 Captains H.J.Johnson and J.O.Sherrard start out with eight other officers under the command of Captain Herbert Stewart of the 3rd Dragoon Guards in pursuit of Cetshwayo.

18th AUGUST 1879 Brev. Major Bradshaw and Lieutenant Hast with "E" Company leave Ulundi to make a road via the Isiahlals and Inhlazatye mountains to Fort Cambridge.

19th AUGUST 1879 "E" Company camps at Langasanis kraal.

20th AUGUST 1879 Lt.Col. C.Tucker placed in command of Headquarter's personal escort of General Sir Garnet Wolseley at Ulundi. The escort consists of five Companies of the 80th Regiment of Foot, two Companies 2/24th Regiment of Foot, three Troops of the King's Dragoon Guards and two nine pounder guns of the Royal Artillery.

22nd AUGUST 1879 Brev. Major Bradshaw with "E" Company encamp in the Isihlals Valley on the Umhlalus River. Captains H.J.Johnson and J.O.Sherrard return from patrol after searching for King Cetshwayo.

23rd-24th AUGUST 1879 Brev. Major Bradshaw with "E" Company remain encamped in the Isihlals Valley on the Umhlalus River.

25th-29th AUGUST 1879 "E" Company encamped at the Inhlazatye Mission Station.

28th AUGUST 1879 The Zulu King Cetshwayo captured at the kraal of Umhlungulu in the Ngome forest.

30th AUGUST 1879 Brev. Major Bradshaw and Lieutenant Hast with "E" Company leave Inhlazatye for Fort George.

31st AUGUST 1879 "E" Company arrive at Fort George.

1st SEPTEMBER 1879 "E" Company march and reach Fort Cambridge and encamp there.

2nd SEPTEMBER 1879 "E" Company remain encamped at Fort Cambridge. Headquarters begin their march from Ulundi past Langasanis kraal, Inhazatye Mission Station, Conference Hill, Van Ruani Farm and proceed towards Utrecht.

5th SEPTEMBER 1879 "E" Company remain encamped at Fort Cambridge. 2nd Lieutenant H.A.Raitt, 2 sergeants, 1 corporal and 32 privates detached at Fort Oliphant from Fort Weeber in the vicinity of Sekukuni's country.

6th SEPTEMBER 1879 "E" Company march and join up with Headquarters.

10th SEPTEMBER 1879 Headquarters reach Utrecht.

11th SEPTEMBER 1879 Headquarters leave Utrecht and go past Doorne Kop, Parade Kop and Slang River towards Whistlestroom. Private Samuel Wassall with Private Robert Jones of the 24th Regiment receive their Victoria Cross medals from Sir Garnet Wolseley at Utrecht.

13th SEPTEMBER 1879 Following despatch received and published in Order of the 13th September 1879:
To Major C. Tucker Army Headquarters Commanding Headquarters Escort Ulundi Zululand 1st September 1879 General Orders:

1) The following despatch conveying Her Majesty's gracious congratulations upon the victory at Ulundi has been received by the General Commanding from the Secretary of State for War and is published for the information of the troops.

"War Office 24th July 1879 Sir, I have to acknowledge the receipt of telegraphs news of the capture and destruction of Ulundi and of the successful action which proceeded it. Having communicated this intelligence to the Queen, Her Majesty has commanded me to express the very great satisfaction and thankfulness with which she has received it and to convey to Lt. Gen. Lord Chelmsford and to the troops under his command a congratulations on the victory they have obtained. Her Majesty is proud of the conduct of her troops and wishes to be informed as soon as possible of the condition of the wounded. I have etc. Fred Stanley"

2) The General Commanding sincerely congratulates the troops under the command upon the capture of the late King of Zululand whose presence at large in the territory over which he ruled was fatal to all hopes of permanent and satisfactory peace. By the exertions of the troops, British and Colonial, European and native that capture of Cetshwayo has been effected. It has become possible to reap the fruits of the previous military operations and the pacification of Zululand has been assured. To Lt.Gen. C.M.Clarke, Commanding Clarke's Column and all of the Officers and men under his command, the thanks of the General Commanding are specially due, though deprived of the opportunity of meeting the enemy in the field they have most carefully carried out the tasks allotted to them, the satisfactory remembrance that their efforts have been attended with complete success.

By Order G.Pomeroy - Colley Brev. General Chief of Staff

15th SEPTEMBER 1879 Headquarters encamp at Whistlestroom in the District of Wakkerstroom.

5th OCTOBER 1879 The distribution of the 80th Regiment of Foot:
Pretoria Headquarters and 1 Company;
Wakkerstroom 5 Companies;
Fort Weeber 1/2 Company;
Fort Oliphant 1/2 Company;
Lydenburg 1 Company.

6th OCTOBER 1879 Lt.Col. C.Tucker leaves Wakkerstroom, Pretoria and the five Companies become a Detachment. The following letter received from the 2nd Battalion 4th King's Own Regiment dated 6th October 1879 to Lt. Col. C.Tucker Commanding 80th Regiment of Foot:

"Sir, I have the honour to forward herewith a Pencil sketch of a monument to the memory of Captain Moriarty and men of the 80th Regiment erected by the 4th King's Own whose work thus recorded their sympathy with their comrades of the 80th Regiment in the loss of so many brave men at the Intombi River. I have the honour to be sir.

Signed W.D.D.Elliot. Major Commanding 2nd Battalion 4th King's Own Regiment"

18th OCTOBER 1879 In reply to the letter received by Lt.Col.Tucker from W.D.D.Elliot 4th King's Own:

"I have the honour to acknowledge the receipt of your letter of 6th October and the accompanying sketch and to thank you, the Officers, non-commissioned officers and men of the 4th King's Own Royal Regiment on behalf of myself and the Regiment which command for your kind thoughtfulness in placing a monument over our poor fellows who fell at the Intombi River and to assure how highly we all appreciate so friendly an act.

Signed C.Tucker Lt.Colonel 80th Regiment"

Twenty-seven non-commissioned officers and men of the 80th Regiment of Foot accompanied General Sir Garnet Wolseley to Fort Weeber as an escort.

6th NOVEMBER 1879 Lieutenant Lindop and 50 non-commissioned officers and men leave Wakkerstroom for Lydenburg.

7th NOVEMBER 1879 2nd Lieutenant B.W.R.Ussher embarks for England on six months' sick leave on *S.S. 'Duart Castle'*.

8th NOVEMBER 1879 Captain J.O.Sherrard embarks for England to join the Depot Companies.

11th NOVEMBER 1879 Lieutenants A.B.Horsbrugh and H.A.Raitt with 33 non-commissioned officers and men of "F" Company leave Fort Weeber and march for Lydenburg. Nineteen non-commissioned officers and men of the 80th Regiment are detached for duty as Gunners with the Transvaal Artillery under the command of Captain Know, Royal Artillery. The men are to be employed in operations against Sekukuni.
2nd Lieutenant R.P. Columb arrives at Pinetown from England on appointment.

12th NOVEMBER 1879 Lieutenant H.C.Savage leaves Pretoria for the purpose of proceeding to England to join the Depot Companies.

The 'makeshift' field
kitchen belonging to
the 80th Regiment.

Captain D.B. Moriarty's
original Grave marker.
Luneburg Cemetery.
The stone was erected by
the 4th King's Own
Regiment.

13th NOVEMBER 1879 Major C.A.F.Creagh is placed in command of troops in the Lydenburg District. Captain W.Howard is ordered to the Lydenburg District to meet his Companies arriving from Fort Weeber.

16th NOVEMBER 1879 Lieutenants A.B.Horsbrugh and H.A.Raitt with 33 non-commissioned officers and men of "F" Company arrive at Lydenburg from Fort Weeber.

17th NOVEMBER 1879 The five companies at Wakkerstroom, strength 4 captains, 2 sub-lieutenants, 15 sergeants, 14 corporals, 9 drummers and 349 privates, march for Pretoria.

18th NOVEMBER 1879 Lieutenant A.H.Lindop and an escort arrive at Middleburg from Wakkerstroom.

19th NOVEMBER 1879 The five Companies arrive at Standerton.

20th NOVEMBER 1879 The five Companies resume the march for Pretoria. Lieutenant T.J.Chamberlain upon the departure of the five companies proceeds to join the Depot Companies.

23rd NOVEMBER 1879 Major Creagh Commanding Column, Captains Howard and Roworth with Lieutenants Horbrugh, Lyons and Raitt with "F" and"G" Companies, strength 5 sergeants, 4 corporals, 2 drummers and 83 privates, proceed from Lydenburg to Sekukuni Hill against Chief Sekukuni.

27th NOVEMBER 1879 An attacking force including Major Creagh and his command leave the fort at 9.00pm to attack Sekukuni Town.

28th NOVEMBER 1879 The force attacks the hills at the back of Sekukuni Town, the 80th and Eckersley's contingent leading. In the face of a heavy fire they reach the hill and clear the ridge as far as the back of the town, and with the Swazis succeed in cutting off the retreat of the Makatees up the gorge at the back enabling the Swazis by dint of numbers to seize and burn the town and thus render possible the subsequent attack upon the "Vecht Koppie". They join the Headquarters camp at the conclusion of the day and leave the Sekukuni Town.

Lt.Colonel Tucker CB commanding 80th Regiment of Foot by London Gazette. Dated 28th November 1879:

"Her Majesty the Queen was graciously pleased to give orders for the following appointments to the most Honourable Order of the Bath Lt. Col. Charles Tucker 80th Regiment to be an ordinary member of the militia division of the 3rd class or Companion of the said most honourable order".

The undermentioned promotion also appears in the same Gazette,

Brevet to be made Major, Captain John Edward Hale Prior, 80th Regiment, dated 29th November 1879 in recognition of his services during the Zulu Campaign.

1st DECEMBER 1879 The five companies reach Pretoria; also Lieutenant Lindop's escort.

Therefore six companies concentrated at Pretoria. The total strength:

1 Field Officer, 5 Captains, 5 Subalterns, 2 Staff,
26 Sergeants, 21 Corporals, 13 Drummers and 501 Privates.

The Officers: Lt. Col. C.Tucker Commanding
Brev. Major J.L.Bradshaw,
Captains A.Saunders, W.T. Anderson, H.J. Johnson, L.C. Potts,
Lieutenants S.W.Cameron, A.W.Hast, A.H.Lindop
2nd Lieutenants E.K.Daubeney, F.M.H.Marshall,
Lieutenant & Adjutant T.E.Griffin,
Quartermaster J. Pendrey

9th DECEMBER 1879 The Personal escort of General Sir Garnet Wolseley arrives at Pretoria and the following letter received,

"They had taken part in the attack on Sekukuni's stronghold and were the first British troops which reached the summit of the Fighting Koppie, gallantly taking at the point of the bayonet"

Letter as follows Army Headquarters Pretoria 9th December 1879 To. Lt.Col. C.Tucker Commanding Her Majesty's 80th Regiment

"Sir, I am directed by General Sir Garnet Wolseley to bring to your special notice the very admirable conduct of Sergeant Horton and the detachment of the 80th Regiment who formed the escort of the General Commanding during the recent operations against the chief Sekukuni. From the day when the General left Pretoria on the 18th October last and until his return today the behaviour of the Regiment has been all that could possibly be desired, it is not only that they gave any trouble or cause for reproof, but they showed a cheerfulness and willingness in their performance of their duties and was beyond praise, no soldier could have done better. Sergeant Horton and the whole of the detachment joined in the storming of the Fighting Koppie at Sekukuni's Town on the morning of the 28th November.

I have re etc., etc. signed Henry Brackenbury Lieutenant Colonel Military Secretary and Acting
Chief of Staff".

One casualty occurred in the escort, Private Calib Chare wounded. "F" & "G" Companies having joined at Lydenburg on the 16th November 1879, the detachment proceeded on the 20th under the command of Captain Walter Howard to join the column under the command of Major Bushman 9th Lancers.

"G" Company with Captain Roworth and Lieutenants Lyons "F" Company, Lieutenant Horsbrugh and Raitt march through the Waterfall Valley and join the force under Major Bushman consisting of 2 companies 94th Regiment, Lydenburg Rifles, Eckersleys Contingent and 8000 Swazis which on the 23rd November 1879 had formed the advanced laager of Fort George to open communications with the force operating from the other side.

14th DECEMBER 1879 For the first time, after taking part in four campaigns since November 1875 and since the first 300 men were sent to Perak from Hong Kong, the Regiment is concentrated at Pretoria, Transvaal. Many hardships and heavy marches were suffered during this period.

16th DECEMBER 1879 By London Gazette dated 16th December 1879 Captain and Brevet Major James Louis Bradshaw promoted to Major via C.J.R.Tyler retired on a pension and Captain John Edward Hale Prior Brev. Major from seconded list appointed Captain via Brev. Major J.L.Bradshaw, both to date from the 15th November 1879.

24th DECEMBER 1879 After a well earned rest, orders to proceed via Kimberley, Beaufort and Cape Town welcomely received!

26th DECEMBER 1879 The Regiment drawn up in close column at 11am with officers and Colours to the front and General Sir Garnet Wolseley taking the general salute. The following General Order is read out to the Regiment by the Chief of Staff:

"General Order by his Excellency Sir Garnet Wolseley G.C.M.G. K.C.B commanding the forces in South Africa. The 80th Regiment will march today from Pretoria by way of Potchefstroom and Kimberley to Beaufort West in the Cape Colony and will hence proceed by rail to Cape Town for England. The General commanding cannot allow this Regiment to enter upon its homeward march without expressing his high sense of its soldier-like bearing and conduct. The 80th Regiment has served for three years in South Africa during which time it has taken part in the Zulu war and in two expeditions against Sekukuni and has become the fatigue of long marches over a great extent of country yet after this varied and trying service its appearance and discipline would do credit to any Regiment in Her Majesty's Army. The General Commanding is well assured that in the march now before it the 80th Regiment under command of Lt.Col.Tucker will show to the inhabitants of the Transvaal, Grigualand West and the Cape Colony an example of what a British Regiment should be, not only in marching power but in loyalty, discipline and orderly conduct.

By Order Signed H. Brackenbury Lt. Col. Acting Chief of Staff Army Headquarters Pretoria
26th December 1879."

Sir Garnet Wolseley addressed Lt.Col.Tucker, the Officers and the Regiment with a few well chosen words and bade God's speed to England. The Regiment moved off from Pretoria, halting and encamping at Humops River, seven miles from Pretoria.

27th DECEMBER 1879 March to Kyokesky's river some twenty and half miles.

28th DECEMBER 1879 March to Groblio's Farm some thirty-five and a half miles distance.

29th DECEMBER 1879 March to Brait Valley approximately fifty and a half miles.

30th DECEMBER 1879 March to Windecfintein Valley some seventy miles.

31st DECEMBER 1879 March to Nia Wolman's Farm covering a distance of eighty-six and a half miles.

1st JANUARY 1880 March and reach Potchefstroom.

2nd JANUARY 1880 At Coumigas Spruit.

3rd JANUARY 1880 March for Klerksdorp.

4th JANUARY 1880 Halt at Klerksdorp, in consequence of the distributed state of the district and for the purposes of arresting Mr.Pretorius, President of the Peoples Committee, Boer Population. Lt.Col.Tucker, Captains Howard and Potts with Lieutenant Raitt in command of 57 non-commissioned officers and men returned to Potchefstroom on mule waggons.

5th JANUARY 1880 Lt.Col.Tucker and his small command reach Potchefstroom early in the morning. During the afternoon Lt.Col.Tucker recalls part of the Regiment to Potchefstroom and directs that the heavy baggage remain at Klerksdorp under an escort of ten men, with Captain Anderson in command and Lieutenant Lindop and 2nd Lieutenant Marshall accompanying.

6th JANUARY 1880 Regiment march from Klerksdorp lightly equipped at 8.00 am and reach Potchefstroom at 9.40pm covering a distance of thirty-three miles.

8th JANUARY 1880 The Regiment encamp at Potchefstroom. Mr.Pretorius admitted to bail.

13th JANUARY 1880 Regiment moves into camp outside the town. The Boers have broken up their encampment and dispersed. Under instructions by Sir Garnet Wolseley the route of the Regiment is changed from Kimberley and Beaufort to Heidelberg and Pietermaritzburg to Durban for embarkation. The following letter was received from the Landdrost of Potchefstroom:

Landdrost's Office Potchefstroom 13th January 1880 The Commanding Officer 80th Regiment, Potchefstroom

"Sir, I have much pleasure in now being able to inform you that Boers who were assembled at the north of the town Potchefstroom have dispersed and have left the place of encampment. As you have now moved your Regiment beyond the limits of the town of Potchefstroom you will allow me to offer you my congratulations on the efficient and orderly conduct of your men while in this place and am highly gratified to be to able say that not a single complaint has been made to me against any of your men and it is with great pleasure that I am able to say that not one case of drunkenness was brought to my notice in my office. Highly appreciating the efficient discipline which must be acknowledged as the distinctive feature of the conduct of your Regiment whilst in the town.

Believe me to be your obedient Servant, Landdrost."

14th JANUARY 1880 The Regiment march for Heidelberg.

16th JANUARY 1880 By local General Order No.122 dated Pietermaritzburg 16th January 1880, Major C.A.F.Creagh appointed to act provisionally as Special Commissioner in the Lydenburg District of the Transvaal Territory, from the 6th January 1880 under article 64 Section 1 of the Royal Warrant for Pay and Promotions dated 1st May 1878.

18th JANUARY 1880 The Regiment reach Heidelberg.

19th JANUARY 1880 The Regiment march for Sugar Bush River and holting and encamp.

20th JANUARY 1880 The Regiment remain encamped.

21st JANUARY 1880 The Regiment resume march and arrive at Newcastle, Natal by way of Standerton, Transvaal.

28th JANUARY 1880 Lt.Col.Tucker and his force encamp at Standerton, Transvaal.

29th JANUARY 1880 The Regiment remains encamped.

30th JANUARY 1880 The Regiment continues march towards Ladysmith.

3rd FEBRUARY 1880 Lt.Col.Tucker and the Regiment arrive at Ladysmith.

5th FEBRUARY 1880 The Regiment leave Ladysmith and march for Colenso and reach it that day. The following letter was received from Sir Garnet Wolseley Government House Pietermaritzburg Natal 30th January 1880

"Sir, I am directed by General Sir Garnet Wolseley to acknowledge the receipt of your letter to me of the 25th instant, forwarding copy of a letter from the Landdrost of Potchefstroom complimenting you upon the conduct of the Regiment under your command during your recent halt at that place. His excellency has read this testimony to the excellent behaviour of the 80th Regiment with much satisfaction and is equally glad to hear that your men have received similar commendation from the Landdrost of Utrecht. I have the honour etc. etc.

Signed Sir Ledger Herbert Private Secretary"

6th FEBRUARY 1880 The Regiment continues march towards Estcourt.

7th FEBRUARY 1880 Lt.Col.Tucker and the Regiment arrive at Estcourt.

8th FEBRUARY 1880 The Regiment encamp at Griffin's Farm eight miles from Estcourt.

9th FEBRUARY 1880 The Regiment march for and reach the Western Mooi River.

10th FEBRUARY 1880 The march is resumed and reaches Currie's Post.

11th FEBRUARY 1880 March and reach Howick.

12th FEBRUARY 1880 Regiment march into Pietermaritzburg and encamp above Fort Napier. After the arrival the following address is read,

Received from the people of Newcastle: Newcastle, Natal January 4th 1880 To the Officer Commanding 80th Regiment

"Sir, We the undersigned the inhabitants of Newcastle take this opportunity of expressing our regret at having to bid adieu to the gallant Regiment under your command for upwards of two years portions of the 80th were stationed here and we have lately watched its movements in the Zulu campaign and in the Transvaal with pride and interest finding that always and everywhere the 80th has behaved with bravery and steadiness and discipline and now finding that the conduct of some portions of Her Majesty's troops is

being called into question we wish to contribute one testimony to the excellent conduct of your Regiment, as far as our acquaintance. With it has gone during the whole time of its stay here the 80th won the respect and goodwill of all alike by the soldier-like qualities of the officers and non-commissioned officers and the admirable discipline which was sustained through all ranks. We do not think a better behaved Regiment ever came to Natal and we wish your stay with us could have been longer but you deserve your long delayed return to the "old country" and we heartily wish you and those under you a safe and pleasant journey home and every prosperity in the future. We are Sir,

Yours faithfully signed T.R.Haddon W.F.Cook D.Moodie"

Captains H.J.Johnson and C.C.Cole with Lieutenant H.H.Harward rejoin Headquarters.

14th FEBRUARY 1880 Lieutenant H.H.Harward is placed under arrest, charged with misbehaving before the enemy at the Intombi River on the 12th March 1879 in shamefully abandoning the party under his command and not taking proper precautions for their safety.

20th-27th FEBRUARY 1880 Lieutenant H.H.Harward brought to trial at Fort Napier, Piertermaritzburg. The Court finds that Lieutenant H.H.Harward is acquitted on all charges and that Lt.Harward be released from arrest.

23rd FEBRUARY 1880 The War Office issues the following statement:

'The Queen has been graciously pleased to signify Her intention to confer the decoration of the Victoria Cross upon the undermentioned non-commissioned officer and men of her Majesty's Army, whose claims have been submitted for Her Majesty's approval, for the gallant conduct displayed by them during the recent operations in South Africa, as recorded against their names:

80th Foot Colour Sergeant Anthony Booth

94th Foot Private Flawn 94th Foot Private Fitzpatrick"

24th FEBRUARY 1880 The London Gazette publishes the award of the Victoria Cross to Colour Sergeant Anthony Booth.

14th MARCH 1880 Lt.Harward returns to duty and continues his army career.

26th MARCH 1880 The Regiment march from Pretoria for embarkation and arrive at Botha's Hill where it encamps.

27th MARCH 1880 The Regiment remains encamped at Botha's Hill.

3rd APRIL 1880 The Regiment is transported by railway in three divisions from Botha's Hill and embarks H.M.S. *'Orontes'* at Durban. Lt.Col.Tucker in command and the following officers accompany the Regiment: Major J.L.Bradshaw; Captains W.Howard, C.E.W.Rowarth, W.T.Anderson, H.J.Johnson, C.C.Cole, L.C.Potts; Lieutenants S.W.Cameron, A.W.Hast, A.B.Horsbrugh, A.H.Lindop, F.W.Lyons, H.A.Raitt; 2nd Lieutenants E.K.Daubeney, F.M.H.Marshall; Lieutenant & Adjutant T.E.Griffin; Quartermaster J.Pendrey.

6th-9th APRIL 1880 H.M.S. *'Orontes'* calls at Simons Bay and refuels with coal.

10th APRIL 1880 The *'Orontes'* calls at Table Bay and here embark Captain and Brevet Major J.E.H.Prior and 2nd Lieutenant R.P.Colornt along with 133 non-commissioned officers and men, including women and children of the Regiment. On leaving Table Bay, the *'Orontes'*, with Captain Kinahan in command, the Regiment numbers 806 non-commissioned officers and men. During the voyage three deaths occur amongst the non-commissioned officers and men. Also on board ship 3 Officers and 240 men of the 2nd Battalion 4th Regiment of Foot with 40 women and 17 children in the charge of Lieutenant Little. On board also invalid detachments who belong to the following drafts:- 9th & 17th Lancers, Kings Dragoons, Royal Artillery, 3rd, 12th, 24th, 58th, 86th, 88th, 91st and 94th and 3rd Battalion 60th Rifles including drafts from both the Army Service and Hospital Corps.

The Embarkation Returns for HMS *"Orontes'* Officers, troops and others on the 2nd 3rd 9th and 10th April

	80th Regt.	Details
Officers & Families		
Officers	21	14
Ladies	2	3
Children		
7 and under 16 years	3	
1 and under 7 years	1	2
Staff Sgts & Families		
Men	8	10
Women	3	3

Children		
Boys		
14 and under 17 years	1	
10 and under 14 years	2	
Girls		
10 and under 17 years	1	2
Boys & Girls		
5 and under 10 years	2	3
1 and under 5 years		3

Troops & Other 3rd Class Passengers & Families N.C.O.'s not being Staff Sgts & Privates

Men	809	341
Women	18	16
Children		
Boys		
14 and under 17 years	1	2
10 and under 14 years	2	1
Girls		
10 and under 17 Years	1	1
Boys and Girls		
5 and under 10 years	9	10
1 and under 5 years	16	11
under 1 year of age	1	1
Horses	4	1

5th MAY 1880 Her Majesty's 80th Regiment of Foot, distribution state:-

2 Field Officers	7 Captains	10 Subalterns	2 Staff	8 Staff Sergeants
36 Sergeants	29 Corporals	14 Drummers	469 Privates	

Officers' families 2 Wives 4 Children   Soldiers' Families 19 Wives 33 Children
To Netley Invalids: 4 Privates.
To Netley Army Reserve: 1 Sgt. 42 Privates.
To Netley Time Expired: 2 Privates

Total   2 Field Officers   7 Captains   10 Subalterns   2 Staff   8 Staff Sergeants
    37 Sergeants   29 Corporals   14 Drummers   517 Privates
    Officers' Families 2 Wives 4 Children   Soldiers' Families 19 Wives 33 Children

Soldiers remaining in South Africa: 1 Field Officer   1 Captain   33 Privates Soldiers' Families   1 Wife

11th MAY 1880 The *'Orontes'* with the 80th Regiment of Foot arrive at King's Town. Lieutenant H.H.Harward resigns his commission.

12th MAY 1880 The Regiment disembark and march to Richmond Barracks. The Bands of the 57th and 84th Regiments played the 80th Regiment through the streets with Major General Glyn CB at the head of the Battalion.

14th MAY 1880 The depot companies 80th Regiment attached to the 38th Regiment join Headquarters.

2nd JUNE 1880 By Horse Guards letter: 200 Privates directed to be transferred to the 38th Regiment, the linked Battalion. Of this number 192 were transferred.

26th JUNE 1880 Colour Sergeant Anthony Booth receives his Victoria Cross at Windsor Castle, which is presented personally by Queen Victoria.

17th AUGUST 1880 The Regiment moves from Richmond Barracks to the Royal Barracks, Dublin and on the same day the depot companies 38th Regiment join Headquarters 80th Regiment. The 38th Regiment of Foot having embarked from Malta on the 9th August 1880, all the men of the 19th Brigade ordered to be transferred to the 80th Regiment of Foot.

18TH AUGUST 1880 180 non-commissioned officers and men transferred.

19TH AUGUST 1880 The annual inspection of the Regiment made by Major General Julius Richard Glyn CB, commanding the Dublin District.

THE BATTLE OF ULUNDI showing Lord Chelmsford's square, 4th July 1879, as depicted in the Illustrated London News.

Chapter 6
THE BATTLES INVOLVING THE 80th REGIMENT OF FOOT

Isandhlwana Wednesday January 22nd 1879

This first disastrous engagement of the Zulu War occurred on Wednesday January 22nd 1879 when the Zulu army attacked and took the British encampment belonging to No.3 Column on the slopes of Isandhlwana. King Cetshwayo had sent one of his Impi's of some twenty thousand warriors to oppose and repel the invading central column. He had planned to attack the invading force after January 22nd - the Impi was to move towards the invaders and rest in the shadows of the Nquthu mountain range.

For the British and Colonial Forces the events leading to the disaster commenced the previous day. On January 21st Lord Chelmsford, the Lieutenant General commanding the British forces in South Africa, ordered out reconnaissance parties with the hope of finding the main Zulu army. One of the patrols consisting of eighty men from the Natal mounted police and some forty volunteers under the command of Major J.Dartnell, made contact with a large number of Zulus during the late afternoon, approximately ten miles from the main camp. Because of the lateness of the day and the failing light Major Dartnell decided to stay out in the 'open' and send a message back to Lord Chelmsford of his findings, with a request for reinforcements prior to engaging the enemy in the morning. Lord Chelmsford decided to split his forces, leaving half of his force at Isandhlwana under the command of Brevet Lieutenant Colonel H.B.Pulliene while he,, himself with Colonel R.Glyn Officer Commanding No. 3 Column proceeded with the remainder to reinforce Major Dartnell with the intention of attacking what was thought to be the main Zulu army.

At approximately 4.00am on the 22nd, Lord Chelmsford and his command left Isandhlwana. Brevet Lt. Colonel Pulliene was left in command until Colonel A.W.Durnford R.E. who had been previously ordered to the camp would arrive. Durnford's and Pulliene's orders were quite simple and clear - 'defend the camp if attacked'.

At about 8.00am, prior to the arrival of Colonel Durnford, Zulus were reported to be advancing from the North East. Buglers sounded the 'fall in' and for over an hour watch was kept. Some two hours later Colonel Durnford arrived. It is assumed at this point in time that Col. Durnford took over command and shortly afterwards an order was given for a company of 1/24th Regiment with their Officer Lieutenant C.W.Cavaye to advance to the higher ground some fifteen hundred yards north of the camp. Shortly after this order was issued and having received further information about the Zulus, he decided to leave the camp himself with his original command. It is thought by some historians that this decision was to prevent any substantial Zulu force getting in between the camp and Lord Chelmsford's 'rear'. At approximately 12 noon mounted Basutos under the command of Lieutenant Raw on reconnoitering patrol spotted some cattle and upon further investigation discovered the main Zulu army in a large valley which had not yet been surveyed. The Zulus had no intentions of attacking on this day, but once they had been discovered there was to be no holding back - the die had been cast!

Back at the camp more gun fire was heard and again the buglers summoned the troops to 'fall in'. Shortly afterwards Captain W.E.Mostyn with his company and Lieutenant Cavaye's company, started to engage the enemy, eventually having to withdraw slowly back towards the camp. At approximately 12.30pm, Zulus were reported to be advancing on the right of the camp. It is generally acknowledged that by 1.00pm all the defenders of the camp were fully occupied in fighting the Zulus.

For the defenders of the camp totalling sixty-seven officers and one thousand seven hundred and seven non-commissioned officers and men, things went disastrously wrong. The Zulus both outnumbered and out-manoeuvered the British forces. By 2.00pm all constructive fighting to defend the camp had ceased, with the survivors endeavouring to make good their escape. At approximately 2.30pm the camp was taken by the Zulus.

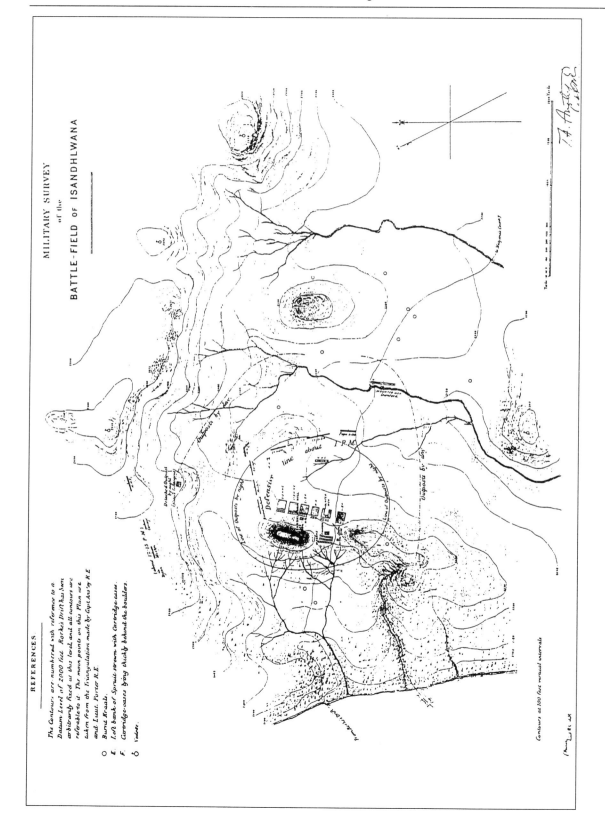

MILITARY SURVEY

of the

BATTLE-FIELD OF ISANDHLWANA

REFERENCES

The Contours are numbered with reference to a
Datum Level of 2000 feet. Rorkes Drift has been
arbitrarily fixed at this level, and all contours are
referable to it. The main points on this Plan are
taken from the Triangulation made by Capt. Anstey R.E.
and Lieut. Porter R.E.

○   Burnt Kraals.
E.   Left bank of Spruit strewn with Cartridge cases.
F.   Cartridge-cases lying thickly behind the boulders.
☒   Vedet.

Contours at 100 Feet vertical intervals.

In the annals of British military history this was to be the most catastrophic annihilation of a modern army by a force whose warriors carried no more than spears and shields. The casualties sustained by the British and Colonial forces on the battlefield were, killed in action fifty-two officers and eight hundred and six non-commissioned officers and men, including four hundred and seventy-one native and non-combatant troops; a total of 1329 men. It is estimated that Zulu casualties were in excess of one thousand men killed in action or dying of their wounds. The 80th Regiment of Foot attached to No.3 Column lost seven men in the action these being:

2081 Private Henry Thompson (Acting Quartermaster Sergeant, Headquarter Staff)
1271 Sergeant William Johnson   1377 Private John Chesterton   1433 Private Edwin Holman
599 Private William McDonald   675 Private William Seymour   9/60 Private Joseph Whitehouse

Two of the survivors who escaped the carnage of Isandhlwana were members of the 80th Regiment, Privates 919 Samuel Wassall and 228 Thomas Westwood, both members of the 1st Squadron Mounted Infantry. Whilst escaping certain death, Samuel Wassall, almost at the point of reaching safety, stopped and rode back into the foaming and fast flowing waters of the Buffalo River to rescue his drowning comrade. Whilst under enemy fire and coping with the perilous waters, Samuel rescued Thomas Westwood. In doing so was later to be awarded the first Victoria Cross of the Zulu campaign.

The Opposing Forces

British and Colonial Forces

No.2 Column.
Officer Commanding, Colonel A.W.Durnford R.E.
No.11 Battery, 7th Brigade, Royal Artillery
Natal Native Horse: Sikali's Horse (No's 1, 2 and 3 Troops)
Hlubi Troop   Edale Troop   1st Battalion 1st Regiment Natal Native Contingent

No.3 Column (part)
Officer Commanding, Brevet Lt.Colonel H.B.Pulliene 1/24th
'N' Battery, 5th Brigade, Royal Artillery
5th (Field) Company, Royal Engineers (Detachment)
1st Battalion 24th Regiment of Foot, ('A', 'C', 'E', 'F' and 'H' Companies)
2nd Battalion 24th Regiment of Foot ('G' Company)   90th Regiment of Foot (Detachment)
Army Service Corps   Army Hospital Corps
Army Medical Department   1st Squadron Mounted Infantry
Natal Mountain Police (Detachment)   Natal Volunteer Corps
Natal Carbineers   Newcastle Mounted Rifles
Buffalo Border Guard   Natal Native Pioneer Corps (No.1 Company-Details)
1st Battalion 3rd Regiment Natal Native Contingent (Detachment)
2nd Battalion 3rd Regiment Natal Native Contingent (Detachment)

Zulu Forces
Chiefs in command, Ntshingwayo and Mavumengwana
Right Horn* - uDududu, isaNgqu, imBube (comprising the uNodwengu 'Corps') and uNokhenke
Chest* - umCijo, umXapho (contingents) and uMbonambi
Left Horn*- inGobamakhosi and uVe
Loins* (Reserve) - uThulwana, inDluyengwe, inDlondlo (comprising of members of the uNdi 'Corps') and
                                                                                         uDloko

(NB. *positions of the various Regiments and Corps at the start of the attack)

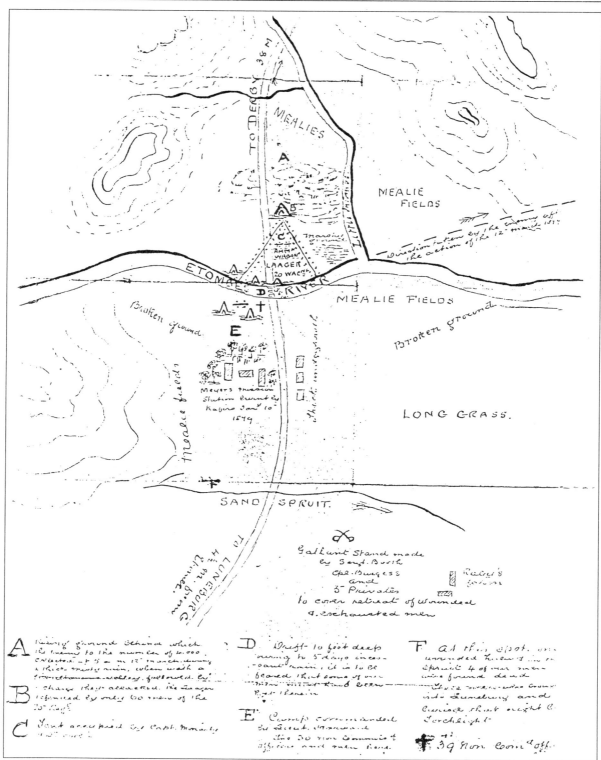

Map of the Intombi River and Mealie Fields, the original of which was found amongst the
papers of Lieutenant-Colonel Charles Tucker (later Major-General)

Intombi River Wednesday March 12th 1879

The second disaster that befell the British and Colonial forces was on Wednesday March 12th 1879 at a river crossing known as Myer's Drift on the Intombi River. The 80th Regiment of Foot (Staffordshire Volunteers) on this day suffered its own private disaster, although on a smaller scale than the Isandhlwana catastrophe.

The lines of communication and transport to Luneburg where the 80th were based was a roadway which stretched some one hundred and thirty miles from Lydenburg, passing the main settlements of Middleburg and Derby. The only means of moving stores and equipment were by cattle-drawn waggons. During late February a convoy of eighteen waggons was commissioned to deliver stores and provisions to Luneburg. Major Tucker, the Officer Commanding at Luneburg, on March 1st ordered out 'D' Company under the command of Captain W.T.Anderson with the instructions to meet these waggons and escort them into Luneburg. However, due to other pressing needs Major Tucker, on March 5th, recalled Captain Anderson and his Company. Two days later Captain Moriarty with a detachment of Company strength was ordered out to locate the waggon convoy and again escort it safely into Luneburg. Captain Moriarty was accompanied by Lieutenant H.J.Johnson and 2nd Lieutenant A.H.Lindop.

The first of the waggons were found at a place called Myer's Drift, a crossing on the Intombi River. They found that following the withdrawal of Captain Anderson's Company, whilst the convoy had no armed escort, Zulus had attacked the waggons and driven off some of the cattle used to pull the waggons. Not having sufficient oxen, the waggoners had decided to try to haul the waggons in relays. This was obviously very unsatisfactory, knowing full well that Prince Mbilini's stronghold was situated quite nearby and that he held allegiance to King Cetshwayo.

Because of the heavy rain the river was swift flowing and had risen to such an extent that it was now approximately forty-five metres across. Several waggons were now stranded on the north bank of the river, following an attempt to get one waggon across, with the result of it becoming marooned mid-stream, unable to be pulled forward or back.

Over the next couple of days, men and animals toiled in the appalling weather conditions and eventually got all the remaining waggons down to the drift. By March 9th all of the waggons were assembled at the river crossing, Lieutenant Lindop and some of the men meanwhile had managed to get two of the waggons across the river but due to the heavy and continuous rain no more were able to be got across and there was no alternative but to sit it out until the waters of the river subsided.

On March 11th Major Tucker accompanied by Lieutenant H.H.Harward, set out to discover the whereabouts of this now overdue convoy. They soon found them encamped on either side of the swollen river, sixteen waggons on the north bank and the other two on the south bank. Major Tucker seeing for himself the plight of the situation, expressed deep concern at the method of laagering of the twin encampments. On the north bank waggons had been lined up to form an inverted 'V' from the river, the waggons were obviously too far apart and the whole scenario was somewhat unorthordox. Captain Moriarty acknowledged the situation, but reciprocated by pointing out the terrain, the ground and the weather conditions, as well as the general state of both the men and animals. As history tells, nothing was done to alter the state of affairs, to the probaleble detriment of the whole encampment.

Major Tucker left the camp taking with him the two Lieutenants Johnson and Lindop, Lieutenant Harward remained to give assistance to the Captain. Later the same day Harward with some men went in search of stray cattle, returning just before dark. Upon his return Lieutenant Harward went to the Captain's tent and fell asleep, only to be awakened and ordered across the river, because a sergeant was the senior ranking soldier in charge on that side of the river.

In South Africa, the time of dusk is extremely limited and just prior to actual darkness sentries were posted to both encampments and the cattle were herded inside the 'V' shaped laager with the soldiers going to their tents and the conductors and drivers going either into or underneath their waggons. All precautions appeared to have been taken and the men and animals settled down for the night. In the early hours of the next day, March 12th., at approximately 4.00am a single shot was heard by the sentries on the south bank. Lieutenant Harward was told and he made his men 'stand to'. A message was sent across the river to inform the Captain. It appears that the only instructions given by Captain Moriarty was for the sentries guarding his side of the river to be on greater alert.

A mist now settled over the encampments and river. Taking advantage of this, at approximately 4.40am, Prince Mbilini and his forces crept undetected to within ninety metres of the main laager and began to attack. Men in various stages of undress and consciousness fell out of their beds, tents and waggons to try and repel the enemy, but to no avail. Within minutes the Zulus were in amongst the tents and animals, and men were being stabbed with assegai or bludgeoned to death with the knobkerry. The men on the south bank, as soon as they had located the enemy, opened fire, this in turn attracting the enemy to them. Part of the Zulu forces started to cross the fast flowing river to attack them as well.

Lieutenant Harward seeing his small element of command starting to disintegrate, ordered his second in command, Sergeant Anthony Booth, to rally as many men as he could and to carry out a fighting retreat to a remote disused farmhouse some three miles from the river. Harward then mounted his horse and left the field to summons help from Major Tucker at Luneburg. Sergeant Booth with great presence of mind, and coolness and discipline, along with several other men under his command, held firm and with steady volleys kept the enemy at bay. This enabled them to retire in an orderly manner and also allow any fleeing survivors to escape from certain death.

Major Tucker was alerted at approximately 6.30am by Lieutenant Harward and immediately ordered as many mounted men as could be mustered to proceed with utmost speed to the Intombi River. A further one hundred and fifty men were to immediately follow on foot. It was not long before Tucker and his mounted force were in sight of the strickened encampments. The Zulus spotting in the distance the advancing 'Red Coats', withdrew back to their stronghold some five kilometres to the North-East. But Mbilini had successfully taken the camps, driven off the cattle and taken most of the supplies and ammunition.

Anthony Booth with his little command of bedraggled survivors were now safe and were ordered to continue into Luneburg. The sight that the rescuers now beheld was a scene of utter carnage; their fellow comrades lay dead in various postures, horrendously mutilated. Captain Moriarty had commanded one hundred and five soldiers, including a civil surgeon; of these, he along with sixty non-commissioned officers and men, including Civil Surgeon Cobbin lay dead. Two white waggon conductors and fifteen black drivers had also been killed. The remainder of the day was spent collecting and burying the dead, the majority to remain forever where they had fallen on the banks of the Intombi River.

Sergeant Anthony Clarke Booth, the next day was promoted to Colour Sergeant and was later to be awarded a most deserved Victoria Cross for the coolness he had displayed whilst heavily outnumbered and saving so many lives on that disastrous day.

Opposing Forces
British Forces
80th Regiment of Foot

North Bank:	Officer Commanding	Captain D.B.Moriarty	
	1 Colour Sergeant	4 Corporals	64 Privates
	1 Civil Surgeon	Conductors and Drivers (exact numbers unknown)	
South Bank	Senior Officer, Lieutenant H.H.Harward		
	1 Sergeant	33 Privates	Conductors and Drivers (exact numbers unknown)

Zulu Forces
Swazi/Zulu Warriors totalled four hundred* Chief in Command Mbilini

* Various witness accounts have indicated that the attacking forces varied from four hundred to four thousand with reports that casualties ranged from twenty-five to two hundred.

Kambula Saturday March 29th 1879

Following the major disaster at Isandhlwana, Colonel H.E.Wood VC CB who was in command of the Left Column (No.4), was instructed to carry out a 'holding position' until such time that Lord Chelmsford could reorganize his forces for the conquest of the Zulu Nation. He established a fortified camp at Kambula providing protection from possible attack on Utrecht and Luneberg. Before the second invasion of Zululand began, Colonel Wood was ordered to create diversionary actions, both to keep the Zulus in the North East occupied and also hopefully to draw other Zulu forces away from Eshowe which was under seige and Ulundi which was the main target of the invasion. The camp at Kambula was six miles from Zungwin Mountain, beyond which lay the Hlobane and Itentika Mountains.

The first diversionary attack was to be an assault on Hlobane Mountain, the reputed stronghold of Mbilini and his followers. This took place on March 28th with disastrous results. The plan was to scale the mountain plateau from two differing points and then, once upon the mountain, to combine forces and flush out the enemy. During the assault both of the attacking forces at differing times spotted a Zulu army moving in five columns on the far side of the mountain. The exact whereabouts of this Impi of some twenty thousand warriors was unknown. But the Impi, once alerted by the gunfire of the assault, moved in to engage Wood's forces on the mountain. Outnumbered and in danger of being cut off from the main camp at Kambula, a somewhat hasty retreat was called and the third of Chelmsford reverses was enacted. Satisfied that the mountain was cleared of the British, the Zulus moved off to rest by the Umvolosi River!

Despite this defeat, Colonel Wood at least now knew the Zulus' exact location and strength, and with fresh intelligence he realised that they were intending to attack him which was further confirmed the next morning when one of Uhamu's men arrived at the camp with a party of Raaf's Corps who had been on patrol. They told him that the Zulu Impi were intending to make their attack on Kambula at about midday that very day (Saturday March 29th). At about 11.00a.m the Zulus were reported to be moving in five columns, the actual direction of their march unclear. At approximately 12.45pm, after the soldiers had had their lunch, tents were dropped and the final preparations for the defence were completed.

King Cetshwayo had instructed his military leaders not to take on the enemy in fortified positions, but to tempt the defenders out into the open. Unconvinced of the Zulus' intentions and commitment to attack and fearing that they might bypass his fortified positions, Wood ordered out his mounted troops to provoke them into attacking. The ruse was complete, the Zulus were well disciplined but with the success of Isandhlwana and more recently Hlobane fresh in their minds, they advanced to attack the fortified positions, against the King's instructions. By 2.15pm, the attacks on Kambula were fully committed on different flanks and at different times without any co-ordination and the defenders easily fought them off. At about 5.00pm, the Zulus appeared to lose some of their zest for the fight and their attacks lost momentum. Consequently Colonel Wood ordered out his mounted troops. The Zulus started to retreat and before long, it turned into a rout. The Zulus were not accustomed to taking prisoners and they asked for no quarter - and none was given!

The encampment at Kambula contained a total of two thousand and eighty-six defenders, of which eighty-eight men were listed as sick. The cost of the battle on the British side amounted to three officers and twenty-six rank and file killed in action and a further five officers and forty-nine men wounded. Only one man belonging to the 80th Regiment was wounded and that was 1387 Lance-Sergeant Thomas Brown who was attached to the 11th Battery, 7th Brigade Royal Artillery. He was severely wounded in the head. The Zulus lost in excess of one thousand in this fierce battle and this was the most critical battle of the war - it is believed that the Zulus finally realised then that they would not be able to vanquish these soldiers from their country.

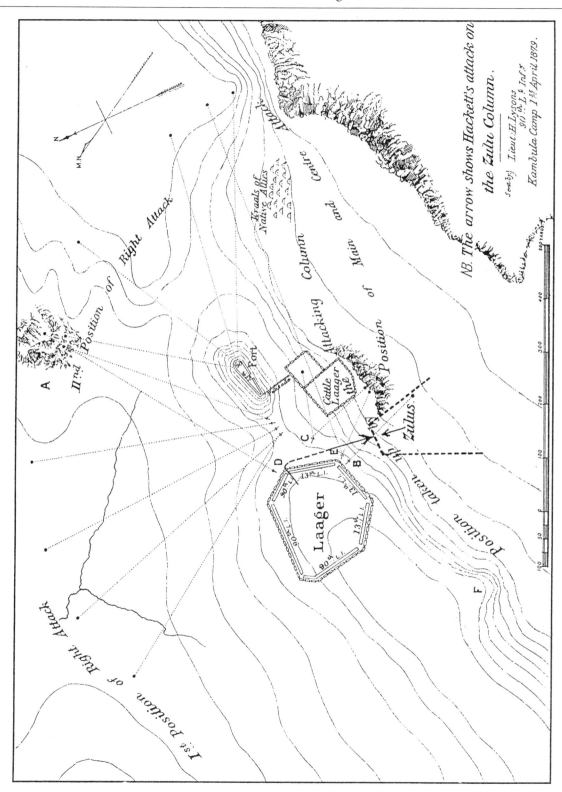

Battle of Kambula

Opposing Forces
British and Colonial Forces
Officer Commanding, Colonel Wood V.C. C.B.

Main Laager

No. 11 Battery, 7th Brigade Royal Artillery   Royal Engineers (Detachments)

1st Battalion 13th Regiment of Foot (7 Companies)   90th Regiment of Foot (7 Companies)

Mounted Infantry (1 Squadron)   Frontier Light Horse (4 Troops)

Raaf's Transvaal Rangers (2 Troops)   Baker's Horse

Kaffrarian Rifles   Dutch Burghers

Border Horse   Mounted Basutos

Wood's Irregulars   Hamu's Warriors

Redoubt   90th Regiment of Foot (1 Company) (With two Guns)

Cattle Laager

1st Battalion 13th Regiment of Foot (1½ Companies)

90th Regiment of Foot (1 Company)

Zulu Forces
Chiefs in Command, Ntshingwayo and Mnyamana

Right Horn* - inGobamakhosi

Chest*

Right - uDloko, uDududu, isaNgqu, imBube, uThulwana, inDluyengwe and inDlondlo

Left - uNokhenke and uMbonambi

Left Horn* - umCijo

(NB. *positions of the various Regiments and Corps at the start of the attack)

The Battle of Kambula portayed by the London Illustrated News

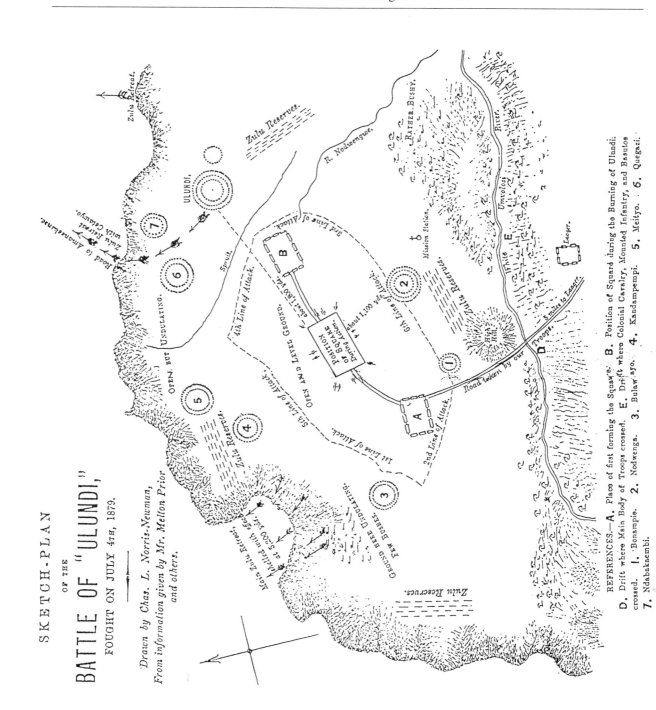

SKETCH-PLAN
OF THE
BATTLE OF "ULUNDI,"
FOUGHT ON JULY 4TH, 1879.

Drawn by Chas. L. Norris-Newman,
From information given by Mr. Melton Prior
and others.

REFERENCES.—A. Place of first forming the Square. B. Position of Square during the Burning of Ulundi. D. Drift where Main Body of Troops crossed. E. Drift where Colonial Cavalry, Mounted Infantry, and Basutos crossed. 1. Bonampie. 2. Nodwenga. 3. Bulawayo. 4. Kandampempi. 5. Meityo. 6. Quegazi. 7. Ndabakaembi.

Ulundi Friday July 4th 1879

Sir Garnet Wolseley had been sent out to take command of the forces in South Africa in an endeavour to bring the war to an early conclusion. He was also commanded to sort out the future of Zululand and its people. Lord Chelmsford knowing that he was being replaced by Wolseley, prior to him taking command wanted one more victory against the Zulus, to leave his military reputation intact - albeit a little tarnished. To finally defeat the Zulu army at Ulundi and destroy the Zulu King's residence would vindicate the reverses suffered by the British and Colonial Forces earlier in the campaign.

The 2nd Division and the Flying Column were still under the direct control of Lord Chelmsford and on July 3rd they marched to the White Umvolosi River. A few days earlier negotiations for peace had been in progress but certain demands had not been fulfilled, and Chelmsford therefore continued his preparations to move forward and take the Zulu King's kraal at Ulundi.

On July 4th, leaving five Companies of 1/24th Regiment of Foot, one Company of Royal Engineers and various detachments from other Regiments to defend his encampment, he ordered the advance to attack and destroy Ulundi. At 6.00am, the mounted men of the Flying Column crossed the Umvolosi River, closely followed by the combined forces of the 2nd Division and the Flying Column. As soon as this attacking force reached suitable ground at about 7.30am, they were formed into one huge hollow rectangle. The 80th Regiment of Foot consisting of five Companies formed the vanguard of this human fighting 'square'. A pair of gattling guns were positioned in the centre of the advancing face of the 'square' with a further twelve pieces of artillery distributed along the other sides and corners. Once the order had been given to continue the march at 8.00am, the band of the 13th Regiment of Foot started to play and the various Colours were unfurled and displayed.

At approximately 8.45am, the Zulu forces which had started to merge together, came into contact with the mounted men whom Chelmsford had sent out in advance. After baiting the Zulus to attack, the mounted men soon retired within the hollow 'Square'. Fifteen to twenty thousand Zulu warriors then manoeuvred to attack the invading force. The British and Colonial soldiers were positioned four deep on each face of the 'square', the front two rows kneeling with the rear two standing. With the use of modern rifles and gattling guns and artillery, the Zulus had no chance. Their attacks became uncoordinated, although some two to three thousand warriors did make a determined attempt to break the ranks at one of the corners held by the 21st and 58th Regiments of Foot.

After experiencing the devastating effect of the fire power at Kambula, the Zulus realised that they could never compete against the whiteman's technology. Some fifty minutes later, at about 9.35am, noting that the momentum of the Zulu attack had lessened, Lord Chelmsford ordered the Cavalry out to attack the retreating Zulus. The retreat turned into a rout and the Zulus were pursued with no quarter asked or given. Shortly after 10.00am, the artillery was ordered to shell Ulundi and then to put Ulundi to the torch. Other kraals were burned and the smoke from the Mahlabathini Plains could be seen for miles around. Following the battle and the burning of the kraals, the wounded were attended to, the dead buried and the troops allowed to have a meal. At 2.00pm the men were ordered to retire to their own encampment. The Zulus were beaten and Isandhlwana had been avenged.!

Of the four thousand, one hundred and sixty-six Europeans and one thousand and five natives who took part in this battle, the British and Colonial casualties amounted to two officers and ten men and three natives killed. Two of the men killed were members of the 80th Regiment of Foot, 1630 Sergeant James Henry Watts and 1892 Private Joseph Floyd. A total of nineteen officers and sixty-nine men including ten natives were wounded. Five of the men wounded belonged to the 80th Regiment of Foot, 1249 Sergeant Thomas O'Neill (severely wounded), 19/636 Corporal Albert Beecroft (severely wounded), 19/669 Private Patrick Tully (dangerously wounded), 1213 Private William Lunt (dangerously wounded) and 1616 Private Michael Duffy (severely wounded).

The Zulu army was beaten in the open and the King's principal residence destroyed. Lord Chelmsford and his forces had completed their objectives. The only thing that remained for complete victory was for the capture of Cetshwayo, the King of the Zulus and this task became the responsibility of Sir Garnet Wolseley.

Opposing Forces

British and Colonial Forces   General Commanding, Lieutenant-General Lord Chelmsford K.C.B.

2nd Division   Officer Commanding, Major-General Edward Newdigate

'N' Battery 6th Brigade, Royal Artillery   'N' Battery 5th Brigade, Royal Artillery
17th Lancers   2/21st Regiment of Foot
58th Regiment of Foot   94th Regiment of Foot
2nd Battalion Natal Native Contigent   Shepstone's Horse
Bettington's Horse   Army Medical Department

Flying Column   Officer Commanding, Colonel Evelyn Wood V.C., C.B.

'10' Battery 7th Brigade, Royal Artillery   '11' Battery 7th Brigade, Royal Artillery
5th (Field) Company, Royal Engineers   1/13th Regiment of Foot
80th Regiment of Foot   90th Regiment of Foot
Wood's Irregulars   Natal Native Pioneers
Mounted Infantry (1st Squadron)   Transvaal Rangers
Frontier Light Horse   Natal Light Horse   Baker's Horse
Edendale Troop, Natal Native Horse   Detachment of Army Hospital Corps.

Zulu Forces   Chiefs in Command,   Ziwedu, Mnyamana, Dabulamanzi and Ntshingwayo

Regiments: inGobamakhosi   umXhapho   isaNgqu   uThulwana
                    iOwa   izinGulube   uDududu   uVe
                    uDloko   inDluyengwe   uNokhenke   inSukamngeni
                    uMbonambi   inDlondlo

N.B. It should be noted that the Zulu forces consisted of elements of all the amabutho except the inDabakawombe and uDlambedlu who were with the King.

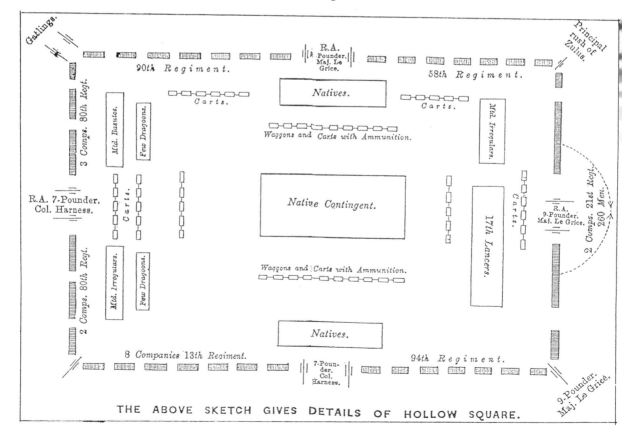

A diagrammatic representation of the Square at Ulundi

Chapter 7
THE INTOMBI RIVER INCIDENT

During March 1879 Major Charles Tucker was in command of five Companies of the 80th Regiment of Foot at Luneburg. Up until this time these companies had no involvement in the actual conflict, although seven members who had volunteered for the mounted section had died at the Battle at Isandhlwana on January 22nd. The main road by which military supplies were transported between the Transvaal and Natal ran up from Luneburg through to Derby and Middleburg, approximately one hundred and thirty miles. This road crossed the Intombi River, a tributary of the Pongola, approximately four and a half miles from Luneburg, at a place called Myer's Drift. The road ran close to the Zulu border and at this time, was subject to attacks by Zulu and Swazi irregulars under the leadership of Mbilini, (Mbilini was a Swazi prince who owed allegiance to the Zulu king Cetswayo).

Late in February one such convoy of eighteen waggons loaded with ammunition, stores and provisions left Lydenburg for Natal. On March 1st Major Tucker sent out Captain W.T.Anderson and Lieutenant Daubeney with "D" Company to meet the convoy at Derby and escort it into Luneburg. On Wednesday March 5th "D" Company was required for other duties and consequently recalled. The convoy was thus left to continue its journey unescorted.

On Friday March 7th Captain D.B.Moriarty accompanied by Lieutenant H.J.Johnson and 2nd Lieutenant A.H.Lindop were ordered out with a detachment of company strength consisting of 103 non-commissioned officers and men. Civil Surgeon William Ingram Cobbin also accompanied this military detachment. Captain Moriarty's orders were to escort the convoy down the dangerous lower sections of the road where it passed within four miles of Mbilini's Kraal.

Within a couple of hours Captain Moriarty and his command reached Myer's Drift about four and a half miles from Luneburg passing the deserted Myer's Farmhouse some two miles back from the river. The river at this time was forty-five metres across, swollen by the continuous heavy rains. The crossing point at the drift was in a large open area, although it was overlooked by high broken ground. Because of the rains the drift was impassable. Seven of the waggons had reached the north side of the river, but were unable to go any further. The approaches to the river had become extremely muddy and one of the seven waggons had become stranded whilst attempting to get it across. Captain Moriarty ordered suitable materials to be gathered and with the equipment they had brought with them, a raft was constructed and used some ninety metres up stream from the drift. At this point the southern bank was less steep. It took the rest of that day to complete the building of the raft and to set up a camp with the waggons on the north side of the river.

On the morning of March 8th, Captain Moriarty with Lieutenant Johnson set out north to search for the rest of the convoy. Lieutenant Lindop and two platoons remained to work on the approaches to the south bank and to guard the waggons on the north bank. Moriarty found the remaining waggons approximately three miles north of the drift with eleven civilian conductors and thirty kaffirs who had formed a laager with the waggons. Josiah Sussens from Pretoria was in charge of the laager and welcomed the Captain and his escort. Sussens reported to Moriarty that the Zulus had previously attacked the laager and driven off forty-six of the oxen.

During the next forty-eight hours the soldiers and civilians struggled in the pouring rain with the remaining oxen to move the waggons to the river and by the end of the next day, March 9th, the remaining section of the convoy had reached Myer's Drift. The river crossing was still impassable, in fact the level was still rising, although by this time the soldiers and civilians who had remained had managed to ferry two of the waggons across. Because of the rising water level and the dangerous current, it was decided that nothing could be done now until the river subsided. Captain Moriarty ordered a laager to be made with the waggons on the north bank but unfortunately they were positioned in a somewhat unorthodox manner. The sixteen waggons were arranged in a 'V' shape, the base legs starting some eighteen metres from the river edge, both sides of the laager approximately

The Intombi River Drift.
During March 1879 the river would have been at least 600mm deeper making the river up to
2.4m-2.7m deep at its centre.

The site of Captain Moriarty's encampment looking towards Mbilini's stronghold.

Sergeant Anthony Booth rallying survivors.

The mass grave the other side of the track, where Lt. Harward's provision waggons
stood at the time of the attack.

sixty metres long with its apex ninety metres from the river. For the soldiers on the north bank, four bell tents were erected between the river bank and the waggons on the upstream leg of the 'V'. The three ammunition carts and draft oxen were positioned inside the 'V'. Captain Moriarty had his own tent erected outside the 'V' by the apex near the road. To the west of the laager lay high broken ground beyond mealie fields and to the east an area of marshy ground leading to the small Little Intombi River and beyond this further mealie fields.

The men on the south bank pitched their three tents in a row next to the two waggons, approximately forty metres from the road and thirty metres from the river.

Throughout the 10th the heavy rains continued and the men took shelter in their tents. The European conductors slept in their own waggons and the voorloopers took shelter underneath. The rains continued during the morning of the 11th eventually stopping in the afternoon. During this break in the weather, Major Tucker arrived at the camp with Lieutenant Harward to find out what had happened to the convoy. He disapproved of the laager that had been formed and pointed out to Captain Moriarty that the waggons were too far apart, the legs of the 'V' being too far from the river and in general that the defensive arrangements were inadequate. Captain Moriarty reported the difficulties he had encountered in the muddy conditions, positioning the waggons and also pointed out that the gap between the waggons and the river had increased due to the water level subsiding. It was hoped to ferry the remaining waggons across the river the following day and therefore Captain Moriarty felt that the existing arrangements need not be changed. Major Tucker left things as they were and rode back to Luneburg with Lieutenant Johnson and 2nd Lieutenant Lindop, leaving Lieutenant H.H.Harward with the Captain.

Later that day Lieutenant Harward rode out of the camp with a few men to search for some oxen which had strayed. The party returned to camp just before dark and Lieutenant Harward went to the Captain's tent and fell asleep. The oxen were inside the laager with the men who were not on guard duty. All precautions appeared to have been taken and all seemed safe and secure. Captain Moriarty had left thirty-four men on the south side (Luneburg side) of the river, with only one non-commissioned officer, Sergeant Anthony Booth in charge, so he woke up the Lieutenant and ordered him across the river to be in command. Throughout the night it rained continually again and gradually a thick mist settled over the river. Just before dawn, around 4.00am on the 12th March, a shot was heard by the sentries on the south bank. Lieutenant Harward was informed and he immediately ordered his men to "stand to" and sent a messenger to the Captain. Captain Moriarty ordered his sentries, who where located approximately fourteen to eighteen metres right and left of his tent to be on the alert and went back to sleep.

The rain eventually stopped and the waggons on the south bank were just visible through the mist. The Zulus crept to within ninety metres of the encampment on the north bank and then fired a volley into the laager. Then they threw down their rifles and charged into the laager, stabbing relentlessly with their assegais. At this point, one of the sentries on the south bank spotted the Zulus and opened fire to raise the alarm. The sentries on the north also located the Zulus and opened fire on them. However, so suddenly had the Zulus appeared that before the men in the laager on the north side could get to their positions the Zulus were amongst them stabbing and killing them as they emerged from their tents. Hearing the alarm, Captain Moriarty rushed from his tent just outside the laager to be surrounded by the enemy. He shot dead three of them, but fell wounded by an assegai which had been thrown and then was hit by gunfire. As he fell, he cried out, "Fire away boys! Death or glory!" Within a matter of minutes, the Doctor, the majority of the enlisted men, the black drivers and the waggon conductors had all been killed.

As soon as Lieutenant Harward and his men opened fire, a large section of the attacking Zulu force broke off their attack on the north bank and started to cross the river. Lieutenant Harward's command seemed to start to disintegrate now and at this point he decided to ride off to Luneburg for help. But before he left the field, he ordered Sergeant Booth to fall back and try to make for the deserted farmhouse approximately three miles away, with as many men as he could muster. Sergeant

Battle at the Intombi River 12th March 1879

Booth with Lance Corporal Burgess and several men retreated from the river slowly, firing controlled volleys and thus holding off the greatly superior enemy force. This enabled his small command and some other fleeing survivors to escape the horrors of the attacking Zulu forces. For the gallant conduct and coolness he displayed in this action he was to win the Victoria Cross. Lieutenant Harward reached Luneberg and alerted Major Tucker at about 6.30am, reporting that the camp at Myer's Drift was in the possession of the enemy.

Major Tucker immediately ordered every man who could be mounted to proceed to Myer's Drift. Instructions were also given that two companies, approximately one hundred and fifty men of 'C' Company under the command of Lieutenant T.J.Chamberlain and 'H' Company under the command of Lt. L.C.Potts were to follow on. Captain W.T.Anderson with 'D' Company were to remain to guard the fort.

When they saw the mounted force of redcoats approaching,, the Zulus made off eastwards, having already by now successfully looted the waggons and driven off the oxen. Major Tucker and his troops rode into the devastated camp and were met by one soldier and two kaffirs who came out of hiding. Sixty-two members of the escort including two white waggon conductors and fifteen black drivers had perished. The bodies which had not been carried away by the river were lying all about the place, the majority naked, some partly clothed, all butchered and badly mutilated by assegai wounds. It did not take long for the remaining troops to reach the stricken camp and they immediately began a search for the missing men. An inspection of the camp revealed that the whole of the ammunition had been captured including blankets and rifles. The rocket equipment and rockets had been removed from their containers but had not been taken.

An enormous burial trench was started which took most of the day. Around 5.00pm, Major Tucker read a burial service over the dead, although twenty men were still missing. The bodies of Captain Moriarty and Doctor Cobbin were brought back into Luneburg and buried on the 13th March. The men were ordered back into Luneburg and en-route they searched all the mealie fields and long grass. Approximately three miles from the river more bodies were found and they too were brought into Luneburg and at about 9.00pm these were laid to rest by torchlight.

The search for the missing men was resumed on the 13th March but no more were found. On the 14th March the river level continued to fall and on the 15th March a party of men were ordered out to reclaim the waggons. They managed to move the remaining waggons across the river and bring in ten waggons and whilst doing so they discovered three bodies along with a number of rifles in the river. On the 16th March the rest of the waggons were transported into Luneburg including a further three bodies found in the river.

Of all the engagements of the Zulu War, this was the most disastrous encounter for the 80th Regiment of Foot. Captain Moriarty with seventy-eight other men of Her Majesty's Forces had perished savagely before the sun had hardly begun its daily journey across the African sky.

The Official returns of the War Office

The following dispatches were received at the War Office on the 21st April 1879, from the Lieutenant-General Commanding the Forces South Africa:

"Sir, It is my sad duty to report to you that on the morning of the 12th March a convoy of waggons, halted on its road from Derby to Luneburg, on the left bank of the Intombi River, was attacked by the Zulus, and with the exception of some ten men who escaped by swimming the river, the whole of the escort who were within the waggon laager on that bank are reported to have been killed. The Officer in command of the detachment on the right bank, Lieutenant Harward, 80th Regiment, appears to have done his utmost to assist his comrades in their unequal struggle, as soon as he was aware of what was occuring. I have the honour to forward the report from this officer, and that of Major Tucker, 80th Regiment, commanding at Luneburg. I have desired that Colonel Wood make further enquiries into the matter. His report, when received, shall be forwarded. As I am leaving for the frontier at the Lower Tugela tomorrow, I have desired my Deputy Adjutant-General, pending the arrival of a General Officer, to forward you any reports that may

arrive during my absence. The reports enclosed are printed, as I considered it advisable to communicate the reports received to the public through the press. I have, &c.

CHELMSFORD Lieutenant-General"

"Luneberg, 12th March 1879

To the Officer Commanding the Troops at Luneburg:

Sir, I have the honour to report as follows, from the camp at Intombi River, where an escort of the 80th Regiment, under Captain Moriaty, were laagered on the 12th March 1879:

Being awake during the night I heard a shot fired in the distance, I got up and ordered the sentry to rouse the detachment on the side of Intombi Drift nearest Luneberg, and to apprise Captain Moriarty of the fact, and ask for his orders; these were that the escort should remain under arms. I afterwards found that this shot was fired about 4 am. I retired to my tent close by, where I waited, dressed, and about an hour afterwards I heard, "Guard turn out" I instantly turned out and saw, as the fog lifted, a dense mass of Zulus about 200 yards from the waggon laager, extending all across the valley with a front of some 2 or 3 miles apparently. I immediately put my men (35 of all ranks) under a waggon near our tents, and directed their fire on the flanks of the enemy, who were endeavouring to surround our waggon laager on the other side of the river. I next observed that the enemy had gained full possession of the camp, and were driving off the cattle. Our men were retiring on the river, which was now full of human beings. On seeing this, I directed my fire entirely with a view to covering the retreat of our men. This was well sustained, and enabled many to get over the river alive. The enemy were now assegaing our men in the water, and also ascending the banks of the river close to us; for fear, therefore, of my men being stabbed under the waggon, and to enable them to retire before their ammunition should be exhausted, I ordered them to retire steadily, and only just in time to avoid a rush of Zulus to our late position. The Zulus came on in dense masses and fell upon our men, who being already broken, gave way, and a hand to hand fight ensued. I endeavoured to rally my men, but they were too much scattered, and finding re-formation impossible, I mounted my horse and galloped into Luneburg at utmost speed, and reported all that had taken place. I estimate the strength of the enemy at not less than 4000 men. I beg to draw attention to the good service rendered by Sergt. A.Booth and the men of the party on the Luneburg side of the river, whose steady fire was instrumental in saving many lives.

(Signed) H. H. HARWARD Lieut., 80th Regt."

"Luneberg, 12th March 1879

From Major C.Tucker, 80th Regiment, Commanding troops to Assistant Military Secretary, Headquarters, Pietermaritzburg:

I have to report, for the information of His Excellency the Lieutenant-General Commanding, that on the 7th instant a party consisting of 104, all ranks, under command of Capt. D.B.Moriarty 80th Regiment, left Luneburg with a view of escorting and bringing into Luneburg 18 waggons, variously loaded on their way from Derby. Some of these waggons were reported as broken down on the Little Intombi River. Captain Moriarty's orders were to bring these waggons or their loads into Luneburg, but if this was impossible, owing to the fearful state of the road, he was to laager his waggons at the Intombi River and wait until he should be able to cross. During the 8th, 9th and 10th, the river was so very high from the constant rains, that nothing could be done. On the 11th the river lowered some 4 feet, but the stream was so rapid nothing could be got across. A light raft consisting of planks and empty barrels had been made, but would carry very little weight. On the morning of the 12th, about 6.30 am Lieut. Harward arrived at Luneburg from the Intombi River reporting that the camp and waggons were in possession of the enemy. I enclose a copy of a report from this officer:- As I have no mounted men under my command, I at once ordered all the horses belonging to the officers of the regiment to be saddled, and proceeded to the camp at the Intombi River, leaving orders for 150 men of the 80th Regiment to follow. On approaching Myers' Mission Station we observed, extending for about two miles under the brow of Umbeline's Hill, a long thick line of Zulus making eastward. I computed the body of the enemy in view at not less than 4000; there were undoubtedly many more; as we could see no cattle being driven, these Zulus were evidently making a hurried retreat. Arriving at the Intombi River, I found the laager completely wrecked, the cattle being taken and the contents of the waggons strewn about the place, and from the bank of the river we could see the dead bodies of our men lying about on the opposite side. On the arrival of the 80th from Luneburg, the bodies were collected and interred on this side of the river. I regret to report that Captain D.B.Moriarty was killed, together with Civil Surgeon Cobbin. Out of a total of 104 Officers and men of the 80th Regt. 40 are known to be killed, 20 are missing, and 44 have escaped to Luneberg - 1 man slightly wounded. In addition to the above Mr.Whittington waggon conductor, a volunteer named Campbell, late of Ferreira's Horse and a native driver, have been killed. With regard to the 20 men reported missing of the 80th Regiment, I fear most of them have been drowned or assegaid in the river, which was running swiftly, and was exceedingly high at the time. A list of the waggon employees will be sent as soon as possible.

It is impossible to ascertain the loss of the enemy, twenty-five bodies were found at the scene of the action, principally on the bank of the river, and doubtless many more were drowned. Two Zulus have been taken prisoner, both wounded severely. From one I gathered the information that the "impi" which attacked the laager was headed by Umbeline, who was instigated to bring this force by Manyanyobe. This prisoner distinctly stated twice that there were 9000 Zulus present, and that there were collected from all parts of the surrounding country; he further stated that Umnyamana was asked to assist, but refused to send his men. From all information I can gather on the subject, the camp was evidently surprised, the enemy taking advantage of the mist to approach the camp unseen. I consider the men fought well and bravely, but were completely outnumbered. The small party under Lieut. Harward, on this side of the river, rendered to a hopeless cause valuable assistance, in covering the retreat across the river of such men as were able to reach it; and I am of the opinion that but for those on this side of the Intombi River, not one man would have escaped, and that had the escort been double it's number, the result must have been the same. The river having subsided about midday, I was enabled to bring across the rockets, gun ammunition and powder untouched by the enemy.

C. TUCKER, Major Commanding 80th Regiment and Troops"

Return of Killed and missing 80th Regiment at Intombi River 12th March 1879
The killed and missing are distinguished by 'k' and 'm'

	Captain D.B. Moriarty ,	Company E,	k
459	Colour-Sergeant Henry Frederick,	Company A,	m
544	Lance-Sergeant Ernest Johnson,	Company E,	k
1726	George Sansam,	Company C,	k
733	Corporal John McCoy,	Company F,	k
1647	Drummer John Leather,	Company A,	m

Privates of the following Companies:

585	John Anthony,	Company A,	k
203	Arthur Banks,	Company A,	k
943	John Banner,	Company A,	m
745	George Broughton,	Company A,	k
488	Henry Brownson,	Company A,	k
1797	James Christie,	Company A,	k
1042	Alfred Day,	Company A,	k
753	John Dodd,	Company A,	m
260	Henry Dutton,	Company A,	k
1028	William Farrell,	Company A,	m
176	William Flyfield,	Company A,	m
	William Fox,	Company A,	k
1925	John Fourneaux,	Company A,	m
500	Edward Gittings,	Company A,	k
1696	Joseph Green,	Company A,	k
526	George Hadley,	Company A,	m
227	George Haines,	Company A,	k
999	Eli Hawkes,	Company A,	m
783	Thomas Healey,	Company A,	m
709	Thomas Hodges,	Company A,	k
902	John Ingham,	Company A,	k
1865	John Luffarty,	Company A,	k
1931	Henry Lodge,	Company A,	m
1976	George Mitchel,	Company A,	k
2048	Robert Moore,	Company A,	k

1032	William Moran,	Company A,	k	
1926	Henry Night,	Company A,	k	
1770	Joseph Silcock,	Company A,	m	
510	Henry Smith,	Company A,	m	
587	Joseph Tibbett,	Company A,	k	
716	Joseph Weaver,	Company A,	k	
48	James Brown,	Company C,	k	
222	William Findley,	Company C,	k	
2008	Julien Hart,	Company C,	m	
1919	Henry Jacobs,	Company C,	k	
999	Ralph Leese,	Company C,	k	
2063	Arthur Middow,	Company C,	k	
2085	Charles Pritchard,	Company C,	m	
2070	Henry Ruffle,	Company C,	k	
546	Jonah Adey,	Company E,	k	
1290	John Chadwick,	Company E,	k	
1163	Arthur Pummell,	Company E,	m	
1291	Richard Tomlinson,	Company E,	m	
1705	George Tucker,	Company E,	m	
104	Thomas Tucker,	Company E,	k	
	John Robinson,	Company E,	k	
370	James Vernon,	Company E,	k	
1605	Herbert Woodward,	Company E,	m	
1021	Henry Hill,	Company B,	k	
1499	John Hughes,	Company B,	k	
1378	Bernard McSherry,	Company B,	k	
220	William Phipps,	Company B,	k	
615	Michael Sheridan,	Company B,	m	
520	Henry Meadous,	Company F,	k	

C.TUCKER, Major 80th Regiment, Commanding Troops."

Court Martial Of Lieutenant Henry Hollingworth Harward (G.O.70)

Lord Chelmsford was notified of the incident on the Intombi River which occurred on the March 12th 1879, the second report of a disaster to his forces. Captain Moriarty was dead but his second in command, Lieutenant Harward was still alive and was subsequently subjected to a Court Martial. On February 14th 1880, Lieutenant Henry Hollingworth Harward was placed under arrest the charges being:

1. **Having misbehaved before the enemy, in shamefully abandoning a party of the Regiment under his command when attacked by the enemy, and in riding off at speed from his men.**
2. **Conduct to the prejudice of good order and military discipline in having at the place and time mentioned in the first charge, neglected to take proper precautions for the safety of a party of a Regiment under his command when attacked.**

The Court Martial of Lieutenant Henry Hollingworth Harward under General Order No.70 was held on February 20th 1880 at Fort Napier, Pietermaritzburg. The trial was in session from February 20th-27th. The Court's findings were that Lieutenant Harward was acquitted of all the charges. His main defence was that he had only joined the convoy escort the night before and that one could not form a proper laager with only two waggons. With regards to leaving his men, his was the only horse and only when his command started to disintegrate had he decided help was required, bearing in mind he was probably better prepared than Captain Moriarty. The Court findings eventually reached Sir Garnet Wolseley for review. Wolseley could not alter the course of justice; however he did not agree with the Court's findings and refused to confirm them. Sir Garnet Wolseley remarked:

"That a Regimental Officer who is the only Officer present with a party of men actually and seriously engaged with the enemy, can, under any pretext whatever, be justified in deserting them, and by so doing, abandoning them to their fate. The more helpless a position in which an officer finds his men, the more it his bounden duty to stay and share their fortune, whether for good or ill".

The Duke of Cambridge the Commander in Chief of the Army supported Sir Garnet Wolseley's comments and instructed them to read out the General Order to the head of every Regiment. Lieutenant H.H.Harward was released from arrest and on March 14th 1880 returned to duty, to continue his army career. However, his career was in ruins and he resigned his commission on May 11th 1880.

Lieutenant H.H.Harward

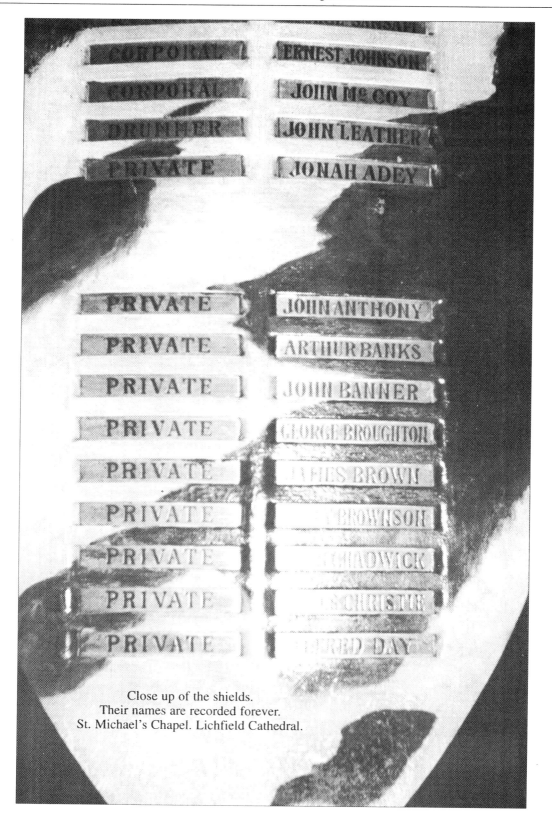

Close up of the shields.
Their names are recorded forever.
St. Michael's Chapel. Lichfield Cathedral.

The mass grave and memorial.

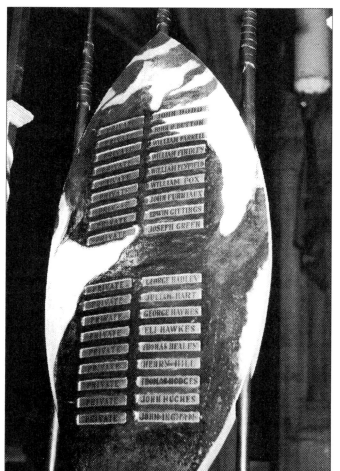

Shield Memorial.
Lichfield Cathedral.

The memorial, the drift and
Captain Moriarty's camp.
The mass grave looking
North East.

The memorial inscription.

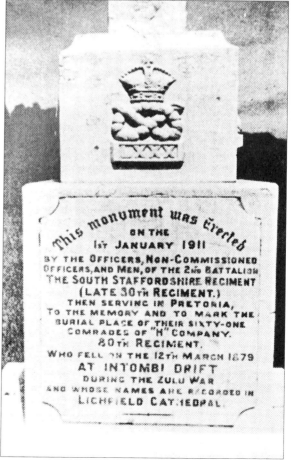

This monument was Erected
ON THE
1st JANUARY 1911
BY THE OFFICERS, NON-COMMISSIONED
OFFICERS, AND MEN, OF THE 2nd BATTALION
THE SOUTH STAFFORDSHIRE REGIMENT
(LATE 80th REGIMENT.)
THEN SERVING IN PRETORIA,
TO THE MEMORY AND TO MARK THE
BURIAL PLACE OF THEIR SIXTY-ONE
COMRADES OF "H" COMPANY.
80th REGIMENT.
WHO FELL ON THE 12TH MARCH 1879
AT INTOMBI DRIFT
DURING THE ZULU WAR
AND WHOSE NAMES ARE RECORDED IN
LICHFIELD CAT.1EDRAL.

THE VICTORIA CROSS

Chapter 8
THE
VICTORIA CROSS

A Brief History

Of all the medals awarded for bravery the most coveted is the Victoria Cross. It is not made of valuable metal or studded with precious gemstones, but is a simple cross design made of bronze. The award is open to any man or woman employed either as a civilian with the armed forces (as described in the Royal Warrant, dated December 13th 1858), or as a soldier, sailor or airman/airwoman employed in one of the armed forces, be he/she of highest or lowest rank.

Britain's highest award for very outstanding deeds of gallantry in the presence of the enemy was named after the sovereign who influenced and implemented the award. The Victoria Cross medal was instituted by Her Majesty Queen Victoria in the year 1856, the Royal Warrant being signed and dated January 29th. Although the medal was introduced during 1856, it was awarded retrospectively to the Autumn of 1854, for actions during the Crimean War, 1853-1856. The commission was placed with the jewellers Hancock's to produce the prestigious medals and when the first batch had been manufactured, Her Majesty Queen Victoria on the morning of June 6th 1857 presented the first sixty-two recipients with their Victoria Crosses at a parade held in Hyde Park, London

To be awarded the Victoria Cross necessitates an act of valour or devotion to duty in the presence of the enemy. Some of the clauses in the Royal Warrant for the Cross are that *'neither rank, nor long service, nor wounds, nor any other circumstances or condition whatsoever save the merit of conspicuous bravery'* thereby placing *'all persons on a perfectly even footing in relation to eligibility for the decoration'*.

In 1858 the Royal Warrant was amended so that the cross could be won by those who *'may perform acts of conspicuous courage and bravery.......in circumstances of extreme danger such as the occurrence of a fire on board ship, or of the foundering of a vessel at sea, or under any other circumstances in which........life or public property may be saved'*. Later in 1881 a further amendment was made, *'Our will and pleasure is that the qualification shall be conspicuous bravery or devotion to the country in the presence of the enemy'*. During 1902 another amendment was made when King Edward VII approved the award being granted posthumously. King George V granted on October 21st 1911 that members of the Indian Army be eligible for the award. On May 22nd 1920, eligibility for the award was extended to incorporate the Royal Air Force and *'Air Forces of the Dominions, Colonies Dependencies or Protectorates of the Commonwealth'*; and *'matrons, sisters, nurses and the staff of the Nursing Services and other Services pertaining to hospitals and nursing, and civilians of either sex serving regularly or temporarily under orders, direction or supervision...'* of the military authorities. The Warrant again emphasised that the Victoria Cross *'shall only be awarded for most conspicuous bravery or some daring pre-eminent act of valour or self sacrifice or extreme devotion to duty in the presence of the enemy'*.

Where a group or body of men, soldiers, sailors or airmen, so display and merit the award of the Victoria Cross, then the officers and non-commissioned officers, rank and file select one person by ballot.

In the heat of battle, men and women carry out many a daring deed and in some cases self sacrifice, quite unnoticed and unrecorded. Since the inauguration of the Victoria Cross, a total of 1354 'Crosses' have been awarded. The earliest recorded deed to merit the Victoria Cross was carried out on June 21st 1854 by Charles Davis Lucas, a Mate on board HMS *'Hecla'*. The last VC was awarded posthumously to Sergeant Ian John McKay of the 3rd Battalion, the Parachute Regiment, for his actions on June 12th 1982. Only on six occasions has the Victoria Cross been awarded for actions not carried out in front of the enemy. Since the introduction of the award, there have only been four occurrences where the award has gone to civilians. Three Victoria Crosses were awarded to

Magistrates for their actions during the Indian Mutiny of 1857-58, the forth civilian being a Clergyman in the Bengal Ecclesiastical Department attached to the Indian Army and granted for his deeds during the Afghan War of 1878-80.

Like any other gallantry award, the award can be conferred more than once. In the history of this particular award only three men have been awarded the Victoria Cross twice, these being Lieutenant Arthur Martin-Leake VC RAMC, Captain Noel Godfrey Chavasse VC MC MA RAMC and Captain Charles Hazlitt Upham VC, New Zealand Military Forces.

When the Victoria Cross was originally awarded the receiver of the award below that of a commissioned rank was also granted a pension of £10 per annum for life with a further £5 per year for any subsequent 'Bar'. Throughout the years these pensions have been increased irrespective of rank or position.

Should a person who receives the Victoria Cross be found guilty of treason, felony, cowardice or any infamous crime, the medal and pension may be confiscated and his name, (no woman has yet received the award), erased from the list of recipients of the Victoria Cross. There has been incidents where such crimes have been committed and consequently the name has been removed from the Victoria Cross list including the confiscation of the medal and the pension. However, due to the comments made by the late King George V on a particular case, all the names were re-entered onto the Victoria Cross Roll, although, in theory, the medal and pension can still be taken away.

The Victoria Cross was awarded to the United States of America Unknown Warrior who is buried in Arlington National Cemetery, Washington D.C., dated October 28th 1920.

Description of the Victoria Cross

The Victoria Cross although highly prized, is not made of valuable metal. The design is that of a cross/patte (Maltese cross), 34mm across with raised edges. On the obverse side in the centre there is a lion passant guardant standing upon the Royal Crest. Below the Crown on a semi-circular scroll there are the words 'FOR VALOUR'. On the reverse side is recorded the date of the act for which the medal is awarded. The cross is suspended by means of a bar which is ornamented with laurel leaves and this bar incorporates a 'V' by which the actual medal is suspended by a plain single link. The name, rank and regiment or ship of the recipient is engraved at the back of the clasp. The ribbon is designed to pass on the back of this clasp. The ribbon which is 40mm wide originally was designed blue for the Navy and crimson for the Army. On May 22nd 1920 by Royal Warrant signed by the Secretary of State for War, Sir Winston Churchill, the colour of crimson was adopted for all branches of the Forces.

When only the medal ribbon is worn, a small replica of the cross is mounted in the centre of the ribbon. This is because other awards and medals have similar coloured ribbons. When the medal is awarded twice i.e. a 'Bar' then a second small replica cross is mounted on the ribbon.

Victoria Crosses awarded to the Staffordshire Regiment(The Prince of Wales's)

Since the inauguration of the Victoria Cross in 1856, members of the Staffordshire Regiment and its antecedent Regiments of Foot have between them received thirteen Victoria Crosses and the thirteen names are recorded in the Garrison Church of St.George's at Whittington Barracks near Lichfield. Six were awarded posthumously.

The earliest Cross awarded to the Regiment went to Drummer Thomas Flynn who was a member of the 64th Regiment of Foot during the Indian Mutiny. Whilst taking part in the last action at Cawnpore on January 28th 1857, he was awarded the medal for outstanding courage when attacking enemy guns. The last two Crosses awarded were to Major R.H Cain and Lance-Sergeant J.D.Baskeyfield, both members of the 2nd Battalion, the South Staffordshire Regiment for their deeds on September 17th and 20th 1944 respectively, at the battle at Arnhem.

Over the years warfare has changed greatly, the weapons of war become increasingly sophisticated and more deadly. To be awarded the Victoria Cross today, and to live to receive it, is truly against all the odds. Due to the nature of mankind, there will always be wars in the world, and there will always be someone willing to perform an act of bravery beyond the call of duty which would warrant consideration for the Victoria Cross. But in all these conflicts there will also be many deeds that would easily merit consideration but are unseen or unrecorded. First and foremost the awards of Victoria Crosses to the soldiers of any regiment including the Staffordshire Regiment, reflect most surely the willingness of all its members to carry out their duties in times of war and 'peace', whether fighting the foe or protecting the innocent.

In addition to the thirteen Victoria Cross holders credited to the Staffordshire Regiment there are two names recorded of men who were attached to other Regiments at the time:

Captain T.De Courcy. 38th Regiment of Foot Crimea 11th May 1855

Captain E.Jotham. The North Staffordshire Regiment Waziristan 7th January 1915

The Regiment's Victoria Cross Medals were awarded for actions during the Indian Mutiny 1857/58, the Zulu War 1879, the Great War 1914/18 and the Second World War 1939/45.

The Staffordshire Regiment's Victoria Crosses

THE INDIAN MUTINY 1857-1858
Flinn, Thomas; Drummer; 64th Regiment of Foot; Cawnpore, India; 28th November 1857

THE ZULU WAR 1879
Wassall, Samuel; Private ; 80th Regiment of Foot; Isandhlwana, Zululand 22nd January 1879
Booth, Anthony Clarke; Colour Sergeant; 80th Regiment of Foot; Intombi River, Zululand 12th March 1879

THE GREAT WAR 1914-1918
Vallentin[*], John Franks; Captain; The South Staffordshire Regiment; 1st Batt. Zillebeke, Belgium;7th November 1914
Kilby[*](MC), Arthur Forbes Gordon; Captain;The South Staffordshire Regiment; 2nd Batt; Loos, France;
25th September 1915
Henderson[*], Edward Elers Delaval;Lt.Colonel; The North Staffordshire Regiment[1]; Mesopotamia;
25th January 1917
Barratt[*], Thomas;Private; The South Staffordshire Regiment, 7th Batt; Ypres, Belgium; 27th July 1917
Carmichael, John; Sergeant; The North Staffordshire Regiment,9th Batt; Zwarteleen, Belgium; 8th Sept
1917
Thomas, John;Lance Corporal; The North Staffordshire Regiment, 5th Batt; Flanders,France;
30th Nov 1917
Coltman(DCM.MM), William Harold; Lance Corporal; The North Staffordshire Regiment, 1/6th Batt.
Mannequin, France; 3rd/4th October 1918

THE SECOND WORLD WAR 1939-1945
Cairns[*], George Albert; Lieutenant; The South Staffordshire Regiment,1st Batt[2]; Henu, Burma; 13th March 1944
Cain, Robert Henry;Major; The South Staffordshire Regiment,2nd Batt[3]; Arnhem, Holland; 17th September 1944
Baskeyfield[*], John Daniel; Lance Sergeant The South Staffordshire Regiment, 2nd Batt[4]; Arnhem, Holland; 20th
September 1944

* Victoria Cross was awarded Posthumously
(1)Lieutenant-Colonel Henderson was attached to the 9th Battalion, Royal Warwickshire Regiment
(2)Lieutenant Cairns of the Somerset Light Infantry was attached to 1st Battalion South Staffordshire Regiment
(3)Major Cain of the Royal Northumberland Fusiliers was attached to the 2nd Battalion South Staffordshire Regiment
(4)Lance Sergeant Baskeyfield was attached to the 1st Airborne Division

The Zulu War Victoria Crosses

The war against the Zulus in 1879 was a small colonial war of no consequence until one of the world's most modern armies was defeated at Isandhlwana on the January 22nd 1879 by a so-called army of savages armed only with shields and spears and a few obsolete rifles.

During the Zulu War of 1879 there was a total of twenty-three Victoria Crosses awarded. Of these, two were awarded posthumously in 1907 - at the time of the war there was no such provision. Of the remaining twenty-one Crosses eleven were earned in a single action at Rorke's Drift on the night of January 22nd and 23rd, a total of seven going to men of the 24th Regiment of Foot. This Regiment was to gain a total of ten Crosses during the Zulu War. The twenty-three Victoria Crosses which were awarded were distributed as follows:

1 -	Royal Engineers	1 -	9th Queen Royal Lancers	1 -	13th Light infantry
10 -	24th Regiment of Foot	1 -	60th Rifles	2 -	80th Regiment of Foot
2 -	90th Light Infantry	1 -	Commissariat and Transport	1 -	Army Medical Corps
2 -	Frontier Light Horse	1 -	Natal Native Contingent		

Name	Rank	Regiment/Department Establishment	Date in London Gazette	Place and date of presentation	Presented by
ISANDHLWANA - 22nd JANUARY 1879					
Melvill*, Teignmouth.	Lieutenant and Adjutant	24th Regiment of Foot	2/5/79[1]		
Coghill*, Nevill. Josiah Ayler	Lieutenant	24th Regiment of Foot	2/5/79[1]		
Wassall, Samuel.	Private	80th Regiment of Foot	17/6/79	Utrecht, 11/9/79	Sir Garnet Wolseley
RORKE'S DRIFT - 22nd/23rd JANUARY 1879					
Chard, John Rouse Merriott	Lieutenant	Royal Engineers	2/5/79	St.Paul's, 16/7/79 Zululand	Sir Garnet Wolseley
Bromhead, Gonville	Lieutenant	24th Regiment of Foot	2/5/79	Utrecht, 22/8/79	Sir Garnet Wolseley
Allan, William Wilson	Corporal	24th Regiment of Foot	2/5/79	Windsor, 9/12/79 Castle	H.M.Queen Victoria
Hitch, Frederick	Private	24th Regiment of Foot	2/5/79	Netley, 12/08/79 Hospital England	H.M. Queen Victoria
Hook, Alfred Henry	Private	24th Regiment of Foot	2/5/79	Rorke's 03/08/79 Drift	Sir Garnet Wolseley
Jones, Robert	Private	24th Regiment of Foot	2/5/79	Utrecht, 11/9/79	Sir Garnet Wolseley
Jones, William	Private	24th Regiment of Foot	2/5/79	Windsor, 13/1/80 Castle	H.M.Queen Victoria
Williams, John	Private	24th Regiment of Foot	2/5/79	Almeda, 1/3/80 Gibraltar	Maj. General Anderson
Reynolds, James Henry	Surgeon	Army Hospital Corps	17/6/79	St.Paul's, 16/7/79 Zululand	Sir Garnet Wolseley
Dalton, James Langley	Asst. Commissary	Commissariat/Transport	17/11/79	Fort Napier, 16/1/80 Zululand	Maj.General Clifford
Schiess, Ferdnand Christian	Corporal	Natal Native Contingent	29/11/79	Pietermaritzburg, Natal 03/02/80	Sir Garnet Wolseley
INTOMBI RIVER - 12th MARCH 1879					
Booth, Anthony Clarke	Sergeant	80th Regiment of Foot	24/2/80	Windsor 26/6/80 Castle,	H.M.Queen Victoria

HLOBANE MOUNTAIN - 28th MARCH 1879

Buller (CB), Redvers Henry.	Lt.Colonel	60th Rifles	17/6/79	St.Paul's,16/7/79 Zululand	Sir Garnet Wolseley
Leet, William Knox	Major	13th Light Infantry	17/6/79	Windsor, 9/12/79 Castle	H.M.Queen Victoria
Browne, Edward Stevenson Lieut.		24th Regiment of Foot	17/6/79	Pine Tree Camp, Zululand 22/08/79	Sir Garnet Wolseley
Lysons, Henry	2nd Lieut.	90th Light Infantry	05/4/82	Cawnpore, India,18/08/82	Colonel Craig
Fowler, Edmund John.	Private	90th Light Infantry	05/04/82	Windsor Castle, 13/05/82	H.M.Queen Victoria

WHITE UMVOLOSI RIVER (ULUNDI) - 3rd JULY 1879

Beresford, Lord William Leslie De La Poer	Captain	9th Queen Lancers	23/8/79	Windsor Castle	H.M.Queen Victoria
D'arcy, Henry Cecil. Dudgeon	Captain	Frontier Light Horse	09/10/79	Pretoria,10/12/79 South Africa	Sir Garnet Wolseley
O'Toole, Edmund	Sergeant	Frontier Light Horse	09/10/79	Fort Napier,16/1/80 Zululand	Maj. General Clifford

* Both Lieutenants Melvill and Coghill were Posthumously awarded the Victoria Cross
[1] The award of the Victoria Cross was confirmed in a later Gazette dated 15/01/07

Samuel Wassall VC (No. 427 Private) 1856-1927

Samuel Wassall was born on April 7th 1856 at Moor Lane, Kingswinford near Dudley in Staffordshire. Samuel was the son of Samuel and Emma, (Hubble) Wassall. His birth was registered in the District of Stourbridge, Sub District Kingswinsford on April 21st 1856, Certificate No.229.

At the age of eighteen years and seven months and having the trade of dyer, Samuel enlisted into the British Army on November 28th 1874, signing his attestation papers in Dudley. It was recorded that Samuel was 5ft4¾ in (1.64m) tall, had a fresh complexion, grey eyes and light brown hair.

On June 13th 1877 Samuel Wassall joined the 80th Regiment of foot in South Africa. The Imperial forces were short of mounted troops at this time and a call went out for volunteers from the various regiments and detachments. Samuel along with a number of soldiers from the 80th Regiment volunteered and was accepted. It was not long before he, along with the Imperial mounted troops assigned to 'Carrington's Horse', saw action against the Kaffirs.

At the outbreak of the war against the Zulus, Samuel was still with the mounted infantry and the squadron he was attached to, were allotted to No.3 (Central) Column. On January 11th 1879 at daybreak the mounted troops and natives of No.3 column crossed into Zululand via the ford (waggon drift) located near to Rorke's Drift, the infantry crossing the Buffalo River by ponts. Following the attack on Sihayo's Kraal on January 12th and after further reconnaissance, the Column eventually arrived at its first major campsite in Zululand at Isandhlwana Hill. As a result of reconnoitering work on January 21st, Lord Chelmsford made the decision to divide his forces and the next day he advanced further into Zululand to reinforce Major Dartnell, hopefully to attack and defeat the Zulu army. Samuel along with other members of the mounted infantry, remained with Brevet Lieutenant-Colonel Pulliene to protect the camp on the slopes of Isandhlwana.

During the late morning of January 22nd a Zulu force of some twenty thousand warriors attacked the encampment. Only those on horseback had any chance of escape and out of over a thousand soldiers left to defend the camp, only seventy-nine Europeans were to survive. With the way to Rorke's Drift cut off, the only means of escape was across the river and the veldt, some six to seven miles distance. To cross to safety, with the river in flood, was a formidable task. This point of the river, known from that day on as 'Fugitive's Drift', was where Samuel saved the life of a fellow comrade who was drowning whilst under enemy fire. For his brave deed, he was to be awarded the Victoria Cross, the first awarded during the Zulu War. In the London Gazette dated June 17th 1879 the War Office gave notice:

Private Samuel Wassall V.C.

VICTORIA CROSS AND SOUTH AFRICA 1877-79
MEDAL OF PRIVATE SAMUEL WASSALL, 80th FOOT
WHO EARNED HIS AWARD IN THE AFTERMATH OF THE
BATTLE OF ISANDHLWANA IN ZULULAND ON 22 JAN 1879
WHILE SERVING WITH A MOUNTED INFANTRY DETACHMENT
ONLY VERY FEW OF THE 80th EARNED THE 1877 CLASP TO THE MEDAL

The medals of Private Samuel
Wassall V.C. 80th Regiment of Foot.
Victoria Cross and South Africa
Medal with clasp '1877-8-9'

The Grave of Samuel
Wassall V.C.
Barrow in Furness.

"that the Queen has been graciously pleased to signify Her intention to confer the decoration of the Victoria Cross on the undermentioned Officers and soldier of Her Majesty's Army, whose claims have been submitted for Her Majesty's approval, for their gallant conduct during the recent operations in South Africa, as recorded against their names" - one of these being Samuel Wassall of the 80th Regiment of Foot.

On July 30th 1879 in General Order No. 23 this was again confirmed and at a place called Utrecht, South Africa, on September 11th 1879, Samuel Wassall along with Robert Jones of the 24th Regiment (for his part in the defence of Rorke's Drift), were presented with their Victoria Cross medals by Sir Garnet Wolseley G.C.M.G., K.C.B. Samuel, at the age of twenty-two years and nine months was the youngest serving soldier at the time to hold the award.

On December 30th 1880 Samuel was transferred to the Army reserve having served six years with the Colours. To show for his short military career, Samuel was entitled to wear the following medals; the Victoria Cross and the South Africa Medal with the clasp '1877-8-9'. For being awarded the Victoria Cross he was also granted a pension of £10 per annum for life.

When he left the Army, seeking to better his prospects of employment, Samuel moved to Barrow-in-Furness and lived with his brother William at 28 Exeter Street. He was for a time employed in the electrical department of the Barrow shipyard. He fell in love with Rebecca Round the daughter of John Round a stocktaker and they were married on April 10th 1882 at the Parish Church of St.Matthew's. Samuel was then aged 23. They were to live first in Melbourne Street and later 32 Lyon Street, Barrow. They were blessed with seven children, sons, Samuel, Albert, Ernest and Henry and daughters Florence, Clara and Minnie, all of whom married. At the age of seventy Samuel was admitted to the North Lonsdale Hospital in Barrow and on Monday January 21st 1927 he succumbed to this illness. He is buried at St.James's Church, Barrow-in-Furness, in the same grave as his wife Rebecca who died after him on May 20th 1937.

SAMUEL WASSALL(No. 427 Private) 1856-1927 CITATION FOR THE VICTORIA CROSS

Private Samuel Wassall 80th Regiment of Foot

"For his gallant conduct in having, at the imminent risk of his own life, saved that of Private Westwood, of the same Regiment. On the 22nd January 1879, when the camp at Isandhlwana was taken by the enemy, Private Wassall retreated towards the Buffalo River, in which he saw a comrade struggling, and apparently drowning. He rode to the bank, dismounted, leaving his horse on the Zulu side, rescued the man from the stream, and again mounted his horse, dragging Private Westwood across the river under a heavy shower of bullets."

Award Published in the London Gazette dated 17th June 1879

Escape from Isandhlwana 22nd January 1879 - Samuels Story

On January 22nd 1879 the main encampment belonging to the No. 3 Column was attacked and successfully taken by the Zulus. When all was lost the remaining survivors made a bid to escape and only those on horseback appeared to have any chance of avoiding the oncoming massed black ranks of Zulu warriors with their ritual cries, slashing spears and bludgeoning knobkerries.

Private Samuel Wassall of the 80th Regiment of Foot, who had volunteered as a Mounted Infantry man, was part of the forces encamped at Isandhlwana. Making his escape from the stricken camp and nearing safety, Private Wassall risked his own life to save that of a fellow soldier, who was drowning. To quote in his own words:

The only way to escape was by the Buffalo River, six or seven miles away and we had to get cross it into our own territory, Natal. A main road led to the river but the road was cut off by the Zulus and I had to take a road across the veldt, I knew nothing about. But, I was not in the mood to care which way I went so long as it took me away from the enemy, and so I went furiously on, stumbling over the rough rocky ground, expecting every instant that my horse, a Basuto pony would fall. In that case I should not have had a chance for the Zulus would have been upon me before I could have got up again. To this day, I cannot understand how a living soul got away from Isandhlwana, because we were seriously harassed by the savages. shots came after us and clouds of spears, but I did escape from the field of the massacre and reached the Zulu bank of the river, and saw on the other side of the Natal territory, where my only hope of safety lay. I knew how dangerous the river was, there was a current running six or seven mile an hour, no ordinary man could swim it. But, the Zulus had a curious way of using there elbows which made them able to get across. I drove my horse into the torrent, thankful even to be in that part and was urging him to the other side, when I heard a cry for help and I saw a man of my own Regiment, a Private named Westwood was being carried away. He was struggling, desperately and was drowning, The Zulus were sweeping down to the river bank, which I had just left and there was a terrible temptation to go ahead and just save one's self, but I turned my horse around on the Zulu bank, got him there, dismounted, tied him upto a tree and I never tied him more swiftly. Then I struggled out to Westwood, got hold of him and struggled back to the horse with him. I scrambled up into the saddle, pulled Westwood after me and plunged into the torrent again, and as I did so the zulus rushed upto the bank and let drive with their firearms and spears, but most mercifully I escaped them all and with a thankful heart urged my gallant horse up the steep bank on the Natal side and then got him to go as hard as he could towards Helpmakaar about fifteen miles from Isandhlwana, where our main camp was. I ought to have gone straight onto Rorke's Drift after escaping from Isandhlwana but the zulus were already surging on towards the drift, which was held by a mere handful of men of the 24th, expected to wipe out its defenders as they had wiped out the camp at Isandhlwana. At this time I was very lightly clad, I had thrown my helmet aside and my red tunic off, the British soldiers fought in the good old red in those days and not in khaki, so that I was clothed in just my shirt and trousers with my bandolier over my shirt and so I rode on as hard as I could, with a few of the fugitives from Isandhlwana.

Private Samuel Wassall unlike so many of his fellow soldiers, lived to tell the tale and his brave rescue of a drowning comrade was an act of bravery which richly deserved an award. For his act of valour in the face of the enemy, Private Samuel Wassall was awarded the Victoria Cross.

Anthony Clarke BOOTH VC (No. 919 Colour Sergeant) 1846-1899

Anthony Clarke Booth was born on April 21st 1846 in a village called Carrington in the Parish of Basford near Nottingham.

During 1864 Anthony tried to join the army in the ranks of the Royal Marine Light Infantry. Following a medical examination he was refused admission to the ranks of the British army due to a heart murmur. Later that same year whilst on a business trip, Anthony at the age of eighteen years and six months and having the trade of tailor, enlisted to join the 80th Regiment of Foot. He signed his attestation in Sheffield before a Justice of the Peace on October 31st 1864 at 10.25am. His enlistment describes him as being 5ft 6in (1.68m) tall, with a fresh complexion, grey eyes and brown hair. His religion was Church of England, however his descendants say that Anthony on his death bed changed to the Roman Catholic Church. He joined the 80th Regiment of Foot at the depot at Buttevant in the County of Cork, Ireland on November 10th 1864 and after three months was moved to Chatham and then onto Fort Tregantle in Devon.

Whilst in the Army, Anthony met Lucy O'Brien from Doneraile in County Cork, Ireland, not far from Buttevant and on September 18th 1866, Anthony Clarke Booth and Lucy were married at Stoke Gabriel in the County of Devon. During thirty-three years of marriage, Lucy had eight children; Herbert born July 12th 1867 at Portland, Dorset; Anthony born September 15th 1868 at Fleetwood, Lancashire; William born November 21st 1870 at Belfast, Northern Ireland; Florence born August 17th 1873 in Hong Kong; Henry Charles born October 3rd 1875, in Hong Kong; Lucy born February 10th 1877 at Cape Town, South Africa; Andrew born May 17th 1881 in Dublin, Ireland and Albert Edward born June 10th 1883 at Tralee, County Kerry, Ireland. Lucy Booth passed away just before her sixty-fifth birthday on June 11th 1912.

Of Anthony's and Lucy's children, the following is known: Lucy died in South Africa March 14th 1879 aged two years, (two days after her father survived the massacre at the Intombi River); Herbert died at the age of thirty-seven years, May 29th 1905 at Great Altcar, near Liverpool. Albert Edward died on December 23rd 1907 at Brierley Hill, West Midlands at the age of twenty-three. Henry Charles died May 15th 1911. Florence married Harry Pearson at Brierley Hill and they emigrated to Canada. William who married Annie Clancey at Brierley Hill on August 20th 1906, died August 7th 1946 aged 75 years. Annie his wife died on November 26th 1968 aged 94.

Colour Sergeant Anthony Clarke Booth V.C.

William and Annie had three children, Edward William born July 16th 1907; Bernard Albert born September 7th 1908 and Victor Charles born December 15th 1910. Bernard Albert and Charles Victor are the only surviving grandsons of Anthony Booth VC and at the time of writing this book, Albert is eighty-five and Charles is eighty-two years young!

During Anthony's army career, he received several promotions and demotions:-

Promoted to Corporal	1st July 1865
Reduced to Private	4th September 1865
Promoted to Corporal	20th April 1869
Promoted to Sergeant	1st January 1872
Appointed Colour Sergeant	3rd April 1876
Reverted to Sergeant	11th February 1879
Appointed Colour Sergeant	13th March 1879
Reverted to Sergeant	19th October 1880
Promoted to Colour Sergeant	15th March 1884

On May 16th 1888, Anthony Booth VC was transferred to the 1st Volunteers Battalion South Staffordshire Regiment as a Sergeant Instructor and Colour Sergeant and served in ''C' Company at Brierley Hill.

Colour Sergeant Booth joined the army on October 31st 1864 and re-engaged at Belfast for the 80th Regiment of Foot on September 5th 1871. He completed twenty-one years of service. From the time of his attestation to January 11th 1872 his service was in the United Kingdom. His overseas service was as follows :-

Straits Settlements	12th January 1872 - 27th November 1872
China	28th November 1872 - 14th February 1876
Straits Settlements	15th February 1876 - 10th March 1877
Cape of Good Hope	11th March 1877 - 11th May 1880

On March 12th 1879, during the Zulu War and at a place called Myer's Drift on the Intombi River, a battle took place. Sergeant Booth was a member of the small force of 152 men, of whom 106 belonged to the 80th Regiment of Foot, the remainder being waggon conductors and drivers. A Zulu force of some 4,000 warriors attacked the waggon convoy which was encamped on either side of the river. The senior officer, Captain D.B.Moriarty was killed immediately and the only remaining officer, Lieutenant H.H.Harward left the field of battle. Sergeant Booth, the senior non-commissioned officer remaining, took command and controlled a fighting retreat. In demonstrating this coolness and steadfastness in a deadly situation, Sergeant Booth was 'Mentioned in Dispatches' and recommended for the award of the Distinguished Conduct Medal.

On March 13th 1879, Anthony was promoted to Colour Sergeant and for his gallant conduct, he was awarded the Victoria Cross on March 12th 1879. The award was published in the London Gazette of February 24th 1880.

On April 10th 1880, the 80th Regiment's officers, non-commissioned officers and men with their families embarked on Her Majesty's Ship 'Orontes' destined for Ireland. On May 11th 1880 the 'Orontes' arrived at Kings Town and the next day the Regiment disembarked and marched to Richmond Barracks, with the bands of the 57th and 84th Regiments of Foot leading them through the streets and Major General Glyn CB at the head of the Battalion.

Whilst stationed in Ireland, Colour Sergeant Anthony Clarke Booth travelled to London and at Windsor Castle on June 26th 1880, Her Majesty Queen Victoria personally presented the Victoria Cross to him.

In September 1883 he left Ireland for Lichfield after twenty-one years service. He was now sent to Brierley Hill as a Sergeant Instructor with the local rifle Company where he remained until April 30th 1898 when he was discharged having attained the maximum age. His total army service was 33 years 182 days (for Pension 33 years 178 days). He had served in the 80th Regiment and on amalgamation with the 38th Regiment had continued his service with the 2nd Battalion South Staffordshire Regiment.

To show for his long army career he was entitled to wear the following medals:- The Victoria Cross, the India General Service Medal with clasp for 'Perak', the South Africa Medal with clasp '1878-79' and the Long Service and Good Conduct medal. With the Victoria Cross, he was awarded a pension of £10 per annum for life. With the Long Service and Good Conduct Medal went a gratuity of five pounds.

When Anthony Clarke Booth VC finally retired from the army in April 1898 he unfortunately did not live to enjoy a long retirement. During the early part of December 1899 he suffered an attack of rheumatic fever and jaundice developed. On December 8th at the age of fifty-four years, Anthony died and is buried in St.Michael's Churchyard, Brierley Hill near Dudley. Lucy his wife is buried in the same grave along with one of their sons, William.

ANTHONY CLARKE BOOTH (No.919 Colour Sergeant) 1846-1899
CITATION FOR THE VICTORIA CROSS

Colour Sergeant ANTHONY CLARKE BOOTH 80th Regiment of Foot

"For his gallant conduct on the 12th March 1879, during the Zulu attack on the Intombi River, in having when considerably outnumbered by the enemy, rallied a few men on the south bank of the river, and covered the retreat of fifty soldiers and others for a distance of three miles. The Officer Commanding 80th Regiment reports that, had it not been for the coolness displayed by this Non-Commissioned Officer, not one man would have escaped."

Award Published in The London Gazette dated 24th February 1880

A LETTER HOME

When a regiment was serving abroad very few wives and children accompanied it, but one such family in South Africa belonged to Sergeant Anthony Booth. Lucy Booth and her children, were housed during the Zulu conflict in Cape Town. After the attack at the Intombi River on the 12th March, Sergeant Anthony Booth, on the 14th March 1879, wrote a letter to his wife in which he described the events of the attack and the sad loss of many of his comrades[*]:

"Luneburg 14th March 1879

My Dear Wife and Children, You must please excuse me not answering your last letter that I received about eight days since. I know you will be thankful for the most miraculous escape I have had - and I know you and our children will be proud of your Husband and father when you will see in papers the account of this Battle at Intombi River. We left Luneburg on the morning of the 7th March to escort a convoy of waggons, about some twenty-four in number. We arrived at the Intombi River some six miles from Luneburg on the road to Derby about 11a.m. the river was very high and we could not cross it only on a raft that me and Mr. Lindop and some of the men constructed. The rain coming down heavens hard which continued for four days successively - I was acting Quarter Master Sergeant for the men, 103 men - Captain Moriarty, Lieutenant Johnson, Lieutenant Lindop and Doctor Cobbin also a lot of volunteers and nigger drivers in all that was engaged in the battle was 154 men, Officers to all told only about forty-one men and some niggers arrived at Luneburg to tell the tale. Mr. Lindop had gone to Luneburg the night before the battle also Lieutenant Johnson and one man Lieutenant Harward came out to relieve them that would leave 152 men all told at the Intombi River. About 4.30 a.m. on the 12th March 1879 I was awoke by hearing a shot fired in the direction of the mountains (I should have told you we were under Umberlines Cave a notorious Chieftain) - Lieutenant Harward called for me to alarm the camp on the other side of the river for there was me and Lieutenant Harward and thirty-three men on one side of the river, the remainder on the other side. I called out for the sentry on the other side to alarm the camp, he did not answer me but a man named Tucker came to the river side and I told him to tell Captain Moriarty that a shot had been fired and to alarm the camp. He sent word back that the men were to get dressed but to remain in their tents. I was in the Commissariat Waggon taking charge of the goods. I went in the waggon again and lit my pipe and looked at my watch, it was 1/4 to 5 a.m. I put on my ammunition belt and me and another man was smoking in the waggon, when about 5 o'clock I heard another shot fired and someone shout Sergeant Johnson. I looked out of the waggon and I shall never

VICTORIA CROSS AND MEDALS OF COLOUR SERGEANT ANTHONY BOOTH, 80th FOOT
HIS AWARD WAS EARNED IN THE ACTION AT
THE INTOMBI DRIFT IN THE ZULU WAR ON 12 MAR 1879
HE WAS ENTITLED TO WEAR THE INDIAN GENERAL SERVICE MEDAL
WITH THE CLASP FOR 'PERAK' BUT IT SEEMS HE DECLINED
TO CLAIM IT AS HE SAW NO ACTION THERE

The medals of Colour Sergeant Anthony
Booth VC 80th Regiment of Foot
Victoria Cross
Indian General Service Medal with clasp
'Parak'
South African Medal with clasp '1878-9'
Long Service and Good Conduct Medal.

The Grave of Anthony Booth VC
St. Michael's churchyard
Brierley Hill

forget the sight. I saw the day was just breaking and there was about five (5) thousand Zulus on the other side, they were close to the tents and shouted their war cry 'Zu Zu'. They fired a volley into us on this side of the river then they commenced assegaing the men as they lay in the tents. I rallied my party by the waggon and poured heavy firing into them as fast as we could, some of the men coming out from the other side of the river and coming across to us. Crawford was one of them, he was the only man out of his tent that got across alive. Captain Moriarty and Doctor Cobbin was murdered in their tents and most of the men also. I commanded the party on this side as Lieutenant Harward saddled his horse and galloped away leaving us to do the best we could, when I saw all our men across, about fifteen in number all as naked as they was born, I sent them on in front and we retired firing at them, there was hundreds of the Kaffirs crossing the river to try and cut us off but we made good our escape to a mission station and expected to be outflanked there but we fought our way to within a mile of Luneburg - the distance we had to run and fight was nearly five miles, so you will have a guess how we were situated - We arrived at Luneburg about fifteen minutes past seven o'clock losing nine men on my side and forty one, on the other side was buried - and all the remainder was assegaied in the river - a party went out to bury them on the same day but they have been and took them up again, I mean the Kaffirs, and skinned them - so we are ordered out again to go and bury them. We go directly, I am one of them.

The names of killed are -	Captain Moriarty	Dr. Cobbin	Sergt. Johnson 'E' Co.
	Sergt. Sansam 'C' Co.	Corpl. McCoy	
Pte. Anthony	'A' Co.	Pte. J. Brown	'C' Co.
Banks'	"	Findley	"
Broughton	"	Jacobs	"
Brounson	"	Leese	"
Christy	"	Middow	"
Dutton	"	Ruffe	"
Fox	' "	Ralphs	"
Gellings	"	Meadows	'E' Co.
Green	"	Adey	"
Haines	"	Chadwick	"
Tom Hodges	"	T. Hicks	"
Hughes	"	J. Robinson	"
Laffarty	"	J. Vernon	"
Mitchell	"	H. Hile	'
Moore	"	P. Hughes	"
Moran	' "	B. McSherry	' "
Knight	"	B. Phipps	"
Teblett	"		
Weaver	"		

Names of men missing, they must have been killed in the river: missing:-

Cr. Sergt. Fredericks	Pte. Silcock
Leather	Smith
Pte. Banner	Hart
Day	Pritchard
Dadd	Purnell
Farnell	Tomlinson
Flyfield	G. Tucker
Fernaux	Wooderard
Hadley	Sheridan
E. Hanks	Lodge
W. Healey	

I am acting Pay Sergeant of a Company now - there was a parade and I and my small party was highly complimented on the bravery we exhibited in saving as many lives as we did and bringing them in with such bitter loss of life. on my side, I am Mentioned in Despatches to the General and to Colonel Wood, there is also a letter sent to the Head of the Natal Argos, I will send you one when I get it.

Now dear wife, I hope you and our children are all well - I hope Lucy is better that she was not so far gone as you thought. With fondest love to you and all the children, I remain trusting God to spare me from all evil and grant me life to see you all again.

I remain,   Your loving husband,

A. Booth

Remember me to all enquiring friends. I received a letter from Terence Bennett and another from Bill and Andrew, with some Christmas cards for all our children, I received them the day before I left for the Intombi River, I could not find it when I returned - Sergeant Else got my Colours, and he was Tried - and reduced. The next day - he was restored. I may get Frederick's Colours."

Sergeant Anthony Booth, unlike so many of his fellow soldiers lived to tell the tale of his successful retreat with a small number of comrades and other survivors. By his coolness and initiative in command he deserved the praise of his peers and senior officers alike.

*For the purpose of this letter, the spellings and rank remain unaltered from Sergeant Booth's original.

Colour-Sergeant Anthony Booth V.C. and his wife Lucy with four of their sons who all served with the Colours.

The South Africa Medal.

Obverse 988 Private John Conway, 80th
Regiment of Foot Clasp '1878-9'
Reverse 1894 Private Thomas Rhoades,
80th Regiment of Foot Clasp '1878'
(Medals - Authors Collection)

Chapter 9
THE SOUTH AFRICA MEDAL

The South Africa Medal was issued to soldiers who served in South Africa between September 25th 1877 and December 2nd 1879. In January 1880 a Royal Warrant was requested for permission to issue a medal to members of Her Majesty's Armed Forces for services in South Africa. Three Royal Warrants were eventually issued and a General Order, G.O.No.103 was published in August 1880. Due to its ambiguous wording, a further General Order, G.O.No.134 was issued in October 1880.

A total of seven 'bars' were issued, 1877;1877-8;1877-8-9;1877-9;1878;1878-9 and 1879. Out of the 36,600 medals which were struck, a total of 5600 were issued with no 'bar' and allocated to officers, non-commissioned officers and men who were part of Her Majesty's forces employed in operations against the Zulus between January 11th and September 1st 1879, _who did not_ cross the borders into Zululand.

Extract from the General Order 103:-

G.O.103 - Medals

I. The Queen in consideration of the arduous duties performed, and the successful conclusion of the operations referred to in the next paragraph, has been graciously pleased to command that a medal be granted to Her Majesty's Imperial Forces and to such of Her Majesty's Colonial Forces, European or Native, as were regularly organized and disciplined as combatants, whether raised by the Colonial Government or by the General Officer Commanding.

II. The medal will be granted to the Forces employed against:
    a. The Galekas, Gaikas, and other Kaffir Tribes from the 26th September 1877 to the 28th June 1877 inclusive.
    b. Against Pokwane, from the 21st to the 28th January 1878 inclusive.
    c. Against the Griquas, from the 24th April to the 12th November 1878 inclusive.
    d. Against the Zulus, from the 11th January to the 1st September 1879 inclusive.
    e. Against Sekukuni, from the 11th Nov to the 2nd Dec 1879, and including the troops who were stationed at Fort Burghers, Fort Albert Edward, Seven Mile Post, Fort Oliphants, Fort Weeber, and in Sekukuni's Valley.
    f. Against Moirosi's stronghold.

III. Her Majesty has also been pleased to approve of a clasp being attached to the said Medal, on which will be incorporated the year or years in which the recipients of the Medal were engaged in the late wars. Thus:

	YEAR ON CLASP
For operations against the Galekas,etc.	1877-8
" " " the Pokwane and the Griquas	1878
" " in the Zulu and Sekukuni Campaigns	1879
" " as specified in paragraph **II** in 1877,78,79	1877-8-9
" " as specified in paragraph **II** in 1878,79	1878-9

The principle being that the year or years on the clasp convey all the operations in which the recipient may have engaged in such year or years.

THE SOUTH AFRICA MEDAL (September 25th 1877-December 2nd 1879)
The periods during which the recipients of the South Africa Medals served are indicated on the clasps - 1877; 1877-8; 1877-8-9; 1877-9; 1878; 1878-9 and 1879.

MEDAL   The medal is a silver disc 35.5mm (1.4in) diameter.
        Obverse: Head of Queen Victoria, diadem,1
        Inscription:- VICTORIA REGINA
        Reverse: A lion crouching behind a Protea bush, the wording above "SOUTH AFRICA"
        exergue:- four assegais and kaffir shield
        Mounting: Silver scroll bar

RIBBON   The ribbon is 32mm wide. The colour of the ribbon is:- watered orange-yellow, with two broad and two narrow blue stripes.

Additional Medal Information
Designers   Obverse   W.Wyon R.A.   Reverse   L.C.Wyon
The medals were struck at the Royal Mint.

THE 80th REGIMENT OF FOOT (STAFFORDSHIRE VOLUNTEERS) MEDAL LIST

The names of the officers, non-commissioned officers and men of the 80th Regiment of Foot (Staffordshire Volunteers) entitled to the South Africa Medal decoration for being part of the forces as in para II of G.O.10: 1880. (soldier's rank at the time the medal was earned in brackets) The spelling of the soldiers names has been taken directly from the medal lists. The names in brackets are the variants in the Regiments Nominal Rolls

Officers, Non-commissioned Officers and Men of the 80th Regiment of Foot

	Anderson, Wilfred Turner. Captain	1687	Bickerton, Joseph. Private
4202	Allen, John. Sergeant Major	1076	Billingham, James Private
894	Allen, Charles. Sergeant	29	Birch, William. Private
1968	Attride, George. (alias George Eve) Sergeant	109	Bird, Francis. Private
93	Arthurs, William. Corporal	412	Blakeway, John. Private
1822	Allen, Amos. Corporal (Private)	719	Boden, John. Private
304	Abbott, John. Private	1015	Bond, William. Private
1505	Adair, Henry. Private	1897	Booker, Alfred. Private
704	Adams, Robert. Private	1155	Booth, Enoch. Private
546	Adey, Jonah. Private	766	Booth, Frederick. Private
976	Adey, Walter. Private	265	Bourn, William. Private
1283	Allison, John. Private	519	Bowen, Thomas. Private
1017	Allsop, Joseph. (George) Private	534	Bown, Ebineger. Private
231	Anderson, Frederick. Private	489	Boyle, Martin. Private
1916	Annals, Alfred. Private	2102	Boyle, Thomas. Private
19/585	Anthony, John. Private	1564	Bradshaw, William. Private
1521	Appleton, Thomas. Private	567	Bramill, William. Private
1437	Arkell, James. Private	1877	Braze, Thomas. Private
7	Armstrong, Thomas W. Private	273	Brereton, Thomas. Private
108	Arthurs, Michael. Private	722	Brew, George. Private
2033	Atkins, Charles. Private	415	Bridgewood, William. Private
1452	Atkinson, James. Private	1664	Broadhurst, Amos. Private
		19/745	Broughton, George. Private
	Bird, H. O. School Master	48	Brown, James. Private
919	Booth (VC), Anthony, Clarke. Colour Sergeant	122	Brown, John Private
1054	Beal, Wallace. Sergeant (Corporal)	542	Brown, John. Private
200	Bailey, John J. Lance Sergeant (Private)	576	Brown, Samuel. Private
1387	Brown, Thomas. Lance Sergeant	1553	Brown, William. Private
19/636	Beecroft, Alfred. Corporal (Private)	19/488	Brownson, Henry. Private
762	Brew, George. Corporal	659	Buckler, Thomas. Private
2038	Barnwell, William. Drummer	1728	Bunday, Henry. Private
759	Backett, John. Private	2054	Burgess, William. Private
779	Bagnall, Thomas. Private	169	Burgwin, Thomas. Private
1998	Bailey, Frederick. Private	2055	Burke, Daniel. Private
1223	Bailey, Thomas. Private	1856	Burnett, John. Private
577	Baker, John. Private	2071	Burrett, William. Private
19/202	Banks, Arthur. Private	99	Burton, Alfred. Private
1049	Banks, Thomas. Private	1737	Burton, Joseph. Private
943	Banner, John. Private	1984	Burton, Thomas. Private
1448	Barber, Alexander. Private	278	Butler, Frederick. Private
1382	Barcklie, Matthew. Private	574	Butler, John. Private
1514	Barnes, James. Private	603	Byrne, Christopher. Private (Sergeant)
531	Barnett, Richard. Private		
1591	Barron, Anthony. Private		**Creagh,** Charles Augustus Fitzgerald Brevet Major
1038	Bateman, William. Private		Cameron, Saumarez William. Lieutenant
349	Baxter, William. Private		Chamberlain, Tankerville James Lieutenant
1358	Baxter, William. Private	995	Cameron, Harry. Sergeant
1028	Beaumont, Alfred. Private	1044	Carter, Samuel. Sergeant
276	Bebbington, William. Private	966	Cooper, Albert. Lance Sergeant (Private)
1164	Bedwith, Alfred. Private	545	Constable, Thomas. Corporal (Private)
736	Bell, James. Private	1241	Corraskry, James. Corporal
1070	Bellerson, Thomas. Private	301	Collier, Alfred. Drummer
680	Bennett, William. Private	1769	Cunningham, Thomas. Drummer
105	Bentley, John. Private	159	Callaghan, Patrick. Private
275	Bentley, John. Private	1129	Cameron, Frederick. Private
975	Benton, Samuel. Private	406	Carberry, Richard. Private
513	Betts, Henry. Private	112	Carpenter, John. Private

1578	Carroll, James. Private
18	Carroll, John. Private
1290	Chadwick, John. Private
1656	Chadwick, Henry. Private
287	Chare, Calib Edwin. Private
1340	Carey, Francis. Private (Corporal)
1914	Chase, Robert. Private
1944	Cherrie, William. Private
1377	Chesterton, John. Private
1797	Christie, (Christy) James. Private
507	Clarke, John. Private
2026	Clarke, Owen. Private (Sergeant)
983	Clarke, Thomas. Private
1497	Clarke, Thomas. Private
1014	Clarke, Thomas. Private
94	Clarke, William. Private
1827	Clay, Isaac. Private
1982	Clayton, George. Private
1658	Clayton, Herbert. Private
487	Cleaton, William. Private
2	Cleaver, John. Private
551	Cluit, John. Private
755	Colclough, George. Private
561	Cole, William. Private
485	Coleman, Thomas. Private
1478	Collier, William. Private
1324	Collinson, Robert. Private
1989	Colyer, William. Private
314	Conlon, John. Private
739	Connell, James. Private
690	Connell, John. Private
988	Convey, John. Private
82	Cooke, George. Private
1913	Cooke, (Cook) George. Private
2072	Cooper, Edwin. Private
696	Cope, Samuel. Private
1051	Corbett, David. Private
753	Corns, John. Private
502	Cowdrell, Richard. Private
1874	Coy, William. Private
123	Coyne, John. Private
499	Crawford, William. Private
1524	Cullen, Peter. Private
232	Cullen, Michael. Private
631	Curtin, John. Private
	Daubeney, Edward Kaye. Lieutenant (2nd Lieut.)
909	Davis, John. Quartermaster Sergeant (Sergeant)
1048	Day, Hugh H. Colour Sergeant (Sergeant)
2101	Davis, Charles G. Sergeant
594	Donovan, William. Drummer
465	Dabbs, Robert. Private
1272	Dagger, Henry. Private
209	Daniels, William. Private
1312	Davis, William. Private
19/1042	Day, Alfred. Private
1930	Day, William. Private
1119	Deacon, William. Private
1115	Delaney, Michael. Private
1464	Dempsey, Andrew. Private
1361	Dermott, James. Private
19/953	Dodd, John. Private
1971	Doe, Joseph. Private
1076	Dollin, Robert. Private (Sergeant)
1071	Done, Benjamin. Private
1330	Doyle, Augustine. (Augustin) Private
243	Drinkwater, Enoch. Private

2005	Dudley, Alfred. Private
274	Dudley, Joseph. Private
1616	Duffy, Michael. Private
2079	Dumbleton, Benjamin. Private
507	Dunn, Charles. Private
260	Dutton, John Henry. Private
895	**Else**, William. Colour Sergeant (Sergeant)
1383	Ermion, George. Sergeant
794	Eady, John. Private
718	Edwards, Edward. Private
379	Edwards, Eli. Private
1624	Edwards, Robert. Private
1035	Edwards, William. Private
1141	Edwards, William. Private
421	Eley, Frederick. Private
84	Ellison, Robert. Private
143	England, William. Private
1003	Evens, (Evans) Evan. Private
214	Evens, (Evans) George. Private
713	Evens, (Evans) Henry. Private
1074	Evens, (Evans) John. Private
570	Everett, William. Private (Corporal)
2109	**Frayling**, William Walter Band Master
1362	Foulks, John. Colour Sergeant (Sergeant)
459	Fredericks, Henry. Colour Sergeant
1026	Fallon, John. Private
1045	Fallon, Josiah. Private (Corporal)
1028	Farnell, William. Private
2019	Farrell, Patrick. Private
467	Fawcett, Thomas. Private
1114	Field, Edward. Private
222	Findley, William. Private
520	Finn, James. Private
1860	Finnegan, Patrick. Private
230	Fisher, John. Private
1947	Fisher, Thomas. Private
1286	Fitzmorris, Thomas. Private
604	Fitzpatrick, Patrick T. Private
233	Fletcher, James. Private
1695	Flewitt, James. Private
1892	Floyd, Joseph. Private
19/176	Flyfield, William. Private
785	Flynn, Robert. Private
490	Foden, Joseph. Private
613	Follows, George. Private
812	Ford, James. Private
340	Ford, Thomas. Private
1820	Foster, Robert. Private
778	Foster, William. Private
1597	Foulk, John. Private
1030	Fox, John. Private
1465	Fox, William. Private
2080	Francis, James. Private
1918	Fricker, Joseph. Private
677	Frighney, Robert. Private
151	Fryer, William. (William, George.) Private
1449	Fulton, William. Private
2089	Furness, Albert. Private
679	Furness, Richard. Private
1925	Furniaux, John. Private
1279	**Grant**, John. Sergeant (Corporal)
1439	Garner, George. Corporal
1915	Green, Henry. Corporal
2015	Gardiner, Charles. Private

469	Giblin, Owen. Private
173	Gibson, John. Private
1335	Gilligan, William. Private
19/500	Gittins, Edwin. Private
1901	Godden, Thomas. Private
699	Godwin, William. Private
1182	Grant, John. Private
603	Gratton, John. Private
743	Greatback, James. Private
1697	Green, Joseph. Private
239	Grey, (Gray) William. Private
1463	Griffiths, Edward. Private
1550	Griffiths, Henry. Private
836	Gubbins, Nicholas. Private
1044	Guest, Joseph. Private
1671	Guilfoy, James. Private
1999	Gutterege, (Guttridge) Arthur. Private
1031	Gutteredge, (Gutalage) George. Private
368	Guy, William. Private
	Howard, Walter. Major (Captain)
	Harward, Henry Hollingworth. Lieutenant
	Hast, Arthur Wellesley. Lieutenant
	Horsbrugh, Archibald Borthwick. Lieutenant
1646	Harcourt, Frederick. Sergeant (Corporal)
889	Horton, Thomas. Sergeant (Corporal)
288	Hanmer, George. Lance Sergeant (Private)
1176	Hacker, William. Private
1502	Hackman, Samuel. Private
19/536	Hadley, George. Private
538	Hale, Charles. Private
539	Hale, William. Private
580	Halford, John. Private
1777	Hall, John. Private
957	Hall, William. Private
1812	Halligan, James. Private
1859	Hamerton, Thomas. Private
1513	Hammonds, Francis. Private
281	Handcox, Joseph. Private
492	Hands, William. Private
702	Hannon, (Hannen) John. Private
512	Harbattle, George. Private
121	Harper, Josiah. Private
643	Harris, Henry. Private
1824	Hart, George. Private
2008	Hart, Julian. Private
135	Hartrick, William. Private
1816	Harvey, John. Private
1073	Hatton, Frederick. Private
19/999	Hawkes, Eli. Private
147	Hawkins, William. Private
1951	Hayden, George. Private
1966	Hayes, Dennis. (Dennies)Private
19/227	Haynes, (Haines) George. Private
761	Haywood, Mark. Private
235	Haywood, (Hayward) Joseph. Private
19/783	Healey, Thomas. Private
599	Heath, William. Private
1906	Herman, George. Private
167	Herryman, Ephraim. Private
19/1021	Hill, Henry. Private
256	Hill, Thomas. Private
721	Hill, Thomas. Private
1068	Hill, Thomas. Private
207	Hince, Thomas. Private
737	Hing, Thomas. Private
604	Hixon, (Hickson) Henry. Private

881	Hockley, Philip. Private
709	Hodges, Thomas. Private
740	Hogan, Martin. Private
498	Holden, Samuel. Private
1433	Holman, Edwin. Private
97	Holmes, Archibald. Private
29	Holmes, James. Private
2094	Hopkins, William Francis. Private
979	Hopley, William. Private
2083	Hopson, John. Private
1522	Hough, John. Private
129	Hoult, Edward. Private
1720	Howard, Charles. Private
1945	Howard, Frank. Private
543	Howard, Henry. Private
1721	Howard, Owen. Private
2067	Howes, John. Private
495	Hughes, Benjamin. Private
552	Hughes, James. Private
1499	Hughes, John. Private
1589	Hughes, Joseph. Private
1898	Hunt, Frederick. Private
1072	Hurd, Walter. Private
945	Hussell, William. Private
535	Husselbee, John. Private
902	**Ingham**, John. Private
1838	Irvine, William Thomas. Private
	Johnson, Henry James. Captain (Lieutenant)
1271	Johnson, William. Sergeant
1783	Joyce, William. Lance Sergeant (Private)
2107	Jennings, Edgar. Corporal
19/544	Johnson, Ernest. Corporal
272	Jackson, Thomas. Private
1919	Jacobs, Henry. Private
1083	Jefferson, William. Private
285	Jenkins, (Jenkin) Henry Charles. Private
241	Jennings, George. Private
1005	Jobbourn, (Jobburn) Henry. Private
653	Johnson, Hubert. Private
1723	Johnson, John. Private
1679	Johnson, Joseph. Private
2058	Johnson, William. Private
226	Jones, Charles. Private
240	Jones, Henry. Private
155	Jones, James. Private
1391	Jones, William. Private
1488	Jones, William John. Private
1814	Jones, William. Private
1964	Jones, William Jas. Private
1251	Joyce, Martin. Private
589	Judd, Thomas. Private
668	**Kelly**, Patrick. Sergeant
1567	King, John. Sergeant (Corporal)
1711	Kelly, Thomas. Corporal
1344	Kilsill, Henry. Corporal
461	Kynaston, John. Corporal
418	Keats, Joseph. Private
115	Keenan, William. Private
682	Kelly, Peter. Private
1477	Kelly, Thomas. Private
578	Kesterton, William. Private
1357	Kettle, John. Private
526	Kilbride, John. Private
456	King, James. Private

	Lindop, Alfred Henry. Lieutenant (2nd Lieutenant)	1799	McGookin, John. Private
	Lyons, Frederick William. Lieutenant (2nd Lieutenant)	1719	McGurk, (McQuirk), Peter. Private
1321	Lynch, Thomas. Colour Sergeant (Sergeant)	2282	McKee, Edward. Private
2065	Lawrence, Robert. Sergeant	1546	McKee, James. Private
374	Lockett, Joseph. Lance Sergeant (Private)	1775	McKenny, William. Private
185	Lowbridge, David. Lance Sergaent (Private)	309	McKenzie, John. Private
1833	Lewis, William. Corporal	77	McNeil, Michael. Private
2066	Little, William, Corporal	19/1378	McSherry, Bernard. (Edward) Private
1647	Leather, John. Drummer	1983	Mead, Thomas. Private
110	Lewis, John. Drummer	19/590	Meadows, Henry. Private
1865	Lafferty, John. Private	1025	Meekin, Edward. Private
357	Lawrence, William. Private	1492	Meers, Edward. Private
1902	Lawton, Henry. Private	432	Melsop, John. Private
1795	Leigh, Ralph. Private	678	Merryman, John. Private
632	Leek, John. Private	83	Middleton, Edward. (Edwin) Private
19/996	Leese, Ralph. Private	2063	Middow, Arthur. Private
1029	Lewis, Henry. Private	49	Millar, John. Private
1506	Lewis, Peter. Private	586	Millington, Thomas. Private
1625	Linkston, Robert. Private	1976	Mitchell, George. Private
1834	Linnett, John. Private	268	Moffatt, John. Private
267	Linskey, Patrick. Private	1057	Moffatt, John. Private
27	Lloyd, (Loyd) William. Private	2106	Monaghan, Patrick. Private
1990	Loage, James. Private	554	Moore, George. Private
19/1931	Lodge, Henry. (Alias Henry Cook)Private	2048	Moore, Robert. Private
583	Longstaff, George. Private	310	Moran, Martin. Private
1657	Lord, William. Private	1032	Moran, William. Private
1653	Lowrie, James. Private	1397	Moreton, William. Private
1213	Lunt, William. Private	787	Morgan, Bernard. Private
		180	Morris, John. Private
	Moriarty, David Barry. Captain	504	Morris, Joseph. Private
	Moore, William. Lieutenant	1821	Morris, Joseph. Private
918	Machin, Frederick. Colour Sergeant	681	Morris, Michael. Private
416	Markwell, Thomas. Sergeant	964	Morris, Thomas. Private
1761	McDonald, Nicholas. Sergeant	161	Morris, William. Private
124	McMullen, John. Sergeant (Corporal)	768	Morris, William. Private
1487	Major, Robert. Corporal	476	Morris, (Morriss) John. Private
2000	Martin, Charles. Corporal	315	Mountford, William. Private
714	Maynard, William J. Corporal	1904	Muddell, Charles. Private
1525	McCready, Robert. Corporal	1678	Mulgrew, James. Private
19/733	McCoy, John. Corporal	1579	Mullholland, Joseph. Private
1303	McDonald, John. Corporal	127	Mullins, Thomas. Private
1372	Moore, George. Corporal	1501	Murphy, William. Private
1319	Moore, Henry. Corporal (Drummer)		
1534	Murch, Samuel. Corporal (Private)	201	**Norton,** William. Colour Sergeant
1767	McQuillan, John. Drummer	157	Navan, John. Private
1336	Moran, William. Drummer	984	Neale, Joseph. Private
2092	Maden, George. Private	758	Newey, William. (John) Private
1426	Makepeace, John. Private	1868	Newton, Henry. Private
1568	Malloy, John. Private	468	Nicklin, Thomas. Private
1351	Manning, Stephen. Private	1926	Night, Henry. Private
1927	Mantell, Henry. Private	263	Nixon, Joseph. Private
1890	Marsdin, (Marsden) Mark. Private	1339	Nolan, Patrick. Private
2103	Marson, William. Private	1681	Nolan, Thomas. Private
206	Martin, Frederick. Private	772	Noonan, Thomas. Private
1909	Martin, Thomas. Private	1062	Norton, John. Private
588	Mason, Edward. Private	1566	Nunnerley, John. Private
1712	Massey, Thomas. Private		
732	Masterson, Peter. Private	692	**O'Day**, Owen. Drum Major
1933	Matthews, Alfred. Private	1249	O'Neill, Thomas. Colour Sergeant (Sergeant)
170	Matthews, Charles. Private	1117	O'Brien, Richard. Private
1846	May, John. Private	1456	O'Neil, John. Private
2108	McAuliffe, Edmond. Private	1736	Ovens, Williams. Private
300	McCaffrey, Hugh. Private	166	Owen, Edward. Private
62	McClearey, (McClarey) Dennis. Private	1840	Owen, James. Private
1349	McCullough, James. Private	165	Owen, William. Private
559	McDonald, William. Private		
1858	McGillan, Thomas. Private		

	Prior, John Edward Hale. Major (Captain)	1337	Rubie, George. Private
	Potts, Lipton Cumming. Captain (Lieutenant)	1085	Rubie, Robert. Private
784	Pendergast, Henry. Sergeant (Corporal)	2070	Ruffle, Henry. Private
1257	Penketh, James. Sergeant (Corporal)	711	Rush, Frank. Private
582	Page, Albert. Private	2010	Russell, James. Private
1027	Parks, Charles. Private	1254	Ryan, Daniel. Private
1256	Parks, Henry. Private	1912	Ryan, Henry. Private
1885	Parrott, George. Private	1423	Ryan, Joseph. Private
172	Parry, Henry. Private		
1160	Patey, John. Private		**Sherrard**, James Ormsby. Captain (Lieutenant)
971	Payne, Thomas. Private	3124	Shore, Edward. Colour Sergeant
698	Pearse, Charles. Private	1503	Stevenson, Joseph. Sergeant
805	Pemberton, Henry. Private	1627	Sansam, George. Lance Sergeant
399	Pepper, John. Private	2062	Stephens, Edward. Corporal
662	Perkins, John. Private	375	Salt, George. Private
116	Perkins, Joseph. Private	1889	Salter, Charles. Private
92	Peters, Frank. Private	972	Sanders, John. Private
246	Phillips, Alfred. Private	439	Sands, (Sandes) William. Private
477	Phillips, Thomas. Private	968	Sargeant, Henry. (William) Private
612	Phillips, Thomas. Private	1533	Satterly, William. Private
220	Phipps, William. Private	962	Saville, Edward. Private
649	Picken, George. Private	1019	Savage, James. Private
286	Pitcher, (Pittcher) Joseph. Private	670	Saxton, (Josiah) Joseph. Private
360	Plant, Henry. Private	2074	Scott, Edward. Private
1604	Plant, William. Private	1253	Seddons, (Seddon) Thomas. Private
1549	Poole, John. Private	377	Sedgeley, William Henry. Private
706	Powell, Edward. Private	262	Senior, John. Private
1234	Powers, John. Private	650	Sergeant, John W. Private
717	Powis, Samuel. Private	675 (695)	Seymour, William. Private
186	Preece, George. Private	484	Shapcott, Henry. Private
2031	Prince, John. Private	970	Shaw, Frederick. Private
2085	Pritchard, Charles. Private	1165	Shaw, Samuel. Private
1053	Proud, Peter. (Robert) Private	2035	Shellock, James. Private
1163	Pummell, Arthur. Private	19/615	Sherridan, Michael. Private
		514	Shirley, Henry William. Private
645	**Queeny**, Owen. Private	508	Sigley, John. Private
2047	Quick, James. Private	1770	Silcock, Joseph. Private
		324	Simcock, John. Private
	Roworth, Charles Edward Whitaker. Captain	511	Simpson, William. Private
	Raitt, Herbert Aveling. Lieutenant (2nd Lieutenant)	607	Sinclair, William. Private
2098	Richardson, William. Colour Sergeant (Sergeant)	378	Sivorns, William. Private
1974	Ralphs, Frederick. Private	1864	Skellam, Thomas.(Thomas Everard) Private
201	Ramsey, George. Private	610	Slack, Edward. Private
414	Randle, Henry. Private	608	Sleigh, Walter. Private
1953	Raymond, Charles. Private	376	Smith, Charles. Private
533	Reid, George Thomas. Private	386	Smith, Daniel. Private
158	Renfrey, Alfred. Private	1018	Smith, Daniel. Private
609	Rhoades, (Rhodes) Roland. Private	1048	Smith, George. Private
1894	Rhoades, (Rhoads) Thomas. Private	479	Smith, Henry. Private
528	Richardson, Charles. Private	19/510	Smith, Henry. Private
2012	Richardson, George. Private	646	Smith, Henry. (Henry George) Private
1108	Rickman, George. Private	725	Smith, Henry. Private
995	Riley, Martin. Private	424	Smith, James. Private
1963	Ring, Edward. Private	144	Smith, John. Private
578	Robbins, William. Private	1050	Smith, John. Private
1960	Roberts, Henry. Private	1350	Smith, John. Private
19/259	Robinson, John. Private	1948	Smith, John. Private
1483	Robinson, Robert. Private	1063	Smith, Johnson. Private
1000	Robinson, Samuel. Private	258	Smith, Joseph. Private
1047	Robson, James. Private	657	Smith, Joseph. Private
1393	Rochell, Henry. Private	61	Smith, Mark. Private
965	Rodgers, Samuel. Private	1240	Smith, Michael. Private
486	Rohen, Peter. Private	1494	Smith, William. Private
358	Rouse, William. Private	2029	Soan, Benjamin. Private
744	Rowan, Thomas. Private	1805	Speers, James. Private
975	Rowe, John. Private	729	Spence, Robert. Private
663	Rowley, Thomas. Private	746	Spink, James. Private

1526	Stacey, Arthur. Private	1924	Waxham, Thomas. Private
2016	Stanley, Alfred. Private	730	Weaver, Benjamin. Private
1776	Sterling, Henry. Private	606	Weaver, Job:, Private
138	Stokes, Frank. Private	1289	Weaver, John. Private
1987	Storas, William. Private	19/716	Weaver, Joseph. Private
225	Storer, Walter. Private	605	Webster, John. Private
1396	Sugden, Richard. Private	1905	Wells, James. Private
2042	Sullivan, Michael. Private	1002	West, Eli. Private
2060	Summersby, Henry. Private	990	Western, Charles. Private
1988	Sutton, James. Private	294	Westwood, James. Private
		228	Westwood, Thomas. Private
	Tucker (C.B.), Charles. Lt. Colonel (Major)	1097	Wheeler, Richard. Private
2003	Thompson, John. Orderly Room	752	While, William. Private
	Clerk (Quartermaster Sergeant)	2061	White, George. Private
1163	Tolley, William. Sergeant	1041	Whitehouse, David. Private
1011	Tidball, Henry. Corporal (Private)	9/60	Whitehouse, Joseph. Private
1757	Terry, Alfred. Drummer	769	Whitehouse, (Whitehead) Richard. Private
120	Tallice, George. Private	774	Whitehouse, William. Private
735	Taylor, John. Private	2097	Whyman, Thomas. Private
720	Taylor, Joshua Thomas. Private	247	Wiley, Charles. Private
1895	Taylor, Thomas. Private	137	Wiley, Thomas. Private
255	Taylor, William. Private	24	Wilkins, Henry. Private
373	Teehan, John. Private	791	Wilkinson, Samuel. Private
816	Tetlow, Edward. Private	1006	Wilkinson, William. Private
1794	Thompson, Alexander. Private	450	Willings, Enoch. Private
2096	Thompson, E.G.A. Private	1039	William, (Williams) William. Private
2081	Thompson, Henry. Private	991	Williams, Charles. Private
1957	Thompson, Robert. Private	1876	Williams, George. Private
811	Thompson, Thomas. Private	691	Williams, Harry. Private
2002	Thompson, (Thomson) William. Private	997	Williams, Shadrack. Private
162	Thorley, Thomas. Private	361	Williams, Thomas. Private
19/587	Tibbott, Joseph. Private	573	Williams, Thomas. Private
1061	Tilley, George. Private	617	Williams, William. Private
1826	Toal, James. Private	2013	Wilmott, (Wilmot) William. Private
649	Tomlin, Thomas. Private	1896	Wilson, Charles. Private
1291	Tomlinson, Richard. Private	627	Wilson, Frederick. Private
1529	Tomlinson, William. Private	1175	Wilson, Henry. Private
19/1705	Tucker, George. Private	1375	Wiltshire, Benjamin. Private
19/104	Tucker, Thomas. Private	686	Winter, John. Private
669	Tully, Patrick. Private	1020	Winwood, Joseph. Private
1887	Turner, Charles. Private	295	Wood, Charles. Private
459	Turner, Edward. Private	446	Wood, David. Private
501	Tyler, James. Private	515	Wood, James. Private
		1486	Wooding, Isaac. Private
	Ussher, Beverley William Reid. Lieutenant	1605	Woodward, Herbert. Private
188	Upperdine, Joseph. Private	1394	Woolcot, (Woolcox) Henry. Private (Corporal)
		1871	Woollams, Frederick. Private
540	**Vyse**, Joseph. Drummer	2078	Worty, James. Private
1046	Vaughan, John. Private	598	Wright, Frederick. Private
423	Varley, John. Private	564	Wright, George. Private
370	Vernon, James. Private	2051	Wright, Joseph. Private
1080	Vickery, Samuel. Private	1023	Wright, William. Private
		566	Wroe, John. Private
336	**Waters**, James. Colour Sergeant		
1665	Walker, Harry. Sergeant	1888	**Young**, Thomas. Private
1217	Ward, Henry. Sergeant	1013	Yoxall, Frederick. Private
1630	Watts, James Henry. Sergeant		
1320	Weldon, Peter. Corporal (Drummer)		Attached to the 80th Regiment of Foot:
1911	Wakeling, George. Private		Whittington, Joseph. Waggon Conductor
563	Walker, Thomas. Private		
549	Welsh, Anthony. Private		
219	Walsh, John. Private		
1495	Walsh, William. Private		
62	Ward, William. Private		
204	Warner, Cornelius. Private		
427	Wassall (VC), Samuel. Private		
1016	Wassall, Charles. Private		

The Battle of Ulundi

The final battle of the Zulu War at Ulundi as depicted by a contemporary Illustrated London News

THE MEN BEHIND THE MEDALS 1 : THE OFFICERS

According to the Medal List for the 80th Regiment of Foot the names of all ranks who were entitled to the South Africa Medal (G.O.103) totalled 21 officers and 729 non-commissioned officers and men. The research of the details of these men attempts to give an insight into the type of man that filled the ranks of a British infantry regiment around 1879. Although the information is primarily up to and including the Zulu War of 1879, any further information obtained has been included.

Eleven of the twenty-one officers were born in England, seven in Ireland, the remainder in Gibraltar, Italy and the East Indies. The youngest recorded age to hold a first commission was C.E.F.Creagh, sixteen years and three months - also the earliest recorded commission, September 8th 1854. The eldest person to hold a first commission was A.H.Lindop who was thirty years, nine months. The last man to be commissioned was B.W.R.Ussher, who received his commission on June 12th 1878. The average age to obtain a commission was twenty years and eleven months. It should be noted however, that in the late 1870s the 'Cardwell Reforms' were still being implemented which included the end of purchasing of commissions and the introduction of short service agreements.

Of the twenty-one officers, two were promoted from the ranks, A.H.Lindop who had served for 12 years, 265 days and B.W.R.Ussher who had served for 2 years, 280 days. The officer to join the 80th Regiment first was W.T.Anderson who joined on August 4th 1865; the last officer to join was T..J.Chamberlain on October 18th 1878. During the Zulu War the Regiment lost only one officer killed in action, Capt.D.B.Moriarty. One officer resigned his commission following the Zulu War. One officer was to die in a hospital in Upper Egypt serving his country. The majority of the men who served as officers were to retire after many years with the 80th Regiment of Foot or following service with other regiments or departments of the British Army.

Five officers were later in their careers to become the Commanding Officer of the Regiment when it was either the 80th Regiment or the 2nd Battalion South Staffordshire Regiment:- C.Tucker, C.A.F.Creagh, J.E.H.Prior, W.Moore, and E.K.Daubeney. During a later campaign, E.K.Daubeney was awarded the Distinguished Service Order for gallantry. C.Tucker was awarded a knighthood (Knight Commander of the Bath, Knight-Grand Cross of the Royal Victorian Order, and the Grand Cross of the Bath). H.A.Raitt was also made a Companion of the Order of the Bath.

N.B. [P] indicates Commission by Purchase.

WilfredTurner ANDERSON (Captain)

Date of Birth   March 24th 1846   Place of Birth   Newcastle upon Tyne, England
Age upon Entering the Service 19 years 5 months   Served as a Cadet at the Royal Military College
Service and Dates of Commission:
Ensign or Cornet 80th Regiment of Foot August 4th 1865[P]
Lieutenant   80th Regiment of Foot October 14th 1868[P]
Captain   80th Regiment of Foot November 9th 1877
Major   80th Regiment of Foot July 9th 1881
Lieutenant Colonel 2nd Battalion South Staffordshire Regiment July 1st 1888
Retired July 1st 1888
Periods of Employment:
Home   August 4th 1865 - January 11th 1872
Strait Settlements   January 12th 1872 - December 27th 1872
China   December 28th 1872 - August 21st 1874
Home   August 22nd 1874 - November 16th 1877
Cape of Good Hope   November 17th 1877 -
Staff Service Record: Served as Superintendent Of Volunteers 1878
Orders and Decorations: South Africa Medal with clasp '1878-9'
Personal Information   Height 5ft 8 ins   Foreign Languages - French
General Information:
Wilfred Turner Anderson took part in the operations against Sekukuni in 1878 and served with Regiment on the Swazi Border during 1879. Wilfred was present at the final Battle of the Zulu War at Ulundi.

Saumarez William CAMERON (Lieutenant)

Date of Birth   May 29th 1850   Place of Birth   Dublin, Ireland
Age upon Entering the Service 21 years 7 months   Hythe, 2nd Class Certificate
Passed for Promotion   Devonport, August 24th 1886

Service and Dates of Commission
Sub-Lieutenant 80th Regiment of Foot January 17th 1872
Lieutenant   80th Regiment of Foot January 17th 1874
Captain   80th Regiment of Foot February 2nd 1881
Retired August 23rd 1887 with Gratuity of £1,200
Periods of Employment
Home   January 17th 1872 - February 10th 1875
China   February 11th 1875 - November 26th 1875
Strait Settlements   November 27th 1875 - January 26th 1877
Home   January 27th 1877 - September 5th 1878
South Africa   September 6th 1878 - May 11th 1880
Home   May 12th 1880 -
Orders and Decorations   Indian General Service Medal with clasp 'Perak'
                                    South African Medal with clasp '1878-9'
Personal Information   Foreign Languages - French and German
General Information
Saumarez William Cameron served with a detachment of the 80th Regiment of Foot in the Perak expedition
during 1875 and 1876. Saumarez also took part in the Kaffir war of 1878 including the operations against
Sekukuni.

Tankerville James CHAMBERLAIN (Lieutenant)

Date of Birth   January 10th 1844   Place of Birth   Dublin, Ireland
Age upon Entering the Service 24 years   Military Law
Passed for Promotion Yes
Service and Dates of Commission
Ensign or Cornet 13th Light Infantry June 20th 1868 [P]
Transferred to   Ceylon Rifles   June 20th 1868
Lieutenant   Ceylon Rifles   October 28th 1871
Transferred to   80th Regiment of Foot October 18th 1873 (Due to Disbandment of the Ceylon Rifles)
Captain   80th Regiment of Foot January 12th 1881
Major   2nd Battalion South Staffordshire Regiment July 9th 1884
Retired March 16th 1889
Periods of Employment
Home   June 20th 1868 - October 23rd 1868
Ceylon   October 24th 1868 - August 9th 1870
Labuau   August 10th 1870 - December 12th 1871
Ceylon   December 13th 1871 - October 10th 1873
Home   October 11th 1873 - January 26th 1874
China   January 27th 1874 - March 21st 1877
Mauritius   March 22nd 1877 - June 24th 1877
South Africa   June 25th 1877 - December 29th 1879
Home   December 30th 1879 -

Staff Service Record
Fort Adjutant, Hong Kong July 10th 1875 - March 21st 1877
Acting Brigade Major, Hong Kong November 11th 1875 - February 29th 1876 (By Local General Order
                                                    No168 November 10th 1875)
Officiating Assistant Military Secretary, Hong Kong January 10th 1876 - February 29th 1876
Special Duties in Natal with H.E. Sir Henry Bulwer, Lt. Governor
Aide de Camp to H.E. Sir Henry Bulwer, Governor in Natal September 7th 1877 - October 27th 1877

Aide de Camp to Governor and Commander in Chief, Natal February 3rd 1882 - March 1886
Regimental Staff Service Record
Acting Paymaster and Quartermaster, Labuau March 8th 1871 - December 6th 1871

Orders and Decorations   South Africa Medal with clasp '1878-9'
Personal Information   Foreign Languages - French, German, Spanish and Malay
General Information
Tankerville James Chamberlain served in the Transvaal and during November and December 1878 and was in charge of two, six pounder guns. Tankerville took part in the operations against Sekukuni in 1878 and during 1879 he served on the Swazi border and took part in the Zulu War and was present at the Battle of Ulundi.

Charles Augustus FitzGerald CREAGH (Captain and Brevet Major)
Date of Birth   June 10th 1838   Place of Birth   Gibraltar
Age upon Entering the Service 16 years 3 months
Military School or College   Hythe, 1st Class Certificate
Service and Dates of Commission
Ensign or Cornet 50th Regiment of Foot September 8th 1854
Lieutenant 50th Regiment of Foot February 9th 1855
Captain 50th Regiment of Foot May 6th 1863
Transferred to 80th Regiment of Foot January 14th 1871
Brevet Major 80th Regiment of Foot October 1st 1877
Major   80th Regiment of Foot July 9th 1879
Lieutenant Colonel 80th Regiment of Foot July 1st 1881
Colonel   2nd Battalion South Staffordshire Regiment July 1st 1885
Honorary Major General   April 23rd 1887
Retired April 23rd 1887

Periods of Employment
Home   September 8th 1854 - September 23rd 1855
Crimea   September 24th 1855 - July 9th 1856
Home   July 10th 1856 - July 1st 1857
Ceylon   July 2nd 1857 - October 18th 1859
Home   October 19th 1859 - July 28th 1863
Ceylon   July 29th 1863 - November 14th 1863
New Zealand   November 15th 1863 - October 14th 1866
Australia   October 15th 1866 - February 6th 1869
Home   (Half pay) February 7th 1869 - January 13th 1871
Home   January 14th 1871 - January 11th 1872
Strait Settlements January 12th 1872 - November 27th 1872
China   November 28th 1872 - November 10th 1875
Perak   November 11th 1875 - April 17th 1876
Home   April 18th 1876 - October 17th 1877
South Africa   October 18th 1877 - November 19th 1880
Home   November 20th 1880 - May 28th 1884
Egypt   May 29th 1884 -

Staff Service Record
Deputy Assistant Commissary General, Kandy, Ceylon October 12th 1857 - October 1st 1859
Aide de Camp to Sir G.F. Bowen GCMG Governor of Queensland(Brisbane), January 1867-July 1868
Staff Officer at Lydenburg, South Africa September 20th 1878 - November 15th 1878
Commandant District of Lydenburg, South Africa November 11th 1878 - December 28th 1878
Commanding Troops at Derby and Lydenburg, South Africa January 1st 1879 - January 31st 1879
Transport Officer No.5 Column Zulu War Forces February 1st 1879 - February 23rd 1879
Commanding Troops Lydenburg, South Africa May 5th 1879 - December 12th 1879
Commanding Irregular Calvalry - Ferreira's Horse July 1879 - September 1879

Staff Officer Transvaal, South Africa September 1879-January 1880
Acting Commissariat Officer North District Transvaal December 12th 1879-August 26th 1880
Regimental Staff Service Record
Acting Paymaster July 1872 - November 1875

Orders and Decorations	New Zealand Medal
	Indian General Service Medal with clasp 'Perak'
	South Africa Medal with clasp '1878-9'
	Mentioned in Despatches
	Egypt Medal with clasp 'The Nile 1884-85'
	Egypt, Khedive Star
Personal Information Height 5 ft 7¹/₂ ins	Foreign Languages - French and Dutch

Married Mary Anna Dodd on July 20th 1863 in the Isle of Wight by the Reverend Bowden, Church of England. Mary died in Lichfield, Staffordshire on July 22nd 1881. Charles and Anna had one child, Charles Hamilton Vandeleur born on August 29th 1865 and christened in Auckland, New Zealand.

General Information
Charles Augustus FitzGerald Creagh no doubt saw more active service than the majority of his fellow Officers. He served with the 50th Regiment of Foot (Royal West Kent) in the Crimea September 11th 1855 to July 9th 1856. He also saw action during the war in New Zealand November 15th 1863 to October 14th 1866 and was present at the storming and capture of Rangiawhia. He was in command of a party of the 50th Regiment which helped repulse an enemy attack on the encampment at Nukumaru. As a Captain he served with the 80th Regiment in the expedition to Perak under General Colbourne 1875/1876. 1878 he served in the Transvaal in the operations against Sekukuni. In the Zulu War he commanded three Companies of the 80th Regiment of Foot and afterwards was appointed to serve as Commandant of the Lydenberg District in South Africa. Also served in the Transvaal. Whilst taking part in further operations against Sekukuni he was invalided. As Lieutenant Colonel he served with the Nile Expedition 1884-85 in command of the 2nd Battalion of the South Staffordshire Regiment. In command July 9th 1884 to 1887.

Edward Kaye DAUBENEY (2nd Lieutenant)
Date of Birth   May 23rd 1858   Place of Birth   Ampney, Cirencester, England
Age upon Entering the Service 19 years 11 months
Military School or College   Served as a Cadet at the Royal Military College, 1878
                                        Hythe, 1st Class Cert. Extra Certificate Musketry 1882
Passed for Promotion
Lieut-Col 1898, G.O.C.C.329 Simla May 12th 1902
107/Aldershot/365/October 18th 1898
Service and Dates of Commission
2nd Lieutenant 80th Regiment of Foot   May 11th 1878
Lieutenant 80th Regiment of Foot   December 1st 1880
Captain   2nd Battalion South Staffordshire Regiment August 7th 1886
Major   2nd Battalion South Staffordshire Regiment November 18th 1896
Lieutenant Colonel 2nd Battalion South Staffordshire Regiment October 16th 1903
Brevet Colonel (Half Pay)   October 16th 1906
Brigade Commander Territorial Division Gloucester & Worcester December 10th 1910
Temporary Brigadier General   August 5th 1914
Temporary Brigadier General   September 1st 1916

Periods of Employment
Home	May 11th 1878 - July 27th 1878
South Africa	July 28th 1878 - May 11th 1880
Home	May 12th 1880 - February 27th 1884
Egypt	February 28th 1884 - August 15th 1885
Staff Egyptian Army	August 16th 1885 - July 21st 1886
Home	July 22nd 1886 - February 17th 1893

ADC to GOC Frontier Forces Egypt February 18th 1893 - October 27th 1896
Home   October 28th 1896 - January 21st 1901
India   January 22nd 1901 - March 25th 1903
Home   March 26th 1903 - July 25th 1903
India   July 26th 1903 -

Staff Service Record
Employed with Egyptian Army February 28th 1884-October 30th 1885
Aide de Camp to Brigadier General Egypt October 31st 1885 - August 6th 1886
Adjutant or Assistant Adjutant 3rd Battalion South Staffordshire Regiment January 21st 1896-January
                                                    22nd 1901

Orders and Decorations   Companion of the Order of the Bath
                                         Distinguished Service Order
                                         South Africa Medal with clasp '1878-9'
                                         Egypt Medal with clasp 'The Nile 1884-85'
                                         Mentioned in Dispatches
                                         Egypt, Khedive Star
Personal Information   Height 5ft 11 ins   Foreign languages - French, German and Arabic
Educated at Wellington College
Edward married Eileen Gertrude FitzGerald, (daughter of Sir P. Fitzgerald, 19th Knight of Kerry), on November
30th 1886 at Valencia Island, Ireland, marriage conducted by the Reverend Delaye, Church of England. Edward
and Eileen had one Child, Thomas Edward born September 9th 1894, christened at the Church of St.Peter's,
Ampney Cirencester.

General Information
Edward Kaye Daubeney served with the 80th Regiment and took part in the campaign against Sekukuni 1878.
Served on the Swazi border and took part in the Zulu War and in the final battle at Ulundi. Later in the Nile
expedition 1884 and 1885. February 28th to October 30th 1885 was employed with the Egyptian Army and
served in the Egyptian Field Force during 1885 and 1886 as ADC. to Brigadier Butler. For his actions in the
engagement at Giniss he was awarded the Distinguished Service Order. Later appointed Commanding Officer
2nd Battalion South Staffordshire Regiment 1903-1907. During Great War commanded the Gloucester and
Worcestershire Brigade, the 182nd Infantry Brigade and the Reserve Highland Brigade. In 1919 awarded the
Companion of the Order of the Bath. His home was at Woodbridge, Suffolk. Edward died on November 3rd
1932 in his seventy-fifth years, leaving a son.

Henry Hollingworth HARWARD (Lieutenant)
Date of Birth   November 25th 1847   Place of Birth   Oak Bank, Sevenoaks, England
Age upon Entering the Service 24 years 1 months
Military School or College   No
Service and Dates of Commission
Cornet or Ensign 1st West India Regiment December 30th 1871
Lieutenant   1st West India Regiment December 30th 1874
Lieutenant   80th Regiment of Foot May 13th 1874
Resigned his Commission on May 11th 1880
Periods of Employment
Home   December 30th 1871 - May 4th 1873
Jamiaca   May 5th 1873 - December 2nd 1873
West Africa   December 3rd 1873 - May 12th 1874
China   May 13th 1874 - February 14th 1876
?   February 15th 1876 - July 4th 1877
South Africa   July 5th 1877 - May 11th 1880

Regimental Staff Service Record
Fort Adjutant C.C. Castle   February - March ⎫   Years not
Fort Adjutant Sierra Leone   March - July   ⎬   Known

General Sir Garnet Wolseley, G.C.M.G., K.C.B., Commander in Chief of the British Forces in South Africa whose early career was with the 80th Regiment and thought highly of them.

Orders and Decorations

Ashantee Medal
South Africa Medal with Clasp '1878-9'

Personal Information   Height 5ft 10ins
General Information
Henry Hollingworth Harward took part in the Ashantee campaign of 1873 and 1874 under command of Major-General Sir Garnet Wolseley. During 1877 he joined the 80th Regiment in South Africa on August 3rd and took part in the campaign against Sekukuni under command of Colonel Rowlands the following year. Henry then in 1879 took part in the Zulu War. He was one of two Officers involved in the Intombi River massacre, the only officer to survive the incident, he was court martialled but later acquitted. Because of his reported actions in this disastrous engagement and subsequent court martial, although acquitted, he felt it necessary to resign his commission on May 11th 1881, after serving eight years and one hundred and thirty-four days with the Colours.

Arthur Wellesley HAST (Lieutenant)

Date of Birth   May 29th 1854   Place of Birth   Southampton, England
Age upon Entering the Service 19 years 9 months
Military School or College   Hythe - no Certificate
                             Military Engineering Chatham - Certificate
Passed through school of Instruction - Field Works Military Topography
Passed for Promotion   Yes

Service and Dates of Commission
Sub-Lieutenant/
2nd Lieutenant 80th Regiment of Foot February 28th 1874
Lieutenant   80th Regiment of Foot February 28th 1874
Captain   80th Regiment of Foot April 1st 1881
Major   2nd Battalion South Staffordshire Regiment January 27th 1885
Retired with Gratuity October 31st 1890
Periods of Employment
Home   February 28th 1874 - December 2nd 1875
Strait Settlements December 3rd 1875 - January 26th 1877
South Africa   January 27th 1877 - May 11th 1880
Home   May 12th 1880 -

Regimental Staff Service Record
Acting Paymaster of Detachment January 27th 1877 - September 30th 1878
Orders and Decorations   Indian General Service Medal with clasp 'Perak'
                                  South Africa Medal with clasp '1878-9'
Personal Information   Foreign Languages - French
Married Janie Eleanor (Hast) at St.Barnabas Church, Church of England, Kensington, London by Reverend F. Hessey D.C.L., on June 24th 1880
General Information
Arthur Hast served with the detachment of the 80th Regiment of Foot in the Perak expedition in 1876. He commanded a mule battery of two seven-pounder guns on Zulu border 1878, for which he received personal thanks of His Excellency, Lieutenant-General Lord Chelmsford re: letter dated September 9th 1878. Served throughout the left attack against Sekukuni, in charge of two guns in the column under command of Colonel Rowlands on Swazi border. In the Zulu War, was present at Ulundi, the final battle of War.

Archibald Borthwick HORSBRUGH (Lieutenant)

Date of Birth   December 26th 1856   Place of Birth   Norwood, Middlesex, England
Age upon Entering the Service 17 years 2 months
Military School or College   Direct Commission
Passed for Promotion
Passed for Captain Special Certificate
D.G.M.E. 107/Gen No/552 1882
Passed for Lieutenant Colonel 107/SE/298, d/W.O. 24/9/1894   Distinction - Military Law

Service and Dates of Commission
Ensign or Cornet 80th Regiment of Foot February 28th 1874
Lieutenant 80th Regiment of Foot February 28th 1874
Captain   80th Regiment of Foot April 5th 1881
Transferred to 1st Battalion South Staffordshire Regiment April 5th 1881
Major   1st Battalion South Staffordshire Regiment February 11th 1884
Transferred to 2nd Battalion South Staffordshire Regiment (2nd in Command) March 11th 1885
Lieutenant Colonel 2nd Battalion South Staffordshire Regiment February 11th 1895
Retired November 25th 1896

Periods of Employment
Home   February 28th 1874 - December 29th 1875
Strait Settlements   December 30th 1875 - March 10th 1877
South Africa   March 11th 1877 - May 11th 1880
Home   May 12th 1880 - August 16th 1881
Malta   August 17th 1881 - July 7th 1882
Egypt   July 8th 1882 - May 16th 1883
Malta   May 17th 1883 - February 21st 1884
Egypt   February 22nd 1884 - September 29th 1886
Gibraltar   September 30th 1886 - March 19th 1891
Home   March 20th 1891 - April 14th 1892
Egypt   April 15th 1892 - June 15th 1893
Home   June 16th 1893 -

Orders and Decorations   South Africa Medal with clasp '1878-9'
                            Egypt Medal with clasps 'The Nile 1884-85' and 'Kirbekan'
                            Egypt, Khedive Star
Personal Information   Foreign Languages - French and German
Archibald Horsbrugh age of thirty-nine years married Gwynyth Dorothea Coyney aged twenty-nine by the
Reverend Dean Luckock, Church of England, Cathedral Church Lichfield, Staffordshire April 22nd 1896.

General Information
Archibald served in the operations against Sekukuni 1878, which were suspended during Zulu War in which he
took part. Following Zulu War, Chief Sekukuni was again challenged and his stronghold finally taken
November 28th 1879 with Archibald taking part in the assault. With the 1st Battalion (38th Regiment of Foot)
in the Egyptian War 1882 and member of the reconnaissance force from Alexandria August 5th. As Captain,
took part in Nile expedition 1884-85 and present in the action at Kirbekan receiving serious wounds.

Walter HOWARD (Captain)
Date of Birth   July 7th 1838   Place of Birth   Portsmouth, England
Age upon Entering the Service 19 years 9 months
Military School or College   Hythe, 1st Class Certificate
                                       Chatham 1st Class Certificate;Field Works and Surveying
Service and Dates of Commission
Cornet or Ensign 80th Regiment of Foot March 16th 1858
Lieutenant 80th Regiment of Foot August 26th 1859ᴾ
Captain   80th Regiment of Foot December 10th 1873
Captain (Paymaster) Pay Department July 13th 1880
Brevet Major
Transferred to The Hampshire Regiment July 24th 1884
Honorary Major   July 13th 1894
Honorary Lieutenant Colonel   February 17th 1897
Retired July 7th 1898

Periods of Employment
Home   March 16th 1858 - February 3rd 1859

East Indies	February 4th 1859 - June 19th 1866
Home	June 20th 1866 - March 11th 1874
China	March 12th 1874 - November 10th 1875
Strait Settlements	November 11th 1875 - January 3rd 1877
Home	January 4th 1877 - February 1st 1878
South Africa	February 2nd 1878 - May 11th 1880
Home	May 12th 1880 -

Staff Service Record
Acting Ordnance, Commissariat Officer & District Pay Master August 26th 1878 - July 4th 1879

Regimental Staff Service Record
Acting Pay Master September 13th 1879 - July 4th 1880

Orders and Decorations   Indian General Service Medal with clasps 'Bhootan' and 'Perak'
                                South Africa Medal with clasp '1878-9'

Personal Information   Foreign Languages - French
Walter Howard married Emily Roselta Budd December 7th 1881 at the Church of England, Church of St.Mary Abbot, Kensington, London by the Reverend W.E. Haigh.
General Information
Walter Howard whilst with the 80th Regiment took part in the left attack during the Bhootan expedition 1865. As a Lieutenant he served in the Perak expedition 1875-76. Walter served throughout operations against Sekukuni 1878 in which he received the thanks of Colonel Rowlands and later in Zulu War 1879. He also took part in the operations against Sekukuni, and was present in the storming of the chief''s stronghold at Ulundi. Mentioned in the London Gazette January 16th 1880 (Despatches - Brevet Major for services rendered). Died at Guildford aged seventy-one years of age.

Henry James JOHNSON (Lieutenant)
Date of birth June 15th 1850   Place of Birth   London, England
Age upon Entering the Service 18 years
Military School or College   Served as a Cadet at the Royal Military CollegeHythe,
                                              1st Class Certificate - Fortifications; Military Language
Service and Dates of Commission
Cornet or Ensign 80th Regiment of Foot July 8th 1868
Lieutenant 80th Regiment of Foot October 28th 1871
Captain 80th Regiment of Foot March 13th 1879
Retired January 12th 1881
Periods of Employment

Home	July 8th 1868 - July 3th 1874
China	July 4th 1874 - February 14th 1876
Strait Settlements	February 15th 1876 - March 10th 1877
South Africa	March 11th 1877 - May 11th 1880
Home	May 12th 1880 -

Staff Service Record
District Adjutant, Lydenburg November 1878-January 1879
Commissariat Officer, Luneburg February 14th 1879-April 11th 1879
Regimental Staff Service Record
Instructor of Musketry November 5th 1874 - March 13th 1879
Orders and Decorations   Indian General Service Medal with clasp 'Perak'
                                South Africa Medal with clasp '1878-9'Personal Information
Personal Information   Foreign Languages - French
General Information
Henry James Johnson served in Perak expedition 1876. Was put in charge of the Maharhah Lela and other Malay prisoners during this campaign. In command of Fort Nameluke in the operations against Chief Sekukuni 1878. District Adjutant at Luneburg and on Swazi border, taking part in the Zulu War, present in the final battle at Ulundi.

Alfred Henry LINDOP (2nd Lieutenant)
Date of Birth   April 25th 1847   Place of Birth   Birr, Ireland
Age upon Entering the Service (Commission) 30 years 9 months
Military Schoo█████████   Non-Commissioned Officers Certificate

Service and Dates of Commission
Sub-Lieutenant 80th Regiment of Foot February 2nd 1878
Lieutenant   80th Regiment of Foot March 28th 1879
Exchanged to   102nd Regiment of Foot September 29th 1880
Captain (Pay Master) 12th Regiment of Foot October 21st 1885
Army Pay Department September 1st 1886
Major (Pay Master) Army Pay Department September 1st 1896
Retired 1904

Periods of Employment
(Commission)
Home   February 2nd 1878 - August 1st 1878
South Africa   August 2nd 1878 - May 11th 1880
Home   May 12th 1880 -
Staff Service Record
Ordnance Officer to No.5 Column (Under Col. Rowlands) February 1st 1878-April 1st 1878

Orders and Decorations (Commission)   South Africa Medal with clasp '1878-9'
Personal Information
Alfred Henry Lindop married Lucy Allen September 22nd 1868 Belfast by the Roman Catholic Priest, the
Reverend I.Canaran. Alfred and Lucy had three children, Lucy Margaret born September 10th 1871, baptized
in Gibraltar, Alfred Henry born June 8th 1873, baptized Malta and Alice Maud born on June 20th 1875 and also
baptized in Malta.

General Information
Alfred Henry Lindop served in the Ranks for a total of twelve years and two hundred and sixty-five days,
attaining rank of Sergeant Major prior to receiving his commission. Served with 28th Regiment of Foot (North
Gloucestershire). 80th Regiment in the Tranvaal during the last two months of 1878 with Colonel Rowlands, in
campaign against Chief Sakukuni.Also in Zulu War, present in the final battle at Ulundi.

Frederick William LYONS (2nd Lieutenant)
Date of Birth   December 26th 1855   Place of Birth   Dublin, Ireland
Age upon Entering the Service 22 years
Military School or College   Hythe, 1st Class Certificate
                                         Chatham, Military Engineering 4152/243/26
                                         Military Topography July 7th 1883
Passed for Promotion
Passed in A & B para 39.Sec H.Q.R., D.O.York No.9, Sept. 9th 1883

Service and Dates of Commission
Cornet or Ensign 80th Regiment of Foot February 16th 1878
Lieutenant 80th Regiment of Foot May 17th 1879
Captain   2nd Battalion South Staffordshire Regiment January 26th 1884
Seconded for Service as Adjutant of Auxiliary Forces (42nd Regiment District) July 1st 1887
Retired May 7th 1890 with Gratuity of £1,200

Periods of Employment
Home   February 16th 1878 - April 10th 1878
South Africa   April 11th 1878 - May 11th 1880
Home   May 12th 1880 - December 1st 1885

Egypt	December 2nd 1885 - October 15th 1886
Gibraltar	October 16th 1886 - April 27th 1887
Home	April 28th 1887 -

Staff Service Record
District Adjutant & Remount Officer, Lydenburg, Transvaal February 6th 1879 - June 30th 1879
Regimental Staff Service Record
Adjutant, 2nd Battalion South Staffordshire Regiment June 28th 1884 - June 9th 1885

Orders and Decorations   South Africa Medal with clasp '1878-9'
       Egyptian Medal

Personal Information   Foreign Languages - French
Frederick Lyons married Alice Gertrude Matterson on January 5th 1882 at the Church of England Church of St.Peter's, Brighton by Archdeacon Hamah.
General Information
Frederick William Lyons took part in the operations against Sekukuni during 1878/1879, present at the storming of the Chiefs' stronghold November 28th 1879. Adjutant and Remount Officer at Lydenburg. In the Zulu War, present at final battle at Ulundi. As Captain, served in Egypt, with the Soudan Frontier Field Force during operations on the Upper Nile in 1885/86

William MOORE (Lieutenant)

Date of Birth   July 10th 1855   Place of Birth   Florence, Italy
Age upon Entering the Service 18 years 7 months
Military School or College   Chatham - School of Military Engineering, 1880
       Distinguished Tactics & Fortifications,
       Authority D.G.M.E. W.O. March 13th 1882
       Special Certificate, Distinction Military Law
       107/Gen. No. 522 W.O. February 13th 1886
Passed for Promotion
For Lieutenant Colonel - Cairo General Orders 1895

Service and Dates of Commission
Sub Lieutenant 75th Regiment of Foot February 28th 1874 (Per War Office)
Transfer to 80th Regiment of Foot April 15th 1874 (By Authority)
Lieutenant 80th Regiment of Foot Feb 28th 1874 (Anti dated, Commission bears date April 15th 1874)
Captain 2nd Battalion South Staffordshire Regiment October 4th 1881
Brevet Major 2nd Battalion South Staffordshire Regiment November 18th 1888
Lieutenant Colonel 2nd Battalion South Staffordshire Regiment October 16th 1895
Retired October 16th 1899

Periods of Employment
Home	February 28th 1874 - December 29th 1875
Strait Settlements	December 30th 1875 - March 10th 1877
South Africa	March 11th 1877 - March 7th 1880
Home	March 8th 1880 - October 2nd 1881
Malta	October 3rd 1881 - July 7th 1882
Egypt	July 8th 1882 - March 22nd 1883
Malta	March 23rd 1883 - February 21st 1884
Egypt	February 22nd 1884 - June 28th 1886
Gibraltar	June 29th 1886 - December 13th 1888
Home	December 14th 1888 - February 17th 1893
Egypt	February 18th 1893 - October 10th 1895
India	October 11th 1895 -

Staff Service Record
Acting Commissariat Officer August 14th 1878
Acting Ordnance Stores Officer to Dist. Pay Master at Standerton, Transvaal January 14th 1879
District Adjutant January 14th 1879 - July 9th 1879
Acting Ordnance Officer Pinetown, Natal August 25th 1879 - September 30th 1879

Orders and Decorations   South Africa Medal with clasp '1878-9'
                                          Egypt Medal with clasps 'The Nile 1884-85' and 'Kirbekan'
                                          Egypt, Khedive Star
Personal Information   Height 5 ft 9 ins Foreign Languages - French
William Moore married Isabel Susan Coyney November 29th 1893 by Rev Percy Mainwaring C. of E. at
Lichfield, County of Staffordshire. One child Isabel Mary born December 17th 1894 baptized at Lichfield.
General Information
William Moore took part in the operations against Chief Sekukuni 1878 and in the Zulu War 1879. Egyptian
War 1882 with the 1st Battalion South Staffordshire Regiment, (38th Regiment of Foot), present with the
reconnaissance force from Alexandria August 5th. Nile expedition 1884/5 and operations of the River Column
under Major General Earle, including action at Kirbekan. Commanding Officer of the 2nd Battalion (80th
Regiment of Foot), The South Staffordshire Regiment 1895-1899.

David Barry MORIARTY (Captain)
Date of Birth   March 6th 1837   Place of Birth Kilmallock, County Limerick, Ireland
Age upon Entering the Service 20 years 9 months

Service and Dates of Commission
Cornet or Ensign 6th West Yorkshire Militia (Accepted Lieutenancy 1853)
Ensign   6th Regiment of Foot December 19th 1857
Unattached Company April 1859
Lieutenant 6th Regiment of Foot July 30th 1859 (Half Pay - April 1st 1870)
Captain 80th Regiment of Foot January 6th 1876

Killed in Action Intombi River - March 12th 1879

Periods of Employment
England   December 19th 1857 - May 16th 1858
Gibraltar   May 17th 1858 - June   1862
South Africa   June   1862 - July   1863
Home   July   1863 - December 1867
India   December 1867 - February 1871
Home   February 1871 - March 6th 1876
Singapore   March 7th 1876 - January 28th 1877
South Africa   January 29th 1877 - March 12th 1879

Orders and Decorations   South Africa Medal with clasp '1878-9'
Personal Information   Foreign Languages - French, Italian and Spanish

General Information

David Barry Moriarty was the sixth son of James Moriarty and his wife Mary Catherine Bridget (nee. Barry),
born at 'The Grange', Kilmallock Ireland. Served in various Mediterranean Stations including Gibraltar, Corfu
and Zante. When waiting to go to Jamaica, accepted an exchange and served for twelve months in the Channel
Islands. December 1867 ordered to embark to Queenstown. During 1868 took part in the Hazala Campaign. As
Captain 80th Regiment of Foot 1878 in South Africa took part in the campaign against Chief Sekukuni. During
the Zulu War, in command of an escort, protecting a waggon convoy, David Barry Moriarty was killed in action
March 12th 1879 at Myer's Drift on the Intombi River. Forty-two years of age when he died, his body is buried
at Luneburg, several miles from battle field.

Captain David Barry Moriarty killed
in action 12th march 1879.
Intombi River - South Africa.

The replacement marker on Captain
Moriarty's Grave.
Luneburg Cemetery.

Lipton Cummings POTTS (Lieutenant)
Date of Birth   December 10th 1848   Place of Birth   Sunderland, England
Age upon Entering the Service 20 years 3 months
Military School or College   Served as Cadet at the Royal Military College
Passed for Promotion
Passed for Major - Military Education Office February 28th 1884

Service and Dates of Commission
Cornet or Ensign
With Graduity from 104th Regiment of Foot March 17th 1869
Cornet or Ensign 80th Regiment of Foot March 17th 1869
Lieutenant   80th Regiment of Foot October 28th 1871
Captain   80th Regiment of Foot July 9th 1879
Brevet Major 80th Regiment of Foot October 2nd 1883
Exchange to Royal Munster Fusiliers October 4th 1884
Hon. Lt. Colonel   October 10th 1885
Retired 1885

Periods of Employment
Home   March 17th 1869 - January 11th 1872
Strait Settlements   January 12th 1872 - November 27th 1872
China   November 28th 1872 - February 14th 1876
Strait Settlements   February 15th 1876 - January 23rd 1877
Home   January 24th 1877 - October 29th 1877
South Africa   October 30th 1877 - May 11th 1880
Home   May 12th 1880 -

Staff Service Record
District Adjutant, Transvaal   } September 11th 1878
Superintendent of Volunteers, Natal   } January 13th 1879
Regimental Staff Service Record
Acting Adjutant, Pietermaritzburg January 25th 1878 - April 30th 1878

Orders and Decorations   South Africa Medal with clasp '1878-9'
Personal Information   Height 5 ft 10 ins   Foreign Languages - French
General Information
Lipton Cummings Potts served with the 80th Regiment of Foot in South Africa and in the Zulu War 1879, and
was present in the final battle at Ulundi.

John Edward Hale PRIOR (Captain)
Date of Birth   December 29th 1848   Place of Birth   Deesa, East Indies
Age upon Entering the Service 19 years 2 months
Military School or College   Cadet at the Royal Military College - 1867
Passed for Promotion
Passed to Rank of Major 107/Gen No. 354

Service and Dates of Commission
Cornet or Ensign 80th Regiment of Foot March 21st 1868[P]
Lieutenant   80th Regiment of Foot August 30th 1871
Captain   80th Regiment of Foot November 18th 1877
Brevet Major 80th Regiment of Foot November 29th 1879
Major   South Staffordshire Regiment July 19th 1882
Lieutenant Colonel South Staffordshire Regiment February 11th 1891
Brevet Colonel   February 11th 1895
Half Pay   October 16th 1895

Colonel   Regimental District October 20th 1895
Major General (local Rank) A.D.C. Infantry 15th Brigade South Africa   December 18th 1899

Periods of Employment
Home	March 21st 1868 - January 11th 1872
Strait Settlements	January 12th 1872 - December 27th 1872
China	December 28th 1872 - November 10th 1875
Strait Settlements	November 11th 1875 - March 8th 1876
Home	March 9th 1876 - August 1st 1878
South Africa	August 2nd 1878 - May 11th 1880
Home	May 12th 1880 - February 17th 1893
Egypt	February 18th 1893 -

Staff Service Record
Frontier Light Horse, Zululand December 9th 1878
Acted as Staff Officer to Colonel Buller April 8th 1879
Orderly & Staff Officer to Colonel Harrison R.E. July 17th 1879
Flying Column and Afterwards toTransvaal District December 1879

Orders and Decorations   Indian General Service Medal with clasp 'Perak'
                                               South Africa Medal with clasp '1878-9'

Personal Information   Height 5 ft 9¹/₂ins   Foreign Languages - French
John Edward Hale Prior married Annie Gadd Mathews at Hanbury Church, Gloucestershire February 1st 1883
by Reverend John Way, C of E. John and Annie had two children, Geraldine Esme Belinda born November 7th
1883, christened at Redland Church, George Edward Redvers born December 3rd 1885, christened at Abbotts
Leigh Church. Annie died October 1st 1929 and is buried in same grave as her husband, who died January 9th
1900, in the church yard of St.Chad's Lichfield, County of Staffordshire.

General Information
80th Regiment of Foot, Perak expedition 1875/76. At commencement of Zulu War proceeded on special duties
to South Africa. Saw action with the Frontier Light Horse in engagement on Hlobane Mountain. Orderly Officer
to Colonel Buller at the affair at the Upoko River. Present at the Battle of Ulundi, including reconnaissance
duties the day before this final battle, being mentioned twice in Dispatches. At the recommencement of the
campaign against Chief Sekukuni, he served as Staff and Orderly Officer to Colonel Harrison. Mentioned on
two occasions in the London Gazette, March 28th 1879 and August 21st 1879 (Mentioned in Dispatches of
Brigadier Wood VC CB and Colonel Buller VC CB).
Commanding Officer of the 2nd Battalion South Staffordshire Regiment 1891-1895.

Herbert Aveling RAITT (2nd Lieutenant)
Date of Birth   August 23rd 1858   Place of Birth   London, England
Age upon Entering the Service 19 years 7 months   Military School or College : Hythe, 1st Class Certificate
Service and Dates of Commission
Sub Lieutenant (From Militia) 80th Regiment of Foot March 27th 1878
Lieutenant 80th Regiment of Foot July 9th 1879
Captain 2nd Battalion South Staffordshire Regiment January 26th 1884
Major   2nd Battalion South Staffordshire Regiment February 12th 1896
Lieutenant Colonel 1st Battalion South Staffordshire Regiment January 1st 1901
Brevet Colonel   February 10th 1904
(Half Pay)   January 1st 1905
Brevet Colonel   February 10th 1907
Colonel (Half Pay)   February 23rd 1907
Brigadier General (Temp) No. 7 District   September 4th 1907
General Officer Commanding (South Midland Division) September 6th 1907- April 1st 1908
Major General   September 12th 1912
Commander Burma Division A.D.C. 1916

Periods of Employment
Home   March 27th 1878 - May 22nd 1878
South Africa   May 23rd 1878 - May 11th 1880
Regimental Staff Service Record
Adjutant October 5th 1880 - February 1st 1881
Adjutant February 2nd 1880 - June 4th 1884

Orders and Decorations   Companion of the Order of the Bath
                                    South Africa Medal with clasp '1878-9'
                                    Queen's South Africa Medal with clasps, 'Orange Free State',
                                         'Transvaal' and 'Wittebergen'
                                    King's South Africa Medal with clasps, 'South Africa 1901' and
                                         'South Africa 1902'
Personal Information   Foreign Languages - French
General Information
Herbert Aveling Raitt Served in the Kaffir War 1878 including both campaigns 1878 and 1879 against Chief
Sekukuni. Present at assault which captured the Chief's stronghold 1879. Bechuanaland Expedition under
command of Sir Charles Warren 1884-85, in command of Troop of the 3rd Mounted Rifles, Diamond Field
Force. Egyptian Army from March 5th 1894 to March 4th 1896. December 1900. In command of the 1st
Battalion South Staffordshire Regiment. Orange Free State April to May 1900, Orange River Colony, May to
November 29th 1900, including actions at Wittebergen (July 1st-29th). Transvaal July 1901. Orange River
Colony November 30th 1900 to May 31st 1902. Mentioned in Dispatches, London Gazette September 10th
1901. For his Services in South Africa during the Boer War awarded the Companion of the Order of the Bath.
On Friday November 8th 1935, Herbert Raitt died in his sleep at his home at 2 Grimstone Gardens, Folkestone.
Principle mourners Lady Raitt, Miss Margaret Raitt (daughter), Mr & Mrs N.H.V.Gigill (son in law & daughter),
Colonel F.J.Raitt (brother) and Col. & Mrs A.G.Haig (brother in law and sister in law).

Charles Edward Whitaker ROWORTH (Captain)
Date of Birth   May 24th 1835   Place of Birth   London, England
Age upon Entering the Service 22 years 7 months
Military School or College   Hythe, 1st Class Certificate (Extra)
                                              Royal Arsenal Woolwich
Service and Dates of Commission
Cornet or Ensign 6th Regiment of Foot December 17th 1857
Lieutenant   6th Regiment of Foot March 18th 1859[P]
Captain (Half Pay)   105th Regiment of Foot April 1st 1870 (Captains Commission anti dated April 1st 1870
but performed duties of Musketry Instructor till August 26th 1870)
Captain   80th Regiment of Foot December 17th 1875
Brevet Major   July 1st 1881
Honorary Lieutenant Colonel   January 1st 1886
Retired January 1st 1886

Periods of Employment
Home   December 17th 1857 - May 16th 1858
Gibraltar   May 17th 1858 - November 16th 1861
Home   November 17th 1861 - January 17th 1864
At sea   January 18th 1864 - May 20th 1864
Jamaica   May 21st 1864 - May 8th 1867
Home   May 9th 1867 - August 26th 1870
Strait Settlements   April 29th 1876 - March 10th 1877
South Africa   March 11th 1877 - May 11th 1880
Home   May 12th 1880 -
Staff Service Record
Acting Staff Officer for Prisoners & Recruiting List, in Sligo, Ireland July 1st 1875 - February 10th 1876
Acting Ordnance at Lydenburg, Transvaal January 25th 1879 - January 1st 1880

Regimental Staff Service Record
Gazetted Instructor of Musketry
6th Regiment of Foot May 11th 1866 - August 26th 1870

Orders and Decorations   South Africa Medal with clasp '1878-9'

Personal Information   Foreign Languages - French & Spanish
Charles Edward Whitaker Roworth married Eleanor Speed Andrews in Gibraltar May 1st 1861 by Reverend
Thomas Hieman, Civil Chaplain, C of E. Charles and Eleanor had six children, Hereward August, born
Colchester May 25th 1863, christened Brockham, Surrey, Frederick Henry, born August 9th 1865, christened
Newcastle, Jamaica, Edward Percy, born July 14th 1867, christened Greenlaw, Scotland, Lilian Ethel, born
September 23rd 1870, christened Penally, South Wales, Lionel, born June 27th 1872 christened at Brighton and
finally Ida Muriel, born March 16th 1874 and christened in Brockham, Surrey.
General Information
Took part in the putting down of the rebellion in Jamaica during 1865. Operations against Chief Sekukuni 1878
and 1879 and capture of the Chief's stronghold. In Hong Kong, Mentioned in Dispatches, letter No.268 dated
Hong Kong August 26th 1876 for services in Perato.

James Ormsby SHERRARD (Lieutenant)
Date of Birth June 14th 1845   Place of Birth Kilcullen, Ireland   Age entering the Service 23 yrs 4 months
Military School or College   Hythe, 1st Class Certificate, School of Musketry
                                           Chatham, School of Military Engineering
Passed for Promotion
Passed for Major, Authority of Military Education Officer February 28th 1884

Service and Dates of Commission
Ensign 80th Regiment of Foot October 15th 1868[P]
Lieutenant 80th Regiment of Foot October 28th 1871
Captain 80th Regiment of Foot March 28th 1879
Major South Staffordshire Regiment January 26th 1884
Died whilst serving with the Colours on September 9th 1884 in Assouau Hospital, Upper Egypt, having served
fifteen years and three hundred and twenty-nine days.
Periods of Employment
Home   October 15th 1868 - January 11th 1872
Strait Settlements   January 12th 1872 - January 23rd 1873
China   January 24th 1873 - February 14th 1876
Strait Settlements   February 15th 1876 - March 10th 1877
South Africa   March 11th 1877 - December 8th 1879
Home   December 9th 1879 - August 28th 1882
Egypt   August 29th 1882 - December 3rd 1882
Home   December 4th 1882 - May 7th 1882
Egypt   May 8th 1882 - September 9th 1884

Staff Service Record
Fort Adjutant, Fort Weeber October 3rd 1878 - December 28th 1878
Acting Commissariat Officer December 29th 1878-February 10th 1879
Acting District Pay Master February 5th 1879 - April 9th 1879

Regimental Staff Service Record
Acting Adjutant Hong Kong February 23rd 1874 - August 23rd 1875
Acting Adjutant & Quartermaster   February 6th 1879 - November 15th 1879
Orders and Decorations   South Africa Medal with clasp '1878-9'
                                           Egypt Medal
                                           Egypt, Khedive Star

Personal Information   Height 5 ft 10 ins
James Ormsby Sherrard married Mary Hussey September 1st 1883 in Ballymacillyatt, County Kerry, Ireland, by Archdeacon Dermy, Church of Ireland. Whilst serving in Egypt 1884 he and his wife were taken ill, and both died in Assouau Hospital, Upper Egypt of Fever and Debility on September 9th 1884.
General Information
Operations against Chief Sekukuni 1878. Zulu War, being present in the battle at Ulundi. Mentioned in Dispatches, reference London Gazette March 15th 1879.

Charles TUCKER (Major)

Date of Birth   December 6th 1838   Place of Birth   Ashburton, England
Age upon Entering the Service 16 years 11 months
Service and Dates of Commission
Ensign or Cornet 22nd Regiment of Foot November 23rd 1855[P]
Lieutenant   22nd Regiment of Foot October 23rd 1857[P]
Captain   22nd Regiment of Foot May 18th 1860
Transferred (By Exchange) 80th Regiment of Foot November 6th 1860
Brevet Major 80th Regiment of Foot December 9th 1872
Major   80th Regiment of Foot November 9th 1877
Lieutenant Colonel 80th Regiment of Foot July 9th 1879
Colonel (Retired on Half Pay)   July 9th 1883
Brevet Colonel Middlesex District (Hounslow) February 1885
Colonel (Half Pay)   August 1891
Major General   September 13th 1893
Commander in Chief Scottish District 1903 - 1905
Colonel   The Cheshire Regiment October 1909 - 1911
Colonel   The South Staffordshire Regiment 1911 - 1935

Periods of Employment
Home   November 23rd 1855 - April 30th 1860
Malta   May 1st 1860 - January 31st 1861
East Indies   February 1st 1861 - June 19th 1866
Home   June 20th 1866 - January 11th 1872
Strait Settlements January 12th 1872 - December 27th 1872
China   December 28th 1872 - November 12th 1873
Home   November 13th 1873 - November 24th 1875
Strait Settlements November 25th 1875 - March 10th 1877
South Africa   March 11th 1877 - May 11th 1880
Home   May 12th 1880 - July 9th 1884

Staff Service Record
Acting Brigade Major, Singapore February 23rd 1876 - April 3rd 1876
Commanded Field Force at Utrecht, South Africa December 9th 1877 - August 25th 1878
Left Attack , Sekukuni Campaign September 25th 1878 - December 23rd 1878
Command of Troops at Lydenberg, South Africa January 1st 1879 - February 12th 1879
Command of Personal Escort to Sir Garnet Wolseley August 20th 1879 - September 15th 1879
Commanded Pretoria Force, South Africa of 2,000 of all areas November 29th 1879 - December 25th 1879

Orders and Decorations   Companion of the Order of the Bath
                                  Knight Commander of the Order of the Bath
                                  Knight Grand Cross of the Royal Victorian Order
                                  Knight Grand Cross of the Bath
                                  Indian General Service Medal with clasps, 'Bhootan' and 'Perak'
                                  South Africa Medal with clasp '1878-9'
                                  Queen's South Africa Medal with clasps, 'Cape Colony' 'Paardeberg'
                                  and 'Johannesburg'

Sir Charles Tucker G.C.B., G.C.V.O.

Sir Charles Tucker Grave.
St. Andrew's churchyard,
Ashburton.

(Photograph Mr. K. Brealey)

King's South Africa Medal with clasps, 'South Africa 1901' and
'South Africa 1902'
Queen Victoria's Diamond Jubilee
King Edward VII Coronation
King George V Silver Jubilee

Personal Information   Height 5 ft 10 ins

The younger son of Mr Robert Tucker born at 'The Hall', Ashburton, Devon. Married Matilda Frederika Hayter, daughter of Mr John Hayter, Painter-in-Ordinary to Queen Victoria October 5th 1865 in Darjeerling, East Indies by the Rev J.Richards, C of E. Charles and Matilda had three children, Edith Augusta Beresford, born October 21st 1866, christened at Ashburton, Leopold Hancock Baillie, born August 6th 1868, christened at Fleetwood and Duncan Hayter Ffoude born January 30th 1870, christened at Birr, Ireland. Matilda Frederika died on July 11th 1897 in Secunderabad, India. In 1902 Charles married again, to Ellen Mary O'Connell, second daughter of Sir Maurice O'Connell, 2nd Baronet.

General Information

Charles Tucker boy and man was highly thought of, forthright with his thoughts and language but well liked and respected. Of the officers researched for this book, he was the most honoured. His army career started in 1855; throughout it he was to see active service throughout the world. Bhootan Campaign 1864-65. Perak Expedition 1876. South Africa in many actions in differing campaigns, the campaigns against Chief Sekukuni in 1878 and 1879 and between these, a prominent part in the Zulu War 1879, being Officer in Command of a number of Companies of the 80th Regiment of Foot. Mentioned in dispatches a number of times (London Gazette April 21st and August 21st 1879). Took part in the final battle at Ulundi July 4th 1879. September 1891 sent out to Natal to take command of the troops. Left South Africa during 1895 to command the First Class District of Secunderabad of the Madras Army in India. Command of the 7th Division in the Boer War; awarded the Queen's South Africa Medal with three clasps. November 27th 1879 awarded the Honour of the Companion of the Order of the Bath. In 1900 the Knight Commander of the Order of the Bath. Knight Grand Cross of the Bath September 18th 1905. Knight Grand Cross of the Royal Victorian Order June 14th 1912.
October 9th 1909 to September 10th 1911, Colonel of the Cheshire Regiment. September 11th 1911 until his death Colonel of the South Staffordshire Regiment.Up until 1933 he made official business trips to the War Office, and after that would still attend functions associated with his favourite regiment, the 'South Staffordshire Regiment' when his health permitted.
Died ninety-seven years of age, at his home in Biarritz, Sunday December 22nd 1935. His body was brought home and lies buried in the local churchyard of St.Andrew's Ashburton and was laid to rest with full military honours, the funeral officiated by the Reverend E.F.Ball and Archdeacon Thompson, Sub-Dean of Exeter; the King was represented by Colonel G.S.Perkin DSO, ADC.
Major General Charles Tucker's awards and medals can be seen at the Staffordshire Regimental Museum.

Beverley William Reid USSHER (2nd Lieutenant)

Date of Birth   April 4th 1854   Place of Birth   Dublin, Ireland
Age upon Entering the Service (Commission) 21 years   Passed for Promotion
G.O.C.C. Simla, April 21st 1884

Service and Dates of Commission
Lieutenant 1st Royal Lancashire Regiment November 25th 1871
(Resigned Commission - October 25th 1875)
2nd Lieutenant 80th Regiment of Foot June 12th 1878
Lieutenant 80th Regiment of Foot January 12th 1881
Captain 20th Hussars December 23rd 1885
Transferred 7th (The Princes Royals) Dragoon Guards March 16th 1887
(Half Pay) April 25th 1894   Retired April 25th 1899

Periods of Employment (Commission)
Home   June 12th 1878 - September 19th 1878
South Africa   September 20th 1878 - December 7th 1879
Home   December 8th 1879 - August 20th 1880

East Indies	August 21st 1880 - March 22nd 1884
Egypt	March 23rd 1884 - December 23rd 1885

Staff Service Record
Transport Officer in Brigadier Wood's Flying Column during the invasion of Zululand

Orders and Decorations
South Africa Medal with clasp '1878-9'
Egypt Medal with clasps, 'The Nile 1884-85' and 'Kirbekan'
Egypt, Khedive Star

Personal Information
Foreign Languages - French and Hindustani

General Information

Beverley William Reid Ussher served in the Ranks for a total of two years and two hundred and twenty-eight days, with the 18th Hussars. With 80th Regiment in South Africa, took part in operations against Sekukuni November and December 1878 and Zulu War following year, present at the final battle Ulundi. Later in Egypt taking part in the Soudan Expedition and seeing action at Kirbekan.

WILLIAM INGRAM COBBIN MRCS (CIVIL SURGEON)

William Ingram Cobbin was the son of John and Mary Ingram. His father married twice, Eliza Smith on December 24th 1832 at Colchester - they had one child Frederick Finden born September 29th 1839 at Camberwell and Mary Day Leeson August 3rd 1843 at the parish church of St.George's, Hanover Square, London. John and Mary Ingram had five children, John Leeson Day born Brixton July 9th 1844, Elizabeth Amelia born 1845, died 1847, Ingram born 1847, died 1849, Marian Elizabeth born 1848 Brixton and lastly William Ingram who was born on June 26th 1851 at 6 Priests Buildings, Lakenham, Norwich.

When William was twenty-five years of age he attended the Royal College of Surgeons of England, Court of Examiners July 31st 1876, unfortunately he was not successful and had to be referred. William eventually passed his examinations to become a Surgeon and was included in the Listings for the Court of Examiners dated January 26th 1877. Although qualified in Surgery it was not until later he became qualified in Medicine - first registered under the Medical Act of 1858 on August 4th 1877.

According to the records of the Royal College of Surgeons, William Ingram Cobbin appeared on their list for the first time on July 11th 1878. He was also included in the Medical Directory for 1878 and was registered as living at 68 Torrington Square, Bloomsbury, London. It is also recorded that William was employed by the Peninsula and Orient Shipping Company, later working in South Africa.

In 1879 during the Zulu War William serving with Her Majesty's Forces he accompanied Captain David Barry Moriarty in command of a Company of the 80th Regiment of Foot, who were ordered out from Luneberg to escort a convoy of eighteen waggons carrying ammunition, stores and provisions. On Wednesday March 12th the waggon convoy was attacked at Myer's Drift on the Intombi River. At the age of twenty-seven years, William was killed in action and his body was laid to rest in the cemetery at Luneburg. Awarded the South African Medal with the Bar '1878-9'.

William Ingram Cobbin MRCS: Last Will and Testament

This is the Last Will and Testament of me William Ingram Cobbin of Torrington Square in the County of Middlesex - Surgeon. I give demise and bequeath unto my Trustees herein - after named their executors administrators and assigns all my shares in the leasehold property situated at No.1 South Molton Lane, No.11 Brook Street Oxford Street and also No.125 Kentish Town Road both in the County of Middlesex for all my estate and interests therein nevertheless to be held by them upon trust to receive the rent issues and profits of the said property and after payment of the outgoings incidental thereto upon trust to pay the nett annual produce unto my sister Marian Elizabeth the wife of John Alexander Miller for her sole and seperate use and free from the debts interference and control of her present or any future husband for and during her natural life and her receipt alone shall be a sufficient discharge to the intent that she shall have any power to deprive herself thereof by way of anticipation And from and after her deceased Upon trust for such person or persons and for such intents and purposes as my said sister shall notwithstanding coverture by Will appoint and in case she shall not make any will or other testamentary disposition then my said trustees are to stand possessed thereon for such person or persons as shall be her next of kin at the time of her death according to the Statutes for the distribution of the estates of intestates And I empower my said trustees to grant and give or join in granting and giving a Lease or Leases of either or both the said properties for any term or terms not exceeding twenty-one years at the best annual rent that can be obtained for the same but so that no premium shall be received in respect of such lease or leases I give and bequeath my medical books to my cousin John Rudd Leeson I also give and bequeath all other my personal effects and trinkets to my said sister absolutely And as to all the rest and residues of my estate and effects real and personal and whether in possession reversion remainder or expectancy Unto my executors hereinafter named And I hereby direct them to sell the same immediately after my deceased and after payment thereout of my just debts funeral and testamentary expenses to divide the same into twenty-two equal portions and as to eight of such portions I give and bequeath the same unto my said sister her executors administrators and assign absolutely in addition to any other bequests in her favour and as to eight other of such portions I give and bequeath the same unto my brother John Leeson Day Cobbin his executors administrators and assigns and as to one other of such portions I give and bequeath the same unto such Treasurers for the time being of the University College Hospital for the uses of the said hospital And as to the remaining five of such portions I give and bequeath one each to my friends John Sidney Lansdon, Margaret Ann Leslie the wife of George Leslie of Quebec Lodge, Blackheath in the County of Kent. Gerald Coleman, Henry Charles Lang and John Hawthorne Lydall And I appoint my cousin George Michael Silley and my friend John Hawthorne Lydall Executors and Trustees of this my will and I declare that the said John Hawthorne Lydall shall be entitled to act as Solicitor in the Trust premises and to charge and be paid for all business whether strictly professional or not transacted by him in relation to the said trust premises as if he had not been a Trustee or Executor of these presents And I hereby revoke all former Wills and Testamentary dispositions at any time heretofore made by me and declare this to be my last Will and Testament

In witness whereof I the said William Ingram Cobbin Have hereunto set my hand this tenth day of August One thousand eight hundred and seventy-seven -   *W I Cobbin -*
Signed by the said Testator as and for his last Will and Testament in the presence of us both present at the same time who at his request in his presence and in the presence of each other have hereunto subscribed our names as witness -   *G Reedston Garthorne 53 Oaeney Crescent N.W.*
           H F Lance Clerk to J H Lydall Solicitor 12 Southampton Building Chancery Lane.
Proved at London 15th July 1879 by the Oath of John Hawthorne Lydall one of the executors to whom Admon was granted George Michael Silley the other executor having renounced.

THE MEN BEHIND THE MEDALS 2: NON-COMMISSIONED OFFICERS AND MEN

The vast majority of the information regarding the rank and file has been taken directly from the 80th Regiment's Nominal Roll Book in the Regimental Museum at Whittington Barracks near Lichfield. The spellings have been taken from the Medal List for the 80th Regiment of Foot for the South Africa Medal (General Order No.103). Some are different between the Medal List and the Regiment's Nominal Roll book - both spellings have been included with the Medal List version taking precedence. The information relating to the individual non-commissioned officers and men has been presented in rank/alphabetical order.

The places of birth have mostly been identified, but due to the inventory spelling of the parishes and towns and the checking of maps proving difficult, it has sometimes been impossible to locate the parish/town of birth. For the sake of consistency where places are not located, the actual spelling of the Nominal Roll has been included. In the course of research and the checking of the Regimental Records, however, it has been noted that the compiler of the Nominal Rolls has often not entered the name of the parish but instead entered a double entry of the parish and town as the same and for consistency the presentation is the same as the Nominal Roll Book. It is also noted that in some cases the place of birth has been entered as a village or town in the 'parish', with the name of the nearest largest town also.

From the information, one can establish their places of birth, their status and trade, etc. The places of birth vary from being born on ship to being born in far away places like Australia, Canada and India. One can also see the counties the men were born in and identify the best recruitment centres and the diverse occupations prior to enlistment in the British Army.

Saving a Comrade.

Private S. Wassall, V.C. of the 80th Regiment. Zululand 1879.

A selotaped and well-worn 'souvenir' from a contemporary periodical owned by the
Wassall family and celebrating their ancestors heroic deed.

THE MEN BEHIND THE MEDALS 2: NON-COMMISSIONED OFFICERS AND MEN

4202 Sergeant- Major   ALLEN John
Born: On board ship
           on passage from India
Enlisted at Chatham on 30/01/56
Aged 14 years 10 months, Ht. 4 ft 6 1/2 ins
Complexion fair, Eyes grey
Hair light brown, Trade None
Joined Regiment 07/02/56 at Aldershot
Discharged 2nd Period 08/07/81

2109 Band-Master FRAYLING William Walter
Born: Parish Market Lavington
Town   Devizes, Wilts.
Enlisted not known,on 15/01/59
Aged 14 years 10months Ht. 4 ft 11 ins
Complexion fair, Eyes grey
Hair light,Trade None
Joined Regiment not known
Invalided 18/03/84
Discharged 04/04/87

School-Master BIRD H. O.
Born: Parish
Town & County
Enlisted at   on
Aged   years   months, Ht. ft   ins
Complexion   Eyes
Hair   Religion
Trade
Joined Regiment

919 Col.Sgt. BOOTH(VC) Anthony Clarke
Born: Parish Basford
Town   Nottingham, Notts.
Enlisted at Sheffield on 28/10/64
Aged 18 years 6 months, Ht. 5 ft 6 ins
Complexion fresh, Eyes grey
Hair brown, Religion C.E
Trade Tailor
Joined Regiment 10/11/64 at Buttevant
Received Victoria Cross and £10pa for
life for conduct 12/03/79 at Intombi River

1048 Col. Sgt. DAY Hugh H.
Born: Parish Huntstile
Town   Bridgewater, Somerset
Enlisted at Taunton on 08/01/67
Aged 18 years, Ht. 5 ft 5 ins
Complexion fair, Eyes blue
Hair light brown,Religion C.E.
Trade Labourer
Joined Regiment 11/01/67 at Devonport.
Discharged 31/01/88

895 Col.Sgt. ELSE William Frederick
Born: Nuzeuaban
           Bengal (India)
Enlisted at Buttevant on 15/08/63
Aged 15 years 4 months, Ht. 4 ft 11 ins
Complexion sallow, Eyes hazel
Hair light brown, Religion C.E.
Trade None
Joined Regiment 23/06/66 at Fort Tregantle Devonport
Discharged pension 25/01/90

918 Col.Sgt. MACHIN Frederick
Born: Parish Gloucester
Town   Gloucester, Glos.
Enlisted at Sheffield on 27/09/64
Aged 22 years 9 months, Ht. 5 ft 6 5/8 ins
Complexion fresh, Eyes grey
Hair brown, Religion C.E. Trade Collier
Joined Regiment 23/06/66 at Fort Tregantle Devonport
To South Staffs Regt. Sept '83

201 Col. Sgt. NORTON William
Born: Parish Wigan
Town   Wigan, Lancs.
Enlisted at Liverpool on 31/07/58
Aged 19 years 9 months, Ht. 5 ft 5 3/4 ins
Complexion fresh, Eyes grey
Hair brown, Trade Labourer
Joined Regiment 12/04/59 at Cawnpore
Discharged 14/11/79

1249 Col. Sgt. O'NEIL Thomas
Born: Parish Arklon
Town   Arklon, Wicklow
Enlisted at Liverpool on 24/05/69
Aged 21 years 9 months, Ht. 5 ft 7 3/8 ins
Complexion fresh, Eyes blue
Hair brown, Trade Clerk
Joined Regiment 31/05/69 at Fleetwood
Died 20/02/83

2003 Orderly Room-Clerk THOMPSON John
Born: Parish St. James's
Town   Poole, Dorset
Enlisted at Westminster on 18/05/72
Aged 22 years 1 month, Ht. 5 ft 5 ins
Complexion fresh, Eyes blue
Hair light, Trade Clerk
Joined Regiment not known

692 Drum-Major O'DAY Owen
Born: Parish Dover
Town   Dover, Kent
Enlisted at Chester on 28/03/60
Aged 14 years 3 months Ht. 4 ft 9 1/2 ins
Complexion fresh, Eyes grey
Hair dark brown, Religion Protestant
Trade None
Joined Regiment 28/01/61
at Saugor (Central India)
Discharged 21/11/87

909 Quarter Master-Sergeant DAVIS John
Born: Montreal, Canada
Enlisted at Buttevant on 07/05/64
Aged 19 years 11 months Ht. 5 ft 7 ins
Complexion fresh, Eyes hazel
Hair light brown, Religion C.E.
Trade Gun Smith
Joined Regiment 23/06/64
at Fort Tregantle, Devonport

1362 Col.Sgt. FOULKS John
Born: Parish Morcott
Town   Uppingham, Rutland
Enlisted at Leicester on 22/08/70
Aged 20 years 5 months, Ht. 5 ft 5 ins
Complexion Swarthy, Eyes hazel
Hair dark brown, Religion C.E.
Trade Groom
Joined Regiment 31/08/70 at Belfast
To 19th Brigade Depot Lichfield 01/12/80

459 Col.Sgt. FREDERICKS Henry
Born: Hanover, Germany
Enlisted at Tower Hill on 27/05/59
Aged 22 years, Ht. 5 ft 5 3/4 ins
Complexion yellow, Eyes blue
Hair light brown, Trade Tailor
Joined Regiment 28/05/61
at Saugor (Central India)
Served in "A" Company
Killed in Action 12/03/79 Intombi River

1321 Col.Sgt. LYNCH Thomas
Born: Parish Dungarvan
Town   Dungarvan, Waterford
Enlisted at Bolton on 27/11/69
Aged 18 years 6 months, Ht. 5 ft 6 1/4 ins
Complexion ruddy, Eyes hazel
Hair dark brown, Religion R.C.
Trade Labourer
Joined Regiment not Known
To Depot 18/05/88

2098 Col.Sgt. RICHARDSON William
Born: Parish St. Margaret's
Town   Leicester, Liecs.
Enlisted at Leicester on 02/11/72
Aged 21 years 6 months, Ht. 5 ft 5 7/8 ins
Complexion fresh, Eyes hazel
Hair brown, Trade Carpenter
Joined Regiment not known Deserted Transvaal 14/01/80

3124 Col. Sgt. SHORE Edward
Born: St. Philip's, Sydney
New South Wales, Australia
Enlisted at not Known on 03/02/54
Aged 11 years 6 months, Ht. 4 ft 6 1/2 ins
Complexion, Eyes & Hair -not Known
Trade None
Joined Regiment 03/02/54 at Calcutta
Discharged 30/08/87
Appointed Canteen Steward

336 Col. Sgt. WATERS James
Born: Parish Manchester
Town   Manchester, Lancs.
Enlisted at Manchester on 03/04/59
Aged 19 years, Ht. 5 ft 5 3/4 ins
Complexion fresh, Eyes hazel
Hair dark brown, Trade Labourer
Joined Regiment 01/04/60
at Saugor (Central India)
Discharged 23/07/80

894 Sergeant ALLEN Charles
Born: Parish Chatham
Town Chatham, Kent
Enlisted at Buttevant on 29/06/63
Aged 14 years 11 months, Ht. 4 ft 6 ins
Complexion fresh, Eyes grey
Hair brown, Religion C.E.
Trade None
Joined Regiment 23/06/66
at Fort Tregantle, Devonport
Transferred to Hants Militia 14/08/80

1968 Sergeant ATTRIDE George
(Alias George Eve)
Born: Parish Dorking
Town Dorking, Surrey
Enlisted at Reading on 18/04/72
Aged 20 years 8 months, Ht. 5 ft 5 ins
Complexion fair, Eyes blue
Hair brown, Trade Labourer
Joined Regiment: not known
Deserted May 1884

1044 Sergeant CARTER Samuel
Born: Parish Kenwyn
Town Truro, Cornwall
Enlisted at Plymouth on 07/01/67
Aged 18 years, Ht. 5 ft 5 ins
Complexion fresh, Eyes grey
Hair light brown, Trade Labourer
Joined Regiment 09/01/67 at Devonport
To 4th Batt. South Staffs Regt. 17/04/84

2101 Sergeant DAVIS Charles G.
Born: Parish
Town
County
Enlisted not known
Aged years months, Ht. ft. ins
Complexion Eyes
Hair Religion
Trade
Joined Regiment
Transferred to Army Reserve 27/12/79

1383 Sergeant ERMION George
Born: Parish Harton
Town Chester, Cheshire
Enlisted at Storenburg on 27/08/70
Aged 18 years 2 months, Ht. 5 ft 6 3/4 ins
Complexion fair, Eyes grey
Hair light brown, Religion C.E.
Trade Labourer
Joined Regiment 03/09/70 at Belfast
Discharged by purchase 14/02/80

1271 Sergeant JOHNSON William
Born: Parish Bolton
Town Bolton, Lancs.
Enlisted at Bolton on 12/06/69
Aged 17 years, Ht. 5 ft 6 1/4 ins
Complexion fresh, Eyes blue
Hair brown, Trade Labourer
Joined Regiment 18/06/69 at Fleetwood
Killed in Action at Isandhlwana
22/01/79 whilst attached to the 1st Squadron Mounted Infantry

668 Sergeant KELLY Patrick
Born: Parish Innesmac
Town Derrygonelly, Fermanagh
Enlisted at Gosport on 16/02/76
Aged 29 years 2 months, Ht. 5 ft 5 1/4 ins
Complexion fair, Eyes blue
Hair fair, Trade Labourer
Joined Regiment 02/02/78 at South Africa
To 19th Brigade Depot 17/07/80
Rejoined Batt. 23/07/84
Transferred to 3rd Battalion South Staffs Regt. 19/03/86

1567 Sergeant KING John
Born: Parish St. Chad's
Town Shrewsbury, Shrops.
Enlisted at Shrewsbury on 26/12/70
Aged 19 years 4 months, Ht. 5 ft 5 1/2 ins
Complexion fair, Eyes grey
Hair brown, Religion R.C.
Trade Labourer
Joined Regiment 06/01/71 at Belfast
(Refer to new Army No. 445)

124 Sergeant McMULLEN John
Born: Parish Longford
Town Longford, Longford
Enlisted at not known on 22/10/57
Aged 18 years, Ht. 5 ft 4 3/4 ins
Complexion fresh, Eyes hazel
Hair sandy,
Trade Labourer
Joined Regiment 02/10/58 at Cawnpore
Discharged 27/07/80

1054 Sergeant BEAL Wallace
Born: Parish Walsall
Town Walsall, Staffs
Enlisted at Walsall on 04/06/77
Aged 20 years 6 months, Ht. 5 ft 4 1/2 ins
Complexion fair, Eyes grey
Hair brown, Trade Stoker
Joined Regiment 03/12/78 at Pretoria,
South Africa
To 19th Battalion 04/10/81

995 Sergeant CAMERON Harry
Born: Melbourne, Australia
Enlisted at Newcastle Under Lyme
on 30/08/66
Aged 20 years 4 months, Ht. 5 ft 6 1/2 ins
Complexion fresh, Eyes hazel
Hair light brown, Religion C.E
Trade Plumber
Joined Regiment 01/09/66
at Fort Tregantle, Devonport   Died 23/02/83

1279 Sergeant GRANT John
Born: Parish Macclesfield
Town Macclesfield, Cheshire
Enlisted at Manchester on 16/06/69
Aged 18 years 8 months, Ht. 5 ft 6 ins
Complexion fresh, Eyes blue
Hair light brown, Trade Dyer
Joined Regiment 21/06/69 at Fleetwood
To 19th Brigade Depot 01/12/80

1646 Sergeant HARCOURT Frederick
Born: Parish Cheltenham
Town Cheltenham, Glos.
Enlisted at Liverpool on 18/01/70
Aged 22 years 1 month, Ht. 5 ft 7 ins
Complexion sallow, Eyes hazel
Hair brown, Religion C.E.
Trade Clerk
Joined Regiment 21/01/71 at Belfast
Discharged 16/11/92
(Refer to new Army No. 400)

889 Sergeant HORTON Thomas
Born: Parish Liverpool
Town Liverpool, Lancs.
Enlisted at Jhansi (India) on 14/03/63
Aged 12 years 11 months, Ht. 4 ft 7 ins
Complexion ruddy, Eyes hazel
Hair light, Trade None
Joined Regiment 14/03/63 at Jhansi (India)
To 4th Batt. South Staffs Regt. 17/04/84

2065 Sergeant LAWRENCE Robert
Born: Parish Salisbury
Town Salisbury, Wilts.
Enlisted at Lambeth on 29/05/72
Aged 24 years 9 months, Ht. 5 ft 6 1/4 ins
Complexion fresh, Eyes grey
Hair dark brown,
Trade Clerk and Dispencer of Medicine
Joined Regiment not known
To Army Reserve 04/10/79 Died on Reserve 30/10/79

416 Sergeant MARKWELL Thomas
Born: Parish Tottenham
Town Tottenham, Middlesex
Enlisted at Westminster on 17/05/59
Aged 18 years, Ht. 5 ft 3 ins
Complexion fresh, Eyes grey
Hair brown, Religion Protestant
Trade Labourer
Joined Regiment 28/01/61
at Saugor (Central India)
Discharged 29/09/79

1761 Sergeant McDONALD Nicholas
Born: Parish Randalstown
Town Randalstown, Antrim
Enlisted at Belfast on 07/09/71
Aged 19 years, Ht. 5 ft 6 ins
Complexion freckled, Eyes blue
Hair brown, Religion R.C.
Trade Tailor
Joined Regiment 09/09/71 at Belfast
To South Staffs Regt.
Discharged invalid 14/05/88 (Ref.new Army No. 450)

1503 Sergeant STEVENSON Joseph
Born: Parish Portnorres
Town Newry, Down
Enlisted at Belfast on 03/12/70
Aged 17 years, Ht. 5 ft 5 ins
Complexion fresh, Eyes grey
Hair brown, Religion C.E.
Trade Hackler
Joined Regiment 03/12/70 at Belfast
(Refer to new Army No. 392)

784 Sergeant PENDERGAST Henry
Born: Parish Newcastle Under Lyme
Town Newcastle Under Lyme, Staffs.
Enlisted at Stafford on 30/08/76
Aged 19 years, Ht. 5 ft 9 1/2 ins
Complexion fresh, Eyes grey
Hair brown, Trade Collier
Joined Regiment 03/12/78
at Pretoria South Africa

1257 Sergeant PENKETH James
Born: Parish St John's
Town Salford, Lancs.
Enlisted at Fleetwood on 11/06/69
Aged 15 years, Ht. 4 ft 9 ins
Complexion fresh, Eyes grey
Hair red, Trade None
Joined Regiment 14/06/69 at Fleetwood
Rejoined after desertion 31/03/80
To 19th Brigade 01/12/80 (Refer to new Army No. 2803)

1217 Sergeant WARD Henry
Born: Parish Blackburn
Town Blackburn, Lancs.
Enlisted at Preston on 24/11/68
Aged 23 years, Ht. 5 ft 7 1/2 ins
Complexion fresh, Eyes hazel
Hair light, Trade Weaver
Joined Regiment 28/11/68 at Fleetwood
Invalided 26/05/85

1630 Sergeant WATTS James Henry
Born: Parish Liverpool
Town Liverpool, Lancs.
Enlisted at Liverpool on 14/01/70
Aged 18 years, Ht. 5 ft 6 7/8 ins
Complexion pale, Eyes grey
Hair light brown, Trade Joiner
Joined Regiment 20/01/81 at Belfast
Served in "H" Company
Killed in Action at Ulundi 04/07/79

288 Lce. Sergeant HANMER George
Born: Parish Chesaseday
Town Newport. Shrops.
Enlisted at Newcastle Under Lyme
on 21/04/74
Aged 19 years 10 months, Ht. 5 ft 5 1/4 ins
Complexion fresh, Eyes grey
Hair brown, Trade Labourer
Joined Regiment 04/11/74 at Hong Kong

1783 Lce. Sergeant JOYCE William
Born: Parish Ballinrobe
Town Ballinrobe, Mayo
Enlisted at Liverpool on 27/09/71
Aged 20 years, Ht. 5 ft 8 5/8 ins
Complexion fresh, Eyes grey
Hair light Brown, Religion R.C.
Trade Labourer
Joined Regiment 27/09/71 at Belfast
Discharged Free 22/11/83
(Refer to new Army No. 396)

374 Lce. Sergeant LOCKETT Joseph
Born: Parish Norton in the Moors
Town Burslem, Staffs.
Enlisted at Newcastle Under Lyme
on 10/05/59
Aged 18 years, Ht. 5 ft 3 1/4 ins
Complexion fresh, Eyes grey
Hair dark brown, Religion Protestant
Trade Potter
Joined Regiment 28/01/61 at Saugor (Central India)
Deserted 28/10/68 Discharged 12/06/83

1822 Corporal ALLEN Amos
Born: Parish Leerefrith
Town Leek, Staffs.
Enlisted at Manchester on 31/10/71
Aged 24 years, Ht. 5 ft 11 ins
Complexion fresh, Eyes grey
Hair light brown, Trade Labourer
Joined Regiment 02/11/71 at Belfast
To 3/13 South Staffs 10/07/87
(Refer to new Army No. 704)

1163 Sergeant TOLLEY William
Born: Parish Bewdley
Town Bewdley, Worcs.
Enlisted at Birmingham on 08/09/64
Aged 20 years, Ht. 5 ft 5 1/4 ins
Complexion Healthy, Eyes grey
Hair brown, Trade Forgeman
Joined Regiment 01/08/77 at South Africa
Transferred to Militia 04/04/82

1665 Sergeant WALKER Harry
Born: Parish St. Mary's
Town Leicester, Liecs.
Enlisted at Leicester on 19/01/71
Aged 18 years, Ht. 5 ft 5 3/4 ins
Complexion fresh, Eyes hazel
Hair brown, Religion C.E.
Trade Hairdresser
Joined Regiment 27/01/71 at Belfast
To Depot 24/02/82

200 Lce. Sergeant BAILEY John J.
Born: Parish Madley
Town Madley, Shrops.
Enlisted at Birmingham on 30/01/74
Aged 19 years 4 months, Ht. 5 ft 6 1/2 ins
Complexion fresh, Eyes light
Hair brown, Trade Bricklayer
Joined Regiment 23/02/76 at Singapore

1387 Lce. Sergeant BROWN Thomas
Born: Parish Knutsford
Town Knutsford, Cheshire
Enlisted at Manchester on 01/09/70
Aged 19 years 9 months, Ht. 5 ft 5 1/4 ins
Complexion fresh, Eyes blue
Hair dark brown, Religion C.E.
Trade Labourer
Joined Regiment 08/09/70 at Belfast
Discharged by purchase 17/01/83

966 Lce. Sergeant COOPER Albert
Born: Parish Worcester
Town Worcester, Worcs.
Enlisted at Lichfield on 10/04/77
Aged 20 years, Ht. 5 ft 7 1/4 ins
Complexion fresh, Eyes dark brown
Hair dark brown, Trade Groom
Joined Regiment 13/06/77
at Cape of Good Hope
To 1st Battalion 19/04/83

185 Lce. Sergeant LOWBRIDGE David
Born: Parish Walsall
Town Walsall, Staffs.
Enlisted at Wolverhampton on 20/01/74
Aged 20 years, Ht. 5 ft 6 3/4 ins
Complexion fresh, Eyes blue
Hair brown, Trade Caster
Joined Regiment 23/02/76 at Singapore
(Refer to new Army No. 704)
Transferred to Army Reserve 24/06/80

1627 Lce. Sergeant SANSAM George
Born: Parish Stoke
Town Market Drayton, Shrops
Enlisted at Liverpool on 13/01/71
Aged 22 years, Ht. 5 ft 7 1/8 ins
Complexion fair, Eyes blue
Hair light brown, Religion C.E.
Trade Labourer
Joined Regiment 20/01/71 at Belfast
Served in "C" Company
Killed in Action 12/03/79 Intombi River

93 Corporal ARTHURS William
Born: Parish Leicester
Town Leicester, Leics.
Enlisted at Birmingham on 22/08/73
Aged 18 years 6 months, Ht. 5 ft 5 3/8 ins
Complexion fresh, Eyes grey
Hair brown, Trade Groom
Joined Regiment 23/02/76 at Singapore
Transferred to Army Reserve 04/10/79

545 Corporal CONSTABLE Thomas
Born: Parish St. Thomas's
Town Birmingham, Warks.
Enlisted at Lichfield on 23/07/75
Aged 21 years, Ht. 5 ft 5 ins
Complexion fresh, Eyes grey
Hair light brown, Trade Engineer
Joined Regiment 25/11/75 at Singapore
Transferred on 31/12/79 to 2/21st Fusiliers

19/636 Corporal BEECROFT Alfred
Born: Parish   Birmingham
Town   Birmingham, Warks.
Enlisted at Birmingham on 11/01/76
Aged 19 years, Ht. 5 ft 7 1/4 ins
Complexion fresh, Eyes blue
Hair brown, Trade Fitter
Joined Regiment 02/02/78 at South Africa
Served in "H" Company   Transferred to Army Reserve 02/02/82

762 Corporal BREW George
Born: Parish   Albrighton
Town   Albrighton, Staffs.
Enlisted at Walsall on 16/08/76
Aged 19 years, Ht. 5 ft 6 3/4 ins
Complexion fresh, Eyes blue
Hair light brown, Trade Labourer
Joined Regiment 02/02/78 at South Africa
Transferred to Army Reserve 26/01/83

1915 Corporal GREEN Henry
Born: Parish   Weasenham
Town   Fakenham, Norfolk
Enlisted at Westminster on 15/03/72
Aged 22 years 7 months, Ht. 5 ft 5 3/4 ins
Complexion fair, Eyes grey
Hair light brown,
Trade Clerk
Joined Regiment not known
Transferred to Army Reserve 04/10/79

2107 Corporal JENNINGS Edgar
Born: Parish   Hayton
Town   Liverpool, Lancs.
Enlisted at Liverpool on 05/02/73
Aged 24 years 10 months, Ht. 5 ft 8 1/2 ins
Complexion fresh, Eyes grey
Hair light brown, Trade Clerk
Joined Regiment not known
Transferred to Army Reserve 04/10/79

19/544 Corporal JOHNSON Ernest
Born: Parish   Lichfield
Town   Lichfield, Staffs.
Enlisted at Lichfield on 26/02/75
Aged 18 years 9 months, Ht. 5 ft 5 ins
Complexion fresh, Eyes brown
Hair brown, Trade Servant
Joined Regiment 13/01/77 at Cape of Good Hope
Served in "E" Company Killed in Action 12/03/79 Intombi River

1833 Corporal LEWIS William
Born: Parish   Kibworth
Town   Kibworth, Leics.
Enlisted at Leicester on 02/11/71
Aged 19 years, Ht. 5 ft 5 3/4 ins
Complexion fresh, Eyes hazel
Hair brown, Trade Groom
Joined Regiment 10/11/71 at Belfast
Transferred to Army Reserve 04/10/79

2066 Corporal LITTLE William
Born: Parish   St. George's
Town   London, Middlesex
Enlisted at Lambeth on 30/05/72
Aged 23 years 2 months, Ht. 5 ft 5 ins
Complexion fresh, Eyes grey
Hair light brown, Trade Labourer
Joined Regiment not known
Transferred to Army Reserve 25/10/79

1487 Corporal MAJOR Robert
Born: Parish   Cookstown
Town   Cookstown, Tyrone
Enlisted at Belfast on 01/12/70
Aged 17 years 2 months, Ht. 5 ft 5 1/2 ins
Complexion dark, Eyes brown
Hair dark brown, Religion C.E.
Trade Labourer
Joined Regiment 01/12/70 at Belfast
To 3rd Batt. South Staffs Regt. 31/03/84

19/733 Corporal McCOY John
Born: Parish Newcastle Under Lyme
Town Newcastle Under Lyme, Staffs.
Enlisted at Newcastle on 13/07/76
Aged 19 years, Ht. 5 ft 7 ins
Complexion fresh, Eyes blue
Hair brown, Trade Tailor
Joined Regiment 13/06/77
at Cape of Good Hope
Served in "C" Company
Killed in Action 12/03/79 Intombi River

1241 Corporal CORRASKRY James
Born: Parish   Athboy
Town   Trim, Meath
Enlisted at Manchester on 15/12/68
Aged 22 years, Ht. 5 ft 8 3/4 ins
Complexion fresh, Eyes blue
Hair dark brown, Trade Labourer
Joined Regiment 19/12/68 at Fleetwood

1439 Corporal GARNER George
Born: Parish Newcastle Under Lyme
Town Newcastle Under Lyme, Staffs
Enlisted atNewcastle Under Lyme on 21/10/70
Aged 19 years 11 months, Ht. 5 ft 6 1/4 ins
Complexion fresh, Eyes grey
Hair brown, Religion C.E.
Trade Labourer
Joined Regiment 27/10/70 at Belfast
Discharged 11/11/82

1711 Corporal KELLY Thomas
Born: Parish   Loughglinn
Town   Loughglinn, Roscommon
Enlisted at Newcastle Under Lyme on 16/02/71
Aged 19 years, Ht. 5 ft 5 1/8 ins
Complexion fresh, Eyes grey
Hair dark brown, Religion R.C.
Trade Labourer
Joined Regiment 23/02/71 at Belfast
Transferred to South Staffs
To R. Hiberman School 17/06/86
Re-transferred/Discharged 21/10/89 (New Army No. 451)

1344 Corporal KILSILL Henry
Born: Parish   Birmingham
Town   Birmingham. Warks.
Enlisted at Birmingham on 17/08/70
Aged 19 years, Ht. 5 ft 6 1/4 ins
Complexion fair, Eyes blue
Hair dark brown, Religion C.E.
Trade Wire Cleaner
Joined Regiment 19/08/70 at Belfast
Discharged free 07/08/83

461 Corporal KYNASTON John
Born: Parish   Shrewsbury
Town   Shrewsbury, Shrops
Enlisted at Wolverhampton on 07/01/75
Aged 19 years, Ht. 5 ft 7 1/2 ins
Complexion fresh, Eyes hazel
Hair brown, Trade Labourer
Joined Regiment 12/02/78 at South Africa
Transferred to Army Reserve 07/01/81

2000 Corporal MARTIN Charles
Born: Parish   St.Pancras
Town   London, Middlesex
Enlisted at Westminster on 14/05/72
Aged 20 years 9 months, Ht. 5 ft 5 ins
Complexion fair, Eyes grey
Hair brown, Trade Carman
Joined Regiment not known
Transferred to Army Reserve 04/10/79

714 Corporal MAYNARD William J.
Born: Parish   Deptford
Town   London, Middlesex
Enlisted at Walsall on 24/06/76
Aged 23 years, Ht. 5 ft 9 1/4 ins
Complexion fair, Eyes grey
Hair light brown, Trade Clerk
Joined Regiment 17/11/76 at Singapore
Transferred to Army Reserve 23/03/84

1525 Corporal McCREADY Robert
Born: Parish   Birkenhead
Town   Birkenhead, Cheshire
Enlisted at Liverpool on 08/12/70
Aged 19 years, Ht. 5 ft 4 3/4 ins
Complexion fresh, Eyes grey
Hair brown, Religion C.E.
Trade Mason
Joined Regiment 15/12/70 at Belfast
Transferred on 01/10/85 to
The Manchester Regiment

1319 Corporal MOORE Henry
Born: Parish   Dundalk
Town   Dundalk, Armagh
Enlisted at Fleetwood on 21/09/69
Aged 14 years 2 months, Ht. 4 ft 7 1/4 ins
Complexion fresh, Eyes brown
Hair dark brown, Trade None
Joined Regiment 21/09/69 at Fleetwood
Discharged free 21/09/82

1303 Corporal McDONALD John
Born: Parish   Forkhill
Town   Dundalk, Armagh
Enlisted at Preston on 29/06/69
Aged 23 years, Ht. 5 ft 6 1/4 ins
Complexion fresh, Eyes brown
Hair dark brown, Trade Puddler
Joined Regiment 03/07/69 at Fleetwood
Disharged 02/08/80

1372 Corporal MOORE George
Born: Parish   Shoreditch
Town   London, Middlesex
Enlisted at Westminster on 26/06/70
Aged 18 years, Ht. 5 ft 7 3/4 ins
Complexion fresh, Eyes grey
Hair brown, Religion C.E.
Trade Bleach Maker
Joined Regiment 31/08/70 at Belfast
Discharged by Purchase 09/05/80

1011 Corporal TIDBALL Henry
Born: Parish   Morebath
Town   Morebath, Devon
Enlisted at Salford on 17/05/77
Aged 19 years Ht. 5 ft 6 1/2 ins
Complexion fresh, Eyes brown
Hair brown, Trade Labourer
Joined Regiment 13/06/77 at Cape Town,
South Africa
Transferred to Army Reserve 19/04/83

1320 Corporal WELDON Peter
Born: Parish   Galway
Town   Galway, Galway
Enlisted at Leeds on 29/09/69
Aged 14 years 6 months, Ht. 4 ft 10 3/4 ins
Complexion fresh, Eyes grey
Hair red, Religion R.C.
Trade None
Joined Regiment 09/10/69 at Fleetwood
Discharged by purchase 13/03/80

2038 Drummer BARNWELL William
Born: Parish   Chelsea
Town   London, Middlesex
Enlisted at Westminster on 04/01/72
Aged 20 years 3 months, Ht. 5 ft 5 ins
Complexion fair, Eyes hazel
Hair dark brown, Trade Bricklayer
Joined Regiment not known
Discharged by Purchase 17/09/79

1647 Drummer LEATHER John
Born: Parish   Warrington
Town   Warrington, Cheshire
Enlisted at Liverpool on 19/01/71
Aged 18 years, Ht. 5 ft 5 3/8 ins
Complexion fair, Eyes blue
Hair light, Trade Labourer
Joined Regiment 21/01/71 at Belfast
Served in "A" Company
Killed in Action 12/03/79 Intombi River

110 Drummer LEWIS John
Born: Parish   Bishop's Castle
Town   Bishop's Castle, Shrops.
Enlisted at Birmingham on 06/09/73
Aged 19 years 6 months, Ht. 5 ft 6 ins
Complexion sandy, Eyes grey
Hair sandy, Trade Engine Driver
Joined Regiment 04/11/74 at Hong Kong
Transferred to Army Reserve 04/10/79

1767 Drummer McQUILLAN John
Born: Parish   Armagh
Town   Armagh, Armagh
Enlisted at Belfast on 19/09/71
Aged 16 years, Ht. 5 ft 3 1/2 ins
Complexion fresh, Eyes blue
Hair brown, Religion R.C.
Trade Labourer
Joined Regiment 22/09/71 at BelfastDischarged 1st Period 29/09/83

304 Private ABBOTT John
Born: Parish   Molecamber
Town   Weymouth, Dorset
Enlisted at Doncaster on 08/08/74
Aged 19 years 2 months, Ht. 5 ft 7 1/2 ins
Complexion fair, Eyes brown
Hair brown, Trade Painter
Joined Regiment 02/02/78at South Africa
Transferred to Army Reserve 27/08/81

1534 Corporal MURCH Samuel
Born: Parish   Ashburton
Town   Ashburton, Devon
Enlisted at Ashburton on 12/12/70
Aged 19 years, Ht. 5 ft 5 1/4 ins
Complexion fresh, Eyes grey
Hair brown, Religion C.E.
Trade Groom
Joined Regiment 23/12/70 at Belfast
To 19th Brigade Depot 01/12/80
Rejoined 17/08/81, Discharged 13/12/82

2062 Corporal STEPHENS Edward
Born: Parish   Stroud
Town   Stroud, Glous.
Enlisted at Barnet on 29/05/72
Aged 21 years, Ht. 5 ft 5 ins
Complexion fresh, Eyes grey
Hair dark brown, Trade Painter
Joined Regiment not known
Transferred to Army Reserve 04/10/79

301 Drummer COLLIER Alfred
Born: Parish   St. Giles
Town   Reading, Berks.
Enlisted at Aldershot on 10/07/74
Aged 15 years 10 months, Ht. 5 ft 1 3/4 ins
Complexion fresh, Eyes grey
Hair light brown, Trade None
Joined Regiment 23/02/76 at Singapore
Transferred to Army Reserve 29/08/81

1769 Drummer CUNNINGHAM Thomas
Born: Parish   Shankhill
Town   Belfast, Antrim
Enlisted at Belfast on 19/09/71
Aged 14 years, Ht. 4 ft 7 ins
Complexion fair, Eyes blue
Hair light brown, Religion R.C.
Trade Labourer
Joined Regiment 22/09/71 at Belfast
Transferred to 3rd Batt. South Staffs 16/10/87
(Refer to new Army No. 521)

594 Drummer DONOVAN William
Born: Parish   Peckham
Town   London, Middlesex
Enlisted at Gosport on 11/12/75
Aged 14 years 8 months, Ht. 4 ft 6 ins
Complexion fresh, Eyes grey
Hair dark brown, Trade Musician
Joined Regiment 02/02/78 at South Africa
To Depot 29/05/83, Rejoined 03/09/85
Discharged by Purchase 18/12/87

1336 Drummer MORAN William
Born: Parish   Isladaim
Town   Castlebar, Mayo
Enlisted at Birr on 04/02/70
Aged 14 years, Ht. 4 ft 6 ins
Complexion fresh, Eyes grey
Hair brown, Trade None
Joined Regiment 04/02/70 at Birr
Discharged 15/02/80

1757 Drummer TERRY Alfred
Born: Parish   St. Saviour's
Town   London, Surrey
Enlisted at London on 20/08/71
Aged 14 years 1 month, Ht. 4 ft 5 1/4 ins
Complexion fair, Eyes blue
Hair brown, Religion C.E.
Trade None
Joined Regiment 02/09/71 at Belfast
Discharged Free 26/04/84(Refer to new Army No. 398)

540 Drummer VYSE Joseph
Born: Parish   Fazeley
Town   Tamworth, Staffs.
Enlisted at Tamworth on 19/07/75
Aged 21 years, Ht. 5 ft 6 ins
Complexion fresh, Eyes dark
Hair brown, Trade Collier
Joined Regiment 25/11/75 at Sinapore
Transferred to Army Reserve 20/07/81

546 Private ADEY Jonah
Born: Parish   Wednesfield
Town   Wednesfield, Staffs.
Enlisted at Walsall on 26/07/75
Aged 23 years 9 months, Ht. 5 ft 5 ins
Complexion dark, Eyes brown
Hair brown, Trade Hay Maker
Joined Regiment 25/11/78 at Singapore
Served in "E" Company
Killed in Action 12/03/79 Intombi River

1505 Private ADAIR Henry
Born: Parish Shankhill
Town Belfast, Antrim
Enlisted at Belfast on 05/12/70
Aged 20 years, Ht. 5 ft 6 1/2 ins
Complexion sallow, Eyes brown
Hair dark brown, Religion C.E.
Trade Labourer
Joined Regiment 07/12/70 at Belfast
To Depot 24/01/93 (Refer to new Army No. 432)

704 Private ADAMS Robert
Born: Parish Matlock
Town Matlock, Derbs.
Enlisted at Lichfield on 09/06/76
Aged 20 years, Ht. 5 ft 5 3/4 ins
Complexion fair, Eyes brown
Hair brown Trade Sadler.
Joined Regiment 19/11/76 at Singapore
Died 14/02/80

1017 Private ALLSOP Joseph
(Nominal Rolls refers to
1017 ALLSOP George)
Born: Parish Whittington
Town Lichfield, Staffs.
Enlisted at Lichfield on 21/05/77
Aged 21 years, Ht. 5 ft 5 ins
Complexion fair, Eyes blue
Hair dark, Trade Farm Labourer
Joined Regiment 13/06/77
at Cape of Good Hope
Transferred to 38th Regt. 19/06/80

231 Private ANDERSON Frederick
Born: Parish Wolverhampton
Town Wolverhampton, Staffs.
Enlisted at Wolverhampton on 23/02/74
Aged 22 years, Ht. 5 ft 6 ins
Complexion fresh, Eyes blue
Hair brown, Trade Iron Caster
Joined Regiment 04/11/74 at Hong Kong
Transferred to Army Reserve 24/06/80

1916 Private ANNALS Alfred
Born: Parish North Walton
Town North Walton, Hamps.
Enlisted at Westminster on 14/03/72
Aged 21 years, Ht. 5 ft 6 ins
Complexion fresh, Eyes hazel
Hair brown, Trade Labourer
Joined Regiment not known
Transferred to Army Reserve 04/10/79

7 Private ARMSTRONG Thomas W.
Born: Parish Armagh
Town Armagh, Armagh
Enlisted at Buttevant on 09/04/73
Aged 14 years 3 months, Ht. 4 ft 6 ins
Complexion fresh, Eyes hazel
Hair light brown, Trade None
Joined Regiment not known
Transferred to 1st Batt. 04/10/81

108 Private ARTHURS Michael
Born: Parish Curragh
Town Kildare, Leimster
Enlisted at Leek on 08/09/73
Aged 19 years 6 months, Ht. 5 ft 4 3/4 ins
Complexion fresh, Eyes grey
Hair brown, Trade Labourer
Joined Regiment 04/11/74 at Hong Kong
Transferred to Army Reserve 08/01/80

2033 Private ATKINS Charles
Born: Parish Isleworth
Town Brentford, Middlesex
Enlisted at Westminster on 14/12/71
Aged 19 years, Ht. 5 ft 5 ins
Complexion fresh, Eyes grey
Hair brown, Trade Labourer
Joined Regiment not known
Transferred to Army Reserve 10/01/81

1998 Private BAILEY Frederick
Born: Parish Cambourne
Town London, Middlesex
Enlisted at Westminster on 07/05/72
Aged 21 years 9 months, Ht. 5 ft 8 ins
Complexion fresh, Eyes blue
Hair brown, Trade Carpenter
Joined Regiment not known
Discharged by Purchase 21/06/83

976 Private ADEY Walter
Born: Parish Darlaston
Town Darlaston, Staffs.
Enlisted at Walsall on 21/04/77
Aged 21 years, Ht. 5 ft 4 3/4 ins
Complexion fresh, Eyes hazel
Hair brown, Trade Labourer
Joined Regiment 13/06/77
at Cape of Good Hope
Discharged Invalid 23/02/80

1283 Private ALLISON John
Born: Parish Devenshulus
Town Devenshulus, Lancs.
Enlisted at Fleetwood on 19/06/69
Aged 24 years 11 months, Ht. 5 ft 8 ins
Complexion sallow, Eyes grey
Hair brown, Trade Tailor
Joined Regiment 23/06/69 at Fleetwood
Discharged 13/07/79

19/585 Private ANTHONY John
Born: Parish Harbourne
Town Birmingham, Warks.
Enlisted at Birmingham on 02/12/75
Aged 18 years 8 months, Ht. 5 ft 5 3/4 ins
Complexion fresh, Eyes blue
Hair light, Trade Labourer
Joined Regiment 17/11/76 at Singapore
Served in "A" Company
Killed in Action 12/03/79 Intombi River

1521 Private APPLETON Thomas
Born: Parish St. Helen's
Town St. Helen's, Lancs.
Enlisted at Liverpool on 08/12/70
Aged 20 years, Ht. 5 ft 5 ins
Complexion fresh, Eyes hazel
Hair brown, Religion C.E.
Trade Labourer
Joined Regiment 15/12/70 at Belfast
Transferred to Army Reserve 27/08/81

1437 Private ARKELL James
Born: Parish not known
Town Gloucester, Glous.
Enlisted at Deptford on 14/10/70
Aged 23 years, Ht. 5 ft 5 3/4 ins
Complexion fresh, Eyes brown
Hair dark brown, Religion C.E.
Trade Labourer
Joined Regiment 22/10/70 at Belfast
Discharged by Purchase 08/03/81

1452 Private ATKINSON James
Born: Parish Cuerdew
Town Preston, Lancs.
Enlisted at Blackburn on 24/10/70
Aged 20 years, Ht. 5 ft 5 3/4 ins
Complexion fresh, Eyes brown
Hair sandy, Religion C.E.
Trade Spinner
Joined Regiment 03/11/70 at Belfast
Discharged 24/09/80

759 Private BACKETT John
Born: Parish Birmingham
Town Birmingham, Warks.
Enlisted at Birmingham on 14/08/76
Aged 19 years 4 months, Ht. 5 ft 6 ins
Complexion sallow, Eyes blue
Hair dark brown, Trade Painter
Joined Regiment 13/06/77
at Cape of Good Hope
Transferred to Army Reserve 26/01/83

779 Private BAGNALL Thomas
Born: Parish Birmingham
Town Birmingham, Warks.
Enlisted at Birmingham on 24/08/76
Aged 19 years, Ht. 5 ft 6 ins
Complexion fair, Eyes grey
Hair brown, Trade Tepinle Maker
Joined Regiment 02/02/78 at South Africa
Transferred to 1st Batt. 04/10/81

19/202 Private BANKS Arthur
Born: Parish Willenhall
Town Willenhall, Staffs.
Enlisted at Walsall on 03/02/74
Aged 18 years, Ht. 5 ft 5 ins
Complexion sallow, Eyes grey
Hair black, Trade Locksmith
Joined Regiment 23/07/76 at Singapore
Served in "A" Company
Killed in Action 12/03/79 Intombi River

1223 Private BAILEY Thomas
Born: Parish
Town
County
Enlisted at
Aged years months, Ht. ft ins
Complexion   Eyes
Hair   Religion
Trade   Joined Regiment

577 Private BAKER John
Born: Parish   Willenhall
Town   Willenhall, Staffs.
Enlisted at Lichfield on 30/11/75
Aged 23 years, Ht. 5 ft 5 3/4 ins
Complexion fresh, Eyes brown
Hair brown, Trade Locksmith
Joined Regiment 17/11/76 at Singapore
Transferred to Army Reserve 02/12/81

1448 Private BARBER Alexander
Born: Parish   Ballymena
Town   Ballymena, Antrim
Enlisted at Belfast on 31/10/70
Aged 18 years 4 months, Ht. 5 ft 5 1/4 ins
Complexion dark, Eyes grey
Hair dark brown, Religion Presbyterian
Trade Plumber & Safe Fitter
Joined Regiment 31/10/70 at Belfast
Discharged 31/10/82

1382 Private BARCKLIE Matthew
Born: Parish   Kilrook
Town   Carrickfergus, Antrim
Enlisted at Belfast on 02/09/70
Aged 19 years, Ht. 5 ft 7 ins
Complexion fresh, Eyes grey
Hair dark brown, Religion C.E.
Trade Bleacher
Joined Regiment 03/09/70 at Belfast
To 1st Batt. South Staffs Regt. 19/04/83
(Refer to new Army No. 378)

1514 Private BARNES James
Born: Parish   Wigan
Town   Wigan, Lancs.
Enlisted at Blackburn on 09/12/70
Aged 20 years, Ht. 5 ft 5 1/8 ins
Complexion fair, Eyes grey
Hair white, Religion C.E.
Trade Stoker
Joined Regiment 13/12/70 at Belfast
Discharged 1st Period 07/12/82

349 Private BAXTER William
Born: Parish   New Linten
Town   New Linten, Notts.
Enlisted at Birmingham on 22/09/74
Aged 23 years 10 months, Ht. 5 ft 4 3/4 ins
Complexion fresh, Eyes grey
Hair brown, Trade Chain Maker
Joined Regiment 13/06/77
at Cape of Good Hope
Transferred to Army Reserve 21/06/81

1358 Private BAXTER William
Born: Parish   Kegworth
Town   Kegworth, Leics.
Enlisted at Derby on 22/08/70
Aged 19 years 6 months, Ht. 5 ft 5 1/4 ins
Complexion fresh, Eyes grey
Hair brown, Trade Labourer
Joined Regiment 30/08/70 at Belfast
Discharged by Purchase 17/07/80

1028 Private BEAUMONT Alfred
Born: Parish
Town
County
Enlisted at
Aged   years   months, Ht. ft   ins
Complexion   Eyes
Hair   Religion
Trade
Joined Regiment

1070 Private BELLERSON Thomas
Born: Parish   Walsall
Town   Walsall, Staffs.
Enlisted at Walsall on 12/06/77
Aged 18 years, Ht. 5 ft 4 1/2 ins
Complexion dark, Eyes hazel
Hair dark brown, Trade Labourer
Joined Regiment 02/02/78 at South Africa
Transferred to 38th Regt. (Date not known)

1049 Private BANKS Thomas
Born: Parish   Willenhall
Town   Willenhall, Staffs.
Enlisted at Walsall on 01/06/77
Aged 18 years 6 months, Ht. 5 ft 4 5/8 ins
Complexion fair, Eyes grey
Hair light brown, Trade Locksmith
Joined Regiment 02/02/78 at South Africa
Transferred to 38th Regt. 19/06/80

943 Private BANNER John
Born: Parish   Congleton
Town   Congleton, Cheshire
Enlisted at Congleton on 24/03/65
Aged 21 years, Ht. 5 ft 6 ins
Complexion dark, Eyes dark
Hair brown, Trade Smith
Joined Regiment 23/06/66
at Fort Tregantle, Devonport Served in "A" Company
Killed in Action 12/03/79 Intombi River

531 Private BARNETT Richard
Born: Parish   Hanley
Town   Stoke, Staffs.
Enlisted at Hanley on 06/07/75
Aged 22 years 6 months, Ht. 5 ft 5 1/4 ins
Complexion fresh, Eyes grey
Hair light brown Trade Labourer
Joined Regiment 25/11/75 at Singapore
Transferred to Army Reserve 08/07/81

1591 Private BARRON Anthony
Born: Parish   Whalley
Town   Accrington, Lancs.
Enlisted at Blackburn on 31/12/70
Aged 19 years, Ht. 5 ft 6 1/4 ins
Complexion sallow, Eyes brown
Hair brown, Religion C.E.
Trade Spinner
Joined Regiment 13/01/71 at Belfast
Discharged 01/01/83

1038 Private BATEMAN William
Born: Parish   Willenhall
Town   Willenhall, Staffs.
Enlisted at Walsall on 30/05/77
Aged 21 years, Ht. 5 ft 6 ins
Complexion sallow, Eyes dark brown
Hair brown, Trade Locksmith
Joined Regiment 13/06/77
at Cape of Good Hope
Transferred to 1st Batt. 04/10/81

276 Private BEBBINGTON William
Born: Parish   Burslem
Town   Burslem, Staffs.
Enlisted at Hanley on 08/04/74
Aged 19 years 6 months, Ht. 5 ft 6 ins
Complexion fresh, Eyes grey
Hair light brown, Trade Forgeman
Joined Regiment 23/02/76 at Singapore
Transferred to Army Reserve 25/06/80

1164 Private BEDWITH Alfred
Born: Parish   Birmingham
Town   Birmingham, Warks.
Enlisted at Birmingham on 04/02/67
Aged 18 years, Ht. 5 ft 7 3/4 ins
Complexion fair, Eyes hazel
Hair brown, Trade Bedstead Maker
Joined Regiment 01/08/77 at South Africa
Discharged by Purchase 14/02/80

736 Private BELL James
Born: Parish
Town
County
Enlisted at
Aged years months, Ht. ft   ins
Complexion   Eyes
Hair   Religion
Trade
Joined Regiment

275 Private BENTLEY John
Born: Parish   Hanley
Town   Hanley, Staffs.
Enlisted at Hanley on 09/04/74
Aged 19 years 10 months, Ht. 5 ft 4 3/4 ins
Complexion fresh, Eyes grey
Hair light brown, Trade Potter
Joined Regiment 04/11/74 at Hong Kong
Transferred to Army Reserve 25/06/80

680 Private BENNETT William
Born: Parish Bullstanton
Town Burslem, Staffs.
Enlisted at Newcastle on 17/05/76
Aged 19 years 11 months, Ht. 5 ft 5 ins
Complexion fresh, Eyes grey
Hair brown, Trade Potter
Joined Regiment 03/12/78 at Pretoria,
South Africa
Transferred to Army Reserve 19/07/82

105 Private BENTLEY John
Born: Parish Stowe
Town Stafford, Staffs.
Enlisted at Newcastle Under Lyme
on 04/09/73
Aged 19 years, Ht. 5 ft 6 ins
Complexion fresh, Eyes blue
Hair brown, Trade Labourer
Joined Regiment 23/02/76 at Singapore
Transferred to Army Reserve 04/10/79

1687 Private BICKERTON Joseph
Born: Parish Hanley
Town Stoke on Trent, Staffs.
Enlisted at Newcastle Under Lyme
on 01/02/71
Aged 19 years, Ht. 5 ft 6 5/8 ins
Complexion fresh, Eyes grey
Hair light brown, Religion C.E.
Trade Potter
Joined Regiment 06/02/71 at Belfast
Discharged 1st Period 01/02/83

1076 Private BILLINGHAM Thomas
(Nominal Roll 1076 BILLINGHAM James)
Born: Parish Birmingham
Town Birmingham, Warks
Enlisted at Birmingham on 18/06/77
Aged 21 years 4 months, Ht. 5 ft 8 ins
Complexion fresh, Eyes grey
Hair brown, Trade Baker
Joined Regiment 02/02/78 at South Africa
Deserted in the Transvaal,
South Africa 10/01/80

29 Private BIRCH William
Born: Parish Broughton
Town Manchester, Lancs.
Enlisted at not known on 18/09/57
Aged 19 years, Ht. 5 ft 5 1/4 ins
Complexion fresh, Eyes hazel
Hair dark brown, Trade Labourer,
Joined Regiment 02/10/58
at Cawnpore (India)
Discharged 30/12/79

1015 Private BOND William
Born: Parish Lichfield
Town Lichfield, Staffs.
Enlisted at Stafford on 19/05/77
Aged 18 years, Ht. 5 ft 4 1/4 ins
Complexion fair, Eyes brown
Hair brown, Trade Collier
Joined Regiment 13/06/77
at Cape of Good Hope
Transferred to 38th Regt. 19/06/80

1897 Private BOOKER Alfred
Born: Parish Dorking
Town Dorking, Surrey
Enlisted at Westminster on 28/02/72
Aged 23 years 4 months, Ht. 5 ft 6 ins
Complexion fresh, Eyes grey
Hair brown, Trade Labourer
Joined Regiment not known
Transferred to Army Reserve 04/10/79

1155 Private BOOTH Enoch
Born: Parish Mancot
Town Mancot, Cheshire
Enlisted at Liverpool on 16/05/68
Aged 22 years, Ht. 5 ft 6 ins
Complexion sallow, Eyes hazel
Hair brown, Trade Carrier
Joined Regiment 23/05/68 at Aldershot
Deserted 18/06/70, Discharged 20/07/82

534 Private BOWN Ebenezer
Born: Parish Stockton
Town Durham, Durham
Enlisted at Walsall on 07/07/75
Aged 19 years 8 months, Ht. 5 ft 6 3/4 ins
Complexion fresh, Eyes brown
Hair brown, Trade Collier
Joined Regiment 25/11/75 at Singapore
Discharged 02/09/80

975 Private BENTON Samuel
Born: Parish Willenhall
Town Willenhall, Staffs.
Enlisted at Walsall on 23/04/77
Aged 19 years, Ht. 5 ft 7 1/2 ins
Complexion fair, Eyes hazel
Hair light brown, Trade Locksmith
Joined Regiment 02/02/78 at South Africa
Transferred to Army Reserve 28/04/83

513 Private BETTS Henry
Born: Parish Hemerfield
Town Bury St. Edmund's, Suffolk
Enlisted at Westminster on 15/06/59
Aged 18 years, Ht. 5 ft 3 ins
Complexion fresh, Eyes grey
Hair brown, Religion Protestant
Trade Labourer
Joined Regiment 28/01/61
at Saugor (Central India)
Discharged 03/08/80

109 Private BIRD Francis
Born: Parish Lambourne
Town Lambourne, Warks.
Enlisted at Birmingham on 08/09/73
Aged 19 years 3 months, Ht. 5 ft 8 3/4 ins
Complexion fresh, Eyes grey
Hair brown, Trade Needle Maker
Joined Regiment 04/11/74 at Hong Kong
Transferred to Army Reserve 04/10/79

412 Private BLAKEWAY John
Born: Parish Bilston
Town Bilston, Staffs.
Enlisted at Walsall on 26/11/74
Aged 19 years, Ht. 5 ft 4 3/4 ins
Complexion fresh, Eyes grey
Hair brown, Trade Labourer
Joined Regiment 13/06/77 at Cape of Good Hope
Transferred to Army Reserve 30/11/80

719 Private BODEN John
Born: Parish Bilston
Town Bilston, Staffs.
Enlisted at Birmingham on 26/06/76
Aged 20 years 3 months, Ht. 5 ft 7 1/4 ins
Complexion fresh, Eyes grey
Hair brown, Trade Tin Maker
Joined Regiment 17/11/76 at Singapore
Transferred to Army Reserve 29/08/81

766 Private BOOTH Frederick
Born: Parish Willenhall
Town Wolverhampton, Staffs.
Enlisted at Wolverhampton on 17/08/76
Aged 23 years 4 months, Ht. 5 ft 6 3/4 ins
Complexion light, Eyes blue
Hair light, Trade Brass Caster
Joined Regiment 17/11/76 at Singapore

265 Private BOURN William
Born: Parish Wednesbury
Town Wednesbury, Staffs.
Enlisted at Walsall on 31/03/74
Aged 22 years, Ht. 5 ft 5 1/2 ins
Complexion fair, Eyes grey
Hair brown, Trade Bolt Maker
Joined Regiment 04/11/74 at Hong Kong
Transferred to Army Reserve 18/06/80

519 Private BOWEN Thomas
Born: Parish Birmingham
Town Birmingham, Warks.
Enlisted at Birmingham on 24/06/75
Aged 19 years, Ht. 5 ft 7 3/4 ins
Complexion fresh, Eyes grey
Hair brown, Trade Labourer
Joined Regiment 17/11/76 at Singapore
Transferred to Army Reserve 26/08/81

1564 Private BRADSHAW William
Born: Parish Whalley
Town Accrington, Lancs.
Enlisted at Blackburn on 30/12/70
Aged 18 years, Ht. 5 ft 7 3/8 ins
Complexion sallow, Eyes grey
Hair dark brown, Religion C.E.
Trade Spinner
Joined Regiment 06/01/71 at Belfast
Discharged 1st Period 30/12/82

489 Private BOYLE Martin
Born: Parish   Walsall
Town   Walsall, Staffs.
Enlisted at Lichfield on 21/05/75
Aged 18 years, Ht. 5 ft 5 ins
Complexion fresh, Eyes brown
Hair brown, Trade Miner
Joined Regiment 13/06/77
at Cape of Good Hope
Discharged 07/12/80

2102 Private BOYLE Thomas
Born: Parish   Oldham
Town   Oldham, Lancs.
Enlisted at Liverpool on 06/11/72
Aged 20 years, Ht. 5 ft 5 3/8 ins
Complexion fresh, Eyes blue
Hair brown, Trade Labourer
Joined Regiment not known
Transferred to Army Reserve 04/10/79

273 Private BRERETON Thomas
Born: Parish   Chester
Town   Chester, Cheshire
Enlisted at Birmingham on 08/04/74
Aged 23 years 8 months, Ht. 5 ft 5 1/2 ins
Complexion fresh, Eyes grey
Hair dark brown ,Trade Labourer
Joined Regiment 04/11/74 at Hong Kong
Transferred to Army Reserve 25/06/80

722 Private BREW George
Born: Parish   St. Mary's
Town   Wolverhampton, Staffs.
Enlisted at Wolverhampton on 29/06/76
Aged 18 years 5 months, Ht. 5 ft 6 3/4 ins
Complexion Sallow, Eyes blue
Hair brown, Trade Puddler
Joined Regiment 02/02/78 at South Africa
Deserted 14/08/80
Transferred to Army Reserve 30/08/81

415 Private BRIDGEWOOD William
Born: Parish   Smethwick
Town   West Bromwich, Staffs.
Enlisted at Dudley on 25/11/74
Aged 21 years, Ht. 5 ft 5 1/2 ins
Complexion ruddy, Eyes hazel
Hair brown, Trade Boat Builder
Joined Regiment 03/12/78 at Pretoria,
South Africa
Transferred to Army Reserve 30/04/81

122 Private BROWN John
Born: Parish   Manchester
Town   Manchester, Lancs.
Enlisted at not known on 22/10/57
Aged 18 years, Ht. 5 ft 5 1/4 ins
Complexion fresh, Eyes hazel
Hair dark brown Trade Piecer
Joined Regiment 02/10/58
at Cawnpore (India)
Discharged 29/09/79

542 Private BROWN John
Born: Parish   Sutton Coldfield
Town   Sutton Coldfield, Warks.
Enlisted at Tamworth on 20/07/75
Aged 19 years 3 months, Ht. 5 ft 5 3/4 ins
Complexion dark, Eyes dark
Hair dark, Trade Baker
Joined Regiment 02/02/78 at South Africa
Deserted 14/08/76
Transferred to 1st Batt. 04/10/81

576 Private BROWN Samuel
Born: Parish
Town
County
Enlisted at
Aged   years months, Ht. ft ins
Complexion   Eyes
Hair   Religion
Trade
Joined Regiment Transferred to 38th Regt. (Date not known)

1728 Private BUNDAY Henry
Born: Parish   Basingstoke
Town   Basingstoke, Hamps.
Enlisted at Aldershot on 23/08/70
Aged 19 years, Ht. 5 ft 6 ins
Complexion fresh, Eyes grey
Hair brown, Religion C.E.
Trade Brick Maker
Joined Regiment 29/05/71 at Belfast
Discharged by Purchase 17/07/80

567 Private BRAMILL William
Born: Parish   Liverpool
Town   Liverpool, Lancs.
Enlisted at Liverpool on 29/06/59
Aged 18 years, Ht. 5 ft 3 1/4 ins
Complexion fresh, Eyes grey
Hair dark brown, Religion Protestant
Trade Caster
Joined Regiment 28/01/61
at Saugor (Central India)
Discharged 03/08/80

1877 Private BRAZE Thomas
Born: Parish   Wolverhampton
Town   Wolverhampton, Staffs.
Enlisted at Liverpool on 09/01/72
Aged 19 years 10 months, Ht. 5 ft 5 3/4 ins
Complexion fair, Eyes light blue
Hair light reddish, Trade Collier
Joined Regiment not known
Transferred to Army Reserve 04/10/79

1664 Private BROADHURST Amos
Born: Parish   All Saints
Town   Leicester, Leics.
Enlisted at Leicester on 19/01/71
Aged 19 years, Ht. 5 ft 4 5/8 ins
Complexion fair, Eyes blue
Hair brown, Religion C.E.
Trade Tailor
Joined Regiment 27/01/71 at Belfast
Deserted 01/11/80

19/745 Private BROUGHTON George
Born: Parish   Wednesbury
Town   Wednesbury, Staffs.
Enlisted at Lichfield on 31/07/76
Aged 19 years, Ht. 5 ft 6 ins
Complexion fresh, Eyes grey
Hair light brown, Trade Labourer
Joined Regiment 13/06/77 at Cape of Good Hope
Served in "A" Company
Killed in Action 12/03/79 Intombi River

48 Private BROWN James
Born: Parish   Dover
Town   Dover, Kent
Enlisted at Dover on 10/06/73
Aged 18 years, Ht. 5 ft 8 ins
Complexion fair, Eyes brown
Hair light brown, Trade Groom
Joined Regiment 23/02/76 at Singapore
Served in "C" Company
Killed in Action 12/03/79 Intombi River

1553 Private BROWN William
Born: Parish   Limerick
Town   Limerick, Limerick
Enlisted at Liverpool on 30/12/70
Aged 19 years, Ht. 5 ft 4 7/8 ins
Complexion fresh, Eyes grey
Hair brown, Religion R.C.
Trade Labourer
Joined Regiment 06/01/71 at Belfast
Transferred to Army Reserve 04/11/79

19/488 Private BROWNSON Henry
Born: Parish   Pannage
Town   Stafford, Staffs.
Enlisted at Tamworth on 17/05/75
Aged 22 years, Ht. 5 ft 5 1/2 ins
Complexion fresh, Eyes blue
Hair light brown, Trade Miner
Joined Regiment 25/11/75 at Singapore
Served in "A" Company
Killed in Action 12/03/79 Intombi River

659 Private BUCKLER Thomas
Born: Parish   Walsall
Town   Walsall, Staffs.
Enlisted at Walsall on 29/01/76
Aged 20 years, Ht. 5 ft 7 5/8 ins
Complexion dark, Eyes dark brown
Hair dark brown, Trade Labourer
Joined Regiment 02/09/78 at South Africa
Transferred to Army Reserve 30/01/82

2055 Private BURKE Daniel
Born: Parish   Aston
Town   Birmingham, Warks.
Enlisted at Lichfield on 09/01/72
Aged 22 years 6 months, Ht. 5 ft 6 ins
Complexion fresh, Eyes grey
Hair sandy, Trade Groom
Joined Regiment not known
Transferred to Army Reserve 20/12/79

2054 Private BURGESS William
Born: Parish Chester
Town Chester, Cheshire
Enlisted at Liverpool on 02/01/72
Aged 18 years 2 months, Ht. 5 ft 5 ins
Complexion sallow
Eyes grey, Hair brown
Trade Billard Maker
Joined Regiment not known
Discharged by Purchase 28/10/79

169 Private BURGWIN Thomas
Born: Parish Shrewsbury
Town Shrewsbury, Shrops.
Enlisted at Newcastle Under Lyme
on 05/01/74
Aged 19 years 7 months, Ht. 5 ft 5 1/4 ins
Complexion fresh, Eyes blue
Hair brown, Trade Miner
Joined Regiment 04/11/74 at Hong Kong
Died at sea on 10/05/80 during passage
home from South Africa

99 Private BURTON Alfred
Born: Parish Birmingham
Town Birmingham, Warks.
Enlisted at Birmingham on 29/08/73
Aged 22 years 4 months, Ht. 5 ft 6 1/4 ins
Complexion fresh, Eyes brown
Hair light brown, Trade Brass Founder
Joined Regiment 04/11/74 at Hong Kong
Transferred to Army Reserve 04/10/79

1737 Private BURTON Joseph
Born: Parish Shankhill
Town Belfast, Antrim
Enlisted at Belfast on 18/01/69
Aged 17 years 2 months, Ht. 5 ft 7 ins
Complexion fresh, Eyes blue
Hair brown, Trade Carpenter
Joined Regiment 01/08/70 at Belfast
Discharged 16/03/80

1984 Private BURTON Thomas
Born: Parish Hilgay
Town Downham Market, Norfolk
Enlisted at Peterborough on 02/05/72
Aged 19 years 11 months, Ht. 5 ft 4 3/4 ins
Complexion florid, Eyes grey
Hair dark brown, Trade Horse Keeper
Joined Regiment not known
Transferred to Army Reserve 04/10/79

159 Private CALLAGHAN Patrick
Born: Parish Wolverhampton
Town Wolverhampton, Staffs.
Enlisted at Wolverhampton on 30/12/73
Aged 22 years, Ht. 5 ft 6 ins
Complexion fresh, Eyes grey
Hair dark brown, Trade Smith
Joined Regiment 04/11/74 at Hong Kong
Transferred to Army Reserve 17/06/80

1129 Private CAMERON Frederick
Born: Melbourne
Australia
Enlisted at Aldershot on 03/12/67
Aged 17 years, Ht. 5 ft 5 3/4 ins
Complexion fair, Eyes hazel
Hair light brown, Trade Miner
Joined Regiment 05/12/67 at Aldershot
Discharged by Purchase 24/12/80

406 Private CARBERRY Richard
Born: Parish Trimslee
Town Whitrant, Waterford
Enlisted at Waterford on 21/05/59
Aged 18 years, Ht. 5 ft 3 1/4 ins
Complexion fresh, Eyes grey
Hair dark brown, Religion R.C.
Trade Labourer
Joined Regiment 28/01/61
Discharged 20/07/80

1290 Private CHADWICK John
Born: Parish Bolton
Town Bolton, Lancs.
Enlisted at Bolton on 21/06/69
Aged 17 years, Ht. 5 ft 6 ins
Complexion fresh, Eyes blue
Hair brown, Trade Labourer
Joined Regiment 26/06/69 at Fleetwood
Served in "E" Company
Killed in Action 12/03/79 Intombi River

1856 Private BURNETT John
Born: Parish Cookstown
Town Cookstown, Tyrone
Enlisted at Belfast on 27/11/71
Aged 21 years, Ht. 5 ft 6 1/2 ins
Complexion fresh, Eyes hazel
Hair dark brown, Trade Weaver
Joined Regiment 29/11/71 at Belfast
Transferred to Army Reserve 27/05/80

2071 Private BURRETT William
Born: Parish Marylebone
Town London, Middlesex
Enlisted at Westminster on 31/05/72
Aged 22 years 6 months,Ht. 5 ft 5 ins
Complexion fresh, Eyes hazel
Hair dark brown, Trade Painter
Joined Regiment not known
Transferred to Army Reserve 04/10/79

278 Private BUTLER Frederick
Born: Parish Lindridge
Town Tenbury, Worcs.
Enlisted at Dudley on 11/04/74
Aged 19 years 11 months, Ht. 5 ft 7 1/2 ins
Complexion ruddy, Eyes hazel
Hair light brown, Trade Labourer
Joined Regiment 23/02/76 at Singapore
Died 18/07/79

574 Private BUTLER John
Born: Parish St. Mary's
Town Stafford, Staffs.
Enlisted at Lichfield on 01/11/75
Aged 18 years 6 months, Ht. 5 ft 6 1/2 ins
Complexion fresh, Eyes brown
Hair dark brown, Trade Labourer
Joined Regiment 03/12/78 at Pretoria, S.A.
To 19th Brigade Depot 01/12/80

603 Private BYRNE Christopher
Born: Parish St. Mary's
Town Dublin, Dublin
Enlisted at Dublin on 11/07/59
Aged 18 years, Ht. 5 ft 3 1/4 ins
Complexion sallow, Eyes brown
Hair brown, Religion R.C.
Trade Labourer
Joined Regiment 28/01/61
at Saugor (Central India)

112 Private CARPENTER John
Born: Parish Shenstone
Town Shenstone, Staffs.
Enlisted at Lichfield on 12/09/73
Aged 21 years, Ht. 5 ft 5 1/4 ins
Complexion fresh, Eyes blue
Hair brown, Trade Miner
Joined Regiment 04/11/74 at Hong Kong
Transferred to Army Reserve 04/10/79

1578 Private CARROLL James
Born: Parish Ballymena
Town Ballymena, Antrim
Enlisted at Belfast on 06/01/71
Aged 22 years, Ht. 5 ft 8 1/2 ins
Complexion fresh, Eyes blue
Hair brown, Religion R.C.
Trade Hackler
Joined Regiment 09/01/71 at Belfast
Discharged Invalid 16/08/81

18 Private CARROLL John
Born: Parish Burslem
Town Burslem, Staffs.
Enlisted at Walsall on 16/04/73
Aged 20 years 2 months, Ht. 5 ft 5 1/4 ins
Complexion fair, Eyes grey
Hair sandy, Trade Labourer
Joined Regiment 18/12/73 at Hong Kong
Deserted 13/02/80

1340 Private CAREY Francis
Born: Parish Armagh
Town Armagh, Armagh
Enlisted at Birr on 02/05/70
Aged 16 years, Ht. 5 ft 2 1/4 ins
Complexion fresh, Eyes grey
Hair brown, Trade Labourer
Joined Regiment at Birr (date not known)
To 1st Battalion South Staffs Regt. 23/09/87

1656 Private CHADWICK Henry
Born: Parish Kirkham
Town Kirkham, Lancs.
Enlisted at Preston on 19/01/71
Aged 19 years, Ht. 5 ft 5 1/4 ins
Complexion fresh, Eyes blue
Hair dark brown, Religion C.E.
Trade Plasterer
Joined Regiment 27/01/71 at Belfast
Discharged 03/02/83

287 Private CHARE Calib Edwin
Born: Parish Studley
Town Studley, Staffs.
Enlisted at Birmingham on 22/04/74
Aged 20 years 1 months Ht. 5 ft 5 1/2 ins
Complexion sallow, Eyes grey
Hair brown, Trade Glass Cutter
Joined Regiment 04/11/74 at Hong Kong
Transferred to Army Reserve 24/06/80

1377 Private CHESTERTON John
Born: Parish St. Pancras
Town London, Middlesex
Enlisted at Westminster on 03/08/70
Aged 19 years, Ht. 5 ft 5 1/2 ins
Complexion fresh, Eyes blue
Hair brown, Religion C.E.
Trade Labourer
Served in 1st Squadron Mounted Infantry
Killed in Action 22/01/79 Isandhlwana

1797 Private CHRISTIE James
(Nominal Roll 1797 CHRISTY James)
Born: Parish Hindley
Town Wigan, Lancs
Enlisted at Liverpool on 06/10/71
Aged 19 years, Ht. 5 ft 5 1/4 ins
Complexion fresh, Eyes hazel
Hair brown, Trade Stoker
Joined Regiment 11/10/71 at Belfast
Served in "A" Company
Killed in Action 12/03/79 Intombi River

507 Private CLARKE John
Born: Parish Birmingham
Town Birmingham, Warks.
Enlisted at Walsall on 17/06/75
Aged 18 years 10 months, Ht. 5 ft 6 ins
Complexion fresh, Eyes brown
Hair dark brown, Trade Fitter
Joined Regiment 17/11/76 at Singapore
Discharged by Purchase 1880

1014 Private CLARKE Thomas
Born: Parish Roscommon
Town Roscommon, Roscommon
Enlisted at Stafford on 19/05/77
Aged 18 years, Ht. 5 ft 7 3/4 ins
Complexion fair, Eyes grey
Hair light brown, Trade Labourer
Joined Regiment 03/12/78 at Pretoria,
South Africa
To 1st Battalion 11/01/82 & 19/09/85

94 Private CLARKE William
Born: Parish Walsall
Town Walsall, Staffs.
Enlisted at Wednesbury on 27/08/73
Aged 18 years 8 months, Ht. 5 ft 5 1/4 ins
Complexion dark, Eyes hazel
Hair light brown, Trade Miner
Joined Regiment 23/02/76 at Singapore
To 1st Battalion 22/09/83

1827 Private CLAY Issac
Born: Parish St. Margaret's
Town Leicester, Leics.
Enlisted at Leicester on 28/10/71
Aged 19 years 6 months, Ht. 5 ft 6 3/4 ins
Complexion fair, Eyes grey
Hair brown, Trade Shoe Finisher
Joined Regiment 09/11/71 at Belfast
Transferred to Army Reserve 24/02/80

2 Private CLEAVER John
Born: Parish Birmingham
Town Birmingham, Warks
Enlisted at Birmingham on 01/04/73
Aged 20 years 3 months Ht. 5 ft 5 1/2 ins
Complexion fresh, Eyes blue
Hair brown, Trade Boot Finisher
Joined Regiment 18/12/73 at Hong Kong
Transferred to Army Reserve 18/06/80

1914 Private CHASE Robert
Born: Parish St. Luke's
Town London, Middlesex
Enlisted at Westminster on 12/03/72
Aged 24 years 8 months, Ht. 5 ft 5 ins
Complexion fair, Eyes brown
Hair dark brown, Trade Servant
Joined Regiment not known
Transferred to Army Reserve 04/10/79

1944 Private CHERRIE William
Born: Parish Glasgow
Town Glasgow, Lanarkshire
Enlisted at Westminster on 10/02/72
Aged 22 years 8 months, Ht. 5 ft 5 ins
Complexion fresh, Eyes hazel
Hair brown, Trade Stoker
Joined Regiment not known
Transferred to Army Reserve 04/10/79

2026 Private CLARKE Owen
Born: Parish Killacara
Town Baillieborough, Cavan
Enlisted at Dublin on 11/10/71
Aged 19 years, Ht. 5 ft 5 ins
Complexion light, Eyes blue
Hair dark brown, Trade Servant
Joined Regiment not known

983 Private CLARKE Thomas
Born: Parish Pavir
Town Knutsford, Cheshire
Enlisted at Newcastle on 23/04/77
Aged 21 years, Ht. 5 ft 6 1/2 ins
Complexion fresh, Eyes hazel
Hair brown, Trade Joiner
Joined Regiment 13/06/77 at Cape of Good Hope
Transferred to Army Reserve 24/04/83

1497 Private CLARKE Thomas
Born: Parish Monaghan
Town Monaghan, Monaghan
Enlisted at Liverpool on 01/12/70
Aged 21 years, Ht. 5 ft 6 ins
Complexion fresh, Eyes hazel
Hair brown, Religion R.C.
Trade Labourer
Joined Regiment 04/12/70 at Belfast
Discharged by Purchase 13/03/80

1982 Private CLAYTON George
Born: Parish St. John's
Town London, Middlesex
Enlisted at Westminster on 30/04/72
Aged 24 years 4 months, Ht. 5 ft 5 ins
Complexion fresh Eyes grey
Hair brown, Trade None
Joined Regiment not known
Transferred to Army Reserve 04/10/79

1658 Private CLAYTON Herbert
Born: Parish Hyde
Town Hyde, Cheshire
Enlisted at Liverpool on 20/01/71
Aged 19 years, Ht. 5 ft 4 3/4 ins
Complexion fair, Eyes blue
Hair light, Religion C.E.
Trade Weaver
Joined Regiment 26/01/71 at Belfast
Discharged 16/01/80

487 Private CLEATON William Thomas
Born: Parish Drumerce
Town Portadown, Armagh
Enlisted at Portadown on 07/06/59
Aged 18 years, Ht. 5 ft 3 1/4 ins
Complexion fresh, Eyes brown
Hair brown, Religion Protestant
Trade Weaver
Joined Regiment 28/01/61 at Saugor (Central India)
Discharged 02/07/81

561 Private COLE William
Born: Parish Coventry
Town Coventry, Warks.
Enlisted at Lichfield on 27/09/75
Aged 18 years, Ht. 5 ft 5 ins
Complexion dark, Eyes dark brown
Hair brown, Trade Chain Maker
Joined Regiment 02/02/78 at South Africa
Transferred to Army Reserve 09/11/81

551 Private CLUIT John
Born: Parish Tettenhall
Town Tettenhall, Staffs.
Enlisted at Lichfield on 02/08/75
Aged 19 years, Ht. 5 ft 6 1/2 ins
Complexion ruddy, Eyes hazel
Hair light brown, Trade Labourer
Joined Regiment 17/11/76 at Singapore
Transferred to Army Reserve 03/08/81

755 Private COLCLOUGH George
Born: Parish Wolstanton
Town Tunstall, Staffs.
Enlisted at Newcastle on 11/08/76
Aged 20 years, Ht. 5 ft 5 1/2 ins
Complexion fresh, Eyes hazel
Hair brown, Trade Sawyer
Joined Regiment 13/06/77
at Cape of Good Hope
Transferred to Army Reserve 26/01/83

1324 Private COLLINSON Robert
Born: Parish Thornton
Town Preston, Lancs.
Enlisted at Fleetwood on 01/12/69
Aged 18 years, Ht. 5 ft 7 ins
Complexion fresh, Eyes grey
Hair sandy, Religion C.E.
Trade Chores
Joined Regiment not known
Discharged Circa £2.00 20/07/82

1989 Private COLYER William
Born: Parish St. Stephen's
Town Canterbury, Kent
Enlisted at Westminster on 06/05/72
Aged 24 years 6 months, Ht. 5 ft 5 3/4 ins
Complexion fresh, Eyes grey
Hair brown, Trade Valet
Joined Regiment not known
Transferred to Army Reserve 04/10/79

314 Private CONLON John
Born: Parish Stone
Town Stone, Staffs.
Enlisted at Lichfield on 01/09/74
Aged 19 years, Ht. 5 ft 7 3/4 ins
Complexion fresh, Eyes grey
Hair brown, Trade Chandler
Joined Regiment 23/02/76 at Singapore
Transferred to Army Reserve 05/09/80

82 Private COOKE George
Born: Parish Bishopgate
Town London, Middlesex
Enlisted at Dover on 29/07/73
Aged 22 years, Ht. 5 ft 5 1/2 ins
Complexion fresh, Eyes hazel
Hair light brown, TradeGlass Cutter/Glazier
Joined Regiment 04/11/74
at Hong Kong
Transferred to Army Reserve 04/10/79

1913 Private COOKE George
(Nominal Roll 1913 COOK George)
Born: Parish Clapham
Town London, Surrey
Enlisted at Westminster on 12/03/72
Aged 21 years 7 months, Ht. 5 ft 5 ins
Complexion fresh, Eyes hazel
Hair light brown, Trade Labourer
Joined Regiment not known
Transferred to Army Reserve 04/10/79

2072 Private COOPER Edwin
Born: Parish Silkstone
Town Barnsley, Yorks.
Enlisted at Westminster on 01/06/72
Aged 20 years 5 months, Ht. 5 ft 5 1/4 ins
Complexion fresh, Eyes grey
Hair brown, Trade Clerk
Joined Regiment not known
Discharged by Purchase 17/09/79

502 Private COWDELL Richard
Born: Parish Smethwick
Town West Bromwich, Staffs.
Enlisted at Birmingham on 01/06/75
Aged 20 years, Ht. 5 ft 5 1/2 ins
Complexion fresh, Eyes grey
Hair brown Trade Blacksmith
Joined Regiment 25/11/75 at Singapore
Deserted 27/11/80

485 Private COLEMAN Thomas
Born: Parish Longton
Town Stoke on Trent, Staffs
Enlisted at Hanley on 15/05/75
Aged 19 years, Ht. 5 ft 5 ins
Complexion fresh, Eyes grey
Hair dark brown, Trade Potter
Joined Regiment 17/11/76 at Singapore
Transferred to Army Reserve 18/05/80

1478 Private COLLIER William
Born: Parish Liverpool
Town Liverpool, Lancs.
Enlisted at Liverpool on 23/11/70
Aged 20 years, Ht. 5 ft 7 1/2 ins
Complexion fresh, Eyes grey
Hair light brown, Religion C.E.
Trade Labourer
Joined Regiment 27/11/70 at Belfast
Discharged 30/11/82

739 Private CONNELL James
Born: Parish Shortheath
Town Erdington, Warks.
Enlisted at Walsall on 24/07/76
Aged 20 years, Ht. 5 ft 6 1/4 ins
Complexion fresh, Eyes grey
Hair brown, Trade Steel Roller
Joined Regiment 17/11/76 at Singapore
Transferred to Army Reserve 29/08/81

690 Private CONNELL John
Born: Parish Wednesbury
Town Walsall, Staffs.
Enlisted at Lichfield on 27/05/76
Aged 20 years, Ht. 5 ft 6 1/4 ins
Complexion dark, Eyes dark brown
Hair dark brown, Trade Puddler
Joined Regiment 17/11/76 at Singapore
Transferred to Army Reserve 29/05/82

988 Private CONVEY John
Born: Parish Shrewsbury
Town Shrewsbury, Shrops.
Enlisted at Newcastle Under Lyme on 30/04/77
Aged 18 years 3 months, Ht. 5 ft 4 5/8 ins
Complexion fresh, Eyes blue
Hair brown, Trade Bricklayer
Joined Regiment 02/02/78 at South Africa
To 1st Battalion 04/10/81

696 Private COPE Samuel
Born: Parish Bloxwich
Town Bloxwich, Staffs.
Enlisted at Lichfield on 02/06/76
Aged 20 years, Ht. 5 ft 6 1/2 ins
Complexion fresh, Eyes hazel
Hair dark brown, Trade Collier
Joined Regiment 03/12/78
at Pretoria, South Africa
Discharged 11/09/80

1051 Private CORBETT David
Born: Parish St. John's
Town Lichfield, Staffs.
Enlisted at Lichfield on 02/06/77
Aged 20 years 6 months, Ht. 5 ft 8 1/4 ins
Complexion fresh, Eyes hazel
Hair brown, Trade Collier
Joined Regiment 02/02/78 at South Africa
Transferred to 38th Regt. (Date not known)

753 Private CORNS John
Born: Parish St. John's
Town Wolverhampton, Staffs.
Enlisted at Lichfield on 09/08/76
Aged 22 years 11 months, Ht. 5 ft 7 1/2 ins
Complexion fresh, Eyes hazel
Hair light brown, Trade Engine Driver
Joined Regiment 13/06/77
at Cape of Good Hope
Discharged Invalid 25/07/82

499 Private CRAWFORD William
Born: Parish Trim
Town Trim, Meath
Enlisted at Bruff on 16/06/59
Aged 18 years, Ht. 5 ft 3 1/2 ins
Complexion fresh, Eyes grey
Hair brown, Religion R.C
Trade Labourer
Joined Regiment 28/01/61
at Saugor (Central India)
Discharged 28/08/83

1874 Private COY William
Born: Parish Northend
Town   Banbury, Warks.
Enlisted at Birmingham on 05/01/72
Aged 19 years 1 months, Ht. 5 ft 6 1/4 ins
Complexion fresh, Eyes blue,
Hair light, Trade Striker
Joined Regiment not known
Transferred to Army Reserve 04/10/79

123 Private COYNE John
Born: Parish Fairhel
Town   Ballinrobe, Galway
Enlisted at Wednesbury on 15/09/73
Aged 23 years, Ht. 5 ft 6 1/2 ins
Complexion fair, Eyes blue
Hair brown, Trade Labourer
Joined Regiment 04/11/74 at Hong Kong
Transferred to Army Reserve 04/10/79

631 Private CURTIN John
Born: Parish Drumcliffe
Town   Ennis, Clare
Enlisted at Buttevant on 08/09/59
Aged 15 years 8 months, Ht. 5 ft 2 ins
Complexion fresh Eyes grey
Hair brown, Religion R.C.
Trade None
Joined Regiment 28/01/61
at Saugor (Central India)
To 19th Brigade Depot 01/12/80

465 Private DABBS Robert
Born: Parish
Town
County
Enlisted at
Aged   years   months, Ht. ft   ins
Complexion   Eyes
Hair   Religion
Joined Regiment

1272 Private DAGGER Henry
Born: Parish Bolton
Town   Bolton, Lancs.
Enlisted at Bolton on 16/06/69
Aged 19 years, Ht. 5 ft 7 1/2 ins
Complexion fair, Eyes brown
Hair brown, Trade Labourer
Joined Regiment 18/06/69 at Fleetwood
To Depot 09/09/85
Discharged 13/07/89

1930 Private DAY William
Born: Parish Willingham
Town   Newmarket, Cambs.
Enlisted at Cambridge on 02/04/72
Aged 25 years 6 months, Ht. 5 ft 5 3/4 ins
Complexion fresh, Eyes grey
Hair black, Trade Labourer
Joined Regiment not known
Transferred to Army Reserve 04/10/79

1119 Private DEACON William
Born: Parish St. Paul's
Town   Bristol, Somerset
Enlisted at Bristol on 17/08/67
Aged 20 years, Ht. 5 ft 5 1/4 ins
Complexion fresh, Eyes hazel
Hair brown, Trade Baker
Joined Regiment 11/11/67 at Aldershot
Discharged Invalid 09/11/86

1115 Private DELANEY Michael
Born: Parish Callan
Town   Callan, Kilkenny
Enlisted at Kilkenny on 03/05/58
Aged 18 years 4 months, Ht. 5 ft 5 3/4 ins
Complexion fresh, Eyes grey
Hair dark brown, Trade Labourer
Joined Regiment 01/06/77 at South Africa
Discharged 04/11/79

1971 Private DOE Joseph
Born: Parish
Town
County
Enlisted at
Aged   years   months, Ht. ft   ins
Complexion   Eyes
Hair
Trade
Joined Regiment

1524 Private CULLEN Peter
Born: Parish
Town
County
Enlisted at
Aged   years months, Ht. ft ins
Complexion   Eyes
Hair   Religion
Trade
Joined Regiment

232 Private CULLEN Michael
Born: Parish Burslem
Town   Burslem, Staffs.
Enlisted at Hanley on 21/02/74
Aged 22 years, Ht. 5 ft 5 1/4 ins
Complexion brown, Eyes dark brown
Hair dark brown, Trade Forgeman
Joined Regiment 04/11/74 at Hong Kong
Transferred to Army Reserve 21/01/81

209 Private DANIELS William
Born: Parish Portway
Town   Oldbury, Worcs.
Enlisted at Wednesbury on 09/02/74
Aged 19 years 11 months, Ht. 5 ft 6 5/8 ins
Complexion dark, Eyes grey
Hair dark brown, Trade Labourer
Joined Regiment 23/02/76 at Singapore
Deserted 15/07/77
Transferred to Army Reserve 17/06/80

1312 Private DAVIS William
Born: Parish Wallasey
Town   Wallasey, Lancs.
Enlisted at Liverpool on 01/07/69
Aged 22 years, Ht. 5 ft 6 1/4 ins
Complexion fresh, Eyes grey
Hair brown, Trade Labourer
Joined Regiment 08/07/69 at Fleetwood

19/1042 Private DAY Alfred
Born: Parish Bicester
Town   Bicester, Oxon.
Enlisted at Birmingham on 28/05/77
Aged 19 years 11 months, Ht. 5 ft 6 3/8 ins
Complexion sallow, Eyes hazel
Hair light brown, Trade Labourer
Joined Regiment 13/06/77
at Cape of Good Hope
Served in "A" Company
Killed in Action 12/03/79 Intombi River

1464 Private DEMPSEY Andrew
Born: Parish Cavan
Town   Cavan, Cavan
Enlisted at Belfast on 10/11/70
Aged 18 years 1 months, Ht. 5 ft 6 ins
Complexion fresh, Eyes grey
Hair brown, Religion R.C.
Trade Labourer
Joined Regiment 10/11/70 at Belfast
Transferred to Army Reserve 27/08/81

1361 Private DERMOTT James
Born: Parish Worcester
Town   Worcester, Worcs.
Enlisted at Birmingham on 24/08/70
Aged 18 years 5 months, Ht. 5 ft 5 1/4 ins
Complexion fresh, Eyes hazel
Hair light brown, Religion R.C.
Trade Labourer
Joined Regiment 31/08/70 at Belfast
To 19th Brigade Depot 01/12/80

19/953 Private DODD John
Born: Parish Melpas
Town   Malpas, Cheshire
Enlisted at Manchester on 20/02/77
Aged 18 years, Ht. 5 ft 4 3/4 ins
Complexion dark, Eyes dark
Hair dark brown, Trade Labourer
Joined Regiment 13/06/77
at Cape of Good Hope
Served in "A" Company
Killed in Action 12/03/79 Intombi River

1330 Private DOYLE Augustine
(Nominal Roll 1330 DOYLE Augustin)
Born: Parish Kilkerrin
Town   Tuam, Galway
Enlisted at Manchester on 09/12/69
Aged 21 years, Ht. 5 ft 6 1/4 ins
Complexion fresh, Eyes dark brown
Hair dark brown, Trade Labourer
Joined Regiment not known

1076 Private DOLLIN Robert
Born: Parish   Dunster
Town   Dunster, Somerset
Enlisted at Taunton on 11/02/67
Aged 18 years 9 months, Ht. 5 ft 5 ins
Complexion fair, Eyes blue
Hair dark brown, Trade Upholsterer
Joined Regiment 12/02/67 at Devonport
Transferred to 3/60th Rifles 01/03/80

1071 Private DONE Benjamin
Born: Parish   St. Mary's
Town   Bilston, Staffs.
Enlisted at Bilston on 08/06/78
Aged 18 years 5 months, Ht. 5 ft 6 ins
Complexion sallow, Eyes brown
Hair brown, Religion C.E.
Trade Miner
Joined Regiment 03/12/78
at Pretoria, South Africa
To Depot 20/06/89
(Refer to new Army No. 2638)

274 Private DUDLEY Joseph
Born: Parish   Dudley
Town   Dudley, Worcs.
Enlisted at Lichfield on 11/04/74
Aged 19 years 6 months, Ht. 5 ft 6 1/2 ins
Complexion fair, Eyes grey
Hair brown, Trade Miner
Joined Regiment 23/02/76 at Singapore
Transferred to Army Reserve 24/06/80

1616 Private DUFFY Michael
Born: Parish   Brusilenyel
Town   Newport, Mayo
Enlisted at Stafford on 12/01/71
Aged 23 years, Ht. 5 ft 6 ins
Complexion light brown, Eyes hazel
Hair light brown, Religion R.C.
Trade Labourer
Joined Regiment 20/01/71 at Belfast
Served in "A" Company

2079 Private DUMBLETON Benjamin
Born: Parish   St. Pancras
Town   London, Middlesex
Enlisted at Westminster on 03/06/72
Aged 19 years 11 months, Ht. 5 ft 4 3/4 ins
Complexion fair, Eyes grey
Hair sandy, Trade Iron Smith
Joined Regiment not known
Transferred to 2/21st Regiment 31/12/79

718 Private EDWARDS Edward
Born: Parish   Stoke
Town   Fenton, staffs.
Enlisted at Newcastle on 22/06/76
Aged 24 years 3 months Ht. 5 ft 6 1/2 ins
Complexion fresh, Eyes hazel
Hair brown, Trade Miner
Joined Regiment 03/12/78 at Pretoria, S.A.
Transferred to Army Reserve 26/01/83

379 Private EDWARDS Eli
Born: Parish   Tipton
Town   Dudley, Staffs.
Enlisted at Lichfield on 19/10/78
Aged 23 years, Ht. 5 ft 5 ins
Complexion ruddy, Eyes hazel
Hair brown, Trade Miner
Joined Regiment 03/12/78
at Pretoria, South Africa
Transferred to Army Reserve 17/05/82

1624 Private EDWARDS Robert
Born: Parish   Liverpool
Town   Liverpool, Lancs.
Enlisted at Liverpool on 12/01/71
Aged 18 years, Ht. 5 ft 5 ins
Complexion fair, Eyes grey
Hair light, Religion C.E.
Trade Printer
Joined Regiment 20/01/71 at Belfast
Transferred to Army Reserve 27/08/81

84 Private ELLISON Robert
Born: Parish   York
Town   York, Yorks.
Enlisted at Birmingham on 19/08/73
Aged 22 years 8 months, Ht. 5 ft 5 3/4 ins
Complexion fair, Eyes grey
Hair brown, Trade Confectioner
Joined Regiment 04/11/74 at Hong Kong
Transferred to Army Reserve 25/10/79

243 Private DRINKWATER Enoch
Born: Parish   Worcester
Town   Worcester, Worcs.
Enlisted at Birmingham on 05/03/74
Aged 22 years, Ht. 5 ft 6 3/4 ins
Complexion fresh, Eyes grey
Hair brown, Trade Fruiterer
Joined Regiment 04/11/76 at Hong Kong
Transferred to Army Reserve 24/06/80

2005 Private DUDLEY Alfred
Born: Parish   Crawley
Town   Crawley, Sussex
Enlisted at Horley on 15/05/72
Aged 20 years 9 months, Ht. 5 ft 4 1/2 ins
Complexion dark, Eyes brown
Hair not known, Trade None
Joined Regiment not known
Transferred to Army Reserve 04/10/79

507 Private DUNN Charles
Born: Parish   Thornton
Town   Thornton, Leics.
Enlisted at Newcastle Under Lyme
on 13/06/59
Aged 18 years, Ht. 5 ft 4 ins
Complexion fresh, Eyes hazel
Hair brown, Religion Protestant
Trade Labourer
Joined Regiment 28/01/61
at Saugor (Central India)
Discharged 20/07/80

260 Private DUTTON John Henry
Born: Parish   Birmingham
Town   Birmingham, Warks.
Enlisted at Birmingham on 26/03/74
Aged 23 years 10 months, Ht. 5 ft 5 1/4 ins
Complexion fresh, Eyes hazel
Hair dark brown, Trade Silver Plater
Joined Regiment 04/11/74 at Hong Kong
Served in "A" Company
Killed in Action 12/03/79 Intombi River

794 Private EADY John
Born: Parish   Crookes
Town   Sheffield, Yorks.
Enlisted at Manchester on 18/09/76
Aged 20 years, Ht. 5 ft 5 1/4 ins
Complexion fresh, Eyes blue
Hair brown, Trade Clerk
Joined Regiment 13/06/77
at Cape of Good Hope
Transferred to 3/60th Rifles 01/03/80

1035 Private EDWARDS William
Born: Parish   Oldbury
Town   Oldbury, Worcs.
Enlisted at Walsall on 28/05/77
Aged 18 years, Ht. 5 ft 4 5/8 ins
Complexion fresh, Eyes grey
Hair dark brown, Trade Labourer
Joined Regiment 13/06/77 at Cape of Good Hope
Deserted 08/01/80, To Depot 19/08/82

1141 Private EDWARDS William
Born: Parish   Sawbridgeworth
Town   Bishop's Stortford, Herts.
Enlisted at Bishop's Stortford on 15/02/68
Aged 18 years, Ht. 5 ft 8 ins
Complexion fair, Eyes grey
Hair fair, Religion C.E.
Trade Labourer
Joined Regiment 22/02/68 at Aldershot
To Depot 21/01/82 (Refer to new Army No 2632)

421 Private ELEY Frederick
Born: Parish   St. John's
Town   Stafford, Staffs.
Enlisted at Lichfield on 30/11/74
Aged 18 years 3 months, Ht. 5 ft 6 1/4 ins
Complexion fresh, Eyes dark hazel
Hair dark brown, Trade Shoe Maker
Joined Regiment 03/12/78
at Pretoria, South Africa
Transferred to Army Reserve 30/11/80

214 Private EVENS George
(Nominal Roll 214 EVANS George)
Born: Parish   Edgmond.
Town   Newport, Shrops.
Enlisted at Hanley on 10/2/74
Aged 19 years 8 months, Ht. 5 ft 4 3/4 ins
Complexion fresh, Eyes grey
Hair brown, Trade Labourer
Joined Regiment 23/02/76 at Singapore
Transferred to Army Reserve 17/06/80

143 Private ENGLAND William
Born: Parish St. Mary's
Town Stafford, Staffs.
Enlisted at Lichfield on 01/10/73
Aged 18 years, Ht. 5 ft 7 1/4 ins
Complexion fair, Eyes blue
Hair light brown, Trade Riveter
Joined Regiment 18/01/77 at Singapore
Transferred to Army Reserve 18/06/80

1003 Private EVENS Even
(Nominal Roll 1003 EVANS Even)
Born: Parish Newtown
Town Newtown, Montgomery
Enlisted at Walsall on 08/05/77
Aged 19 years, Ht. 5 ft 5 3/4 ins
Complexion fresh, Eyes grey
Hair brown, Trade Miner
Joined Regiment 13/06/77
at Cape of Good Hope
Transferred to 38th Regiment 19/06/80

570 Private EVERITT William
(Nominal Roll 570 EVERETT William)
Born: Parish Messing
Town Colchester, Essex
Enlisted at Colchester on 11/10/65
Aged 18 years, Ht. 5 ft 4 3/4 ins
Complexion fresh, Eyes grey
Hair light brown, Trade Labourer
Joined Regiment 25/11/75 at Singapore
To Depot 18/11/85

1026 Private FALLON John
Born: Parish Walsall
Town Walsall, Staffs.
Enlisted at Lichfield on 26/05/77
Aged 19 years, Ht. 5 ft 4 1/2 ins
Complexion fresh, Eyes dark
Hair dark, Trade Puddler
Joined Regiment 13/06/77
at Cape of Good Hope
Deserted 18/08/79

1045 Private FALLON Josiah
Born: Parish St. Mary's
Town Lichfield, Staffs.
Enlisted at Lichfield on 01/06/77
Aged 19 years 9 months, Ht. 5 ft 5 ins
Complexion fair, Eyes dark brown
Hair sandy, Trade Painter
Joined Regiment 02/02/78 at South Africa
Transferred to Army Reserve 20/06/83

1114 Private FIELD Edward
Born: Parish
Town
County
Enlisted at
Aged years months, Ht. ft ins
Complexion Eyes
Hair Religion
Trade
Joined Regiment
Transferred to 91st Regt. (Date not known)

222 Private FINDLEY William
Born: Parish Manchester
Town Manchester, Lancs.
Enlisted at Manchester on 11/10/58
Aged 28 years, Ht. 5 ft 11 1/2 ins
Complexion fresh, Eyes hazel
Hair light brown, Trade Joiner
Joined Regiment 19/06/66 at Fort Freemantle, Devonport
Served in "C" Company
Killed in Action 12/03/79 Intombi River

520 Private FINN James
Born: Parish Stoke on Trent
Town Hanley, Staffs.
Enlisted at Newcastle under Lyme
on 21/06/75
Aged 19 years 10 months, Ht. 5 ft 5 1/4 ins
Complexion sallow, Eyes hazel
Hair dark brown, Trade Miner
Joined Regiment 13/06/77 at Cape of Good Hope
Transferred to Army Reserve 21/06/81

1286 Private FITZMORRIS Thomas
Born: Parish Liverpool
Town Liverpool, Lancs.
Enlisted at Liverpool on 17/06/69
Aged 20 years, Ht. 5 ft 6 3/4 ins
Complexion fresh, Eyes blue
Hair brown, Trade Carter
Joined Regiment 23/06/69 at Fleetwood
Discharged 20/07/89

713 Private EVENS Henry
(Nominal Roll 713 EVANS Henry)
Born: Parish Birmingham
Town Birmingham, Warks.
Enlisted at Birmingham on 20/06/76
Aged 19 years 6 months, Ht. 5 ft 5 3/4 ins
Complexion fresh, Eyes brown
Hair brown, Trade Labourer
Joined Regiment 13/06/77 at Cape of Good Hope
Transferred to Army Reserve 29/08/81

1074 Private EVENS John
(Nominal Roll 1074 EVANS John)
Born: Parish Darleston
Town Darleston, Staffs.
Enlisted at Walsall on 13/06/77
Aged 18 years, Ht. 5 ft 4 1/2 ins
Complexion sallow Eyes hazel
Hair light brown, Trade Miner
Joined Regiment 02/02/78 at South Africa
Transferred to 38th Regiment 19/06/80

1028 Private FARNELL William
Born: Parish Wednesbury
Town Wednesbury, Staffs.
Enlisted at Walsall on 29/05/77
Aged 19 years, Ht. 5 ft 5 ins
Complexion fresh, Eyes grey
Hair brown, Trade Labourer
Joined Regiment 13/06/77
at Cape of Good Hope
Served in "A" Company
Killed in Action 12/03/79 Intombi River

2019 Private FARRELL Patrick
Born: Parish Ashford
Town Wicklow, Wicklow
Enlisted at Dublin on 29/08/71
Aged 21 years, Ht. 5 ft 8 1/2 ins
Complexion fresh, Eyes hazel
Hair dark brown, Trade Dyer
Joined Regiment not known
Transferred to Army Reserve 04/10/79

467 Private FAWCETT Thomas
Born: Parish Richmond
Town Richmond, Staffs.
Enlisted at Walsall on 09/01/75
Aged 22 years, Ht. 5 ft 5 1/2 ins
Complexion light, Eyes grey
Hair light brown, Trade Labourer
Joined Regiment 02/02/78 at South Africa
Transferred to Army Reserve 12/01/81

1860 Private FINNEGAN Patrick
Born: Parish Killmegrow
Town Castlewellan, Down
Enlisted at Belfast on 08/12/71
Aged 23 years, Ht. 5 ft 6 1/4 ins
Complexion fresh, Eyes blue
Hair light brown, Trade Baker
Joined Regiment 09/12/71 at Belfast
Transferred to Army Reserve 01/10/79

230 Private FISHER John
Born: Parish Wolverhampton
Town Wolverhampton, Staffs.
Enlisted at Wolverhampton on 21/02/74
Aged 20 years 6 months, Ht. 5 ft 6 1/8 ins
Complexion fresh, Eyes brown
Hair dark brown, Trade Miner
Joined Regiment 23/02/76 at Singapore
Transferred to Army Reserve 18/06/80

1947 Private FISHER Thomas
Born: Parish Liverpool
Town Liverpool, Lancs.
Enlisted at Westminster on 13/04/72
Aged 24 years 7 months, Ht. 5 ft 5 ins
Complexion fair, Eyes hazel
Hair brown, Trade Shoe Maker
Joined Regiment not known
Transferred to Army Reserve 04/10/79

1695 Private FLEWITT James
Born: Parish Ombersley
Town Droitwich, Worcs.
Enlisted at Stourbridge on 01/02/71
Aged 20 years, Ht. 5 ft 6 ins
Complexion fresh, Eyes grey
Hair dark brown, Religion C.E.
Trade Groom
Joined Regiment 13/02/71 at Belfast
Discharged by Purchase 17/07/80

604 Private FITZPATRICK Patrick T.
Born: Parish   Poerstown
Town   Clonmel, Tipperary
Enlisted at Westminster on 24/02/72
Aged 19 years 6 months, Ht. 5 ft 6 ins
Complexion fresh, Eyes hazel
Hair brown, Trade Porter Trade Labourer
Joined Regiment 28/01/61 at Saugor (Central India)
Transferred to 91st Highlanders 31/03/80

233 Private FLETCHER James
Born: Parish   Burslem
Town   Burslem, Staffs.
Enlisted at Hanley on 20/02/74
Aged 19 years 6 months, Ht. 5 ft 4 3/4 ins
Complexion brown, Eyes grey
Hair dark brown, Trade Potter
Joined Regiment 23/02/76 at Singapore
Transferred to Army Reserve 18/06/80

785 Private FLYNN Robert
Born: Parish Newcastle Under Lyme
Town Newcastle Under Lyme, Staffs
.Enlisted at Stafford on 30/08/76
Aged 22 years, Ht. 5 ft 5 3/4 ins
Complexion fresh, Eyes grey
Hair brown, Trade Collier
Joined Regiment 17/11/76 at Singapore
Discharged 17/08/80

490 Private FODEN Joseph
Born: Parish   Stoke
Town   Longton, Staffs.
Enlisted at Newcastle on 20/05/75
Aged 19 years, Ht. 5 ft 5 3/4 ins
Complexion fresh, Eyes hazel
Hair light brown, Trade Potter
Joined Regiment 25/11/75 at Singapore
Transferred to Army Reserve 25/05/81

613 Private FOLLOWS George
Born: Parish   Rugby
Town   Stafford, Staffs.
Enlisted at Lichfield on 03/01/76
Aged 19 years 6 months, Ht. 5 ft 6 1/2 ins
Complexion fresh, Eyes grey
Hair sandy, Trade Miner
Joined Regiment 02/02/78 at South Africa
Transferred to Army Reserve 10/03/82

778 Private FOSTER William
Born: Parish   Stoke on Trent
Town   Longton, Staffs.
Enlisted at Newcastle Under Lyme
on 22/08/76
Aged 18 years 6 months, Ht. 5 ft 5 ins
Complexion fresh, Eyes hazel
Hair brown, Trade Miner
Joined Regiment 13/06/77
at Cape of Good Hope
Transferred to Army Reserve 26/01/83

1597 Private FOULK John
Born: Parish   Hodnet
Town   Market Drayton, Shrops.
Enlisted at Shrewsbury on 03/01/71
Aged 18 years 6 months, Ht. 5 ft 9 ins
Complexion fresh, Eyes grey
Hair brown, Religion Wesleyan
Trade Labourer
Joined Regiment 16/01/71 at Belfast
(Refer to new Army No. 459)

1030 Private FOX John
Born: Parish   St. John's
Town   Tamworth, Warks.
Enlisted at Lichfield on 29/05/77
Aged 21 years, Ht. 5 ft 6 ins
Complexion fresh, Eyes blue
Hair light brown, Trade Weaver
Joined Regiment 13/06/77
at Cape of Good Hope
Transferred to 38th Regt. (Date not known)

677 Private FRIGHNEY Robert
Born: Parish   Mallow
Town   Mallow, Cork
Enlisted at Buttevant on 17/02/60
Aged 19 years, Ht. 5 ft 5 1/2 ins
Complexion sallow, Eyes dark grey
Hair brown, Religion R.C.
Trade Labourer
Joined Regiment 28/01/61
at Saugor (Central India)
To 19th Brigade Depot 01/12/80

1892 Private FLOYD Joseph
Born: Adelaide Australia
Enlisted at Clonmel on 14/07/59
Aged 18 years, Ht. 5 ft 3 ins
Complexion fresh, Eyes grey
Hair brown, Religion R.C.
Joined Regiment not known
Served in "H" Company
Killed in Action 04/07/79 Ulundi

19/176 Private FLYFIELD William
Born: Parish   Bilston
Town   Wolverhampton, Staffs.
Enlisted at Dudley on 07/01/74
Aged 23 years, Ht. 5 ft 7 ins
Complexion pallid, Eyes hazel
Hair light brown, Trade Labourer
Joined Regiment 04/11/74 at Hong Kong
Served in "A" Company
Killed in Action 12/03/79 Intombi River

812 Private FORD James
Born: Parish   Wolverhampton
Town   Wolverhampton, Staffs
Enlisted at Wolverhampton on 11/10/76
Aged 20 years 10 months, Ht. 5 ft 5 1/4 ins
Complexion fresh, Eyes grey
Hair dark brown, Trade Galvaniser
Joined Regiment 03/12/78 at Pretoria, S.A.
Transferred to Army Reserve 27/01/73

340 Private FORD Thomas
Born: Parish   Newcastle
Town   Newcastle, Staffs.
Enlisted at Hanley on 16/09/74
Aged 18 years 6 months, Ht. 5 ft 5 ins
Complexion fresh, Eyes grey
Hair light, Trade Potter
Joined Regiment 23/02/76 at Singapore
Transferred to Army Reserve 18/09/80

1820 Private FOSTER Robert
Born: Parish   Liverpool
Town   Liverpool, Lancs.
Enlisted at Liverpool on 26/10/71
Aged 19 years, Ht. 5 ft 6 5/8 ins
Complexion fair, Eyes brown
Hair light brown, Trade Labourer
Joined Regiment 31/10/71 at Belfast
Transferred to Army Reserve 29/03/79

1465 Private FOX William
Born: Parish   Leek
Town   Leek, Staffs.
Enlisted at Newcastle Under Lyme
on 08/11/70
Aged 19 years, Ht. 5 ft 63/4 ins
Complexion fresh, Eyes grey
Hair brown, Religion C.E.
Trade Collier
Joined Regiment 19/06/70 at Belfast
Served in "A" Company
Killed in Action 12/03/79 Intombi River

2080 Private FRANCIS James
Born: Parish   Hammersmith
Town   London, Middlesex
Enlisted at Westminster on 08/06/72
Aged 24 years, Ht. 5 ft 5 3/4 ins
Complexion fair, Eyes grey
Hair brown, Trade Clerk
Joined Regiment not known
Transferred to Army Reserve 09/09/79

1918 Private FRICKER Joseph
Born: Parish   Dartford
Town   Dartford, Kent
Enlisted at Woolwich on 14/03/72
Aged 20 years, Ht. 5 ft 6 1/2 ins
Complexion swarthy, Eyes hazel
Hair dark brown, Trade Labourer
Joined Regiment not known
Transferred to Army Reserve 04/10/79

2089 Private FURNESS Albert
Born: Parish   Brighouse
Town   Bradford, Yorks.
Enlisted at Warrington on 11/06/72
Aged 21 years 2 months, Ht. 5 ft 6 1/2 ins
Complexion light, Eyes hazel
Hair brown, Trade Wire Drawer
Joined Regiment not known
Transferred to Army Reserve 04/10/79

151 Private FRYER William
(Nominal Rolls
151 FRYER William George)
Born: Parish   Wickham
Town   Canterbury, Kent Enlisted at Canterbury on 13/11/73
Aged 18 years 6 months, Ht. 5 ft 5 1/2 ins
Complexion fresh Eyes blue
Hair light brown, Trade Labourer
Joined Regiment 23/02/76 at Singapore
Transferred to Army Reserve 18/06/80

1449 Private FULTON William
Born: Parish   Tartaraghan
Town   Portadown, Armagh
Enlisted at Portadown on 22/10/70
Aged 18 years, Ht. 5 ft 5 1/2 ins
Complexion fresh, Eyes brown
Hair dark brown, Religion C.E.
Trade Weaver
Joined Regiment 02/11/70 at Belfast
Transferred to Army Reserve 30/08/81

2015 Private GARDINER Charles
Born: Parish   Bethnal Green
Town   London, Middlesex
Enlisted at Westminster on 24/05/72
Aged 24 years 11 months, Ht. 5 ft 5 3/4 ins
Complexion fresh, Eyes hazel
Hair brown, Trade Paper Hanger
Joined Regiment not known
Transferred to Army Reserve 04/10/79

469 Private GIBLIN Charles
Born: Parish   Tamworth
Town   Tamworth, Warks.
Enlisted at Lichfield on 14/01/75
Aged 19 years, Ht. 5 ft 6 1/2 ins
Complexion fresh, Eyes grey
Hair light brown, Trade Collier
Joined Regiment 03/12/78 at Pretoria,
South Africa
Transferred to Army Reserve 12/04/81

173 Private GIBSON John
Born: Parish   Wiginton
Town   Wiginton, Warks.
Enlisted at Walsall on 06/01/74
Aged 19 years, Ht. 5 ft 5 ins
Complexion fresh, Eyes brown
Hair brown, Trade Labourer
Joined Regiment 23/04/76 at Singapore
Transferred to Army Reserve 17/06/80

699 Private GODWIN William
Born: Parish   Portsmouth
Town   Portsmouth, Hamps.
Enlisted at Walsall on 22/05/71
Aged 18 years, Ht. 5 ft 5 ins
Complexion fresh, Eyes blue
Hair auburn, Trade Painter
Joined Regiment 13/06/77
at Cape of Good Hope
Transferred to Army Reserve 29/08/81

1182 Private GRANT John
Born: Parish   Bristol
Town   Bristol, Glos.
Enlisted at Aldershot on 21/08/68
Aged 20 years, Ht. 5 ft 5 1/2 ins
Complexion fresh, Eyes grey
Hair dark brown, Trade Labourer
Joined Regiment 25/08/68 at Aldershot
Discharged free 27/09/83

603 Private GRATTON John
Born: Parish   Stoke on Trent
Town   Hanley, Staffs.
Enlisted at Newcastle on 20/12/75
Aged 18 years 7 months, Ht. 5 ft 6 ins
Complexion fresh, Eyes grey
Hair brown, Trade Miner
Joined Regiment 02/02/78 at South Africa
Transferred to Army Reserve 26/01/83

1463 Private GRIFFITHS Edward
Born: Parish   Chester
Town   Chester, Cheshire
Enlisted at Oldham on 03/11/70
Aged 20 years 11 months, Ht. 5 ft 5 1/4 ins
Complexion fresh, Eyes light grey
Hair brown, Religion C.E.
Trade Shoe Maker
Joined Regiment 11/11/70 at Belfast
Discharged 11/11/82

679 Private FURNESS Richard
Born: Parish   Wolstanton
Town   Tunstall, Staffs.
Enlisted at Newcastle Under Lyme 17/05/76
Aged 23 years, Ht. 5 ft 5 ins
Complexion fresh, Eyes hazel
Hair brown, Trade Potter
Joined Regiment 17/11/76 at Singapore
Transferred to Army Reserve 17/05/82

1925 Private FURNIAUX John
Born: Parish   Bethnal Green
Town   London, Middlesex
Enlisted at Westminster on 20/03/72
Aged 21 years 8 months, Ht. 5 ft 5 ins
Complexion fair, Eyes grey
Hair Light brown, Trade Tin Plate Worker
Joined Regiment not known
Served in "A" Company
Killed in Action 12/03/79 Intombi River

1335 Private GILLIGAN William
Born: Parish   Drumenllen
Town   Birr, Kings (Offally)
Enlisted at Birr on 01/01/70
Aged 14 years 4 months, Ht. 4 ft 7 ins
Complexion fresh, Eyes grey
Hair light brown, Trade None
Joined Regiment date not known
at Birr
Discharged free 07/08/83

19/500 Private GITTINS Edwin
Born: Parish   Clay Hill
Town   Ludlow, Shrops.
Enlisted at Walsall on 02/06/75
Aged 21 years, Ht. 5 ft 5 1/8 ins
Complexion fresh, Eyes grey
Hair light brown, Trade Collier
Joined Regiment 25/11/75 at Singapore
Served in "A" Company
Killed in Action 12/03/79 Intombi River

1901 Private GODDEN Thomas
Born: Parish   Portsmouth
Town   Portsmouth, Hamps.
Enlisted at Westminster on 06/03/72
Aged 23 years 9 months, Ht. 5 ft 6 3/4 ins
Complexion fresh, Eyes brown
Hair dark brown, Trade Clerk
Joined Regiment not known
Transferred to Army Reserve 04/10/79

743 Private GREATBACK James
Born: Parish   Tong
Town   Shifnal, Shrops.
Enlisted at Walsall on 27/07/76
Aged 19 years 2 months, Ht. 5 ft 6 3/4 ins
Complexion fresh, Eyes dark brown
Hair dark brown, Trade Engine Driver
Joined Regiment 13/06/77
at Cape of Good Hope
To 19th Brigade Depot 01/12/80

1697 Private GREEN Joseph
Born: Parish   Chesterfield
Town   Chesterfield, Derbs.
Enlisted at Chesterfield on 07/02/71
Aged 20 years 4 months, Ht. 5 ft 6 3/8 ins
Complexion pale, Eyes hazel
Hair light brown, Religion C.E.
Trade Collier
Joined Regiment 13/02/71 at Belfast
Served in "A" Company
Killed in Action 12/03/79 Intombi River

239 Private GREY William
(Nominal Roll 239 GRAY William)
Born: Parish   Willenhall
Town   Willenhall, Staffs.
Enlisted at Walsall on 02/03/74
Aged 23 years, Ht. 5 ft 5 1/4 ins
Complexion fresh, Eyes grey
Hair brown, Trade Stamper
Joined Regiment 04/11/74 at Hong Kong
Transferred to Army Reserve 06/01/81

1044 Private GUEST Joseph H.
Born: Parish   Aston
Town   Birmingham, Warks.
Enlisted at Lichfield on 31/05/77
Aged 18 years 9 months, Ht. 5 ft 5 3/8 ins
Complexion fair, Eyes blue
Hair dark, Trade Carpenter
Joined Regiment 13/06/77
at Cape of Good Hope
Discharged Invalid 20/12/81

1550 Private GRIFFITHS Henry
Born: Parish St. Julian's
Town Shrewsbury, Shrops.
Enlisted at Manchester on 28/12/70
Aged 19 years, Ht. 5 ft 5 1/2 ins
Complexion fresh, Eyes grey
Hair dark brown, Religion C.E.
Trade Carrier
Joined Regiment 02/01/71 at Belfast
Transferred to Army Reserve 30/08/81

836 Private GUBBINS Nicholas
Born: Parish St. Thomas's
Town Dublin, Dublin
Enlisted at Not known, on 28/03/59
Aged 18 years, Ht. 5 ft 3 ins
Complexion fresh, Eyes blue
Hair fair, Trade Labourer
Joined Regiment not known
Discharged 20/07/80

1031 Private GUTTEREDGE George
(Nominal Roll
1031 GUTALAGE George)
Born: Parish Willenhall
Town Willenhall, Staffs.
Enlisted at Walsall on 29/05/77
Aged 22 years, Ht. 5 ft 4 1/2 ins
Complexion fair, Eyes grey
Hair brown, Trade Lock Smith
Joined Regiment 13/06/77
at Cape of Good Hope
Transferred to 38th Regt. 19/06/80

368 Private GUY William
Born: Parish
Town
County
Enlisted at
Aged years months, Ht. ft ins
Complexion Eyes
Hair Religion
Trade
Joined Regiment

1176 Private HACKER William
Born: Parish Berrick
Town Lrusdon, Wilts.
Enlisted at Aldershot on 25/07/68
Aged 18 years 9 months, Ht. 5 ft 5 ins
Complexion fresh, Eyes blue
Hair red, Trade Labourer
Joined Regiment 28/07/68 at Aldershot
Discharged 26/07/89

538 Private HALE Charles
Born: Parish Loughborough
Town Moulton, Glos.
Enlisted at West Bromwich on 14/07/75
Aged 21 years 4 months, Ht. 5 ft 6 ins
Complexion fair, Eyes hazel
Hair light, Trade Labourer
Joined Regiment 25/11/75 at Singapore
Transferred to Army Reserve 27/07/81

539 Private HALE William
Born: Parish Loughborough
Town Moulton, Glos.
Enlisted at West Bromwich on 12/07/75
Aged 19 years 9 months, Ht. 5 ft 8 3/4 ins
Complexion dark, Eyes brown
Hair brown, Trade Labourer
Joined Regiment 25/11/75 at Singapore
Discharged by Purchase 14/02/86

580 Private HALFORD John
Born: Parish St. Mark's
Town Walsall, Staffs.
Enlisted at Lichfield on 03/12/75
Aged 19 years, Ht. 5 ft 6 3/4 ins
Complexion fresh, Eyes grey
Hair brown, Trade Collier
Joined Regiment 17/11/76 at Singapore
Transferred to Army Reserve 25/05/81

1859 Private HAMERTON Thomas Jas:
Born: Parish Coventry
Town Coventry, Warks.
Enlisted at Birmingham on 30/11/71
Aged 19 years, Ht. 5 ft 5 1/8 ins
Complexion fresh, Eyes grey
Hair dark brown, Trade Painter
Joined Regiment 08/12/71 at Belfast
Transferred to Army Reserve 14/10/79

1671 Private GUILFOY James
Born: Parish Mountrath
Town Mountrath, Queens (Laois)
Enlisted at Manchester on 23/01/71
Aged 22 years, Ht. 5 ft 5 3/4 ins
Complexion fresh, Eyes hazel
Hair dark brown, Trade Labourer
Joined Regiment 30/01/71 at Belfast
Discharged 1st Period 24/01/83

1999 Private GUTTEREGE Arthur
(Nominal Roll 1999 GUTTRIDGE Arthur)
Born: Parish Shoreditch
Town London, Middlesex
Enlisted at Westminster on 14/05/72
Aged 23 years, Ht. 5 ft 5 ins
Complexion fresh, Eyes blue
Hair brown, Trade Labourer
Joined Regiment not known
Transferred to Army Reserve 04/10/79

1502 Private HACKMAN Samuel
Born: Parish Chester
Town Chester, Cheshire
Enlisted at Liverpool on 01/12/70
Aged 21 years, Ht. 5 ft 6 3/8 ins
Complexion fresh, Eyes grey
Hair light brown, Religion C.E.
Trade Labourer
Joined Regiment 04/12/70 at Belfast
Transferred to Army Reserve 29/08/81

19/536 Private HADLEY George
Born: Parish Gost Hill
Town Dudley, Worcs.
Enlisted at Birmingham on 12/07/75
Aged 22 years 6 months, Ht. 5 ft 6 3/4 ins
Complexion sallow, Eyes brown
Hair brown, Trade Labourer
Joined Regiment 25/11/75 at Singapore
Served in "A" Company
Killed in Action 12/03/79 Intombi River

19/227 Private HAYNES George
(Nominal Roll 19/227 HAINES George)
Born: Parish Birmingham
Town Birmingham, Warks.
Enlisted at Birmingham on 20/02/74
Aged 23 years 4 months, Ht. 5 ft 6 1/4 ins
Complexion dark, Eyes hazel
Hair light brown, Trade Gunstock Maker
Joined Regiment 04/11/74 at Hong Kong
Served in "A" Company
Killed in Action 12/03/79 Intombi River

1777 Private HALL John
Born: Parish Sibstaff
Town Market Harborough, Leics.
Enlisted at Market Harborough on 19/09/71
Aged 24 years 8 months, Ht. 5 ft 6 1/8 ins
Complexion fresh, Eyes grey
Hair dark brown, Trade Labourer
Joined Regiment 28/09/71 at Belfast
Died 07/03/80

957 Private HALL William
Born: Parish Bury
Town Bury, Lancs.
Enlisted at Manchester on 09/03/77
Aged 23 years, Ht. 5 ft 8 1/4 ins
Complexion fair, Eyes blue
Hair fair, Trade Labourer
Joined Regiment 13/06/77
at Cape of Good Hope
To 38th Regiment 19/06/80

1812 Private HALLIGAN James
Born: Parish London
Town London, Middlesex
Enlisted at Liverpool on 24/10/71
Aged 19 years, Ht. 5 ft 6 1/8 ins
Complexion fresh, Eyes grey
Hair brown, Trade Mason
Joined Regiment 20/10/71 at Belfast
Deserted 16/06/74
Transferred to Army Reserve 11/10/79

492 Private HANDS William
Born: Parish Birmingham
Town Birmingham, Warks.
Enlisted at Birmingham on 20/05/75
Aged 18 years 5 months, Ht. 5 ft 7 ins
Complexion fresh, Eyes brown
Hair brown, Trade Jeweller
Joined Regiment 13/06/77
at Cape of Good Hope
Transferred to Army Reserve 25/05/87

1513 Private HAMMONDS Francis
Born: Parish   Sand Mary
Town   Shrewsbury, Shrops.
Enlisted at Shrewsbury on 09/12/70
Aged 19 years 8 months, Ht. 5 ft 5 1/2 ins
Complexion fresh, Eyes hazel
Hair brown, Religion C.E.
Trade Butcher
Joined Regiment 13/12/70 at Belfast
Discharged by Purchase 05/08/80

281 Private HANDCOX Joseph
Born: Parish   Tipton
Town   Tipton,Staffs.
Enlisted at Newcastle Under Lyme
on 15/04/74
Aged 19 years 6 months, Ht. 5 ft 4 1/2 ins
Complexion fresh, Eyes blue
Hair brown, Trade Mechanic
Joined Regiment 23/02/76 at Singapore
Transferred to Army Reserve 24/06/80

121 Private HARPER Josiah
Born: Parish   Birmingham
Town   Birmingham,Warks.
Enlisted at Birmingham on 15/09/73
Aged 20 years 8 months, Ht. 5 ft 5 ins
Complexion fresh,
Eyes brown,
Hair dark brown, Trade Labourer
Joined Regiment 04/11/74 at Hong Kong
Transferred to Army Reserve 04/10/79

643 Private HARRIS Henry
Born: Parish   Astwood Bank
Town   Astwood Bank, Worcs.
Enlisted at Walsall on 18/01/76
Aged 18 years, Ht. 5 ft 5 ins
Complexion sandy, Eyes blue
Hair sandy, Trade Labourer
Joined Regiment 02/02/78 at South Africa
Transferred to Army Reserve 03/02/82

1824 Private HART George
Born: Parish St. Patrick's
Town Manchester,Lancs.
Enlisted at Manchester on 27/10/71
Aged 21 years, Ht. 5 ft 6 1/4 ins
Complexion fresh, Eyes grey
Hair dark brown, Trade Mechanic
Joined Regiment 04/11/71 at Belfast
Transferred to Army Reserve 04/10/79

1073 Private HATTON Frederick
Born: Parish   Walsall
Town   Walsall, Staffs.
Enlisted at Walsall on 06/06/77
Aged 18 years, Ht. 5 ft 4 3/8 ins
Complexion fresh, Eyes hazel
Hair brown, Trade Labourer
Joined Regiment 02/02/78 at South Africa
To 1st Battalion 19/09/85
Transferred to Army Reserve 04/10/87

19/999 Private HAWKES Eli
Born: Parish   St. Mary's
Town   Redditch, Worcs.
Enlisted at Wolverhampton on 08/05/77
Aged 19 years 5 months, Ht. 5 ft 6 1/4 ins
Complexion fresh, Eyes blue
Hair light, Trade Bricklayer
Joined Regiment 13/06/77
at Cape of Good Hope
Served in "A" Company
Killed in Action 12/03/79 Intombi River

147 Private HAWKINS William
Born: Parish   Birmingham
Town   Birmingham, Warks.
Enlisted at Birmingham on 29/09/73
Aged 19 years 4 months, Ht. 5 ft 5 1/8 ins
Complexion fresh, Eyes grey
Hair dark brown, Trade Striker
Joined Regiment 04/11/74 at Hong Kong
Transferred to Army Reserve 18/06/80

235 Private HAYWOOD Joseph
(Nominal Roll 235 HAYWARD Joseph)
Born: Parish   Church Aston
Town   Newport, Shrops.
Enlisted at Hanley on 25/02/74
Aged 23 years, Ht. 5 ft 5 1/2 ins
Complexion fair, Eyes dark
Hair dark brown, Trade Bricklayer
Joined Regiment 04/11/74 at Hong Kong
Transferred to Army Reserve 25/06/80

702 Private HANNON John
(Nominal Roll 702 HANNEN John)
Born: Parish   St. Mary's
Town   Manchester, Lancs.
Enlisted at Lichfield on 10/06/76
Aged 23 years, Ht. 5 ft 5 ins
Complexion fair, Eyes hazel
Hair dark brown, Trade Labourer
Joined Regiment 17/11/76 at Singapore
Deserted at Potchefstroom
South Africa 09/01/80

512 Private HARBATTLE George
Born: Parish   Beverley
Town   Beverley, Yorks.
Enlisted at Hanley on 22/06/75
Aged 20 years, Ht. 5 ft 5 3/4 ins
Complexion fresh, Eyes brown
Hair brown, Trade Farm Labourer
Joined Regiment 25/11/75 at Singapore
To 38th Regiment 19/06/80

2008 Private HART Julian
Born: Parish   Cirencester
Town   Cirencester, Glos.
Enlisted at Westminster on 20/05/72
Aged 21 years 11 months, Ht. 5 ft 6 1/8 ins
Complexion fair, Eyes grey
Hair brown, Trade Shopman
Joined Regiment not known
Served in "C" Company
Killed in Action 12/03/79 Intombi River

135 Private HARTRICK William
Born: Parish   Shrewsbury
Town   Shrewsbury, Shrops.
Enlisted at Wolverhampton on 24/09/73
Aged 23 years, Ht. 5 ft 5 ins
Complexion fresh, Eyes grey
Hair brown, Trade Brazier
Joined Regiment 04/11/74 at Hong Kong
Transferred to Army Reserve 18/06/80

1816 Private HARVEY John
Born: Parish   Birmingham
Town   Birmingham, Warks.
Enlisted at Birmingham on 17/10/71
Aged 20 years, Ht. 5 ft 5 3/8 ins
Complexion fair, Eyes grey
Hair brown, Trade Gold Beater
Joined Regiment 30/10/71 at Belfast
Transferred to Army Reserve 18/06/80

1951 Private HAYDEN George
Born: Parish   Great Morden
Town   Royston, Cambs.
Enlisted at Cambridge on 13/04/72
Aged 20 years 6 months, Ht. 5 ft 5 ins
Complexion fresh, Eyes grey
Hair dark brown, Trade Miller & Baker
Joined Regiment not known
Transferred to Army Reserve 04/10/79

1966 Private HAYES Dennis
(Nominal Roll 1966 HAYES Dennies)
Born: Parish   Winchester
Town   Winchester, Hamps.
Enlisted at Westminster on 09/04/72
Aged 20 years, Ht. 5 ft 6 ins
Complexion fresh, Eyes blue
Hair dark brown, Trade Labourer
Joined Regiment not known
Discharged 04/12/80

761 Private HAYWOOD Mark
Born: Parish   Darleston
Town   Darleston, Staffs.
Enlisted at Walsall on 16/08/76
Aged 18 years, Ht. 5 ft 6 1/2 ins
Complexion fresh, Eyes blue
Hair brown, Trade Miner
Joined Regiment 13/06/77
at Cape of Good Hope
Transferred to Army Reserve 26/01/83

1906 Private HERMAN George
Born: Parish   Lambeth
Town   London, Surrey
Enlisted at Westminster on 09/03/72
Aged 21 years, Ht. 5 ft 6 ins
Complexion fresh, Eyes grey
Hair brown, Trade Carpenter
Joined Regiment not known
Transferred to Army Reserve 04/10/79

19/783 Private HEALEY Thomas
Born: Parish   St. Mary's
Town   Dregheda, Neath
Enlisted at Dublin on 14/10/71
Aged 18 years, Ht. 5 ft 5 1/4 ins
Complexion sallow, Eyes grey
Hair brown, Trade Labourer
Joined Regiment 04/07/74 at Singapore
Served in "A" Company
Killed in Action 12/03/79 Intombi River

599   Private HEATH William
Born: Parish   Stoke on Trent
Town   Longton, Staffs.
Enlisted at Hanley on 15/12/75
Aged 19 years 6 months, Ht. 5 ft 6 3/4 ins
Complexion fresh, Eyes brown
Hair sandy, Trade Blacksmith's Striker
Joined Regiment 17/11/76 at Singapore
Transferred to 38th Regt. (Date not known)

256   Private HILL Thomas
Born: Parish   Leigh
Town   Malvern, Worcs.
Enlisted at Lichfield on 21/03/74
Aged 19 years 6 months, Ht. 5 ft 4 3/4 ins
Complexion fair, Eyes grey
Hair light brown, Trade Labourer
Joined Regiment 03/12/78
at Pretoria, South Africa
Transferred to Army Reserve 30/08/81

721   Private HILL Thomas
Born: Parish   Portobello
Town   Willenhall, Staffs.
Enlisted at Lichfield on 28/06/76
Aged 24 years, Ht. 5 ft 7 1/4 ins
Complexion fresh, Eyes brown
Hair brown, Trade Labourer
Joined Regiment 17/11/76 at Singapore
To 1st Battalion 04/10/81
To 1st Battalion 19/09/85

1068 Private HILL Thomas
Born: Parish   Birmingham
Town   Birmingham, Warks.
Enlisted at Walsall on 12/06/77
Aged 18 years 1 months, Ht. 5 ft 5 3/4 ins
Complexion fair, Eyes brown
Hair light, Trade Labourer
Joined Regiment 02/02/78 at South Africa
To 38th Regiment 19/06/80

881   Private HOCKLEY Philip
Born: Parish   Wolverhampton
Town   Wolverhampton, Staffs.
Enlisted at Wolverhampton on 04/11/76
Aged 18 years 10 months, Ht. 5 ft 6 3/4 ins
Complexion fresh, Eyes hazel
Hair dark brown, Trade Labourer
Joined Regiment 03/12/78
at Pretoria, South Africa
To 38th Regiment 19/06/81

709   Private HODGES Thomas
Born: Parish   Little Whitley
Town   Stourport, Worcs.
Enlisted at Worcester on 23/05/60
Aged 23 years, Ht. 5 ft 4 3/4 ins
Complexion fresh, Eyes brown
Hair dark brown, Trade Labourer
Joined Regiment 28/01/61
at Saugor (Central India)
Served in "A" Company
Killed in Action 12/03/79 Intombi River

740   Private HOGAN Martin
Born: Parish   Newcastle
Town   Newcastle, Staffs.
Enlisted at Newcastle on 24/07/76
Aged 18 years 11 months, Ht. 5 ft 5 ins
Complexion fresh, Eyes grey
Hair brown, Trade Labourer
Joined Regiment 13/06/77
at Cape of Good Hope
Discharged Invalid 18/04/82

29 Private HOLMES James
Born: Parish   Pelsall
Town   Walsall, Staffs.
Enlisted at Walsall on 07/05/73
Aged 20 years 8 months, Ht. 5 ft 6 3/4 ins
Complexion fair, Eyes grey
Hair light brown, Trade Labourer
Joined Regiment 04/11/74 at Hong Kong
Transferred to Army Reserve 25/10/79

167 Private HERRYMAN Ephraim
Born: Parish   Instock
Town   Newport, Shrops.
Enlisted at Newcastle Under Lyme
on 02/01/74
Aged 18 years 8 months, Ht. 5 ft 8 3/4 ins
Complexion fresh, Eyes dark hazel
Hair brown, Trade Labourer
Joined Regiment 23/02/76 at Singapore
Transferred to Army Reserve 25/06/80

19/1021 Private HILL Henry
Born: Parish   Rugeley
Town   Rugeley, Staffs.
Enlisted at Lichfield on 20/05/77
Aged 18 years 7 months, Ht. 5 ft 5 1/2 ins
Complexion fresh, Eyes brown
Hair brown, Trade Collier
Joined Regiment 13/06/77 at Cape of Good Hope
Served in "A" Company
Killed in Action 12/03/79 Intombi River

207 Private HINCE Thomas
Born: Parish   St. John's
Town   Chesterfield, Derbys.
Enlisted at Lichfield on 06/02/74
Aged 18 years, Ht. 5 ft 4 3/4 ins
Complexion fair, Eyes dark brown
Hair dark brown, Trade Collier
Joined Regiment 02/02/78 at South Africa
Transferred to Army Reserve 01/12/80

737 Private HING Thomas
Born: Parish   St. Saviour's
Town   London, Middlesex
Enlisted at Newcastle Under Lyme
on 22/07/76
Aged 22 years 5 months, Ht. 5 ft 5 3/4 ins
Complexion fresh, Eyes grey
Hair brown, Trade Miner
Joined Regiment 17/11/76 at Singapore
Transferred to Army Reserve 30/08/81

604 Private HIXON Henry
(Nominal Roll 604 HICKSON Henry)
Born: Parish   St. Luke's
Town   Wolverhampton, Staffs.
Enlisted at Wolverhampton on 20/12/75
Aged 19 years 2 months, Ht. 5 ft 6 ins
Complexion fresh, Eyes hazel
Hair dark brown, Trade Iron Brazier
Joined Regiment 17/11/76 at Singapore
To 38th Regiment 19/06/80

498 Private HOLDEN Samuel
Born: Parish   not known
Town   Dudley, Staffs.
Enlisted at Lichfield on 01/06/75
Aged 21 years, Ht. 5 ft 5 7/8 ins
Complexion fresh, Eyes grey
Hair light brown, Trade Miner
Joined Regiment 02/02/78 at South Africa
Transferred to Army Reserve 17/07/81

1433 Private HOLMAN Edwin
Born: Parish   Welford
Town   Northampton, Northants.
Enlisted at Leicester on 08/10/70
Aged 21 years, Ht. 5 ft 6 5/8 ins
Complexion fresh, Eyes hazel
Hair brown, Religion C.E.
Trade Labourer
Joined Regiment 21/10/70 at Belfast
Killed in Action 22/01/79 Isandhlwana

97   Private HOLMES Archibald
Born: Parish   Ellastone
Town   Stanton, Staffs.
Enlisted at Leek on 27/08/73
Aged 21 years, Ht. 5 ft 6 ins
Complexion fresh, Eyes hazel
Hair light brown, Trade Labourer
Joined Regiment 04/11/74 at Hong Kong
Transferred to Army Reserve 04/10/79

2083 Private HOPSON John
Born: Parish   Bethnal Green
Town   London, Middlesex
Enlisted at Westminster on 10/06/72
Aged 21 years, Ht. 5 ft 5 3/4 ins
Complexion fresh, Eyes grey
Hair brown, Trade Cabinet Maker
Joined Regiment not known
Transferred to Army Reserve 04/10/79

2094 Private HOPKINS William, Francis
Born: Parish St. Martin's
Town   London, Middlesex
Enlisted at Westminster on 06/03/72
Aged 19 years, Ht. 5 ft 5 ins
Complexion fresh, Eyes grey
Hair brown, Trade Labourer
Joined Regiment not known
Transferred to Army Reserve 04/10/79

979 Private HOPLEY William
Born: Parish Bilston
Town   Wolverhampton, Staffs.
Enlisted at Lichfield on 23/04/78
Aged 21 years 8 months, Ht. 5 ft 6 1/2 ins
Complexion fresh, Eyes grey
Hair brown, Trade Miner
Joined Regiment 02/02/78 at South Africa
To 38th Regiment 19/06/80

1720 Private HOWARD Charles
Born: Parish Loughborough
Town   Loughborough, Leics.
Enlisted at Loughborough on 11/04/71
Aged 20 years, Ht. 5 ft 5 3/4 ins
Complexion fair, Eyes brown
Hair brown, Religion C.E.
Trade Labourer
Joined Regiment 26/04/71 at Belfast
To 19th Brigade Depot 01/12/80

1945 Private HOWARD Frank
Born: Parish Lambeth
Town   London, Surrey
Enlisted at Westminster on 12/04/72
Aged 23 years 3 months Ht. 5 ft 7 ins
Complexion fair, Eyes hazel
Hair brown, Trade Piano Forte Maker
Joined Regiment not known
Transferred to Army Reserve 04/10/79

543 Private HOWARD Henry
Born: Parish Hinton
Town   Brackley, Northants.
Enlisted at Wednesbury on 23/07/75
Aged 24 years 9 months, Ht. 5 ft 7 1/8 ins
Complexion grey, Eyes brown
Hair brown, Trade Groom
Joined Regiment 25/11/75 at Singapore
Transferred to Army Reserve 26/01/82

552 Private HUGHES James
Born: Parish King's Norton
Town   King's Norton, Staffs.
Enlisted at Lichfield on 30/07/75
Aged 19 years 4 months, Ht. 5 ft 6 3/4 ins
Complexion fair, Eyes blue
Hair light brown, Trade Brickmaker
Joined Regiment 02/02/78 at South Africa
Transferred to Army Reserve 11/07/82

1499 Private HUGHES John
Born: Parish Liverpool
Town   Liverpool, Lancs.
Enlisted at Liverpool on 01/12/70
Aged 18 years, Ht. 5 ft 5 1/2 ins
Complexion sallow, Eyes hazel
Hair light brown, Religion C.E.
Trade Labourer
Joined Regiment 04/12/70 at Belfast
Served in "B" Company
Killed in Action 12/03/79 Intombi River

1589 Private HUGHES Joseph
Born: Parish West Bromwich
Town   West Bromwich, Staffs.
Enlisted at Newcastle Under Lyme
on 05/01/71
Aged 19 years 7 months, Ht. 5 ft 5 1/4 ins
Complexion fresh, Eyes hazel
Hair brown, Religion C.E.
Trade Puddler
Joined Regiment 13/01/71 at Belfast
Transferred to Army Reserve 29/08/81

535 Private HUSSELBEE John
Born: Parish Settenhall
Town   Wolverhampton, Staffs.
Enlisted at Wolverhampton on 12/07/75
Aged 21 years 8 months, Ht. 5 ft 5 1/4 ins
Complexion fresh, Eyes hazel
Hair light brown, Trade Labourer
Joined Regiment 25/11/75 at Singapore
Transferred to Army Reserve 12/07/81

1522 Private HOUGH John
Born: Parish Newcastle Under Lyme
Town Newcastle Under Lyme, Staffs.
Enlisted at Newcastle Under Lyme
on 07/12/70
Aged 19 years, Ht. 5 ft 7 5/8 ins
Complexion fair, Eyes dark blue
Hair light brown, Religion Wesleyan Trade Labourer
Joined Regiment 15/12/70 at Belfast
Discharged 16/12/82

129 Private HOULT Edward
Born: Parish Longton
Town   Longton, Staffs.
Enlisted at Lichfield on 20/09/73
Aged 18 years 4 months, Ht. 5 ft 6 ins
Complexion fresh, Eyes hazel
Hair light brown, Trade Fitter
Joined Regiment 23/02/76 at Singapore
Transferred to Army Reserve 17/06/80

1721 Private HOWARD Owen
Born: Parish Loughborough
Town   Loughborough, Leics.
Enlisted at Loughborough on 12/04/71
Aged 18 years, Ht. 5 ft 5 1/4 ins
Complexion sallow, Eyes brown
Hair brown, Religion C.E.
Trade Labourer
Joined Regiment 26/04/71 at Belfast
To 19th Brigade Depot 01/12/80

2067 Private HOWES John
Born: Parish Lambeth
Town   London, Surrey
Enlisted at Westminster on 01/06/72
Aged 22 years 6 months, Ht. 5 ft 5 3/4 ins
Complexion fresh, Eyes grey
Hair dark brown, Trade Fireman
Joined Regiment not known
Transferred to Army Reserve 25/10/79

495 Private HUGHES Benjamin
Born: Parish Birmingham
Town   Birmingham, Warks.
Enlisted at Birmingham on 24/05/75
Aged 19 years, Ht. 5 ft 5 1/2 ins
Complexion fair, Eyes grey
Hair light brown, Trade Chandelier Maker
Joined Regiment 17/11/76 at Singapore
Transferred to Army Reserve 25/05/81

1898 Private HUNT Frederick
Born: Parish Alton
Town   Alton, Hamps.
Enlisted at Westminster on 29/02/72
Aged 24 years 11 months, Ht. 5 ft 5 ins
Complexion fresh, Eyes grey
Hair brown, Trade Labourer
Joined Regiment not known
Transferred to Army Reserve 04/10/79

1072 Private HURD Walter
Born: Parish Stoke on Trent
Town   Stoke on Trent, Staffs.
Enlisted at Hanley on 11/06/77
Aged 18 years 6 months, Ht. 5 ft 6 1/4 ins
Complexion fresh, Eyes grey
Hair light brown, Trade Clerk
Joined Regiment 02/02/78 at South Africa
Transferred to Army Reserve 12/06/83

945 Private HUSSELL William
Born: Parish Shooter's Hill
Town   Woolwich, Kent
Enlisted at Manchester on 15/01/77
Aged 20 years, Ht. 5 ft 7 3/4 ins
Complexion fresh, Eyes brown
Hair dark brown, Trade Labourer
Joined Regiment 13/06/77
at Cape of Good Hope
To 38th Regiment 19/06/80

272 Private JACKSON Thomas
Born: Parish Aston
Town   Birmingham, Warks.
Enlisted at Walsall on 08/04/74
Aged 25 years, Ht. 5 ft 5 1/4 ins
Complexion fair, Eyes grey
Hair brown, Trade Painter & Glazier
Joined Regiment 04/11/74 at Hong Kong
Transferred to Army Reserve 24/06/80

902 Private INGRAM John
Born: Parish Huddesfield
Town Huddesfield, Yorks.
Enlisted at Leeds on 12/11/63
Aged 24 years, Ht. 5 ft 7 ins
Complexion sallow, Eyes grey
Hair light brown, Religion C.E.
Trade Spinner
Joined Regiment 23/06/66
at Fort Tregantle (Devonport)
Served in "A" Company Killed in Action 12/03/79 Intombi River

1838 Private IRVINE William Thomas
Born: Parish Tullyaughlish
Town Hamilton, Donegal
Enlisted at Belfast on 10/11/71
Aged 20 years 6 months, Ht. 5 ft 8 ins
Complexion fresh, Eyes hazel
Hair dark brown, Trade School Master
Joined Regiment 13/11/71 at Belfast
Transferred to Army Reserve 04/10/79

285 Private JENKINS Henry, Charles
(Nominal Roll 285 JENKIN Henry, Charles)
Born: Parish Bearwood
Town Wolverhampton, Staffs.
Enlisted at Walsall on 21/04/74
Aged 21 years 11 months, Ht. 5 ft 4 7/8 ins
Complexion fresh, Eyes blue
Hair brown, Trade Engineer
Joined Regiment 04/11/74 at Hong Kong
Transferred to Army Reserve 25/06/80

241 Private JENNINGS George
Born: Parish Newcastle
Town Newcastle, Staffs.
Enlisted at Hanley on 03/03/74
Aged 19 years 6 months, Ht. 5 ft 4 3/4 ins
Complexion brown, Eyes brown
Hair brown, Trade Potter
Joined Regiment 18/06/77 at Singapore
Transferred to Army Reserve 12/01/81

1005 Private JOBBOURN Henry
(Nominal Roll 1005 JOBBURN Henry)
Born: Parish Brownhills
Town Lichfield, Staffs.
Enlisted at Walsall on 09/05/77
Aged 18 years 4 months, Ht. 5 ft 6 1/4 ins
Complexion fresh, Eyes dark brown
Hair dark brown,
Trade Miner, Joined Regiment 13/06/77
at Cape of Good Hope
Struck off Strength by Order, Kingstown Dublin 14/07/77
To 38th Regiment 19/06/81

2058 Private JOHNSON William
Born: Parish Liverpool
Town Liverpool, Lancs.
Enlisted at Liverpool on 04/06/72
Aged 19 years 4 months, Ht. 5 ft 6 1/2 ins
Complexion fresh, Eyes blue
Hair brown, Trade Labourer
Joined Regiment not known
Transferred to Army Reserve 25/10/79

226 Private JONES Charles
Born: Parish Ledbury
Town Ledbury, Hereford.
Enlisted at Walsall on 19/02/74
Aged 19 years 11 months, Ht. 5 ft 5 1/4 ins
Complexion fresh, Eyes grey
Hair brown, Trade Labourer
Joined Regiment 04/11/74 at Hong Kong
Transferred to Army Reserve 18/06/80

240 Private JONES Henry
Born: Parish Worcester
Town Worcester, Worcs.
Enlisted at Birmingham on 02/03/74
Aged 19 years 6 months, Ht. 5 ft 4 5/8 ins
Complexion fresh, Eyes grey
Hair dark brown, Trade Sawyer
Joined Regiment 23/02/76 at Singapore
Transferred to Army Reserve 09/07/80

1814 Private JONES William
Born: Parish Wallasey
Town Birkenhead, Cheshire
Enlisted at Liverpool on 25/10/71
Aged 18 years, Ht. 5 ft 5 3/8 ins
Complexion fair, Eyes blue
Hair brown, Trade Coach Wheel Wright
Joined Regiment 30/10/71 at Belfast
Transferred to Army Reserve 04/10/79

1919 Private JACOBS Henry
Born: Parish Brentwood
Town Brentwood, Essex
Enlisted at Westminster on 18/03/72
Aged 24 years 10 months, Ht. 5 ft 8 ins
Complexion fair, Eyes grey
Hair brown, Trade File Cutter
Joined Regiment not known at Hong Kong
Served in "C" Company
Killed in Action 12/03/79 Intombi River

1083 Private JEFFERSON William John
Born: Parish Lisburn
Town Lisburn, Antrim
Enlisted at Devonport on 16/02/67
Aged 15 years 3 months, Ht. 4 ft 9 1/2 ins
Complexion fresh, Eyes grey
Hair dark brown, Trade None
Joined Regiment 19/02/67 at Devonport
Died 30/08/81

653 Private JOHNSON Hubert
Born: Parish Walsall
Town Walsall, Staffs.
Enlisted at Lichfield on 25/01/76
Aged 18 years, Ht. 5 ft 5 3/4 ins
Complexion fresh, Eyes blue
Hair dark brown, Trade Labourer
Joined Regiment 02/02/78 at South Africa
Deserted 15/08/80

1723 Private JOHNSON John
Born: Parish Ochiltree
Town Ayr, Ayrshire
Enlisted at Belfast on 22/05/71
Aged 21 years, Ht. 5 ft 8 ins
Complexion sallow, Eyes hazel
Hair dark brown, Religion Presbyterian
Trade Miner
Joined Regiment 24/05/71 at Belfast
Transferred to Army Reserve (six years) 24/06/80

1679 Private JOHNSON Joseph
Born: Parish Ansley
Town Atherstone, Warks.
Enlisted at Leicester on 24/01/71
Aged 21 years, Ht. 5 ft 4 3/4 ins
Complexion fresh, Eyes grey
Trade Labourer
Hair brown, Religion C.E.
Joined Regiment 02/02/71 at Belfast
Discharged 1st Period 25/01/83

155 Private JONES James
Born: Parish Newcastle
Town Newcastle, Staffs.
Enlisted at Newcastle Under Lyme
on 22/12/73
Aged 21 years 4 months, Ht. 5 ft 8 ins
Complexion fresh, Eyes hazel
Hair brown, Trade Labourer
Joined Regiment 04/11/74 at Hong Kong
Transferred to Army Reserve 02/08/80

1391 Private JONES William
Born: Parish Lydham
Town Lydham, Shrops.
Enlisted at Newcastle Under Lyme
on 31/08/70
Aged 18 years, Ht. 5 ft 5 1/2 ins
Complexion fresh, Eyes Hazel
Hair brown, Religion C.E.
Trade Labourer
Joined Regiment 09/09/70 at Belfast
Discharged Free 20/01/93 (Refer to new Army No. 393)

1488 Private JONES William, John
Born: Parish Hillsborough
Town Belfast, Down
Enlisted at Belfast on 01/12/70
Aged 18 years, Ht. 5 ft 5 1/4 ins
Complexion fresh, Eyes grey
Hair brown, Religion C.E.
Trade Labourer
Joined Regiment 01/12/70 at Belfast
Discharged 02/12/82

589 Private JUDD Thomas
Born: Parish Birmingham
Town Birmingham, Warks.
Enlisted at Walsall on 08/12/75
Aged 19 years, Ht. 5 ft 5 1/2 ins
Complexion fresh, Eyes brown
Hair brown, Trade Glass Cutter
Joined Regiment 17/11/76 at Singapore
Discharged 27/07/80

1964 Private JONES William, James
Born: Parish   St. Clements
Town   London, Middlesex
Enlisted at Westminster on 22/04/72
Aged 24 years 8 months, Ht. 5 ft 6 ins
Complexion fresh, Eyes grey
Hair dark brown, Trade Clerk
Joined Regiment not known
Transferred to Army Reserve 04/10/79

1251 Private JOYCE Martin
Born: Parish   Myeus
Town   Clifden, Galway
Enlisted at Manchester on 27/05/69
Aged 18 years Ht. 5 ft 8 1/2 ins
Complexion fresh, Eyes grey
Hair dark brown, Trade Labourer
Joined Regiment 02/06/69 at Fleetwood
To Depot 21/03/89

682 Private KELLY Peter
Born: Parish   Stone
Town   Stone, Staffs.
Enlisted at Newcastle Under Lyme
on 17/05/76
Aged 19 years, Ht. 5 ft 6 ins
Complexion fresh, Eyes grey
Hair brown, Trade Labourer
Joined Regiment 17/11/76 at Singapore
Transferred to Army Reserve 30/08/81

1477 Private KELLY Thomas
Born: Parish   Birkenhead
Town   Birkenhead, Cheshire
Enlisted at Newcastle Under Lyme
on 23/11/70
Aged 19 years, Ht. 5 ft 53/8 ins
Complexion fresh, Eyes blue
Hair brown, Religion R.C.
Trade Collier
Joined Regiment 27/11/70 at Belfast
Deserted 18/11/71
Transferred to Army Reserve 27/08/81

578 Private KESTERTON William
Born: Parish
Town
County
Enlisted at
Aged years months Ht. ft ins
Complexion   Eyes
Hair   Religion
Trade
Joined Regiment

1865 Private LAFFERTY John
Born: Parish   Templemoor
Town   Londonderry, Derry
Enlisted at Belfast on 15/12/71
Aged 19 years, Ht. 5 ft 6 ins
Complexion fresh, Eyes brown
Hair dark brown, Trade Labourer
Joined Regiment 18/12/71 at Belfast
Served in "A" Company
Killed in Action 12/03/79 Intombi River

357 Private LAWRENCE William
Born: Parish   Stafford
Town   Stafford, Staffs.
Enlisted at Birmingham on 03/10/74
Aged 18 years 2 months, Ht. 5 ft 4 5/8 ins
Complexion fresh, Eyes grey
Hair brown, Trade Forgeman
Joined Regiment 13/06/77
at Cape of Good Hope
Transferred to Army Reserve 05/10/80

1902 Private LAWTON Henry
Born: Parish   St. George's
Town   London, Middlesex
Enlisted at Westminster on 06/03/72
Aged 22 years 1 months, Ht. 5 ft 6 3/4 ins
Complexion sallow, Eyes brown
Hair light brown, Trade Carman
Joined Regiment not known
Transferred to Army Reserve 04/10/79

1029 Private LEWIS Henry
Born: Parish   Ilkeston
Town   Ilkeston, Derbs.
Enlisted at Birmingham on 26/05/77
Aged 19 years 3 months Ht. 5 ft 5 1/4 ins
Complexion fresh, Eyes grey
Hair brown, Trade Collier
Joined Regiment 13/06/77
at Cape of Good Hope
Died at Dublin 11/04/81

418 Private KEATS Joseph
Born: Parish   Hanley
Town   Burslem, Staffs.
Enlisted at Dudley on 27/11/74
Aged 20 years, Ht. 5 ft 5 1/2 ins
Complexion ruddy, Eyes light brown
Hair light brown, Trade Butcher
Joined Regiment 13/06/77
at Cape of Good Hope
Transferred to Army Reserve 26/11/80

115 Private KEENAN William
Born: Parish   Wolverhampton
Town   Wolverhampton, Staffs.
Enlisted at Walsall on 10/09/73
Aged 19 years 6 months, Ht. 5 ft 5 3/8 ins
Complexion fresh, Eyes grey
Hair dark brown, Trade Brass Caster
Joined Regiment 04/11/74 at Hong Kong
Transferred to Army Reserve 25/10/79

1357 Private KETTLE John
Born: Parish   Birmingham
Town   Birmingham, Warks.
Enlisted at Birmingham on 20/08/70
Aged 22 years, Ht. 5 ft 6 3/4 ins
Complexion fair, Eyes grey
Hair dark brown, Religion C.E.
Trade Bedstead Maker
Joined Regiment 20/08/70 at Belfast
Discharged 21/08/82

526 Private KILBRIDE John
Born: Parish   Wigan
Town   Wigan, Lancs.
Enlisted at Walsall on 29/06/75
Aged 24 years 9 months, Ht. 5 ft 6 ins
Complexion fresh, Eyes grey
Hair brown, Trade Labourer
Joined Regiment 17/11/76 at Singapore
Transferred to Army Reserve 02/07/81

456 Private KING James
Born: Parish   West Bromwich
Town   Smethwick, Staffs.
Enlisted at Dudley on 01/01/75
Aged 22 years, Ht. 5 ft 5 1/2 ins
Complexion ruddy, Eyes hazel
Hair dark brown, Trade Puddler
Joined Regiment 13/06/77
at Cape of Good Hope
Discharged Invalid 11/05/80

1795 Private LEIGH Ralph
Born: Parish   Stoke on Trent
Town   Hanley, Staffs.
Enlisted at Newcastle Under Lyme
on 02/10/71
Aged 19 years, Ht. 5 ft 6 1/4 ins
Complexion fresh, Eyes grey
Hair brown, Trade Potter
Joined Regiment 11/10/71 at Belfast
Transferred to Army Reserve 04/10/79

632 Private LEEK John
Born: Parish   Radnor
Town   Radnor, Radnorshire
Enlisted at Walsall on 10/01/76
Aged 18 years, Ht. 5 ft 5 1/4 ins
Complexion fresh, Eyes dark brown
Hair dark brown, Trade Labourer
Joined Regiment 02/02/78 at South Africa
Transferred to Army Reserve 30/08/81

19/996 Private LEESE Ralph
Born: Parish   Leek
Town   Leek, Staffs.
Enlisted at Hanley on 05/05/77
Aged 18 years 6 months, Ht. not known
Complexion fresh, Eyes hazel
Hair brown, Trade Collier
Joined Regiment 13/06/77
at Cape of Good Hope
Served in "C" Company
Killed in Action 12/03/79 Intombi River

1834 Private LINNETT John
Born: Parish   Smeeton
Town   Leicester, Leics.
Enlisted at Leicester on 27/10/71
Aged 20 years Ht. 5 ft 4 7/8 ins
Complexion fresh, Eyes grey
Hair brown, Trade Labourer
Joined Regiment 10/11/71 at Belfast
Deserted in South Africa 03/02/80

1506 Private LEWIS Peter
Born: Parish   Bootle
Town   Bootle, Lancs.
Enlisted at Liverpool on 02/12/70
Aged 19 years, Ht. 5 ft 6 1/2 ins
Complexion fresh, Eyes grey
Hair brown, Religion C.E.
Trade Smith
Joined Regiment 08/12/70 at Belfast
Deserted 28/02/71
To Depot 21/03/82

1625 Private LINKSTON Robert
Born: Parish   Kirkliston
Town   Edinburgh, Midlothian
Enlisted at Carlisle on 12/01/71
Aged 23 years, Ht. 5 ft 6 1/4 ins
Complexion sallow, Eyes blue
Hair dark brown, Religion C.E.
Trade Gardener
Joined Regiment 20/01/71 at Belfast
Discharged 1st Period 25/01/83

1990 Private LOAGE James
Born: Parish   Wick
Town   Wick, Caithness
Enlisted at Westminster on 08/05/72
Aged 22 years 10 months, Ht. 5 ft 6 1/2 ins
Complexion fresh, Eyes grey
Hair brown, Trade None
Joined Regiment not known
Discharged by Purchase 17/09/79

19/1931 Private LODGE Henry
(Nominal Roll Alias COOK Henry)
Born: Parish   Great Canford
Town   Dunmow, Essex
Enlisted at Bishop Stortford on 23/03/72
Aged 20 years 10 months, Ht. 5 ft 6 3/4 ins
Complexion fair, Eyes light blue
Hair brown, Trade Labourer
Joined Regiment not known
Served in "A" Company
Killed in Action 12/03/79 Intombi River

583 Private LONGSTAFF George
Born: Parish   Walsall
Town   Walsall, Staffs.
Enlisted at Walsall on 04/12/75
Aged 23 years, Ht. 5 ft 5 ins
Complexion fair, Eyes blue
Hair brown, Trade Slater
Joined Regiment 17/11/76 at Singapore
Transferred to Army Reserve 30/08/81

2092 Private MADEN George
Born: Parish   Brighton
Town   Brighton, Sussex
Enlisted at Westminster on 11/06/72
Aged 21 years 1 months, Ht. 5 ft 5 ins
Complexion fair, Eyes hazel
Hair brown, Trade Barman
Joined Regiment not known
Transferred to Army Reserve 04/11/79

1426 Private MAKEPEACE John
Born: Parish   St. Hargh's
Town   Leicester, Leics.
Enlisted at Leicester, on 26/09/70
Aged 23 years, Ht. 5 ft 7 1/8 ins
Complexion fresh, Eyes hazel
Hair brown, Religion C.E.
Trade Shoe Finisher
Joined Regiment 07/10/70 at Belfast
Discharged 04/10/82

1568 Private MALLOY John
Born: Parish   Up Holland
Town   Wigan, Lancs.
Enlisted at Doncaster on 27/12/70
Aged 18 years, Ht. 5 ft 5 1/2 ins
Complexion fresh, Eyes grey
Hair dark brown, Religion R.C.
Trade Labourer
Joined Regiment 06/01/71 at Belfast
To Depot 21/03/82

2103 Private MARSON William
Born: Parish   Beverley
Town   Beverley, Yorks.
Enlisted at Newcastle Under Lyme
on 20/11/72
Aged 24 years 4 months, Ht. 5 ft 7 ins
Complexion fresh, Eyes hazel
Hair brown, Trade Bricklayer
Joined Regiment not known
Transferred to Army Reserve 18/06/80

267 Private LINSKEY Patrick
Born: Parish   Keylongnes
Town   Castlebar, Mayo
Enlisted at Newcastle Under Lyme
on 02/04/74
Aged 20 years, Ht. 5 ft 7 3/4 ins
Complexion fresh, Eyes grey
Hair auburn, Trade Labourer
Joined Regiment 04/11/74 at Hong kong
To 19th Brigade Depot 01/11/80
Discharged by Purchase 30/04/83

27 Private LLOYD William
(Nominal Roll 27 LOYD William)
Born: Parish   Wolverhampton
Town   Wolverhampton, Staffs.
Enlisted at Lichfield on 06/05/73
Aged 20 years 11 months, Ht. 5 ft 7 ins
Complexion sallow, Eyes grey
Hair brown, Trade Puddler
Joined Regiment 18/12/73 at Hong Kong
Deceased 24/09/79

1657 Private LORD William
(Nominal Roll LORD William H.)
Born: Parish   Liverpool
Town   Liverpool, Lancs.
Enlisted at Liverpool on 20/01/71
Aged 19 years, Ht. 5 ft 5 1/4 ins
Complexion fresh, Eyes grey
Hair light, Religion C.E.
Trade Plasterer
Joined Regiment 26/01/71 at Belfast To Depot 21/03/82

1653 Private LOWRIE James
Born: Parish   Chesterfield
Town   Chesterfield, Derbs.
Enlisted at Chesterfield on 18/01/71
Aged 19 years, Ht. 5 ft 6 3/4 ins
Complexion fresh, Eyes grey
Hair dark brown, Religion R.C.
Trade Collier
Joined Regiment 26/01/71 at Belfast
Discharged 02/09/80

1213 Private LUNT William
Born: Parish   Chester
Town   Chester, Cheshire
Enlisted at Bolton on 10/11/68
Aged 18 years 6 months, Ht. 5 ft 6 ins
Complexion ruddy, Eyes brown
Hair brown, Trade Bricklayer
Joined Regiment 16/11/68 at Fleetwood
Served in "E" Company, Deserted 16/06/74
Rejoined from Desertion 04/11/74
Discharged to Pension 08/06/80

1351 Private MANNING Stephen
Born: Parish   Tipperary
Town   Tipperary, Tipperary
Enlisted at Birmingham on 20/08/70
Aged 19 years, Ht. 5 ft 5 1/4 ins
Complexion fair, Eyes grey
Hair light brown, Religion R.C. Trade Labourer
Joined Regiment 22/08/70 at Belfast
Discharged 1st Period 18/12/82

1927 Private MANTELL Henry
Born: Parish   Brighton
Town   Brighton, Sussex
Enlisted at Westminster, on 26/03/72
Aged 20 years 1 months, Ht. 5 ft 6 1/2 ins
Complexion fair, Eyes grey
Hair brown, Trade Butcher
Joined Regiment Not known
Discharged by Purchase 03/08/80

1890 Private MARSDIN Mark
(Nominal Roll 1890 MARSDEN Mark)
Born: Parish   Newington Butts
Town   London, Surrey
Enlisted at Westminster on 22/02/72
Aged 24 years 6 months, Ht. 5 ft 5 ins
Complexion fresh, Eyes grey
Hair brown, Trade Painter
Joined Regiment not known
Transferred to Army Reserve 04/10/79

588 Private MASON Edward
Born: Parish   St. John's
Town   Wolverhampton, Staffs.
Enlisted at Wolverhampton on 06/12/75
Aged 19 years 9 months, Ht. 5 ft 5 ins
Complexion fresh, Eyes blue
Hair light, Trade Puddler
Joined Regiment 17/11/76 at Singapore
Transferred to Army Reserve 30/08/81

206 Private MARTIN Frederick
Born: Parish   Wolstanton
Town   Burslem, Staffs.
Enlisted at Newcastle Under Lyme
on 02/02/74
Aged 18 years 9 months, Ht. 5 ft 4 3/4 ins
Complexion sallow, Eyes grey
Hair brown, Trade Collier
Joined Regiment 23/02/76 at Singapore
Transferred to Army Reserve 07/08/80

1909 Private MARTIN Thomas
Born: Parish   Whitechapel
Town   London, Middlesex
Enlisted at Westminster on 12/03/72
Aged 19 years 4 months, Ht. 5 ft 5 ins
Complexion fresh, Eyes grey
Hair brown, Trade Smith
Joined Regiment not known
Transferred to Army Reserve 22/09/79

1933 Private MATTHEWS Alfred
Born: Parish   Chelsea
Town   London, Middlesex
Enlisted at Westminster on 02/04/72
Aged 22 years, Ht. 5 ft 5 ins
Complexion fresh, Eyes grey
Hair brown, Trade Plasterer
Joined Regiment not known
Transferred to Army Reserve 04/10/79

170   Private MATTHEWS Charles
Born: Parish   St. Paul's
Town   Wolverhampton, Staffs.
Enlisted at Wolverhampton on 05/01/74
Aged 18 years 9 months, Ht. 5 ft 6 ins
Complexion fresh, Eyes hazel
Hair dark brown, Trade Bricklayer
Joined Regiment 23/02/76 at Singapore
Transferred to Army Reserve 18/06/80

1846 Private MAY John
Born: Parish   Liverpool
Town   Liverpool, Lancs.
Enlisted at Liverpool on 13/11/71
Aged 19 years, Ht. 5 ft 5 3/8 ins
Complexion sallow, Eyes grey
Hair light brown, Trade Moulder
Joined Regiment 18/11/71 at Belfast
Discharged 1st Period 22/11/83

1349 Private McCULLOUGH James
Born: Parish   Ballymena
Town   Ballymena, Antrim
Enlisted at Belfast on 22/08/70
Aged 17 years 3 months, Ht. 5 ft 5 1/4 ins
Complexion fresh, Eyes grey
Hair light brown, Religion R.C.
Trade Labourer
Joined Regiment 23/08/70 at Belfast
Discharged 24/08/82

559   Private McDONALD William
Born: Parish   Walsall
Town   Walsall, Staffs.
Enlisted at Walsall on 24/09/75
Aged 19 years, Ht. 5 ft 5 ins
Complexion & Eyes not known
Hair not known, Trade Labourer
Joined Regiment 13/06/77
at Cape of Good Hope
Attached to 1st Squadron
Mounted Infantry
Killed in Action 22/01/79 Isandhlwana

1858 Private McGILLAN Thomas
Born: Parish   Domewarse
Town   Newtown Cavaly, Derry
Enlisted at Belfast on 04/12/71
Aged 19 years, Ht. 5 ft 5 1/2 ins
Complexion fresh, Eyes grey
Hair dark brown, Trade Labourer
Joined Regiment 05/12/71
at Belfast

1546 Private McKEE James
Born: Parish   Armagh
Town   Armagh, Armagh
Enlisted at Belfast on 28/12/70
Aged 19 years, Ht. 5 ft 5 1/2 ins
Complexion fresh, Eyes blue
Hair dark brown, Religion R.C.
Trade Butcher
Joined Regiment 30/12/70 at Belfast
Discharged 02/01/83

1712 Private MASSEY Thomas
Born: Parish   Stoke on Trent
Town   Hanley, Staffs.
Enlisted at Newcastle Under Lyme on 17/02/71
Aged 19 years, Ht. 5 ft 4 7/8 ins
Complexion fresh, Eyes grey
Hair sandy, Religion Wesleyan
Trade Collier
Joined Regiment 23/02/71 at Belfast
Transferred to Army Reserve 27/08/81

732   Private MASTERSON Peter
Born: Parish   West Bromwich
Town   West Bromwich, Staffs.
Enlisted at Longton on 13/07/76
Aged 18 years, Ht. 5 ft 5 3/4 ins
Complexion fresh Eyes grey
Hair brown, Trade Miner
Joined Regiment 13/06/77 at Cape of Good Hope
Transferred to Army Reserve 30/08/81

2108 Private McAULIFFE Edmond
Born: Parish
Town   County
Enlisted at
Aged   years   months,   Ht. ft   ins
Complexion   Eyes
Hair   Religion
Trade
Joined Regiment
To 19th Brigade Depot 03/01/81
Discharged Invalid 18/03/84

300   Private McCAFFREY Hugh
Born: Parish   Aghalucker
Town   Lisnaskea, Fermanagh
Enlisted at Enniskillen, on 10/05/65
Aged 19 years, Ht. 5 ft 5 3/4 ins
Complexion fresh, Eyes grey
Hair brown, Trade Labourer
Joined Regiment 04/11/74 at Hong Kong
Discharged (Claimed after having extented
awarded Pension £3 for Life)

62   Private McCLEARY Dennis
(Nominal Roll 62 McCLAREY Dennis)
Born: Parish   Manchester
Town   Manchester, Lancs.
Enlisted at not known on 06/10/57
Aged 18 years, Ht. 5 ft 4 1/2 ins
Complexion fresh, Eyes hazel
Hair dark brown, Trade Weaver
Joined Regiment 02/10/58 at Cawnpore (India)
Discharged 14/10/79

1799 Private McGOOKIN John
Born: Parish   Glasgow
Town   Glasgow, Ayrshire
Enlisted at Belfast on 09/10/71
Aged 20 years, Ht. 5 ft 6 1/4 ins
Complexion fresh, Eyes grey
Hair dark brown, Trade Hair Dresser
Joined Regiment 11/10/71 at Belfast
Transferred to Army Reserve 04/10/79

1719 Private McGURK Peter
(Nominal Roll 1719 McQUIRK Peter)
Born: Parish   Derrylones
Town   Cookstown, Tyrone
Enlisted at Belfast on 24/03/71
Aged 19 years, Ht. 5 ft 71/4 ins
Complexion fresh, Eyes grey
Hair sandy, Religion R.C.
Trade Glazier
Joined Regiment 25/03/71 at Belfast
Discharged Invalid 30/05/82

2282 Private McKEE Edward
Born: Parish
Town   County
Enlisted at
Aged   years   months,   Ht. ft   ins
Complexion   Eyes
Hair   Religion
Trade
Joined Regiment

77   Private McNEIL Michael
Born: Parish   Dudley
Town   Dudley, Worcs.
Enlisted at Wednesbury on 27/06/73
Aged 21 years 3 months, Ht. 5 ft 5 3/8 ins
Complexion fresh, Eyes grey
Hair light brown, Trade Iron Worker
Joined Regiment 18/12/73 at Hong Kong
Transferred to Army Reserve 04/10/79

1775 Private McKENNY William
Born: Parish Leeds
Town   Leeds, Yorks.
Enlisted at Manchester on 20/09/71
Aged 20 years 8 months, Ht. 5 ft 5 1/8 ins
Complexion fresh, Eyes grey
Hair brown, Religion R.C.
Trade Moulder
Joined Regiment 25/09/71 at Belfast
Transferred to Army Reserve 04/10/79

309 Private McKENZIE John
Born: Parish St. John's
Town   Wolverhampton, Staffs.
Enlisted at Lichfield on 01/09/74
Aged 20 years, Ht. 5 ft 7 1/2 ins
Complexion fresh, Eyes grey
Hair light brown, Trade Boot Closer
Joined Regiment 23/02/76 at Singapore
Transferred to Army Reserve 05/09/80

19/590 Private MEADOWS Henry
Born: Parish St. George's
Town   Birmingham, Warks.
Enlisted at Birmingham on 07/12/75
Aged 23 years, Ht. 5 ft 6 5/8 ins
Complexion fresh, Eyes grey
Hair dark brown, Trade Labourer
Joined Regiment 17/11/76 at Singapore
Served in "B" Company
Killed in Action 12/03/79 Intombi River

1025 Private MEEKIN Edward
Born: Parish Walsall
Town   Walsall, staffs.
Enlisted at Lichfield on 26/05/77
Aged 18 years, Ht. 5 ft 5 ins
Complexion fresh, Eyes grey
Hair brown, Trade Lath Cleaver
Joined Regiment 13/06/77
at Cape of Good Hope
To 1st Battalion 04/10/81

1492 Private MEERS Edward
Born: Parish Manchester
Town   Manchester, Lancs.
Enlisted at Liverpool on 26/11/70
Aged 21 years, Ht. 5 ft 5 ins
Complexion fair-pitted, Eyes blue
Hair light, Religion C.E.
Trade Carter
Joined Regiment 02/12/70 at Belfast
Discharged 11/09/80

2063 Private MIDDOW Arthur
Born: Parish St. Peter's
Town   Ipswich, Suffolk
Enlisted at Westminster on 30/05/72
Aged 20 years 3 months, Ht. 5 ft 5 ins
Complexion fresh, Eyes grey
Hair brown, Trade Carpenter
Joined Regiment not known
Served in "C" Company
Killed in Action 12/03/79 Intombi River

49 Private MILLAR John
Born: Parish St. Mary's
Town   Dover, Kent
Enlisted at Dover, on 10/06/73
Aged 18 years, Ht. 5 ft 6 ins
Complexion fresh, Eyes grey
Hair brown, Trade Labourer
Joined Regiment 23/02/76 at Singapore
Transferred to Army Reserve 17/06/80

586 Private MILLINGTON Thomas
Born: Parish Wolstanton
Town   Wolstanton, Staffs.
Enlisted at Newcastle Under Lyme
on 06/12/75
Aged 23 years, Ht. 5 ft 9.3/4 ins
Complexion fresh, Eyes grey
Hair brown, Trade Collier
Joined Regiment 17/11/76 at Singapore
Transferred to Army Reserve 08/12/81

2106 Private MONAGHAN Patrick
Born: Parish
Town
County
Enlisted at
Aged   years months Ht. ft ins
Complexion   Eyes
Hair   Religion
Trade
Joined Regiment
Transferred to Army Reserve 04/10/79

19/1378 Private McSHERRY Bernard
(Nominal Roll 19/1378 McSHERRY Edward)
Born: Parish Tyrone
Town   Tyrone, Tyrone
Enlisted at Glasgow, on 18/08/70
Aged 18 years, Ht. 5 ft 6 ins
Complexion fresh, Eyes grey
Hair dark brown, Trade Labourer
Joined Regiment 31/08/70 at Belfast
Served in "B" Company
Killed in Action 12/03/79 Intombi River

1983 Private MEAD Thomas
Born: Parish Bushey
Town   Watford, Herts.
Enlisted at St.George's Barracks on 30/04/72
Aged 25 years, Ht. 5 ft 7 3/4 ins
Complexion fresh, Eyes hazel
Hair light brown, Trade Smith
Joined Regiment not known
Discharged Invalid 18/03/8

432 Private MELSOP John
Born: Parish Ballybuff
Town   Birr, Kings (Offaly)
Enlisted at Birr on 28/04/59
Aged 18 years, Ht. 5 ft 3 ins
Complexion light, Eyes grey
Hair light brown, Religion R.C.
Trade Labourer
Joined Regiment 28/01/61at Saugor (Central India)
Discharged 15/10/80

678 Private MERRYMAN John
Born: Parish Stoke on Trent
Town   Hanley, Staffs.
Enlisted at Newcastle Under Lyme
on 13/05/76
Aged 19 years, Ht. 5 ft 6 ins
Complexion fresh, Eyes hazel
Hair brown, Trade Butcher
Joined Regiment 17/11/76 at Singapore
Transferred to Army Reserve 30/08/81

83 Private MIDDLETON Edward
(Nominal Roll 83 MIDDLETON Edwin)
Born: Parish Leamington
Town   Leamington, Warks.
Enlisted at Birmingham on 19/08/73
Aged 22 years 5 months, Ht. 5 ft 5 ins
Complexion fair, Eyes grey
Hair brown, Trade Gas Fitter
Joined Regiment 04/11/74 at Hong Kong
Transferred to Army Reserve 18/06/80

1976 Private MITCHELL George
Born: Parish St. Mary's
Town   Sheffield, Yorks.
Enlisted at Westminster on 26/04/72
Aged 21 years, Ht. 5 ft 6 3/4 ins
Complexion sallow, Eyes brown
Hair dark brown, Trade Labourer
Joined Regiment not known
Served in "A" Company
Killed in Action 12/03/79 Intombi River

268 Private MOFFATT John
Born: Parish Scrabbey
Town   Mirlut, Cavan
Enlisted at Newcastle Under Lyme
on 02/04/74
Aged 20 years, Ht. 5 ft 6 1/4 ins
Complexion fresh, Eyes grey
Hair brown, Trade Labourer
Joined Regiment 04/11/74 at Hong kong
Transferred to Army Reserve 22/01/81

1057 Private MOFFATT John
Born: Parish Walsall
Town   Walsall, Staffs.
Enlisted at Walsall on 31/05/77
Aged 18 years 2 months, Ht. 5 ft 6 1/2 ins
Complexion dark grey, Eyes dark grey
Hair dark brown, Trade Blacksmith
Joined Regiment 02/02/78 at South Africa
To 1st Battalion 04/10/81

310 Private MORAN Martin
Born: Parish Stone
Town   Stone, Staffs.
Enlisted at Lichfield on 02/09/74
Aged 20 years, Ht. 5 ft 7 ins
Complexion fresh, Eyes grey
Hair light brown, Trade Bricklayer
Joined Regiment 13/06/77
at Cape of Good Hope
Transferred to Army Reserve 06/09/80

554 Private MOORE George
Born: Parish
Town
County
Enlisted at
Aged   years   months,   Ht.   ft   ins
Complexion   Eyes
Hair   Religion
Trade
Joined Regiment

2048 Private MOORE Robert
Born: Parish   Clerkswell
Town   London, Middlesex
Enlisted at Westminster on 28/05/72
Aged 20 years 3 months, Ht. 5 ft 6 1/2 ins
Complexion fresh, Eyes hazel
Hair brown, Trade Groom
Joined Regiment not known
Served in "A" Company
Killed in Action 12/03/79 Intombi River

787 Private MORGAN Bernard
Born: Parish Newcastle Under Lyme
Town Newcastle Under Lyme, Staffs.
Enlisted at Newcastle Under Lyme
on 31/08/76
Aged 19 years, Ht. 5 ft 7 ins
Complexion fresh, Eyes grey
Hair brown, Trade Labourer
Joined Regiment 02/02/78 at South Africa
Transferred to Army Reserve 26/01/83

180 Private MORRIS John
Born: Parish   Walsall
Town   Walsall, Staffs.
Enlisted at Walsall on 14/01/74
Aged 21 years, Ht. 5 ft 6 ins
Complexion fresh, Eyes grey
Hair brown, Trade Labourer
Joined Regiment 04/11/74 at Hong Kong
Transferred to Army Reserve 05/09/80

476 Private MORRIS John
(Nominal Roll 476 MORRISS John)
Born: Parish   Knighton
Town   Knighton, Radnor
Enlisted at Hanley on 04/05/75
Aged 22 years 4 months, Ht. 5 ft 5 3/4 ins
Complexion brown, Eyes brown
Hair dark brown, Trade Labourer
Joined Regiment 17/11/76 at Singapore
Transferred to Army Reserve 08/07/81

964 Private MORRIS Thomas
Born: Parish   Newport
Town   Newport, Lincs.
Enlisted at Burton on Trent
on 09/04/77
Aged 18 years 4 months, Ht. 5 ft 4 1/2 ins
Complexion fresh, Eyes grey
Hair brown, Trade Labourer
Joined Regiment 13/06/77
at Cape of Good Hope
Died 19/11/79

161 Private MORRIS William
Born: Parish
Town
County
Enlisted at
Aged   years   months,   Ht.   ft   ins
Complexion   Eyes
Hair   Religion
Trade
Joined Regiment

768 Private MORRIS William
Born: Parish   St. Mary's
Town   Wolverhampton, Staffs.
Enlisted at Lichfield on 21/08/76
Aged 20 years 2 months, Ht. 5 ft 6 ins
Complexion fair, Eyes blue
Hair light brown, Trade Grinder
Joined Regiment 17/11/76 at Singapore
Transferred to Army Reserve 26/01/83

1579 Private MULLHOLLAND Joseph
Born: Parish   Fleetwood
Town   Fleetwood, Lancs.
Enlisted at Blackburn on 31/12/70
Aged 19 years, Ht. 5 ft 5 1/2 ins
Complexion fresh, Eyes grey
Hair dark brown, Religion R.C.
Trade Labourer
Joined Regiment 09/01/71 at Belfast
Discharged Invalid 14/09/80

1032 Private MORAN William
Born: Parish   Wednesbury
Town   Walsall, Staffs.
Enlisted at Walsall on 29/05/77
Aged 22 years, Ht. 5 ft 5 ins
Complexion dark, Eyes dark brown
Hair brown, Trade Labourer
Joined Regiment 13/06/77
at Cape of Good Hope
Served in "A" Company
Killed in Action 12/03/79 Intombi River

1397 Private MORETON William
Born: Parish   Wellington
Town   Wellington, Shrops.
Enlisted at Shrewsbury on 01/09/70
Aged 18 years 10 months, Ht. 5 ft 6 ins
Complexion fair, Eyes grey
Hair brown, Religion C.E.
Trade   Labourer
Joined Regiment 14/09/70 at Belfast
Discharged 02/09/82

504 Private MORRIS Joseph
Born: Parish   Stone
Town   Stone, Staffs.
Enlisted at Lichfield on 07/06/75
Aged 19 years, Ht. 5 ft 5 ins
Complexion fresh, Eyes brown
Hair brown, Trade Metal Roller
Joined Regiment 17/11/76 at Singapore
Discharged 31/03/80

1821 Private MORRIS Joseph
Born: Parish   Preston
Town   Preston, Lancs.
Enlisted at Liverpool on 27/10/71
Aged 20 years, Ht. 5 ft 63/4 ins
Complexion fair, Eyes blue
Hair light, Trade Labourer
Joined Regiment 02/11/71 at Belfast
Transferred to Army Reserve 04/10/79

681 Private MORRIS Michael
Born: Parish   St. Peter's
Town   Manchester, Lancs.
Enlisted at Newcastle on 13/05/76
Aged 23 years, Ht. 5 ft 5 1/4 ins
Complexion fresh, Eyes hazel
Hair brown, Trade Labourer
Joined Regiment 13/06/77
at Cape of Good Hope
Transferred to Army Reserve 11/07/82
To Reserve 18/10/85

315 Private MOUNTFORD William
Born: Parish   Stone
Town   Stone, Staffs.
Enlisted at Hanley on 01/09/74
Aged 19 years, Ht. 5 ft 6 ins
Complexion fresh, Eyes blue
Hair light, Trade Collier
Joined Regiment 23/02/76 at Singapore
Deserted 09/01/80

1904 Private MUDDELL Charles
Born: Parish   Fletching
Town   Woking, Sussex
Enlisted at Westminster on 07/03/72
Aged 22 years 3 months, Ht. 5 ft 5 ins
Complexion fresh, Eyes hazel
Hair brown, Trade Grocer
Joined Regiment not known
Transferred to Army Reserve 04/10/79

1678 Private MULGREW James
Born: Parish   Liverpool
Town   Liverpool, Lancs.
Enlisted at Stourbridge on 21/01/71
Aged 18 years, Ht. 5 ft 5 1/2 ins
Complexion fresh, Eyes grey
Hair dark brown, Religion R.C.
Trade Labourer
Joined Regiment 02/02/71 at Belfast
To 19th Brigade Depot 01/12/80

157 Private NAVAN John
Born: Parish   Walsall
Town   Walsall, Staffs.
Enlisted at Walsall on 30/12/73
Aged 19 years, Ht. 5 ft 5 ins
Complexion fresh, Eyes blue
Hair brown, Trade Labourer
Joined Regiment 23/02/76 at Singapore
Transferred to Army Reserve 17/06/80

127 Private MULLINS Thomas
Born: Parish Birmingham
Town   Birmingham, Warks.
Enlisted at Birmingham on 16/09/73
Aged 19 years 9 months, Ht. 5 ft 5 3/8 ins
Complexion fresh, Eyes grey
Hair brown, Trade Metal Roller
Joined Regiment 04/11/74 at Hong Kong
Transferred to Army Reserve 04/10/79

1501 Private MURPHY William
Born: Parish Wexford
Town   Wexford, Wexford
Enlisted at Liverpool on 29/11/70
Aged 23 years Ht. 5 ft 4 1/2 ins
Complexion fresh, Eyes hazel
Hair brown, Religion R.C.
Trade Porter
Joined Regiment 04/12/70 at Belfast
Discharged Pension 19/05/91
(Refer to new Army No. 460)

1868 Private NEWTON Henry
Born: Parish Preston
Town   Preston, Lancs.
Enlisted at Warrington on 04/01/72
Aged 20 years, Ht. 5 ft 5 5/8 ins
Complexion fresh, Eyes grey
Hair brown, Trade Moulder & Fitter
Joined Regiment not known
Transferred to Army Reserve 04/10/79

468 Private NICKLIN Thomas
Born: Parish Wolverhampton
Town   Wolverhampton, Staffs.
Enlisted at Walsall on 12/01/75
Aged 22 years 10 months, Ht. 5 ft 6 1/2 ins
Complexion fresh, Eyes blue
Hair brown, Trade Puddler
Joined Regiment 02/02/78 at South Africa
Transferred to Army Reserve 12/01/81

1926 Private NIGHT Henry
Born: Parish St. Mary's
Town   Colchester, Essex
Enlisted at Westminster on 22/03/72
Aged 24 years, Ht. 5 ft 5 1/2 ins
Complexion swarthy, Eyes hazel
Hair dark brown, Trade Tailor
Joined Regiment not known
Served in "A" Company
Killed in Action 12/03/79 Intombi River

772 Private NOONAN Thomas
Born: Parish Everton
Town   Liverpool, Lancs.
Enlisted at Manchester on 21/08/76
Aged 22 years, Ht. 5 ft 9 1/2 ins
Complexion fresh, Eyes grey
Hair light, Trade Labourer
Joined Regiment 03/12/78
at Pretoria, South Africa
Transferred to Army Reserve 26/01/83

1062 Private NORTON John
Born: Parish Birmingham
Town   Birmingham, Warks.
Enlisted at Wolverhampton on 07/06/77
Aged 20 years 2 months, Ht. 5 ft 4 1/2 ins
Complexion fresh, Eyes blue
Hair light, Trade Tin Plate Maker
Joined Regiment 03/12/78
at Pretoria, South Africa
Served in "D" Company
Died at Whistlestroom 16/09/79

1566 Private NUNNERLEY John
Born: Parish St. Mary's
Town   Shrewsbury, Shrops.
Enlisted at Shrewsbury on 26/12/70
Aged 19 years 7 months, Ht. 5 ft 7 ins
Complexion fresh, Eyes light brown
Hair brown, Religion R.C.
Trade Labourer
Joined Regiment 06/01/71 at Belfast
To Depot 31/10/81

166 Private OWEN Edward
Born: Parish Holyhead
Town   Holyhead, Anglesey
Enlisted at Newcastle Under Lyme
on 01/01/74
Aged 19 years 8 months, Ht. 5 ft 6 3/4 ins
Complexion fresh, Eyes hazel
Hair brown, Trade Miner
Joined Regiment 04/11/74 at Hong Kong
Transferred to Army Reserve 17/06/80

984 Private NEALE Joseph
Born: Parish Wilfinde
Town   Stratfindonlloon, Warks.
Enlisted at Birmingham on 23/04/77
Aged 18 years 9 months, Ht. 5 ft 7 ins
Complexion fair, Eyes brown
Hair dark brown, Trade Labourer
Joined Regiment 13/06/77
at Cape of Good Hope
Discharged by Purchase 29/12/80

758 Private NEWEY William
(Nominal Roll 758 Newey John)
Born: Parish Great Barr
Town   Walsall, Staffs.
Enlisted at Walsall on 14/08/76
Aged 18 years 6 months, Ht. 5 ft 5 1/4 ins
Complexion fresh, Eyes grey
Hair dark brown, Trade Labourer
Joined Regiment 13/06/77
at Cape of Good Hope
Transferred to Army Reserve 27/01/83

263 Private NIXON Joseph
Born: Parish Hanley
Town   Hanley, Staffs.
Enlisted at Lichfield on 30/03/74
Aged 21 years 10 months, Ht. 5 ft 6 1/8 ins
Complexion fair, Eyes grey
Hair light brown, Trade Miner
Joined Regiment 04/11/74 at Hong Kong
Transferred to Army Reserve 25/06/80

1339 Private NOLAN Patrick
Born: Parish St. Michael's
Town   Limerick, Limerick
Enlisted at not known on 14/02/54
Aged 14 years, Ht. 4 ft 8 3/4 ins
Complexion fresh, Eyes blue
Hair sandy, Trade Shoe Maker
Joined Regiment not known
Discharged 29/09/79

1681 Private NOLAN Thomas
Born: Parish Stone
Town   Stone, Staffs.
Enlisted at Newcastle Under Lyme
on 25/01/71
Aged 19 years, Ht. 5 ft 4 3/4 ins
Complexion fresh, Eyes greyish blue
Hair dark brown, Religion R.C.
Trade Shoe Maker
Joined Regiment 02/02/71 at Belfast
Discharged 1st Period 01/02/83

1117 Private O'BRIEN Richard
Born: Parish Cowes
Town   Cowes, Isle of Wight
Enlisted at Aldershot on 19/10/67
Aged 18 years, Ht. 5 ft 5 ins
Complexion sallow, Eyes light brown
Hair dark, Trade Servant
Joined Regiment 22/10/67 at Aldershot
To Depot 24/01/93
(Refer to new Army No. 2512)

1456 Private O'NEIL John
Born: Parish Dublin
Town   Dublin, Dublin
Enlisted at Manchester on 31/10/70
Aged 19 years 3 months, Ht. 5 ft 7 1/2 ins
Complexion pale, Eyes grey
Hair light brown, Religion R.C.
Trade Boiler Maker
Joined Regiment 06/11/70 at Belfast
Discharged by Purchase 14/02/80

1736 Private OVENS William
Born: Parish Islington
Town   London, Middlesex
Enlisted at Westminster on 18/10/69
Aged 20 years, Ht. 5 ft 8 1/4 ins
Complexion fresh, Eyes grey
Hair dark brown, Trade Carpenter
Joined Regiment 01/08/70 at Belfast
Died at Millstreet County Cork 22/07/80

582 Private PAGE Albert
Born: Parish Birmingham
Town   Birmingham, Warks.
Enlisted at Birmingham on 03/12/75
Aged 21 years 6 months, Ht. 5 ft 5 1/4 ins
Complexion fresh, Eyes grey
Hair light brown, Trade Fitter
Joined Regiment 17/11/76 at Hong Kong
Transferred to Army Reserve 30/08/81

1840 Private OWEN James
Born: Parish Liverpool
Town Liverpool, Lancs.
Enlisted at Liverpool on 06/11/71
Aged 19 years, Ht. 5 ft 5 3/8 ins
Complexion fresh, Eyes hazel
Hair brown, Trade Labourer
Joined Regiment 15/11/71 at Belfast
Discharged 12/01/84

165 Private OWEN William
Born: Parish Holyhead
Town Holyhead, Anglesey
Enlisted at Newcastle Under Lyme
on 01/01/74
Aged 21 years 9 months, Ht. 5 ft 5 ins
Complexion fresh, Eyes light blue
Hair brown, Trade Miner
Joined Regiment 04/11/74 at Hong Kong
Transferred to Army Reserve 17/06/80

1885 Private PARROTT George
Born: Parish Marylebone
Town London, Middlesex
Enlisted at Westminster on 22/02/72
Aged 24 years 9 months, Ht. 5 ft 5 ins
Complexion fresh, Eyes grey
Hair not known, Trade Labourer
Joined Regiment not known
Reformed from Desertion 25/08/74
Transferred to Army Reserve 04/10/79

172 Private PARRY Henry
Born: Parish Wolverhampton
Town Wolverhampton, Staffs.
Enlisted at Wolverhampton on 05/01/74
Aged 21 years, Ht. 5 ft 5 3/4 ins
Complexion fresh, Eyes grey
Hair dark brown, Trade Tinner
Joined Regiment 04/11/74 at Hong Kong
Transferred to Army Reserve 17/06/80

1160 Private PATEY John
Born: Parish Faringdon
Town Faringdon, Berks.
Enlisted at Reading on 23/05/68
Aged 18 years 9 months, Ht. 5 ft 7 1/4 ins
Complexion fresh, Eyes hazel
Hair dark brown, Religion Weslyan
Trade Labourer
Joined Regiment 01/08/77 at South Africa
Transferred to 3rd Vol.Batt.
South Staffs Regt. 19/09/91
(Refer to new Army No. 2653)

399 Private PEPPER John
Born: Parish Birmingham
Town Birmingham, Warks.
Enlisted at Birmingham on 30/10/74
Aged 20 years, Ht. 5 ft 5 1/8 ins
Complexion fresh, Eyes grey
Hair brown, Trade Picture Frame Maker
Joined Regiment 02/02/78 at South Africa
Transferred to Army Reserve 03/10/80

662 Private PERKINS John
Born: Parish Stoke on Trent
Town Longton, Staffs.
Enlisted at Newcastle Under Lyme
on 26/01/76
Aged 19 years, Ht. 5 ft 7 ins
Complexion fresh, Eyes blue
Hair brown, Trade Miner
Joined Regiment 02/02/78 at South Africa
Transferred to Army Reserve 29/08/81

116 Private PERKINS Joseph
Born: Parish Lambourne
Town Lambourne, Warks.
Enlisted at Birmingham on 10/09/73
Aged 18 years 1 month, Ht. 5 ft 6 ins
Complexion fresh, Eyes grey
Hair brown, Trade Needle Maker
Joined Regiment 23/02/76 at Singapore
Transferred to Army Reserve 04/10/79

612 Private PHILLIPS Thomas
Born: Parish Haywood
Town Haywood, Staffs.
Enlisted at Lichfield on 01/01/76
Aged 19 years, Ht. 5 ft 9 1/2 ins
Complexion fresh, Eyes grey
Hair light brown, Trade Miner
Joined Regiment 03/12/78 at Pretoria,
South Africa
Transferred to Army Reserve 02/01/82

1027 Private PARKS Charles
Born: Parish Oldbury
Town Bilston, Staffs.
Enlisted at Walsall on 29/05/77
Aged 24 years 10 months, Ht. 5 ft 8 1/4 ins
Complexion fresh, Eyes hazel
Hair brown, Trade Miner
Joined Regiment 13/06/77
at Cape of Good Hope
To 38th Regiment 07/08/80
To 80th Regiment 17/08/80 To Depot 04/10/81

1256 Private PARKS Henry
Born: Parish Inskip
Town Garstang, Lancs.
Enlisted at Fleetwood on 11/06/69
Aged 17 years 9 months, Ht. 5 ft 6 1/4 ins
Complexion fresh, Eyes grey
Hair brown, Trade Labourer
Joined Regiment 14/06/69 at Fleetwood
Discharged by Pension 01/08/81

971 Private PAYNE Thomas
Born: Parish Harpole
Town Northampton, Northants.
Enlisted at Wednesbury on 18/04/77
Aged 20 years 7 months, Ht. 5 ft 4 3/4 ins
Complexion fair, Eyes grey
Hair light brown, Trade Labourer
Joined Regiment 13/06/77 at South Africa
Struck off strength by Order of Lt-General 18/05/79
To Battalion 22/10/81

698 Private PEARSE Charles
Born: Parish Tipton
Town Tipton, Staffs.
Enlisted at Lichfield on 03/06/76
Aged 23 years, Ht. 5 ft 7 1/8 ins
Complexion fresh, Eyes grey
Hair brown, Trade Collier
Joined Regiment 03/12/78 at Pretoria, South Africa
Transferred to Army Reserve 17/07/82

805 Private PEMBERTON Henry
Born: Parish Birmingham
Town Birmingham, Warks.
Enlisted at Walsall on 04/10/76
Aged 28 years, Ht. 5 ft 8 3/4 ins
Complexion dark, Eyes hazel
Hair brown, Trade Brass Founder
Joined Regiment 03/12/78 at Pretoria,
South Africa
To Battalion 04/10/81

92 Private PETERS Frank
Born: Parish Wolverhampton
Town Wolverhampton, Staffs.
Enlisted at Walsall on 21/08/73
Aged 19 years, Ht. 5 ft 6 ins
Complexion fair, Eyes grey
Hair light brown, Trade Striker
Joined Regiment 03/12/78 at Pretoria,
South Africa
Transferred to Army Reserve 18/06/80

246 Private PHILLIPS Alfred
Born: Parish Thornbury
Town Thornbury, Glos.
Enlisted at Walsall on 10/03/74
Aged 24 years, Ht. 5 ft 5 1/4 ins
Complexion dark, Eyes hazel
Hair dark brown, Trade Labourer
Joined Regiment 04/11/74 at Hong Kong
Transferred to Army Reserve 18/06/80

477 Private PHILLIPS Thomas
Born: Parish Stoke on Trent
Town Longton, Staffs.
Enlisted at Newcastle Under Lyme
on 06/05/75
Aged 18 years 2 months, Ht. 5 ft 5 3/4 ins
Complexion fresh, Eyes grey
Hair brown, Trade Miner
Joined Regiment 17/11/76 at Singapore
Transferred to Army Reserve 30/08/81

286 Private PITCHER Joseph
(Nominal Roll 286 PITCHER Joseph)
Born: Parish Leicester
Town Leicester, Leics.
Enlisted at Birmingham on 22/04/74
Aged 19 years, Ht. 5 ft 4 7/8 ins
Complexion fresh, Eyes dark
Hair brown, Trade Labourer
Joined Regiment 04/11/74 at Hong Kong
Transferred to Army Reserve 29/08/81

220 Private PHIPPS William
Born: Parish Harbourne
Town   Birmingham, Warks.
Enlisted at Birmingham on 10/02/74
Aged 23 years, Ht. 5 ft 4 5/8 ins
Complexion fresh, Eyes brown
Hair black, Trade Sawyer
Joined Regiment 23/02/76 at Singapore
Killed in Action 12/03/79 Intombi River

649 Private PICKEN George
Born: Parish
Town
County
Enlisted at
Aged   years   months, Ht. ft   ins
Complexion   Eyes
Hair   Religion
Trade
Joined Regiment

1549 Private POOLE John
Born: Parish Wrexham
Town   Wrexham, Denbighshire
Enlisted at Brixham on 26/12/70
Aged 19 years, Ht. 5 ft 5 ins
Complexion fresh, Eyes grey
Hair dark brown, Religion C.E.
Trade Tailor
Joined Regiment 02/01/71 at Belfast
Discharged 1st Period 27/12/82

706 Private POWELL Edward
Born: Parish Bilston
Town   Bilston, staffs.
Enlisted at Lichfield on 12/06/76
Aged 18 years 6 months, Ht. 5 ft 5 ins
Complexion fresh, Eyes grey
Hair light, Trade Collier
Joined Regiment 02/02/78 at South Africa
Transferred to Army Reserve 11/07/82

1234 Private POWERS John
Born: Parish Preston
Town   Preston, Lancs.
Enlisted at Preston on 14/12/68
Aged 18 years, Ht. 5 ft 7 ins
Complexion fresh, Eyes grey
Hair light brown, Trade Mason
Joined Regiment 17/12/68 at Fleetwood
Discharged 17/12/80

2085 Private PRITCHARD Charles
Born: Parish Bishopgate
Town   London, Middlesex
Enlisted at Westminster on 07/06/72
Aged 21 years 11 months, Ht. 5 ft 5 ins
Complexion dark, Eyes hazel
Hair brown, Trade Labourer
Joined Regiment not known
Served in "C" Company
Killed in Action 12/03/79 Intombi River

1053 Private PROUD Peter
(Nominal Roll 1053 PROUD Robert)
Born: Parish Walsall
Town   Walsall, Staffs.
Enlisted at Walsall on 29/05/77
Aged 18 years 6 months, Ht. 5 ft 5 1/2 ins
Complexion fair, Eyes hazel
Hair brown, Trade Collier
Joined Regiment 03/12/78
at Pretoria, South Africa

1163 Private PUMMELL Arthur
Born: Parish Basingstoke
Town   Basingstoke, Hamps.
Enlisted at Aldershot on 13/06/68
Aged 17 years, Ht. 5 ft 5 1/2 ins
Complexion fresh, Eyes brown
Hair dark brown, Trade Labourer
Joined Regiment 13/06/68 at Aldershot
Served in "E" Company
Killed in Action 12/03/79 Intombi River

201 Private RAMSEY George
Born: Parish Worcester
Town   Worcester, Worcs.
Enlisted at Birmingham on 02/02/74
Aged 20 years 5 months, Ht. 5 ft 6 5/8 ins
Complexion fresh, Eyes grey
Hair light brown, Trade Labourer
Joined Regiment 04/11/74 at Hong Kong
Transferred to Army Reserve 05/10/80

360 Private PLANT Henry
Born: Parish Dudley
Town   Dudley, Staffs.
Enlisted at Wednesbury on 01/10/74
Aged 20 years 8 months, Ht. 5 ft 7 3/4 ins
Complexion fair, Eyes brown
Hair light brown, Trade Axle Tree Polisher
Joined Regiment 02/02/78 at South Africa

1604 Private PLANT William
Born: Parish Stoke on Trent
Town   Hanley, Staffs.
Enlisted at Newcastle Under Lyme
on 09/01/71
Aged 21 years 2 months, Ht. 5 ft 5 ins
Complexion fresh, Eyes hazel
Hair brown, Religion C.E.
Trade   Collier
Joined Regiment 16/01/71 at Belfast
Transferred to Army Reserve 27/08/81

717 Private POWIS Samuel
Born: Parish Audley
Town   Halmer End, Staffs.
Enlisted at Newcastle on 23/06/76
Aged 21 years 10 months, Ht. 5 ft 6 1/4 ins
Complexion fresh, Eyes hazel
Hair brown, Trade Collier
Joined Regiment 03/12/78 at Pretoria,
South Africa
Transferred to Army Reserve 30/08/82

186 Private PREECE George
Born: Parish Enville
Town   Wolverhampton, Staffs.
Enlisted at Wolverhampton on 20/01/74
Aged 18 years 10 months, Ht. 5 ft 5 ins
Complexion fresh, Eyes hazel
Hair dark brown, Trade Labourer
Joined Regiment 23/02/76 at Singapore
Transferred to Army Reserve 18/06/80

2031 Private PRINCE John
Born: Parish Cullompton
Town   Exeter, Devon.
Enlisted at Bristol on 02/12/71
Aged 19 years 2 months, Ht. 5 ft 5 1/4 ins
Complexion fresh, Eyes grey
Hair light brown, Trade Mason
Joined Regiment not known

645 Private QUEENY Owen
Born: Parish St. Peter's
Town   Wolverhampton, Staffs.
Enlisted at Wolverhampton on 19/01/76
Aged 18 years 1 month, Ht. 5 ft 5 ins
Complexion fresh, Eyes brown
Hair dark, Trade Galvaniser
Joined Regiment 02/02/78 at South Africa
Transferred to Army Reserve 17/07/82

2047 Private QUICK James
Born: Parish Bricket Wood
Town   Watford, Herts.
Enlisted at St. Alban's on 23/05/72
Aged 24 years, Ht. 5 ft 8 1/2 ins
Complexion fresh, Eyes grey
Hair brown, Trade Farm Labourer
Joined Regiment Not known
Transferred to Army Reserve 04/10/79

1974 Private RALPHS Frederick
Born: Calcutta
          India
Enlisted at Westminster on 23/04/72
Aged 21 years, Ht. 5 ft 6 ins
Complexion fresh, Eyes grey
Hair dark brown, Trade Porter
Joined Regiment not known
Served in "C" Company
Killed in Action 12/03/79 Intombi River

533 Private REID George Thomas
Born: Parish Glasgow
Town   Glasgow, Lanarkshire
Enlisted at Birmingham on 09/07/75
Aged 23 years 9 months, Ht. 5 ft 6 3/4 ins
Complexion fair, Eyes grey
Hair brown, Trade Labourer
Joined Regiment 25/11/75 at Singapore
Transferred to Army Reserve 12/07/81
Rejoined 15/08/85
To 1st Battalion 19/09/85

414 Private RANDLE Henry
Born: Parish   Dudley
Town   Dudley, Staffs.
Enlisted at Dudley on 24/11/74
Aged 18 years 6 months, Ht. 5 ft 4 1/2 ins
Complexion sallow, Eyes dark
Hair brown, Trade Striker
Joined Regiment 03/12/78 at Pretoria,
South Africa
Discharged 05/10/80

1953 Private RAYMOND Charles
Born: Parish   Dublin
Town   Dublin, Dublin
Enlisted at Tower Hill on 15/04/72
Aged 24 years 11 months, Ht. 5 ft 6 1/4 ins
Complexion fresh, Eyes grey
Hair auburn, Trade Labourer
Joined Regiment not known
Transferred to Army Reserve 04/10/79

1894 Private RHOADES Thomas
(Nominal Roll 1894 RHOADS Thomas)
Born: Parish   Grandon
Town   Aylesbury, Bucks.
Enlisted at Westminster on 24/02/72
Aged 22 years 9 months, Ht. 5 ft 5 1/2 ins
Complexion fresh, Eyes grey
Hair brown, Trade Groom
Joined Regiment not known
Transferred to Army Reserve 04/10/79

528   Private RICHARDSON Charles
Born: Parish   Wednesbury
Town   Wednesbury, Staffs.
Enlisted at Walsall on 30/06/75
Aged 19 years 2 months, Ht. 5 ft 5 ins
Complexion fair, Eyes grey
Hair light brown, Trade Tube Maker
Joined Regiment 13/06/77
at Cape of Good Hope
Transferred to Army Reserve 05/07/81

2012 Private RICHARDSON George
Born: Parish   Holburn
Town   London, Middlesex
Enlisted at Westminster on 21/05/72
Aged 21 years 7 months, Ht. 5 ft 5 3/4 ins
Complexion fresh, Eyes hazel
Hair brown, Trade Printer
Joined Regiment not known
Transferred to Army Reserve 12/10/79

578   Private ROBBINS William
Born: Parish   St. John's
Town   Coventry, Warks.
Enlisted at Lichfield on 02/12/75
Aged 18 years 2 months, Ht. 5 ft 5 3/4 ins
Complexion fair, Eyes blue
Hair light brown, Trade Bolt Maker
Joined Regiment 17/11/76 at Singapore
Transferred to Army Reserve 30/08/81

1960 Private ROBERTS Henry
Born: Parish   Mogerhanger
Town   Sands, Beds.
Enlisted at Huntingdon on 15/04/72
Aged 20 years, Ht. 5 ft 5 ins
Complexion fresh, Eyes dark blue
Hair light brown, Trade Labourer
Joined Regiment not known
Transferred to Army Reserve 04/10/79

19/259 Private ROBINSON John
Born: Parish   Cambridge
Town   Cambridge, Cambs.
Enlisted at Birmingham on 23/03/74
Aged 23 years, Ht. 5 ft 4 1/2 ins
Complexion sallow, Eyes hazel
Hair brown, Trade Striker
Joined Regiment 04/11/74 at Hong Kong
Served in "E" Company
Killed in Action 12/03/79 Intombi River

1393 Private ROCHELL Henry
Born: Parish   St. Mary's
Town   Stafford, Staffs.
Enlisted at Stafford on 29/08/70
Aged 18 years, Ht. 5 ft 9 ins
Complexion light brown, Eyes hazel
Hair brown, Religion C.E.
Trade Labourer
Joined Regiment 12/09/70 at Belfast
Discharged 30/08/82

158 Private RENFREY Alfred
Born: Parish   Redruth
Town   Redruth, Cornwall
Enlisted at Wolverhampton on 29/12/73
Aged 20 years 2 months, Ht. 5 ft 6 1/2 ins
Complexion fresh, Eyes grey
Hair light brown, Trade Smith
Joined Regiment 04/11/74 at Hong Kong
Transferred to Army Reserve 17/06/80

609 Private RHOADES Roland
(Nominal Roll 609 RHODES Roland)
Born: Parish   Lye
Town   Brierley Hill, Staffs.
Enlisted at Dudley on 30/12/75
Aged 19 years, Ht. 5 ft 6 ins
Complexion fair, Eyes grey
Hair light, Trade Labourer
Joined Regiment 02/02/78 at South Africa
Transferred to Army Reserve 30/08/81

1108 Private RICKMAN George
Born: Parish   Blandford
Town   Blandford, Dorset.
Enlisted at Aldershot on 28/09/67
Aged 19 years, Ht. 5 ft 10 ins
Complexion fresh, Eyes brown
Hair dark brown, Trade Labourer
Joined Regiment 29/09/67 at Aldershot
Discharged 14/10/79

995 Private RILEY Martin
Born: Parish   Stoke on Trent
Town   Longton, Staffs.
Enlisted at Hanley on 02/05/77
Aged 18 years 3 months, Ht. 5 ft 5 1/2 ins
Complexion fresh, Eyes grey
Hair brown, Trade Porter
Joined Regiment 02/02/78 at South Africa
To 1st Battalion 11/01/82

1963 Private RING Edward
Born: Parish   Bermondsey
Town   London, Surrey
Enlisted at Westminster on 19/04/72
Aged 20 years 8 months, Ht. 5 ft 5 3/4 ins
Complexion fresh, Eyes hazel
Hair light brown, Trade Labourer
Joined Regiment not known
Transferred to Army Reserve 04/10/79

1483 Private ROBINSON Robert
Born: Parish   Liverpool
Town   Liverpool, Lancs.
Enlisted at Liverpool on 24/11/70
Aged 20 years, Ht. 5 ft 6 1/4 ins
Complexion fresh, Eyes brown
Hair brown, Religion C.E.
Trade Painter
Joined Regiment 01/12/70 at Belfast
Discharged 30/11/82

1000 Private ROBINSON Samuel
Born: Parish   Cheadle
Town   Longton, Staffs.
Enlisted at Lichfield on 07/05/77
Aged 20 years 1 month, Ht. 5 ft 5 1/4 ins
Complexion fresh, Eyes dark brown
Hair dark brown, Trade Labourer
Joined Regiment 13/06/77
at Cape of Good Hope
To Depot 21/03/82

1047 Private ROBSON James
Born: Parish   Oldbury
Town   West Bromwich, Staffs.
Enlisted at Stafford on 01/06/77
Aged 24 years 6 months, Ht. 5 ft 6 3/4 ins
Complexion light, Eyes light grey
Hair light brown, Trade Labourer
Joined Regiment 02/02/78 at South Africa
To 38th Regiment 19/06/80

358 Private ROUSE William
Born: Parish   Harrow
Town   Harrow, Warks.
Enlisted at Birmingham on 30/09/74
Aged 21 years 2 months, Ht. 5 ft 5 ins
Complexion fresh, Eyes grey
Hair light brown, Trade Labourer
Joined Regiment 13/06/77
at Cape of Good Hope

965 Private RODGERS Samuel
Born: Parish Wolverhampton
Town Wolverhampton, Staffs.
Enlisted at Walsall on 09/04/77
Aged 19 years 6 months, Ht. 5 ft 3 3/4 ins
Complexion fresh, Eyes hazel
Hair brown, Trade Locksmith
Joined Regiment 13/06/77 at Cape of Good Hope
To 38th Regiment 07/08/80
To 80th Regiment 17/08/80
Discharged with Ignominy 20/11/80

486 Private ROHEN Peter
Born: Parish Limerick
Town Limerick, Limerick
Enlisted at Buttevant, on 15/06/59
Aged 18 years, Ht. 5 ft 4 1/4 ins
Complexion fresh, Eyes hazel
Hair red, Religion R.C.
Trade Labourer
Joined Regiment 28/01/61 at Sauger (Central India)
Died at Netley 29/03/80

663 Private ROWLEY Thomas
Born: Parish Stoke
Town Hanley, Staffs.
Enlisted at Newcastle on 25/01/76
Aged 18 years 9 months, Ht. 5 ft 5 1/2 ins
Complexion fresh, Eyes hazel
Hair brown, Trade Miner
Joined Regiment 03/12/78 at Pretoria, S.A.
To 38th Regiment 19/06/80
To 80th Regiment 17/08/80
To 1st Bn. South Staffordshire 04/10/81

1337 Private RUBIE George
Born: Parish St. Paul's
Town London, Middlesex
Enlisted at Liverpool on 17/11/69
Aged 18 years, Ht. 5 ft 8 3/4 ins
Complexion fresh, Eyes blue
Hair brown, Religion C.E.
Trade Porter
Joined Regiment 21/11/69 at Birr
(Refer to new Army No. 394)

1085 Private RUBIE Robert
Born: Parish St. Mary's
Town London, Middlesex
Enlisted at Liverpool on 19/02/67
Aged 18 years, Ht. 5 ft 6 1/2 ins
Complexion fresh, Eyes hazel
Hair brown, Religion C.E.
Trade Labourer
Joined Regiment 21/02/67 at Portland
Transferred to Army Reserve 06/10/79

1254 Private RYAN Daniel
Born: Parish St. Martin's
Town Liverpool, Lancs.
Enlisted at Liverpool on 03/06/69
Aged 18 years, Ht. 5 ft 6 7/8 ins
Complexion fresh, Eyes blue
Hair brown, Trade Labourer
Joined Regiment 08/06/69 at Fleetwood
To Depot 21/03/82
Discharged 14/06/89

1912 Private RYAN Henry
Born: Parish St. Saviour's
Town London, Middlesex
Enlisted at Westminster on 11/03/72
Aged 21 years 6 months, Ht. 5 ft 6 ins
Complexion sallow, Eyes brown
Hair black, Trade Leather Cutter
Joined Regiment not known
Transferred to Army Reserve 04/10/79

1423 Private RYAN Joseph
Born: Parish Cavan
Town Cavan, Cavan
Enlisted at Belfast on 30/09/70
Aged 17 years, Ht. 5 ft 5 1/2 ins
Complexion dark, Eyes hazel
Hair dark brown, Religion R.C.
Trade Labourer
Joined Regiment 04/10/70 at Belfast
Transferred to Army Reserve 21/04/83

439 Private SANDS William
(Nominal Roll 439 SANDES William)
Born: Parish Stockport
Town Stockport, Cheshire
Enlisted at Manchester on 23/05/59
Aged 18 years, Ht. 5 ft 4 1/2 ins
Complexion fresh, Eyes grey
Hair light brown, Religion Protestant
Trade Weaver
Joined Regiment 28/01/61 at Saugor (Central India)
Discharged 20/07/80

744 Private ROWAN Thomas
Born: Parish St. James's
Town Wolverhampton, Staffs.
Enlisted at Walsall on 25/07/76
Aged 21 years, Ht. 5 ft 6 1/4 ins
Complexion fresh, Eyes hazel
Hair brown, Trade Iron Worker
Joined Regiment 17/11/76 at Singapore
To 19th Brigade Depot 01/12/80

975 Private ROWE John
Born: Parish Kidderminster
Town Kidderminster, Worcs.
Enlisted at not known, on 09/10/57
Aged 18 years, Ht. 5 ft 4 ins
Complexion sallow, Eyes hazel
Hair brown, Religion C.E.
Trade Labourer
Joined Regiment not known
Discharged 04/11/79

2070 Private RUFFLE Henry
Born: Parish Whitechapel
Town London, Middlesex
Enlisted at Westminster on 01/06/72
Aged 24 years 6 months, Ht. 5 ft 5 ins
Complexion dark, Eyes hazel
Hair dark brown, Trade Clerk
Joined Regiment not known
Served in "C" Company
Killed in Action 12/03/79 Intombi River

711 Private RUSH Frank
Born: Parish St. Patrick's
Town Walsall, Staffs.
Enlisted at Wolverhampton on 17/06/76
Aged 19 years, Ht. 5 ft 5 ins
Complexion fresh, Eyes grey
Hair light brown, Trade Labourer
Joined Regiment 13/06/77
at Cape of Good Hope
To 38th Regiment 19/06/80

2010 Private RUSSELL James Taylor
Born: Parish St. Clement's
Town Oxford, Oxon
Enlisted at Westminster on 21/05/72
Aged 24 years, Ht. 5 ft 5 1/2 ins
Complexion fresh, Eyes grey
Hair brown, Trade Tailor & Cutter
Joined Regiment not known
Transferred to Army Reserve 04/10/79

375 Private SALT George
Born: Parish Kingsley
Town Cheadle Whiston, Staffs.
Enlisted at Newcastle Under Lyme on 10/05/59
Aged 18 years, Ht. 5 ft 6 5/8 ins
Complexion fresh, Eyes grey
Hair dark brown, Religion Protestant
Trade Labourer
Joined Regiment 28/01/61 at Saugor (Central India)
Discharged 03/08/80

1889 Private SALTER Charles
Born: Parish St. Pancras
Town London, Middlesex
Enlisted at Westminster on 23/02/72
Aged 20 years, Ht. 5 ft 5 ins
Complexion fresh, Eyes grey
Hair brown, Trade Labourer
Joined Regiment not known
Transferred to Army Reserve 04/10/79

972 Private SANDERS John
Born: Parish Checkley
Town Uttoxeter, Staffs.
Enlisted at Uttoxeter on 19/04/77
Aged 18 years, Ht. 5 ft 6 1/4 ins
Complexion fresh, Eyes blue
Hair brown, Trade Labourer
Joined Regiment 13/06/77 at Cape of Good Hope
Died - date not known

962 Private SAVILLE Edward
Born: Parish Leeds
Town Leeds, Yorks
Enlisted at Sheffield on 15/08/65
Aged 19 years, Ht. 5 ft 8 1/2 ins
Complexion fair, Eyes blue
Hair light, Religion C.E.
Trade Cutter
Joined Regiment 23/06/66
at Fort Tregantle, Devonport
To Depot 21/03/82

968 Private SARGEANT Henry
(Nominal Roll 967 SARGEANT Henry)
Born: Parish Tamworth
Town   Tamworth, Staffs.
Enlisted at Lichfield on 16/04/77
Aged 20 years 4 months, Ht. 5 ft 7 1/2 ins
Complexion fresh, Eyes grey
Hair light brown, Trade Labourer
Joined Regiment 13/06/77
at Cape of Good Hope
To Depot 05/05/82

1533 Private SATTERLEY William
Born: Parish Ashburton
Town   Ashburton, Devon.
Enlisted at Ashburton on 12/12/70
Aged 19 years, Ht. 5 ft 4 1/2 ins
Complexion fresh, Eyes grey
Hair dark brown, Religion C.E.
Trade Labourer
Joined Regiment 23/12/70 at Belfast
Discharged 13/12/82

2074 Private SCOTT Edward
Born: Parish St. Andrew's The Less
Town   Cambridge, Cambs.
Enlisted at Cambridge on 01/06/72
Aged 22 years, Ht. 5 ft 5 1/4 ins
Complexion fresh, Eyes hazel
Hair dark, Trade Labourer
Joined Regiment not known
Transferred to Army Reserve 04/10/79

1253 Private SEDDONS Thomas
(Nominal Roll 1253 SEDDON Thomas)
Born: Parish Shelford
Town   Shelford, Lancs.
Enlisted at Bolton on 03/06/69
Aged 18 years, Ht. 5 ft 7 3/4 ins
Complexion fair, Eyes blue
Hair brown, Trade Labourer
Joined Regiment 08/06/69 at Fleetwood
Discharged by Purchase 03/08/80

377 Private SEDGELEY William Henry
Born: Parish Dudley
Town   Dudley, Staffs.
Enlisted at Walsall on 19/10/74
Aged 19 years, Ht. 5 ft 4 1/2 ins
Complexion fresh, Eyes hazel
Hair dark brown, Trade Labourer
Joined Regiment 02/02/78 at South Africa
Deserted at Potchefstroom
South Africa 14/06/80

484 Private SHAPCOTT Henry
Born: Parish Worcester
Town   Worcester, Worcs.
Enlisted at Hanley on 15/05/75
Aged 21 years, Ht. 5 ft 5 3/4 ins
Complexion sallow, Eyes light blue
Hair dark brown, Trade Potter
Joined Regiment 25/11/76 at Singapore
Transferred to Army Reserve 18/05/81

970 Private SHAW Frederick
Born: Parish St. Pancras
Town   London, Middlesex
Enlisted at Westminster on 12/10/65
Aged 15 years, Ht. 4 ft 11 ins
Complexion fair, Eyes blue
Hair brown, Religion C.E.
Trade None
Joined Regiment 23/06/66
at Fort Tregantle, Devonport
Discharged 17/08/80

1165 Private SHAW Samuel
Born: Parish Alford
Town   Alford, Lincs.
Enlisted at Birmingham on 19/09/66
Aged 23 years, Ht. 5 ft 6 1/2 ins,
Complexion sallow, Eyes brown
Hair black, Trade Puddler
Joined Regiment 01/08/77 at South Africa
Discharged by Purchase 14/02/80

508 Private SIGLEY John
Born: Parish Wolstanton
Town   Burslem, Staffs.
Enlisted at Hanley on 19/06/75
Aged 22 years, Ht. 5 ft 6 ins
Complexion fresh, Eyes blue
Hair light brown, Trade Forgeman
Joined Regiment 25/11/75 at Singapore
Transferred to Army Reserve 20/06/81

1019 Private SAVAGE James
Born: Parish Dudley
Town   Dudley, Staffs.
Enlisted at Lichfield on 26/03/77
Aged 18 years, Ht. 5 ft 4 1/2 ins
Complexion fresh, Eyes grey
Hair dark brown, Trade Collier
Joined Regiment 13/06/77
at Cape of Good Hope
To 1st Battalion 04/10/81

670 Private SAXTON Josiah
(Nominal Roll 670 SAXTON Joseph)
Born: Parish Erdington
Town   Sutton Coldfield, Warks.
Enlisted at Lichfield on 09/03/76
Aged 18 years, Ht. 5 ft 7 ins
Complexion fair, Eyes blue
Hair light, Trade Brick Maker
Joined Regiment 02/02/78 at South Africa
Transferred to Army Reserve 09/03/82

262 Private SENIOR John
Born: Parish Newcastle
Town   Newcastle, Staffs.
Enlisted at Hanley on 27/03/74
Aged 20 years 6 months, Ht. 5 ft 4 3/4 ins
Complexion fresh, Eyes blue
Hair light brown, Trade Wire Worker
Joined Regiment 04/11/74 at Hong Kong
Transferred to Army Reserve 24/06/80

650 Private SERGEANT John W.
Born: Parish Gosport
Town   Gosport, Hamps.
Enlisted at Walsall on 24/01/76
Aged 19 years 2 months, Ht. 5 ft 8 3/4 ins
Complexion fresh, Eyes brown
Hair dark brown, Trade Labourer
Joined Regiment 03/12/78 at Pretoria,
South Africa
Transferred to Army Reserve 29/03/82

675 Private SEYMOUR William
(Nominal Roll 695 SEYMOUR William)
Born: Parish St. John's
Town   Manchester, Lancs.
Enlisted at Lichfield on 13/05/76
Aged 18 years, Ht. 5 ft 5 1/2 ins
Complexion fair, Eyes brown
Hair light brown, Trade Labourer
Joined Regiment 13/06/77
at Cape of Good Hope
Attached to 1st Squadron Mounted
Infantry Killed in Action 22/01/79 Isandhlwana

2035 Private SHELLOCK James
Born: Parish Colchester
Town   Colchester, Essex
Enlisted at Westminster on 21/12/71
Aged 19 years 10 months, Ht. 5 ft 5 1/2 ins
Complexion fresh, Eyes grey
Hair brown, Trade Labourer
Joined Regiment not known
Transferred to Army Reserve 04/10/79

19/615 Private SHERRIDAN Michael
Born: Parish St. Mary's
Town   Wolverhampton, Staffs.
Enlisted at Wolverhampton on 07/01/76
Aged 18 years, Ht. 5 ft 5 3/4 ins
Complexion sallow, Eyes hazel
Hair dark brown, Trade Labourer
Joined Regiment 02/02/78 at South Africa
Served in "B" Company
Killed in Action 12/03/79 Intombi River

514 Private SHIRLEY Henry, William
Born: Parish Wolstanton
Town   Burslem, Staffs.
Enlisted at Hanley on 21/06/75
Aged 18 years 6 months, Ht. 5 ft 6 3/4 ins
Complexion fresh, Eyes light blue
Hair light brown, Trade Labourer
Joined Regiment 17/06/76 at Singapore
Transferred to Army Reserve 27/06/81

511 Private SIMPSON William
Born: Parish Wolstanton
Town   Burslem, Staffs.
Enlisted at Hanley on 21/06/75
Aged 18 years, Ht. 5 ft 5 1/4 ins
Complexion fresh, Eyes brown
Hair brown, Trade Collier
Joined Regiment 17/11/76 at Singapore
To 19th Brigade Depot 01/12/80

1770 Private SILCOCK Joseph
Born: Parish Brampton
Town Chesterfield, Derbs.
Enlisted at Chesterfield on 11/09/71
Aged 20 years 11 months, Ht. 5 ft 5 1/8 ins
Complexion fair, Eyes grey
Hair brown, Religion R.C.
Trade Labourer
Joined Regiment 22/09/71 at Belfast
Served in "A" Company
Killed in Action 12/03/79 Intombi River

324 Private SIMCOCK John
Born: Parish
Town
County
Enlisted at
Aged years months, Ht. ft ins
Complexion Eyes
Hair Religion
Trade
Joined Regiment

1864 Private SKELLAM Thomas
(Nominal Roll
1864 SKELLAM Thomas Everard)
Born: Parish Dritchington
Town Uppingham, Rutland
Enlisted at Leicester on 05/12/71
Aged 19 years 6 months, Ht. 5 ft 5 1/2 ins
Complexion fresh, Eyes hazel
Hair brown, Trade Farm Servant
Joined Regiment 16/12/71 at Belfast
Transferred to Army Reserve 29/08/81

610 Private SLACK Edward
Born: Parish Manchester
Town Manchester, Lancs.
Enlisted at Manchester on 06/07/59
Aged 18 years, Ht. 5 ft 3 1/8 ins
Complexion sallow, Eyes grey
Hair brown, Religion Protestant
Trade Labourer
Joined Regiment 28/01/61
at Saugor (Central India)
Discharged 03/08/80

608 Private SLEIGH Walter
Born: Parish St. Mary's
Town Wolverhampton, Staffs.
Enlisted at Wolverhampton on 29/12/75
Aged 24 years 9 months, Ht. 5 ft 6 ins
Complexion fresh, Eyes blue
Hair light, Trade Machinist
Joined Regiment 02/02/78 at South Africa
Transferred to Army Reserve 30/12/81

1048 Private SMITH George
Born: Parish Cannock
Town Cannock, Staffs.
Enlisted at Newcastle Under Lyme
on 31/05/77
Aged 23 years, Ht. 5 ft 4 1/2 ins
Complexion fresh, Eyes blue
Hair brown, Trade Labourer
Joined Regiment 02/02/78 at South Africa
To 38th Regiment 07/03/80
To 1st Battalion 11/05/82

479 Private SMITH Henry
Born: Parish Birmingham
Town Birmingham, Warks.
Enlisted at Lichfield on 13/05/75
Aged 18 years 8 months, Ht. 5 ft 5 1/4 ins
Complexion fresh, Eyes hazel
Hair light brown, Trade Tube Drawer
Joined Regiment 17/11/76 at Singapore
Transferred to Army Reserve 30/05/81

19/510 Private SMITH Henry
Born: Parish Birmingham
Town Birmingham, Warks.
Enlisted at Walsall on 17/06/75
Aged 19 years 7 months, Ht. 5 ft 5 1/2 ins
Complexion fresh, Eyes brown
Hair dark brown, Trade Stoker
Joined Regiment 25/11/75 at Singapore
Served in "A" Company
Killed in Action 12/03/79 Intombi River

144 Private SMITH John
Born: Parish St. Mary's
Town Stafford, Staffs.
Enlisted at Lichfield on 30/09/73
Aged 19 years, Ht. 5 ft 5 1/2 ins
Complexion fresh, Eyes hazel
Hair brown, Trade Shoe Maker
Joined Regiment 23/02/76 at Singapore
Transferred to Army Reserve 18/06/80

607 Private SINCLAIR William
Born: Parish Stoke on Trent
Town Hanley, Staffs.
Enlisted at Newcastle on 27/12/75
Aged 23 years 11 months, Ht. 5 ft 5 3/4 ins
Complexion fresh, Eyes hazel
Hair brown, Trade Puddler
Joined Regiment 02/02/78 at South Africa
Transferred to Army Reserve 04/03/82
To 1st Battalion 19/09/85

378 Private SIVORNS William
Born: Parish Willenhall
Town Willenhall, Staffs.
Enlisted at Lichfield on 20/10/74
Aged 20 years, Ht. 5 ft 6 1/4 ins
Complexion fresh, Eyes hazel
Hair dark brown, Trade Locksmith
Joined Regiment 03/12/78 at Pretoria,
South Africa
Transferred to Army Reserve 29/11/80

376 Private SMITH Charles
Born: Parish Dalehalls
Town Burslem, Staffs.
Enlisted at Newcastle Under Lyme
on 10/05/59
Aged 18 years Ht. 5 ft 4 ins
Complexion fresh, Eyes brown
Hair light brown, Religion Protestant
Trade Potter
Joined Regiment 28/01/61
at Saugor (Central India)
Discharged 27/07/80

386 Private SMITH Daniel
Born: Parish Eccleshall
Town Eccleshall, Staffs.
Enlisted at Hanley on 24/10/74
Aged 18 years 10 months, Ht. 5 ft 6 1/2 ins
Complexion fresh, Eyes brown
Hair brown, Trade Labourer
Joined Regiment 13/06/77
at Cape of Good Hope
Transferred to Army Reserve 15/11/80

1018 Private SMITH Daniel
Born: Parish Wilnecote
Town Tamworth, Staffs.
Enlisted at Lichfield on 24/05/77
Aged 18 years 3 months, Ht. 5 ft 5 1/4 ins
Complexion fair, Eyes brown
Hair light brown, Trade Miner
Joined Regiment 13/06/77 at Cape of Good Hope
To 38th Regiment 19/06/80

646 Private SMITH Henry
(Nominal Roll 646 SMITH Henry George)
Born: Parish Hanley
Town Hanley, Staffs.
Enlisted at Leek on 19/10/59
Aged 26 years 9 months, Ht. 5 ft 6 1/2 ins
Complexion sallow, Eyes dark
Hair dark brown, Religion Protestant
Trade Printer
Joined Regiment 28/01/61 at Saugor (Central India)
Discharged 21 Years 11/01/81

725 Private SMITH Henry
Born: Parish Blakenhall
Town Walsall, Staffs.
Enlisted at Walsall on 30/06/76
Aged 18 years 8 months, Ht. 5 ft 7 ins
Complexion dark, Eyes brown
Hair brown, Trade Collier
Joined Regiment 03/12/78 at Pretoria, South Africa
Transferred to Army Reserve 27/08/81

424 Private SMITH James
Born: Parish Stone
Town Stone, Staffs.
Enlisted at Lichfield on 30/11/74
Aged 18 years, Ht. 5 ft 5 3/4 ins
Complexion fresh, Eyes blue
Hair dark brown, Trade Shoe Maker
Joined Regiment 03/12/78 at Pretoria,
South Africa
Transferred to Army Reserve 30/11/80

1948 Private SMITH John
Born: Parish St. Pancras
Town London, Middlesex
Enlisted at Westminster on 13/04/72
Aged 19 years 5 months, Ht. 5 ft 5 1/2 ins
Complexion fresh, Eyes hazel
Hair brown, Trade Plasterer
Joined Regiment not known
Transferred to Army Reserve 04/10/79

1050 Private SMITH John
Born: Parish Burgshill
Town   Dudley, Staffs.
Enlisted at Walsall, on 01/06/77
Aged 19 years, Ht. 5 ft 6 1/4 ins
Complexion fair, Eyes brown
Hair brown, Trade Labourer
Joined Regiment 02/02/78 at South Africa
To 38th Regiment 19/06/80

1350 Private SMITH John
Born: Parish Coleshill
Town   Coleshill, Warks.
Enlisted at Birmingham on 20/08/70
Aged 20 years 5 months, Ht. 5 ft 5 1/2 ins
Complexion dark, Eyes hazel
Hair dark brown, Religion C.E.
Trade Labourer
Joined Regiment 22/08/70 at Belfast
To 19th Brigade Depot 01/12/80

657 Private SMITH Joseph
Born: Parish Birmingham
Town   Birmingham, Warks.
Enlisted at Birmingham on 24/01/76
Aged 18 years 6 months, Ht. 5 ft 6 1/2 ins
Complexion fresh, Eyes blue
Hair light brown, Trade Engine Driver
Joined Regiment 03/12/78 at Pretoria,
South Africa
Died 14/10/79

61   Private SMITH Mark
Born: Parish Coleshill
Town   Coleshill, Warks.
Enlisted at Wednesbury on 05/06/73
Aged 19 years 6 months, Ht. 5 ft 6 1/8 ins
Complexion fair, Eyes light blue
Hair light brown, Trade Labourer
Joined Regiment 04/11/74 at Hong Kong
Transferred to Army Reserve 11/10/79

1240 Private SMITH Michael
Born: Parish Salford
Town   Manchester, Lancs.
Enlisted at Manchester on 04/12/68
Aged 21 years, Ht. 5 ft 7 1/8 ins
Complexion marked, with small nose,
Eyes grey, Hair dark brown
Trade Labourer
Joined Regiment 19/12/68 at Fleetwood
Discharged 10/12/80

729 Private SPENCE Robert
Born: Parish Edinburgh
Town   Edinburgh, Lothian
Enlisted at Walsall on 10/07/76
Aged 26 years 8 months, Ht. 5 ft 7 1/2 ins
Complexion fair, Eyes grey
Hair light brown, Trade Butcher
Joined Regiment 17/11/76 at Singapore
Transferred to Army Reserve 17/07/82

746 Private SPINK James
Born: Parish Walsall
Town   Walsall, Staffs.
Enlisted at Walsall on 27/07/76
Aged 19 years, Ht. 5 ft 6 1/4 ins
Complexion fresh, Eyes blue
Hair brown, Trade Lace Maker
Joined Regiment 03/12/78 at Pretoria,
South Africa
Transferred to Army Reserve 27/01/83

1526 Private STACEY Arthur
Born: Parish Blythe
Town   Worksop, Notts.
Enlisted at Leicester on 09/12/70
Aged 19 years, Ht. 5 ft 4 7/8 ins
Complexion fresh, Eyes dark hazel
Hair auburn, Religion Wesleyan
Trade Sadler
Joined Regiment 19/12/70 at Belfast
To 19th Brigade Depot 01/12/80

1987 Private STORAS William
Born: Parish Camberwell
Town   London, Surrey
Enlisted at Westminster on 03/05/72
Aged 24 years 1 month, Ht. 5 ft 5 3/4 ins
Complexion fresh, Eyes grey
Hair brown, Trade Brick Maker
Joined Regiment not known
Transferred to Army Reserve 04/10/79

1063 Private SMITH Johnson
Born: Parish St. Thomas's
Town   Nottingham, Notts.
Enlisted at Reading, on 25/01/67
Aged 21 years, Ht. 5 ft 5 ins
Complexion fresh, Eyes hazel
Hair brown, Religion C.E.
Trade Iron Turner
Joined Regiment 01/02/67 at Devonport
Died at Fort Weeber, Transvaal
South Africa 10/12/79

258 Private SMITH Joseph
Born: Parish High Wycombe
Town   High Wycombe, Bucks.
Enlisted at Aldershot on 23/03/74
Aged 18 years 3 months, Ht. 5 ft 5 1/2 ins
Complexion fair, Eyes brown
Hair light brown, Trade Chain Maker
Joined Regiment 23/02/76 at Singapore
Transferred to Army Reserve 29/04/80

1494 Private SMITH William
Born: Parish Liverpool
Town   Liverpool, Lancs.
Enlisted at Liverpool on 28/11/70
Aged 19 years Ht. 5 ft 5 3/8 ins
Complexion fair, Eyes grey
Hair light, Religion C.E.
Trade Labourer
Joined Regiment 02/12/70 at Belfast
(Refer to new Army No. DSR401)

2029 Private SOAN Benjamin James
Born: Parish Bethnal Green
Town   London, Middlesex
Enlisted at Westminster on 19/10/71
Aged 24 years, Ht. 5 ft 5 ins
Complexion fresh, Eyes grey
Hair brown, Trade Labourer
Joined Regiment not known
Transferred to Army Reserve 04/10/79

1805 Private SPEERS James
Born: Parish Shankhill
Town   Belfast, Antrim
Enlisted at Belfast on 17/10/71
Aged 19 years 6 months, Ht. 5 ft 7 ins
Complexion sallow, Eyes grey
Hair light brown, Trade Turner
Joined Regiment 20/10/71 at Belfast
Transferred to Army Reserve 04/10/79

2016 Private STANLEY Alfred
Born: Parish Lambeth
Town   London, Middlesex
Enlisted at Westminster on 24/05/72
Aged 21 years 9 months, Ht. 5 ft 5 ins
Complexion fresh, Eyes hazel
Hair dark brown, Trade Whitesmith
Joined Regiment not known
Transferred to Army Reserve 30/08/81

1776 Private STERLING Henry
Born: Parish St. George's
Town   Stamford, Lincs.
Enlisted at Lincoln on 20/09/71
Aged 19 years 2 months, Ht. 5 ft 7 ins
Complexion fresh, Eyes blue
Hair brown, Religion C.E.
Trade Blacksmith
Joined Regiment 29/09/71 at Belfast
Discharged by Purchase 14/02/80

138 Private STOKES Frank
Born: Parish St. John's
Town   Wolverhampton, Staffs.
Enlisted at Lichfield on 25/09/73
Aged 19 years 2 months, Ht. 5 ft 6 3/4 ins
Complexion fresh, Eyes hazel
Hair brown, Trade Brass Founder
Joined Regiment 04/11/74 at Hong Kong
Transferred to Army Reserve 04/10/79

2042 Private SULLIVAN Michael
Born: Parish Curragh
Town   Tralee, Kerry
Enlisted at Westminster on 14/02/72
Aged 25 years, Ht. 5 ft 5 1/2 ins
Complexion fresh, Eyes grey
Hair brown, Trade Labourer
Joined Regiment not known
Transferred to Army Reserve 04/10/79

225 Private STORER Walter
Born: Parish   Drayton
Town   Tamworth, Staffs.
Enlisted at Newcastle Under Lyme
on 18/02/74
Aged 18 years 10 months, Ht. 5 ft 6 1/4 ins
Complexion fresh, Eyes grey
Hair light brown, Trade Collier
Joined Regiment 23/02/76 at Singapore
Transferred to Army Reserve 24/06/80

1396 Private SUGDEN Richard
Born: Parish   Halifax
Town   Halifax, Yorks.
Enlisted at Manchester on 01/09/70
Aged 23 years 4 months, Ht. 5 ft 6 ins
Complexion fresh, Eyes hazel
Hair dark brown, Religion C.E.
Trade Wood Sorter
Joined Regiment 12/09/70 at Belfast
Discharged 11/09/82

120   Private TALLICE George
Born: Parish   Shenstone
Town   Shenstone, Staffs.
Enlisted at Lichfield on 15/09/73
Aged 18 years, Ht. 5 ft 5 ins
Complexion fresh, Eyes grey
Hair brown, Trade Labourer
Joined Regiment 23/02/76 at Singapore
Transferred to Army Reserve 24/06/80

735 Private TAYLOR John
Born: Parish   Walsall
Town   Wednesbury, Staffs.
Enlisted at Walsall on 18/07/76
Aged 18 years, Ht. 5 ft 5 1/2 ins
Complexion fresh, Eyes hazel
Hair black, Trade Puddler
Joined Regiment 03/12/78 at Pretoria,
South Africa
To 1st Battalion 11/01/82

720   Private TAYLOR Joshua Thomas
Born: Parish   St. James
Town   Wolverhampton, Staffs.
Enlisted at Wolverhampton on 27/06/76
Aged 19 years 9 months Ht. 5 ft 5 1/4 ins
Complexion fresh, Eyes grey
Hair brown, Trade Labourer
Joined Regiment 17/11/76 at Singapore
Transferred to Army Reserve 30/08/81

816   Private TETLOW Edward
Born: Parish   Salford
Town   Salford, Lancs.
Enlisted at Manchester on 09/10/76
Aged 20 years 5 months, Ht. 5 ft 5 1/2 ins
Complexion fresh, Eyes hazel
Hair dark brown, Trade Cloth Finisher
Joined Regiment 03/12/78 at Pretoria,
South Africa
Transferred to Army Reserve 27/01/83

1794 Private THOMPSON Alexander
Born: Parish   Ballyfarleigh
Town   Donaghadee, Down
Enlisted at Belfast on 07/10/71
Aged 19 years 4 months, Ht. 5 ft 6 1/4 ins
Complexion fresh, Eyes blue
Hair dark brown, Trade Labourer
Joined Regiment 10/10/71 at Belfast
Transferred to Army Reserve 04/10/79

2096 Private THOMPSON E. G. A.
Born: Parish
Town
County
Enlisted at
Aged   years   months, Ht. ft   ins
Complexion   Eyes
Hair   Religion
Trade
Joined Regiment

2002 Private THOMPSON William
(Nominal Roll
2002 THOMSON William)
Born: Parish   Greenwich
Town   Greenwich, Kent
Enlisted at Westminster on 19/05/72
Aged 21 years 7 months, Ht. 5 ft 5 ins
Complexion fair, Eyes grey
Hair brown, Trade Labourer
Joined Regiment not known
Transferred to Army Reserve 04/10/79

2060 Private SUMMERSBY Henry
Born: Parish   Walton
Town   London, Surrey
Enlisted at Westminster on 21/05/72
Aged 20 years, Ht. 5 ft 5 1/2 ins
Complexion fresh, Eyes hazel
Hair brown, Trade Groom
Joined Regiment not known
Transferred to Army Reserve 10/10/79

1988 Private SUTTON James
Born: Parish   Slieverve
Town   Waterford, Kilkenny
Enlisted at Barnet on 04/05/72
Aged 24 years 5 months, Ht. 5 ft 5 1/2 ins
Complexion fresh, Eyes grey
Hair brown, Trade None
Joined Regiment not known
Transferred to Army Reserve 20/12/79

1895 Private TAYLOR Thomas
Born: Parish   Lambeth
Town   London, Surrey
Enlisted at Lambeth on 24/02/72
Aged 20 years, Ht. 5 ft 5 1/2 ins
Complexion fair, Eyes hazel
Hair brown, Trade Porter
Joined Regiment not known
Transferred to Army Reserve 04/10/79

255 Private TAYLOR William
Born: Parish   St. Mary's
Town   Stafford, Staffs.
Enlisted at Lichfield on 21/03/74
Aged 19 years 6 months, Ht. 5 ft 6 1/2 ins
Complexion ruddy, Eyes hazel
Hair brown, Trade Shoe Maker
Joined Regiment 18/01/77 at Singapore
Transferred to Army Reserve 25/06/80

373 Private TEEHAN John
Born: Parish   Salford
Town   Salford, Lancs.
Enlisted at Middleton on 09/05/59
Aged 18 years Ht. 5 ft 3 ins
Complexion fresh, Eyes hazel
Hair dark brown, Trade Labourer
Joined Regiment 28/01/61
at Saugor (Central India)
Discharged 10/02/82

2081 Private THOMPSON Henry
Born: Parish   Bromley
Town   Bromley, Kent
Enlisted at Westminster on 08/06/72
Aged 19 years 5 months, Ht. 5 ft 5 3/4 ins
Complexion fresh, Eyes grey
Hair brown, Trade not known
Joined Regiment not known
Attached to Headquarter Staff.
Appointed Acting Quartermaster Sergeant
Killed in Action 22/01/79 at Isandhlwana

1957 Private THOMPSON Robert
Born: Parish   Marylebone
Town   London, Middlesex
Enlisted at Westminster on 17/04/72
Aged 24 years 4 months, Ht. 5 ft 5 ins
Complexion fresh, Eyes grey
Hair brown, Trade Clerk
Joined Regiment not known
Transferred to Army Reserve 04/10/79

811 Private THOMPSON Thomas
Born: Parish   Birmingham
Town   Birmingham, Warks.
Enlisted at Walsall on 09/10/76
Aged 18 years, Ht. 5 ft 8 ins
Complexion dark, Eyes hazel
Hair brown, Trade Brass Founder
Joined Regiment 03/12/78 at Pretoria,
South Africa
To 38th Regiment 19/06/80

1061 Private TILLEY George
Born: Parish   St. George's
Town   Wolverhampton, Staffs.
Enlisted at Wolverhampton on 07/06/77
Aged 20 years, Ht. 5 ft 4 3/4 ins
Complexion fresh, Eyes blue
Hair light, Trade Farrier
Joined Regiment 02/02/78 at South Africa
To 38th Regiment 19/06/80

162 Private THORLEY Thomas
Born: Parish   Cheadle
Town   Cheadle, Staffs.
Enlisted at Newcastle Under Lyme
on 01/01/74
Aged 19 years 10 months, Ht. 5 ft 4 1/2 ins
Complexion fresh, Eyes light blue
Hair brown, Trade Miner
Joined Regiment 04/11/74 at Hong Kong
Deserted 13/01/80

19/587 Private TIBBOTT Joseph
Born: Parish   Brierley Hill
Town   Dudley, Staffs.
Enlisted at Newcastle Under Lyme
on 06/12/75
Aged 22 years 4 months, Ht. 5 ft 6 3/4 ins
Complexion fresh, Eyes hazel
Hair brown, Trade Miner
Joined Regiment 17/11/76 at Singapore
Served in "A" Company
Killed in Action 12/03/79 Intombi River

1529 Private TOMLINSON William
Born: Parish   St. Mary's
Town   Leicester, Leics.
Enlisted at Leicester on 12/12/70
Aged 21 years, Ht. 5 ft 5 1/2 ins
Complexion fresh, Eyes hazel
Hair brown, Religion C.E.
Trade Shoe Finisher
Joined Regiment 19/12/70 at Belfast
Transferred to Army Reserve 30/08/81

649 Private TOMLIN Thomas
Born: Parish   Wolverhampton
Town   Wolverhampton, Staffs.
Enlisted at Wolverhampton date not known
Aged 18 years, Ht. 5 ft 5 1/4 ins
Complexion sallow, Eyes hazel
Hair dark brown, Trade Puddler
Joined Regiment 02/02/78 at South Africa
Transferred to Army Reserve 27/08/81

19/1705 Private TUCKER George
Born: Parish   Birmingham
Town   Birmingham, Warks.
Enlisted at Birmingham on 13/02/71
Aged 19 years 3 months, Ht. 5 ft 5 5/8 ins
Complexion fresh, Eyes hazel
Hair brown, Religion C.E.
Trade Shoe Finisher
Joined Regiment 20/02/71 at Belfast
Served in "E" Company
Killed in Action 12/03/79 Intombi River

1887 Private TURNER Charles
Born: Parish   Waltham
Town   Waltham, Essex
Enlisted at Westminster on 23/02/72
Aged 20 years, Ht. 5 ft 5 ins
Complexion fresh, Eyes hazel
Hair brown, Trade Labourer
Joined Regiment not known
Transferred to Army Reserve 04/10/79

459 Private TURNER Edward
Born: Parish   Bradley
Town   Wolverhampton, Staffs.
Enlisted at Wolverhampton on 04/01/75
Aged 18 years Ht. 5 ft 5 3/4 ins
Complexion fresh, Eyes hazel
Hair brown, Trade Miner
Joined Regiment 02/02/78 at South Africa
Transferred to Army Reserve 22/07/—

501 Private TYLER James
Born: Parish   Tamworth
Town   Tamworth, Warks.
Enlisted at Lichfield on 02/06/75
Aged 23 years, Ht. 5 ft 6 3/4 ins
Complexion fresh, Eyes blue
Hair light brown, Trade Collier
Joined Regiment 13/06/77
at Cape of Good Hope
Transferred to Army Reserve 03/06/81

370 Private VERNON James
Born: Parish   Manchester
Town   Manchester, Lancs.
Enlisted at Middleton on 30/04/59
Aged 20 years, Ht. 5 ft 4 1/4 ins
Complexion fresh, Eyes grey
Hair brown, Trade Book Binder
Joined Regiment 01/04/60
at Saugor (Central India)
Served in "E" Company
Killed in Action 12/03/79 Intombi River

1826 Private TOAL James
Born: Parish   Loughgall
Town   Loughgall, Armagh
Enlisted at Dublin on 02/11/71
Aged 19 years, Ht. 5 ft 6 3/8 ins
Complexion fresh, Eyes grey
Hair brown, Trade Labourer
Joined Regiment 07/11/71 at Belfast
Transferred to Army Reserve 04/10/79

1291 Private TOMLINSON Richard
Born: Parish   Wheelton
Town   Chorley, Lancs.
Enlisted at Preston on 23/06/69
Aged 18 years, Ht. 5 ft 7 1/4 ins
Complexion fresh, Eyes brown
Hair brown, Trade Labourer
Joined Regiment 26/06/69 at Fleetwood
Served in "E" Company
Killed in Action 12/03/79 Intombi River

19/104 Private TUCKER Thomas
Born: Parish   Birmingham
Town   Birmingham, Warks.
Enlisted at Birmingham on 01/09/73
Aged 21 years 8 months, Ht. 5 ft 6 1/4 ins
Complexion fresh, Eyes grey
Hair brown, Trade Wood Carver
Joined Regiment 04/11/74 at Hong Kong
Served in "E" Company
Killed in Action 12/03/79 Intombi River

487 Private TULLY Charles
Born: Parish   Ballinasloe
Town   Ballinasloe, Roscommon
Enlisted at Lichfield on 15/05/77
Aged 18 years, Ht. 5 ft 5 1/4 ins
Complexion dark, Eyes brown
Hair brown, Trade Miner
Joined Regiment 02/02/78 at South Africa
Transferred to Army Reserve 25/05/81

669 Private TULLY Patrick
Born: Parish   Walsall
Town   Walsall, Staffs.
Enlisted at Walsall on 15/02/76
Aged 19 years, Ht. 5 ft 5 ins
Complexion fresh, Eyes hazel
Hair brown, Trade Labourer
Joined Regiment 03/12/78 at Pretoria,
South Africa
Served in "D" Company
To 38th Regiment 19/06/80

188 Private UPPERDINE Joseph
Born: Parish   St. John's
Town   Wolverhampton, Staffs.
Enlisted at Walsall on 26/01/74
Aged 18 years, Ht. 5 ft 5 ins
Complexion fresh, Eyes brown
Hair brown, Trade Labourer
Joined Regiment 23/02/76 at Singapore
Transferred to Army Reserve 19/06/80

1046 Private VAUGHAN John
Born: Parish   Shrewsbury
Town   Shrewsbury, Shrops.
Enlisted at Lichfield on 31/05/77
Aged 18 years 8 months, Ht. 5 ft 4 3/4 ins
Complexion fresh, Eyes hazel
Hair light brown, Trade Fitter
Joined Regiment 02/02/78 at South Africa
Transferred to 38th Regt. (Date not known)

423 Private VARLEY John
Born: Parish   St. John's
Town   St. John's, Staffs.
Enlisted at Lichfield on 30/01/74
Aged 19 years, Ht. 5 ft 7 1/4 ins
Complexion fresh, Eyes hazel
Hair dark brown, Trade Butcher
Joined Regiment 02/02/78 at South Africa
Died at Pietermaritzburg,
South Africa 22/07/80

563 Private WALKER Thomas
Born: Parish   St. Mary's
Town   Portsmouth, Hamps.
Enlisted at Lichfield on 27/09/75
Aged 18 years, Ht. 5 ft 7 1/2 ins
Complexion fresh, Eyes grey
Hair light brown, Trade Labourer
Joined Regiment 03/12/78 at Pretoria,
South Africa
Transferred to Army Reserve 27/09/81

1080 Private VICKERY Samuel
Born: Parish Chard
Town Chard, Somerset
Enlisted at Crewkerne on 06/02/67
Aged 18 years, Ht. 5 ft 6 ins
Complexion sallow, Eyes blue
Hair light brown, Trade Lace Maker
Joined Regiment 13/02/67 at Portland
Invalided 26/05/85

1911 Private WAKELING George
Born: Parish Haverhill
Town Clare, Suffolk
Enlisted at Bury St. Edmunds on 11/03/72
Aged 19 years 9 months, Ht. 5 ft 6 ins
Complexion fresh, Eyes grey
Hair brown, Trade Hair Weaver
Joined Regiment not known
Transferred to Army Reserve 04/10/79

1495 Private WALSH William
Born: Parish Ormskirk
Town Ormskirk, Lancs.
Enlisted at Liverpool on 28/11/70
Aged 21 years, Ht. 5 ft 6 3/8 ins
Complexion fresh, Eyes grey
Hair brown, Religion R.C.
Trade Labourer
Joined Regiment 02/12/70 at Belfast
Deserted 13/01/80

62 Private WARD William
Born: Parish Stourbridge
Town Stourbridge, Worcs.
Enlisted at Wednesbury on 06/06/73
Aged 22 years 3 months, Ht. 5 ft 5 1/4 ins
Complexion dark, Eyes brown
Hair dark brown, Trade Labourer
Joined Regiment 18/12/73 at Hong Kong
Transferred to Army Reserve 04/10/79

204 Private WARNER Cornelius
Born: Parish Whaley Town
Town Walsall, Staffs.
Enlisted at Newcastle Under Lyme
on 04/02/74
Aged 21 years 11 months, Ht. 5 ft 7 3/4 ins
Complexion fresh, Eyes grey
Hair brown, Trade Labourer
Joined Regiment 04/11/74 at Hong Kong
Transferred to Army Reserve 25/06/80

730 Private WEAVER Benjamin
Born: Parish Netherton
Town Dudley, Staffs.
Enlisted at Walsall on 13/07/76
Aged 23 years 2 months, Ht. 5 ft 7 5/8 ins
Complexion dark, Eyes grey
Hair light brown, Trade Chain Maker
Joined Regiment 17/11/76 at Pretoria,
South Africa
Transferred to Army Reserve 27/01/83

606 Private WEAVER Job:
Born: Parish Cradley
Town Rowley, Staffs.
Enlisted at Dudley on 31/12/75
Aged 19 years, Ht. 5 ft 5 1/4 ins
Complexion fair, Eyes dark grey
Hair light brown, Trade Chain Maker
Joined Regiment 03/12/78 at Pretoria,
South Africa
Transferred to Army Reserve 29/08/81

1289 Private WEAVER John
Born: Parish Macclesfield
Town Macclesfield, Cheshire
Enlisted at Preston, on 19/06/69
Aged 19 years, Ht. 5 ft 6 ins
Complexion fair, Eyes grey
Hair light brown, Trade Silk Dyer
Joined Regiment 23/06/69 at Fleetwood
Died 26/03/80

1002 Private WEST Eli
Born: Parish London
Town London, Middlesex
Enlisted at Birmingham on 07/05/77
Aged 18 years 8 months, Ht. 5 ft 5 1/2 ins
Complexion fresh, Eyes grey
Hair brown, Trade Boatman
Joined Regiment 13/06/77
at Cape of Good Hope
To 38th Regiment 19/06/80

549 Private WALSH Anthony
(Nominal Roll 549 WELSH Anthony)
Born: Parish Kildare
Town Kildare, Kildare
Enlisted at Newcastle Under Lyme
on 19/07/75
Aged 19 years, Ht. 5 ft 7 1/4 ins
Complexion fresh, Eyes hazel
Hair brown, Trade Labourer
Joined Regiment 17/11/76 at Singapore
Transferred to Army Reserve 20/10/81

219 Private WALSH John
Born: Parish Birmingham
Town Birmingham, Warks.
Enlisted at Birmingham on 10/02/74
Aged 19 years 9 months, Ht. 5 ft 5 3/4 ins
Complexion fresh, Eyes blue
Hair dark brown, Trade Labourer
Joined Regiment 04/11/74 at Hong Kong
Transferred to Army Reserve 27/08/80

427 Private WASSALL(VC) Samuel
Born: Parish Dudley
Town Dudley, Staffs.
Enlisted at Dudley on 28/11/74
Aged 18 years, Ht. 5 ft 4 3/4 ins
Complexion fair, Eyes grey
Hair light brown, Trade Dyer
Joined Regiment 13/06/77 at South Africa
Received Victoria Cross and £10 pa for life
for gallant conduct at Isandhlwana 22/01/79
Transferred to Army Reserve 30/11/80

1016 Private WASSALL Charles
Born: Parish Birmingham
Town Birmingham, Warks.
Enlisted at Birmingham on 18/05/77
Aged 21 years 1 month, Ht. 5 ft 5 1/4 ins
Complexion fresh, Eyes blue
Hair brown, Trade Labourer
Joined Regiment 02/06/77 at South Africa
Transferred to 38th Regt. (Date not known)

1924 Private WAXHAM Thomas
Born: Parish Frimley
Town Ely, Cambs.
Enlisted at Westminster on 20/03/72
Aged 22 years, Ht. 5 ft 5 ins
Complexion fresh, Eyes grey
Hair brown, Trade Shoe Maker
Joined Regiment not known
Transferred to Army Reserve 04/10/79

19/716 Private WEAVER Joseph
Born: Parish Castlechurch
Town Stafford, Staffs.
Enlisted at Stafford on 24/06/76
Aged 20 years, Ht. 5 ft 5 1/2 ins
Complexion fresh, Eyes grey
Hair brown, Trade Labourer
Joined Regiment 17/11/76 at Singapore
Served in "A" Company
Killed in Action 12/03/79 Intombi River

605 Private WEBSTER John
Born: Parish Walsall
Town Walsall, Staffs.
Enlisted at Walsall on 30/12/75
Aged 21 years, Ht. 5 ft 6 ins
Complexion fresh, Eyes grey
Hair brown, Trade Engine Fitter
Joined Regiment 17/11/76 at Singapore
Transferred to Army Reserve 26/03/82

1905 Private WELLS James
Born: Parish Whitechapel
Town London, Middlesex
Enlisted at Westminster on 09/03/72
Aged 22 years, Ht. 5 ft 6 ins
Complexion fresh, Eyes grey
Hair brown, Trade Shoe Maker
Joined Regiment not known
Discharged 03/07/80

228 Private WESTWOOD Thomas
Born: Parish Birmingham
Town Birmingham, Warks.
Enlisted at Birmingham on 20/02/74
Aged 19 years 6 months, Ht. 5 ft 7 1/4 ins
Complexion sallow, Eyes dark brown
Hair dark brown, Trade Screw Maker
Joined Regiment 23/02/76 at Singapore
Transferred to Army Reserve 25/06/80

990   Private WESTERN Charles
Born: Parish Wolverhampton
Town   Wolverhampton, Staffs.
Enlisted at Walsall on 02/05/77
Aged 22 years, Ht. 5 ft 5 1/2 ins
Complexion fair, Eyes grey
Hair light brown, Trade Labourer
Joined Regiment 13/06/77
at Cape of Good Hope
To Depot 19/08/82

294   Private WESTWOOD James
Born: Parish Birmingham
Town   Birmingham, Warks.
Enlisted at Birmingham on 29/04/74
Aged 19 years 10 months, Ht. 5 ft 6 1/2 ins
Complexion fresh, Eyes brown
Hair brown, Trade Screw Maker
Joined Regiment 23/02/76 at Singapore
Transferred to Army Reserve 25/06/80

2061 Private WHITE George
Born: Parish Camden Town
Town   London, Sussex
Enlisted at Dunstable on 27/05/72
Aged 20 years, Ht. 5 ft 8 ins
Complexion fair, Eyes blue
Hair light brown, Trade Labourer
Joined Regiment not known
Transferred to Army Reserve 04/10/79

1041 Private WHITEHOUSE David
Born: Parish Tividale
Town   Rowley, Worcs.
Enlisted at Tipton on 30/05/77
Aged 22 years 4 months, Ht. 5 ft 11 1/2 ins
Complexion dark, Eyes grey
Hair black, Trade Labourer
Joined Regiment 13/06/77
at Cape of Good Hope
To 1st Battalion 04/10/81

9/60 Private WHITEHOUSE Joseph
Born: Parish Warwick
Town   Warwick, Warks.
Enlisted at Walsall on 31/05/73
Aged 20 years 9 months, Ht. 5 ft 5 ins
Complexion fair, Eyes grey
Hair brown, Trade Puddler
Joined Regiment 04/11/74 at Hong Kong
Mounted Infantry
Killed in Action 22/01/79 Isandhlwana

247   Private WILEY Charles
Born: Parish Wolverhampton
Town   Wolverhampton, Staffs.
Enlisted at Worcester on 20/02/74
Aged 19 years 3 months, Ht. 5 ft 9 1/2 ins
Complexion fresh, Eyes grey
Hair brown, Trade Corkscrew Maker
Joined Regiment 23/02/76 at Singapore
Transferred to Army Reserve 29/08/81

137   Private WILLEY Thomas
Born: Parish Wolverhampton
Town   Wolverhampton, Staffs.
Enlisted at Wolverhampton on 24/09/73
Aged 21 years, Ht. 5 ft 6 3/4 ins
Complexion fresh, Eyes grey
Hair brown, Trade Iron Brazier
Joined Regiment 04/11/74 at Hong Kong
Transferred to Army Reserve 17/06/80

24 Private WILKINS Henry
Born: Parish Fazeley
Town   Tamworth, Staffs.
Enlisted at Birmingham on 01/05/73
Aged 24 years Ht. 5 ft 7 1/2 ins
Complexion fresh, Eyes grey
Hair light brown, Trade Oil Cake Maker
Joined Regiment 04/11/74 at Hong Kong
Transferred to Army Reserve 04/10/79

1039 Private WILLIAM William
(Nominal Roll 1039 Williams William)
Born: Parish Dudley
Town   Dudley, Staffs.
Enlisted at Walsall on 30/05/77
Aged 19 years, Ht. 5 ft 5 1/2 ins
Complexion fresh, Eyes grey
Hair dark brown, Trade Miner
Joined Regiment 13/06/77
at Cape of Good Hope Invalided 03/08/80

1097 Private WHEELER Richard
Born: Parish Reading
Town   Reading, Berks.
Enlisted at Aldershot on 27/08/67
Aged 17 years, Ht. 5 ft 6 ins
Complexion fresh, Eyes grey
Hair dark brown, Trade Labourer
Joined Regiment 28/08/67 at Aldershot
To Depot 21/06/82

752 Private WHILE William
Born: Parish Shrewsbury
Town   Shrewsbury, Shrops.
Enlisted at Newcastle Under Lyme
on 03/08/76
Aged 24 years, Ht. 5 ft 5 ins
Complexion fresh, Eyes hazel
Hair brown, Trade Nailer
Joined Regiment 17/11/76 at Singapore
Transferred to Army Reserve 31/01/83

769 Private WHITEHOUSE Richard
(Nominal Roll 769 WHITEHEAD Richard)
Born: Parish
Town   County
Enlisted at
Aged   years   months, Ht.   ft   ins
Complexion   Eyes
Hair   Religion
Trade
Joined Regiment
Transferred to Army Reserve 26/01/83

774 Private WHITEHOUSE William
Born: Parish
Town
County
Enlisted at
Aged   years   months, Ht.   ft   ins
Complexion   Eyes
Hair   Religion
Trade
Joined Regiment
Transferred to Army Reserve 26/01/83

2097 Private WHYMAN Thomas
Born: Parish Nutshend
Town   Royston, Hereford.
Enlisted at Cambridge on 28/10/72
Aged 19 years 6 months, Ht. 5 ft 5 1/2 ins
Complexion fresh, Eyes brown
Hair dark brown, Trade Labourer
Joined Regiment not known

791 Private WILKINSON Samuel
Born: Parish Wolstanton
Town   Newcastle, Staffs.
Enlisted at Manchester on 09/09/76
Aged 19 years 11 months, Ht. 5 ft 6 ins
Complexion fresh, Eyes grey
Hair dark brown, Trade Collier
Joined Regiment 02/02/78 at South Africa
To 1st Battalion 04/10/81
Transferred to Army Reserve 10/11/81

1006 Private WILKINSON William
Born: Parish Silverdale
Town   Newcastle, Staffs.
Enlisted at Newcastle Under Lyme
on 11/05/77
Aged 18 years 2 months, Ht. 5 ft 5 1/4 ins
Complexion fresh, Eyes brown
Hair brown, Trade Engine Driver
Joined Regiment 13/06/77
at Cape of Good Hope
Transferred to Army Reserve 13/05/83

450 Private WILLINGS Enoch
Born: Parish Bilston
Town   Wolverhampton, Staffs.
Enlisted at Dudley on 28/12/74
Aged 18 years Ht. 5 ft 6 1/4 ins
Complexion ruddy, Eyes grey
Hair light brown, Trade Collier
Joined Regiment 02/02/78 at South Africa
Transferred to Army Reserve 13/05/81

691 Private WILLIAMS Harry
Born: Parish Southall
Town   Southall, Warks.
Enlisted at Birmingham on 29/05/76
Aged 20 years 1 month, Ht. 5 ft 6 1/2 ins
Complexion fair, Eyes blue
Hair light brown, Trade Labourer
Joined Regiment 17/11/76 at Singapore
Transferred to Army Reserve 29/05/82

991 Private WILLIAMS Charles
Born: Parish Birmingham
Town Birmingham, Warks.
Enlisted at Wednesbury on 17/05/77
Aged 18 years 3 months, Ht. 5 ft 5 1/2 ins
Complexion fair, Eyes grey
Hair light brown, Trade Brass Draper
Joined Regiment 13/06/77
at Cape of Good Hope
To 38th Regiment 19/06/80

1876 Private WILLIAMS George
Born: Parish Bridgenorth
Town Bridgenorth, Shrops.
Enlisted at Liverpool on 27/12/71
Aged 21 years, Ht. 5 ft 5 3/8 ins
Complexion fresh, Eyes hazel
Hair brown, Trade Painter
Joined Regiment not known
Transferred to Army Reserve 04/10/79

573 Private WILLIAMS Thomas
Born: Parish Clements
Town Cambridge, Cambs.
Enlisted at Cambridge on 24/06/59
Aged 20 years, Ht. 5 ft 4 3/4 ins
Complexion fresh, Eyes hazel
Hair brown, Religion Protestant
Trade Porter
Joined Regiment 28/01/61
at Saugor (Central India)
Discharged 20/07/80

617 Private WILLIAMS William
Born: Parish St. Peter's
Town Wolverhampton, Staffs.
Enlisted at Shipton on 05/01/76
Aged 18 years 7 months, Ht. 5 ft 5 ins
Complexion fresh, Eyes hazel
Hair dark brown, Trade File Cutter
Joined Regiment 02/02/78 at South Africa
To 38th Regiment 19/06/80

2013 Private WILMOTT William
(Nominal Roll 2013 WILMOT William)
Born: Parish St. Andrew's
Town Plymouth, Devon.
Enlisted at Westminster on 23/05/72
Aged 20 years 5 months, Ht. 5 ft 6 ins
Complexion fair, Eyes grey
Hair brown, Trade Coachsmith
Joined Regiment not known
Transferred to Army Reserve 08/11/79

1375 Private WILTSHIRE Benjamin
Born: Parish Bow
Town London, Middlesex
Enlisted at Westminster on 04/08/70
Aged 18 years, Ht. 5 ft 7 ins
Complexion fresh, Eyes blue
Hair brown, Religion C.E.
Trade Labourer
Joined Regiment 31/08/70 at Belfast
Deserted 14/11/71 and 19/10/79

686 Private WINTER John
Born: Parish Nuneaton
Town Nuneaton, Warks.
Enlisted at Lichfield on 25/05/76
Aged 23 years, Ht. 5 ft 7 3/4 ins
Complexion fresh, Eyes blue
Hair brown, Trade Miner
Joined Regiment 17/11/76 at Singapore
Transferred to Army Reserve 25/05/82

1020 Private WINWOOD Joseph
Born: Parish Blackheath
Town Blackheath, Kent
Enlisted at Lichfield on 24/05/77
Aged 19 years, Ht. 5 ft 8 3/4 ins
Complexion fresh, Eyes blue
Hair dark brown, Trade Miner
Joined Regiment 13/06/77
at Cape of Good Hope
To 1st Battalion 04/10/81

1486 Private WOODING Isaac
Born: Parish New Mills
Town Newtown, Montgomery
Enlisted at Bolton on 24/11/70
Aged 18 years, Ht. 5 ft 6 ins
Complexion fresh, Eyes blue
Trade Labourer
Joined Regiment 01/12/70 at Belfast
Transferred to Army Reserve 29/08/81

997 Private WILLIAMS Shadrack
Born: Parish Wolstanton
Town Newcastle, Staffs.
Enlisted at Newcastle on 07/05/77
Aged 24 years, Ht. 5 ft 10 1/2 ins
Complexion fresh, Eyes blue
Hair brown, Trade Miner
Joined Regiment 13/06/77
at Cape of Good Hope
To 38th Regiment 19/06/80

361 Private WILLIAMS Thomas
Born: Parish St. Mary's
Town Leeds, Yorks.
Enlisted at Tower Hill on 02/05/59
Aged 22 years Ht. 5 ft 3 1/8 ins
Complexion fresh, Eyes grey
Hair sandy, Religion Protestant
Trade Labourer
Joined Regiment 28/01/61
at Saugor (Central India)
Discharged 20/07/80

1896 Private WILSON Charles
Born: Parish Wanstead
Town Wanstead, Essex
Enlisted at Westminster on 26/02/72
Aged 23 years 10 months, Ht. 5 ft 5 3/4 ins
Complexion fresh, Eyes blue
Hair light brown, Trade Bricklayer
Joined Regiment not known
Transferred to Army Reserve 04/10/79

627 Private WILSON Frederick
Born: Parish Stone
Town Stone, Staffs.
Enlisted at Wolverhampton on 08/01/76
Aged 20 years 9 months, Ht. 5 ft 5 1/4 ins
Complexion sallow, Eyes hazel
Hair dark brown, Trade Fireman
Joined Regiment 02/02/78 at South Africa
To 38th Regiment 19/06/80

1175 Private WILSON Henry
Born: Parish Mansfield
Town Mansfield, Notts.
Enlisted at Liverpool on 07/07/68
Aged 24 years, Ht. 5 ft 7 1/2 ins
Complexion sallow, Eyes blue
Hair light brown, Trade Clerk
Joined Regiment 16/07/68 at Aldershot
To Depot 21/03/82

295 Private WOOD Charles
Born: Parish Stoke on Trent
Town Fenton, Staffs.
Enlisted at Newcastle Under Lyme
on 30/04/74
Aged 20 years, Ht. 5 ft 4 3/4 ins
Complexion fresh, Eyes blue
Hair light brown, Trade Miner
Joined Regiment 23/02/76 at Singapore
Transferred to Army Reserve 09/07/80

446 Private WOOD David
Born: Parish Gornal
Town Dudley, Staffs.
Enlisted at Wolverhampton on 19/12/74
Aged 20 years 1 month, Ht. 5 ft 5 1/2 ins
Complexion fresh, Eyes blue
Hair light brown, Trade Miner
Joined Regiment 03/12/78 at Pretoria,
South Africa
Transferred to Army Reserve 15/07/82

515 Private WOOD James
Born: Parish Clanger
Town Walsall, Staffs.
Enlisted at Lichfield on 26/06/75
Aged 18 years 1 month, Ht. 5 ft 5 ins
Complexion fresh, Eyes hazel
Hair light brown, Trade Collier
Joined Regiment 13/06/77
at Cape of Good Hope
Transferred to Army Reserve 30/06/81

1871 Private WOOLLAMS Frederick
Born: Parish Pershore
Town Worcester, Worcs.
Enlisted at Worcester on 28/12/71
Aged 20 years, Ht. 5 ft 5 1/2 ins
Complexion fresh, Eyes grey
Joined Regiment not known
Transferred to Army Reserve 09/03/80

1605 Private WOODWARD Herbert
Born: Parish Barnton
Town   Barnton, Lancs.
Enlisted at Liverpool on 10/01/71
Aged 18 years, Ht. 5 ft 5 7/8 ins
Complexion fresh, Eyes blue
Hair brown, Religion C.E.
Trade Labourer
Joined Regiment 16/01/71 at Belfast
Served in "E" Company
Killed in Action 12/03/79 Intombi River

1394 Private WOOLCOT Henry
(Nominal Roll 1394 WOOLCOX Henry)
Born: Parish St. Giles
Town   London, Middlesex
Enlisted at Newcastle Under Lyme
on 30/08/70
Aged 19 years, Ht. 5 ft 6 3/4 ins
Complexion fresh, Eyes grey
Hair light brown, Religion C.E.
Trade Carpenter
Joined Regiment 12/09/70 at Belfast
Discharged 31/08/82

564 Private WRIGHT George
Born: Parish Bushbury
Town   Wolverhampton, Staffs.
Enlisted at Wolverhampton on 28/09/75
Aged 20 years 6 months Ht. 5 ft 6 1/4 ins
Complexion fresh, Eyes blue
Hair light brown, Trade Striker
Joined Regiment 02/02/78 at South Africa
Transferred to Army Reserve 30/08/81

2051 Private WRIGHT Joseph
Born: Parish St. Michael's
Town   Lichfield, Staffs.
Enlisted at not known on 29/11/71
Aged 22 years, Ht. 5 ft 7 3/4 ins
Complexion fresh, Eyes blue
Hair brown, Trade Labourer
Joined Regiment not known
Transferred to Army Reserve 04/10/79

1023 Private WRIGHT William
Born: Parish St. Mary's
Town   Walsall, Staffs.
Enlisted at Lichfield on 29/05/77
Aged 19 years 6 months, Ht. 5 ft 5 1/4 ins
Complexion fresh, Eyes grey
Hair brown, Trade Miner
Joined Regiment 13/06/77
at Cape of Good Hope
To 38th Regiment 17/06/80

2078 Private WORTY James
Born: Parish Liverpool
Town   Liverpool, Lancs.
Enlisted at Liverpool on 10/06/72
Aged 19 years 4 months, Ht. 5 ft 5 3/8 ins
Complexion dark, Eyes grey
Hair dark brown, Trade Labourer
Joined Regiment not known
Transferred to Army Reserve 04/10/79

598 Private WRIGHT Frederick
Born: Parish Stoke on Trent
Town   Longton, Staffs.
Enlisted at Hanley on 16/12/75
Aged 18 years 8 months, Ht. 5 ft 5 ins
Complexion fair, Eyes blue
Hair brown, Trade Potter
Joined Regiment 02/02/78 at South Africa
Transferred to 38th Regt. (Date not known)

566 Private WROE John
Born: Parish Ashton
Town   Ashton, Lancs.
Enlisted at Manchester on 28/06/59
Aged 18 years Ht. 5 ft 3 ins
Complexion fair, Eyes grey
Hair brown, Religion R.C.
Trade Cotton Piecer
Joined Regiment 28/01/61
at Saugor (Central India)
Discharged 03/08/80

1888 Private YOUNG Thomas
Born: Parish Lambeth
Town   London, Surrey
Enlisted at Lambeth on 23/02/72
Aged 24 years 2 months, Ht. 5 ft 5 ins
Complexion fair, Eyes grey
Hair brown, Trade Whip Maker
Joined Regiment not known
Transferred to Army Reserve 04/10/79

1013 Private YOXALL Frederick
Born: Parish Church Coppsubott
Town   Crewe, Cheshire
Enlisted at Hanley on 24/05/77
Aged 22 years, Ht. 5 ft 4 1/2 ins
Complexion fresh, Eyes grey
Hair dark brown, Trade Farm Labourer
Joined Regiment 13/06/77
at Cape of Good Hope
Transferred to Army Reserve 19/04/83

C.E. Fripps' impressive painting of Isandhlwana It was from this carnage that Samuel Wassall of the 80th Regiment escaped and with outstanding bravery whilst doing so, won the first of the Zulu War Victoria Crosses.

THE 80th REGIMENT OF FOOT (STAFFORDSHIRE VOLUNTEERS)
SOUTH AFRICA MEDAL LIST

Non commissioned officers and men of the 80th Regiment of Foot (Staffordshire Volunteers) who were entitled to the South Africa Medal (General Order No.134 dated October 1880). Their names do not appear on the previous list - they were not entitled under G O No.103 dated August 1880. Nb. The soldiers whose names appeared on the previous list were entitled to the South Africa Medal under both general orders 103 & 134.

G.O.134 - Medals   **Extracts from the General Order No.134:**

 I. The provisions of G.O.103 of 1880 will apply to the forces engaged against Sekukuni in 1878.

 II. In the applications for medals on behalf of such forces, a column will be inserted in the rolls, showing that they were employed in the operations referred to.

OFFICERS, NON-COMMISSIONED OFFICERS AND MEN OF THE 80th REGIMENT OF FOOT

1206	**Ainsworth**, Henry. Private	101	Donovan, Thomas. Private
1850	Allen, Frederick. Private	1900	Dyball, William. Private
1444	Allen, Victor. Private	8	Dyer, George. Private
573	Andrews, William. Private	376	**Ellis**, George. Private
1058	Archer, Harry. Private	1543	Ellis, George. Private
441	Armstrong, John. Private	1162	Ellis, Henry. Private
1055	Armstrong, William. Private	1917	**Ferguson**, Donald. Drummer
1907	Austin, Edward. Private	1830	Farmer, William. Private
1103	**Baxter**, James. Sergeant (Corporal)	1643	Faulkner, William. Private
36	Beverley, James. Sergeant	1228	Fisher, John. Private
98	Butler, John. Sergeant	701	Flint, John. Private
1065	Bagnall, John. Private	303	Foreman, Henry. Private
1788	Bailey, Robert. Private		**Griffin**, Thomas Edward. Lieutenant &Adjutant
560	Baker, William. Private	3642	Graham, Ewen. Lance Corporal
22	Bale, Robert. Private	854	Grantley, Thomas. Private (Paymaster Sergeant)
2056	Balshaw, Albert Edward. Private	700	Gillham, James. Private
1928	Barr, Thomas. Private	1390	Goddard, William. Private
2053	Barrett, Denis. Private	1800	Gretton, William. Private
1872	Barsby, Thomas. Private	1034	Guy, Peter. Private
865	Baxter, Samuel. Private	1802	**Hopkins**, Harry. Colour Sergeant (Corporal)
1535	Beamer, John. Private	3	Hancox, Samuel. Private (Sergeant)
1110	Beatson, Matthew. Private	1558	Hankinson, Richard. Private
280	Biernes, Thomas. Private	1368	Hanson, William. Private
16	Bond, William. Private	1325	Hardy, William. Private
1138	Bow, Spencer. Private	1231	Harvey, William. Private
1277	Bowker, Robert. Private	1562	Haslem, Richard. Private
1358	Brisbane, William. Private	134	Hawkes, Charles. Private
1172	Bunday, David. Private	1975	Hayelton, William. Private
2044	Burden, Joseph. Private	1576	Heavey, Bartholomew. Private
736	Burns, Hugh. Private	1032	Holman, Charles. Private
1609	Burtenshaw, Henry. Private	820	Hopkins, George. Private
3244	**Collins**, John. Sergeant	1994	Hopkins, John T. Private
1063	Cox,George William. Sergeant (Corporal)	890	Horn, William. Private (Corporal)
210	Carr, Joseph. Private	925	Hunt, John. Private
986	Carter, Charles. Private	229	Hutchinson, Thomas. Private
1043	Cheshire, John. Private	366	**Jones**, Nicholas. Sergeant Instructor Musketry
2171	Childs, Edward. Private	566	Jackson, Joseph. Private
1884	Clarke, Alfred George. Private	742	Jackson, Thomas. Private
413	Clulec, Thomas. Private	776	Johnson, Harry. Private
298	Cole, Frederick. Private	997	Jones, Joel. Private
1935	Cooke, Albert. Private	1619	Jones, John. Private
1371	Cooke, Charles. Private	1632	**Kitchen**, Joseph. Private
601	Cox, Joseph. Private	999	**Lovegrove**, Richard. Corporal (Private)
1111	Cruite, George. Private	595	Lawrence, Charles. Drummer
1650	Culley, Frederick. Private	1376	Lacy, John. Private
947	**Davis**, Peter. Sergeant	393	Lawley, Henry. Private
488	Dickey, William. Sergeant	271	Lowe, Samuel. Private
1804	Duncan, John. Sergeant	773	Lunn, John. Private
900	Duggan, Myles. Lance Sergeant	1645	Lynch, William. Private
1364	Daniels, George. Private	1771	Lyons, Thomas. Private
614	Davis, John. Private		**Marshall**, Francis Macleod Hastings. Lieutenant
1633	Delaney, Michael J. Private	1500	McGuiness, Christopher. Orderly Room Clerk
256	Dobson, Edward. Private	1012	Machin, Joseph. Private

1161	Marlow, James. Private	473	Stokes, David. Private
2007	McCall, Martin. Private	1067	Stokes, John. Private
2017	McCann, Patrick. Private	229	Street, Walter. Private
1314	McCormack, Michael. Private	1792	Sturges, Warren. Private
1159	McMahon, Robert. Private		**Tyler**, Charles John Roper. Major
1580	Meachin, Alfred. Private	63	Trott, Charles. Private (Sergeant)
1010	Mead, Isaac. Private	630	Tarver, Jonathan. Private
1683	Mercer, George. Private	1330	Taylor, Robert. Private
1033	Monckton, Edward. Private	1536	Taylor, William. Private
1493	**Nayler**, George. Private	435	Terry, Joseph. Private
555	Nichols, Benjamin. Private	329	Topp, Charles. Private
2023	Nolan, John. Private	487	Tulley, Charles. Private
548	Nolan, Phillip. Private	782	Turner, William. Private
119	**Oakley**, Thomas. Private	1322	Tyldesley, Thomas. Private
478	O'Gera, William. Private	993	**Vanston**, Francis. Private
1162	Owen, George. Private	1941	Vaughan, Henry. Private
	Pendrey, James. Quartermaster	1965	**Woods**, Alfred H. Colour Sergeant
98	Perkins, Benjamin. Sergeant	124	Walkley, Thomas. Private
527	Payne, Edward. Private	803	Walsh, John. Private
685	Perkins, Albert. Private	1009	Wedge, Henry. Private
757	Prince, Joseph. Private	987	Welch, John H. Private
1007	**Ryder**, Thomas. Private	1704	Wells, Edward. Private
	Saunders, Allan. Captain	624	White, John. Private
	Savage, Henry Charles. Lieutenant & Adjutant	1095	White, William. Private
149	Smallwood, Samuel. Armourer Sergeant	1069	Whitby, Charles. Private
819	Simpson, Arthur. Private	2091	Whittaker, William. Private
684	Smallman, John. Private	442	Williamson, Frank. Private
664	Smith, Thomas. Private	1535	Woodford, Joseph. Private
705	Smith, Thomas. Private	977	Woodward, James. Private
200	Snape, James. Private	724	Woodward, Jason. Private
1077	Spencer, Henry. Private	980	Woodward, John. Private
1107	Stevenson, George. Private	1972	**Young,** Henry. Private
1137	Stevenson, Thomas. Private		

THE 80th REGIMENT OF FOOT (STAFFORDSHIRE VOLUNTEERS) SUPPLEMENTARY MEDAL LIST

This supplementary medal list contains the names of 290 officers, non-commissioned officers and men of the 80th Regiment of Foot who are not included in the preceding lists and are taken from the South Africa Medal Rolls produced by D.R.Forsyth. A total of one hundred and twenty were issued with no 'clasp', the rest were entitled to the clasp '1879' or as otherwise stated.Nb. Some soldiers army numbers have been amended to match the 80th Regiment's Nominal Roll Book. The surnames contained within the brackets are the spellings contained within the Regiment's Nominal Roll Book.

OFFICERS, NON-COMMISSIONED OFFICERS AND MEN OF THE 80th REGIMENT OF FOOT

1188	**Appleby**, James. Drummer	1859	Bartley, Myles W. Private No clasp
1856	Adams, George. Private No clasp	1520	Baskoth, Thomas. Private
1916	Aher, James. Private No clasp	1259	Baverstock, George. Private
1968	Allen, John. Private No clasp	1145	Bayless, John. Private
1236	Allport, Cornelius. Private	1081	Biddle, James. Private
1817	Ansell, Joseph. Private No clasp	1251	Bills, Thomas. Private
857	Archer, Richard. Private	1174	Birch, Joseph. Private
922	Archer, Thomas. Private	1854	Blackham, William. Private No clasp
1970	Archer, William. Private No clasp	349	Boyd, Thomas. Private
1874	Atkinson, Seymour. Private No clasp	1919	Brady, Robert. Private No clasp
1918	Attwater, John. Private No clasp	633	Brindley, Alfred. Private
		647	Brindley, William. Private
	Bradshaw, James Lewis. Brevet Major	1556	Britton, Edward. Private
1199	Bailey, Jno. Davies. Private	1914	Brown, George. Private No clasp
397	Baker, Philip. Private	1134	Bullock, George. Private
1870	Ball, John. Private No clasp	907	Bullock, William. Private
1086	Banks, William. Private	79	Burns, H. Private
1883	Bannon, Patrick. Private No clasp	323	Burns, Harry. Private
1908	Bargery, Henry. Private No clasp	1078	Burnes, William. Private
1935	Barker, William. Private No clasp	1922	Bursnell, James. Private No clasp
1634	Barter, Robert. Private	1936	Bush, John. Private

	Cole, Charles Christopher. Captain
222	Cleaver, William. Sergeant
1389	Carter, Henry. Lance Sergeant
1139	Cairns, Edward. Private
1222	Callaghan, Michael. Private
1938	Camp, Daniel. Private No clasp
387	*Carter, John. Private
1140	Cartwright, Samuel. Private
818	Cash, William. Private
1913	Cassidy, William. Private No clasp
387	*Cater, John. Private
1974	Champion, John P. Private No clasp
1906	Childerstone, Stephen. Private No clasp
1967	Cinamond, Thomas E. Private No clasp
1052	Clarke, John. Private
1911	Clarke, John. Private No clasp
1934	Clarke, William. Private No clasp
2044	Colbridge, William. Private No clasp
1550	Cole, Charles Edwin. Private
1969	Coleman, John. Private No clasp
1098	Concaly, John. Private
1221	Connolly, William. Private
1232	Cook, Thomas. Private
1245	Cooper, Jas. Frederick. Private
736	Cope, Thomas. Private
1871	Corbett, Thomas. Private No clasp
1169	Corry, John. Private
1029	Costello, S. Private
1966	Cox, William. Private No clasp
1905	Creagh, William. Private No clasp
194	Crudington, Richard. Private
1198	Cruise, Samuel. Private
1889	Cullum, John. Private No clasp
78	**Dailey**, John. Private No clasp
1158	Dakin, George. Private
410	Dale, Henry. Private
1728	Daniels, Samuel. Private
1213	Darby, William. Private
846	Davis, Samuel. Private No clasp
1271	Donnelly, Patrick. Private
1879	Donohoe, Michael. Private No clasp
1901	Double, Charles. Private No clasp
1231	Dudley, Thomas. Private
1219	Dudwell, John. Private
1202	Dutton, Noah. Private
1876	**Eaton**, William. Private No clasp
1973	Ede, Thomas. Private No clasp
1554	Edwards, Emanuel. Private
1094	Edwards, Michael. Private
750	Egerton, Samuel. Private
1884	**Feltwell**, John. Private No clasp
2052	Ferris, James. Private
1857	Fitton, James. Private No clasp
1512	Fletcher, Albert. Private
1342	Ford, Patrick. Private
1886	Foster, Benjamin. Private No clasp
754	Foster, Thomas. Private
1552	Frayne, Joseph. Private
1196	**Gallagher**, James. Private
1544	Gallagher, Patrick. Private
1024	Garford, Edward. Private No clasp
1813	Garvey, Thomas. Private No clasp
925	Gibbons, Joseph. Private
1261	Glinnon, (Glennon) Thomas. Private No clasp

1184	Goulden, Patrick. Private
936	Granger, Thomas. Private
1131	Greatrix, Benjamin. Private
1851	Griffin, George W. Private No clasp
1538	Griffiths, Jas. Thornton. Private
639	Griffiths, Thomas. Private
835	Griffiths, William. Private
1239	Guest, Thomas. Private
	Huskisson, Samuel George Capt &
	Brevet Major No clasp
820	Hackley, James. Private
1518	Hadley, William. Private
1539	Halligan, Thomas. Private
1937	Hall, James. Private No clasp
1853	Hamilton, James. Private No clasp
1891	Hammonds, William. Private
937	Hanes, E. Private
1880	Harbridge, George. Private No clasp
1253	Hart, John. Private
1864	Haven, John. Private No clasp
1129	Hawksworth, George. Private No clasp
1818	Hayes, Edward. Private No clasp
1268	Haynes, John. Private
921	Haywood, Charles. Private
1267	Haywood, Henry. Private
871	Heath, Robert. Private
1868	Hickey, Joseph. Private No clasp
1848	Hill, Joseph. Private
2047	Hippenstall, John. Private No clasp
894	Hope, James. Private
1933	Hoyle, Joseph. Private No clasp
525	Hughes, George. Private
1814	Hughes, Richard. Private No clasp
1060	Hughes, Thomas. Private
1132	Hughes, William. Private
1900	Hunt, William. Private No clasp
1887	Hyem, Henry. Private
442	**Jervis**, James. Sergeant
1965	Jackman, Eli. Private No clasp
1509	Jackson, Benjamin. Private
823	James, Joseph. Private
1059	Jenkins, Richard. Private
223	Jennings, Thomas. Private
891	Johnson, William. Private
1819	Jones, Daniel. Private No clasp
437	Jones, John. Private
1961	Jones, Samuel. Private No clasp
1214	Jones, Thomas. Private
1260	Jones, Thomas. Private
1976	Joyce, Eli. Private No clasp
1907	**Keen**, John. Private No clasp
2045	Kelly, John. Private No clasp
914	King Charles. Private
1217	King, Peter. Private
182	Knowles, Henry. Private
1885	**Lawson**, John. Private No clasp
1958	Lineham, Jeremiah. Private No clasp
917	Locker, George Thomas. Private
1903	Loney, Thomas. Private No clasp
1863	Loomes, Reuban Thomas. Private
1230	Lowder, John. Private
1532	Luck, John. Private No clasp
1618	**McMullen**, Henry. Corporal

1867	Mellon, James. Corporal No clasp	1296	Rodgers, John. Private
1866	Moon, Richard. Corporal No clasp	1881	Roe, John. Private No clasp
596	Maker, James. Drummer	1540	Rollason, Henry. Private
305	Mace, John. Private	1811	Rose, Richard W. Private No clasp
1981	Macklin, (Macklan) James. Private	1573	Rowe, James. Private
879	Manning, John. Private	853	Rowley, George. Private
963	Mannison, Michael. Private	1923	Rutledge, John. Private No clasp
181	Manson, Alexander. Private	1263	Ryan, John. Private
2046	Marshall, Henry. Private No clasp	1971	Ryan, John. Private No clasp
1397	Martin, William. Private	1878	Ryan, Richard. Private No clasp
1522	Mason, John. Private		
1801	Mayfield, Frank. Private No clasp	1863	**Searl**, Henry. Sergeant No clasp
1253	McClennon, Jno. Private No clasp	1873	Sample, Thomas. Private No clasp
1120	McCue, John. Private	972	Saunders(Sanders) John Private Clasp '1878-9'
765	McDermott, John. Private	1888	Selby, George. Private No clasp
1975	McGlocklin, James. Private No clasp	1904	Sewell, John. Private No clasp
1972	McGrath, Dennis. Private No clasp	1535	Shaw, Jonathan. Private
1875	McGrath, William. Private No clasp	1534	Shaw, Robert. Private
1960	McLoughlin, John. Private No clasp	1810	Shaw, William. Private No clasp
1177	McNichols, Nicholas. Private	323	Shea, Cornelius. Private No clasp
344	Merrill, Thomas. Private	1557	Slater, John. Private
1910	Midgley, James. Private No clasp	893	Smith, David. Private
851	Millership, William. Private	1171	Smith, George. Private No clasp
1109	Mills, Henry. Private	1523	Smith, John. Private
1083	Moffatt, Thomas. Private	1902	Southworth, Benjamin. Private No clasp
924	Moran, James. Private	2009	Stabbs, John. Private No clasp
1084	Morley, Michael. Private	1274	Summers, Jonathan. Private
2049	Morris, George. Private No clasp		
1920	Morris, William. Private No clasp	1245	**Tansley**, Jas. Frederick. Private
2043	Mulligan, John. Private No clasp	1244	Taylor, Alfred. Private
1964	Murphy, Peter. Private No clasp	1121	Taylor, James. Private
1226	Musson, William. Private	1207	Taylor, James. Private
		368	Taylor, William. Private
1555	**Newman**, J. Corporal No clasp	162	Thirley, Thomas Private Clasp '1878-9'
1962	Nash, George. Private No clasp	1511	Thomas, Daniel. Private
958	Newman, Alfred. Private	1108	Toy, James. Private
1963	Newman, Edward. Private No clasp	1091	Tunstall, Arthur. Private
1508	Nicholl, George. Private		
		1872	**Upsdale**, Henry. Private No clasp
1812	**O'Gilvie**, James. Private No clasp	902	Upton, Henry. Private
2087	Owens, Henry. Private No clasp		
1240	Owens, Richard. Private	1516	**Vaughan**, Frank. Private
1858	Owens, Thomas. Private No clasp		
			Williams, George Albanus. 2nd Leiutenant
1401	**Pritchard**, Samuel. Corporal No clasp	530	Walker, Edward. Private No clasp
1147	Parker, Thomas. Private	1546	Walker, George. Private
1903	Parson, John W. Private No clasp	1851	Ward, Issac. Private No clasp
719	Parsons, Richard. Private No clasp	1530	Ward, John. Private
1225	Picken, James. Private No clasp	1921	Ward, John. Private No clasp
1917	Plummer, Peter. Private No clasp	1144	Ware, William. Private
904	Potts, John. Private No clasp	1092	Washington, William. Private
1852	Powis, Noah. Private No clasp	1815	Westcloth, James R. Private No clasp
1909	Preston, John. Private No clasp	1269	Weston, Patrick. Private
1265	Price, John. Private	1506	Wheat, Clement. Private
1816	Price, John. Private No clasp	1536	White, Joseph R. Private
		1250	Whittaker, David. Private
824	**Quinn**, John. Private	1555	Wilkes, William. Private
829	**Rafferty**, James. Private	815	Wilkinson, David. Private
1094	Ratcliffe, George. Private No clasp	1549	Wilks, John. Private
869	Reilly, Michael. Private	1915	Williams, John. Private No clasp
1183	Reeves, James. Private No clasp	1809	Williams, (Williamson) Thomas. Private No clasp
1541	Reynolds, John. Private	1551	Worrolls, Henry. Private
1093	Rice, Andrew. Private	1912	Worth, Richard. Private No clasp
1099	Richardson, Robert. Private	2048	Wrick, (Wride)William. Private No clasp
933	Riley, Albert. Private	1882	Wright, John. Private No clasp
878	Roach, Thomas. Private		
1959	Robertson, Samuel. Private No clasp		*387 Carter John and 387 Cater John probably same person

Ships in port - in this picture, waiting to carry the body of Prince Louis Napoleon home to England

Chapter 10
Analysis: 80th Regiment of Foot and the Zulu War

A total of seven hundred and twenty-nine rank and file soldiers who are entered on the Medal Roll for the South Africa Medal as described in the General Order No.103 have been included in the following research. At the time of going to press, no information was available for twenty-two men (3%).

Places of Birth

A total of 608 men (86%), 63 N.C.O.s (74%) and 545 privates (87%) were born in England, spread over thirty-six counties. Some 222(31%) Staffordshire men filled the ranks of the 80th, thus proving that this was truly a Staffordshire regiment. The next highest represented counties were Warwickshire and Lancashire, each having 66 men(9%). Northern Ireland(as now) provided 31 men(4%) from six counties. 44 men(6%) were born in Southern Ireland (as now Eire), from twenty-two counties. In total 75 men(10%), 16 N.C.O.s(19%) and 59 privates(9%) were born in Ireland. 8 men(1%), were born in five counties of Wales. Scotland was represented by 7 men(1%), from seven counties north of the border.

2 non-commissioned officers were born in Australia, another non-commissioned officer and a private were born in India. One non-commissioned officer was born in Canada and another was born in Germany. Sergeant Major John Allen 4202 was born on board ship on passage home from India.

Places of Enlistment

The earliest recorded date of enlistment was that of Colour Sergeant Edward Shore 3124 who signed his attestation papers on February 3rd 1854. He joined the 80th Regiment on the same day. Patrick Nolan 1339 is the earliest private soldier recorded to have signed attestation papers, on February 14th 1854. Privates John Brown 122, Dennis McCleary 62 and John Birch 29 who all joined the 80th on October 2nd 1858 at Cawnpore, Central India, were the earliest recorded private soldiers.

The youngest age at enlistment was Private Patrick Nolan 1339 who was only fourteen. Privates William Findley 222 and Henry Pemberton 805 were twenty-eight years old when they signed attestation papers, the oldest recorded. There was a total of six 'boy' soldiers recorded, all under sixteen years of age. The average age at enlistment for the non-commissioned officer and the private soldier was 19.05 years and 20.15 years of age respectively.

A total of 32 men(4%) have not had their place of attestation and enlistment established. Some 647 men(93%) enlisted in England in a total of seventy-six locations. One man enlisted in Glasgow, Scotland. In Ireland ten places saw a total of 48 men(7%) enlist. Only one is recorded as joining the army abroad - in Saugor, Central India. Outside Staffordshire the most popular place of enlistment for the 80th Regiment was London; a total of 85 men(12%). But the major recruitment by far was from within its own boundaries, a total of 305 men(44%) being enlisted in Staffordshire. This latter total can be further refined to reflect that 16(19%) became non-commissioned officers, the remaining 289(47%) staying as private soldiers.

Trades and Occupations

87 non-commissioned officers (12%) and 642 privates (88%) have been researched. The trades and occupations of 3 N.C.O.s(3%) and 21 privates(3%), 24 men in total have not been confirmed. A total of 143 trades and occupations have been identified, this excludes labourers, farm labourers and those described as having 'no trades'. The most common occupation prior to enlistment (excluding labourer), was that of a miner/collier, some 80 men (11%). This no doubt reflected the large coalmining industry in Staffordshire in the latter part of the 19th Century. 147 men had the description, 'trade none'. Labourers, farm-labourers and those with the description of 'Trade none' amounted to 277 men (39%). The soldiers of the 80th Regiment of Foot were clearly a widely skilled body of men.

Places of Birth (Counties)

COUNTY	N.C.O.s	PRIVATES	TOTALS
Bedfordshire	-	1	1
Berkshire	1	2	3
Buckinghamshire	-	2	2
Cambridgeshire	-	6	6
Cheshire	5	15	20
Cornwall	1	1	2
Derbyshire	-	6	6
Devon	2	3	5
Dorset	1	2	3
Durham	-	1	1
Essex	-	7	7
Gloucestershire	3	6	9
Hampshire	-	9	9
Herefordshire	-	2	2
Hertfordshire	-	3	3
Isle of Wight	-	1	1
Kent	2	9	11
Lancashire	8	58	66
Leicesterhire	4	11	15
Lincolnshire	-	3	3
Middlesex	8	39	47
Norfolk	1	1	2
Northamptonshire	-	3	3
Nottinghamshire	1	4	5
Oxfordshire	-	2	2
Rutland	1	1	2
Shropshire	6	17	23
Somerset	1	3	4
Staffordshire	10 (12%)	212 (34%)	222 (31%)
Suffolk	-	3	3
Surrey	1	11	12
Sussex	-	5	5
Warwickshire	3	63	66
Wiltshire	2	1	3
Worcestershire	2	20	22
Yorkshire	-	12	12
Total Counties 36	63 (74%)	545 (88%)	608 (86%)

NORTHERN IRELAND

	N.C.O.s	PRIVATES	TOTALS
Antrim	2	8	10
Armagh	3	6	9
Down	1	3	4
Derry	-	2	2
Fermanagh	1	1	2
Tyrone	1	3	4
Total Counties 6	8 (9%)	23 (4%)	31 (4%)

SOUTHERN IRELAND

	N.C.O.s	PRIVATES	TOTALS
Cavan	-	4	4
Clare	-	1	1
Cork	-	1	1
Donegal	-	1	1
Dublin	-	4	4
Galway	1	3	4
Kerry	-	1	1
Kildare	-	1	1
Kilkenny	-	2	2
Laois (Queens)	-	1	1
Leimster	-	1	1
Limerick	-	3	3
Longford	1	-	1
Mayo	2	2	4
Meath	1	1	2
Monaghan	-	1	1
Offaly (Kings)	-	2	2
Roscommon	1	2	3
Tiperrary	-	2	2
Waterford	1	1	2

Wexford	-	1	1
Wickford	1	1	2
Total Counties 22	8 (9%)	36 (6%)	44(6%).

WALES

Anglesey	-	2	2
Denbighshire	-	1	1
Montgomeryshire	-	2	2
Neath	-	1	1
Radnorshire	-	2	2
Total Counties 5	-	8 (1%)	8 (1%)

SCOTLAND

Ayrshire	-	2	2
Caithness	-	1	1
Lanarkshire	-	2	2
Lothian	-	1	1
Midlothian	-	1	1
Total Counties 5	-	7 (1%)	7 (1%)

BORN ABROAD

Australia	2	2	4
Canada	1	-	1
Germany	1	-	1
India	1	1	2
Born on Board ship (passage home from India) 1		-	1
Total	6 (7%)	3 (0.5%)	9 (1%).

N.B. Percentages are based on the known information on places of birth

TOTAL NUMBER OF MEN   Rank and File   729 men   Non commissioned Officers   87 (12%)

Privates   642 (88%)

Places of Enlistment

PLACE OF ENLISTMENT	N.C.O.s	PRIVATES	TOTALS
Aldershot	1	9	10
Ashburton	1	1	2
Barnet	1	1	2
Bilston*	-	1	1
Birmingham	6	60	66
Bishop Stortford	-	2	2
Blackburn	-	4	4
Bolton	2	5	7
Bristol	-	2	2
Brixham	-	1	1
Burton on Trent*	-	1	1
Bury St.Edmunds	-	1	1
Cambridge	-	5	5
Canterbury	-	1	1
Carlisle	-	1	1
Chatham	1	-	1
Chester	1	-	1
Chesterfield	-	3	3
Colchester	-	1	1
Congleton	-	1	1
Crewekerne	-	1	1
Deptford	-	1	1
Derby	-	1	1
Devonport	-	1	1
Doncaster	-	2	2
Dover	-	3	3
Dudley*	-	10	10
Dunstable	-	1	1
Fleetwood	2	3	5
Gosport	2	-	2
Hanley*	-	25	25
Horley	-	1	1
Huntingdon	-	1	1
Kirkham	-	1	1
Leek*	-	3	3
Leeds	1	1	2

Leicester	4	8	12
Lichfield*	3	69	72
Lincoln	-	1	1
Liverpool	9	37	46
London	1	-	1
(Lambeth)	2	2	4
(Tower Hill)	1	2	3
(Westminster)	6	71	77
Longton*	-	1	1
Loughborough	-	2	2
Manchester	5	20	25
Market Harborough	-	1	1
Middleton	-	2	2
Newcastle Under Lyme*	6	57	63
Northampton	-	1	1
Oldham	-	1	1
Peterborough	-	1	1
Plymouth	1	-	1
Preston	2	3	5
Reading	1	2	3
Salford	1	-	1
Sheffield	2	1	3
Shipton	-	1	1
Shrewsbury	1	4	5
Stafford*	1	7	8
Storenburg	1	-	1
Stourbridge	-	2	2
St. Alban's	-	1	1
St.George's Barracks	-	1	1
Tamworth**	1	2	3
Taunton	1	1	2
Tipton*	-	1	1
Uttoxeter*	-	1	1
Walsall*	3	70	73
Warrington	-	2	2
Wednesbury*	-	10	10
West Bromwich*	-	2	2
Wolverhampton*	2	29	31
Woolwich	-	1	1
Worcester	-	3	3
Totals	72 (88%)	575 (93%)	647(93%)
NORTHERN IRELAND			
Belfast	5	20	25
Enniskillen	-	1	1
Portadown	-	2	2
Totals	5 (6%)	23 (4%)	28 (4%) .
SOUTHERN IRELAND			
Birr	1	3	4
Bruff	-	1	1
Buttevant	3	4	7
Clonmel	-	1	1
Dublin	-	5	5
Kilkenny	-	1	1
Waterford	-	1	1
Totals	4 (5%)	16 (3%)	20 (3%) .
SCOTLAND			
Glasgow	-	1	1
Totals	-	1	1
ABROAD			
Central India - Saugor	1	-	1
Totals	1	-	1

Total enlisted within the County of Staffordshire 16 (20%)   289 (47%)   305 (44%)

* Places within Staffordshire
**Circa 1879 Tamworth, was divided, part in Staffordshire and part in Warwickshire. It has been taken that the soldiers who are recorded to have been born in the Staffordshire part of Tamworth have enlisted in the same sector of the town.

Trades and Occupations

	N.C.O.s	PRIVATES	TOTALS
Axle Tree Polisher	-	1	1
Baker	-	4	4
Baker & Miller	-	1	1
Barman	-	1	1
Bedstead Maker	-	2	2
Billard Maker	-	1	1
Blacksmith	-	3	3
Blacksmith's Striker	-	1	1
Bleacher	-	1	1
Bleach Maker	1	-	1
Boat Builder	-	1	1
Boatman	-	1	1
Boiler Maker	-	2	2
Bolt Maker	-	2	2
Book Binder	-	1	1
Boot Closer	-	1	1
Boot Finisher	-	1	1
Brass Caster	-	2	2
Brass Draper	-	1	1
Brass Founder	-	4	4
Brick Maker	-	3	3
Bricklayer	2	8	10
Brazier	-	1	1
Butcher	-	7	7
Cabinet Maker	-	1	1
Carman	1	1	2
Carpenter	1	7	8
Carrier	-	2	2
Carter	-	2	2
Caster	1	1	2
Chain Maker	-	5	5
Chandelier Maker	-	1	1
Chandler	-	1	1
Chores	-	1	1
Clerk	6	9	15
Clerk and Dispenser of Medicine	1	-	1
Coachsmith	-	1	1
Coach Wheelwright	-	1	1
Collier/Miner	3	77	80
Confectioner	-	1	1
Corkscrew Maker	-	1	1
Cloth Finisher	-	1	1
Cotton Piecer	-	1	1
Cutler	-	1	1
Dyer	1	2	3
Engine Driver	1	4	5
Engine Fitter	-	1	1
Engineer	1	1	2
Farm Labourer	-	4	4
Farm Servant	-	1	1
Farrier	-	1	1
File Cutter	-	2	2
Fireman	-	2	2
Fitter	1	4	5
Forgeman	1	4	5
Fruiterer	-	1	1
Galvaniser	-	2	2
Gas Fitter	-	1	1
Gardener	-	1	1
Glass Cutter	-	2	2
Glass Cutter & Glazier	-	1	1
Glazier	-	1	1
Gold Beater	-	1	1
Grinder	-	1	1
Grocer	-	1	1
Groom	5	7	12
Gunsmith	1	-	1
Gunstock Maker	-	1	1
Hackler	1	1	2
Hairdresser	1	1	2
Hair Weaver	-	1	1
Hay Maker	-	1	1
Horse Keeper	-	1	1
Iron Brazier	-	2	2

Bakers in camp

Farriers in camp

Trade	NCOs	Privates	Total
Iron Caster	-	1	1
Iron Turner	-	1	1
Iron Worker	-	2	2
Ironsmith	-	1	1
Jeweller	-	1	1
Joiner	1	2	3
Labourer	26	224	250
Lace Maker	-	2	2
Lath Cleaver	-	1	1
Leather Cutter	-	1	1
Locksmith	-	8	8
Machinist	-	1	1
Mason	1	3	4
Mechanic	-	2	2
Metal Roller	-	2	2
Moulder	-	2	2
Moulder & Fitter	-	1	1
Musician	1	-	1
Nailer	-	1	1
Needle Maker	-	2	2
Oil Cake Maker	-	1	1
Painter	1	9	10
Painter & Glazier	-	1	1
Paper Hanger	-	1	1
Piano Forte Maker	-	1	1
Picture Frame Maker	-	1	1
Piecer	-	1	1
Plasterer	-	4	4
Plumber	1	-	1
Plumber & Safe Fitter	-	1	1
Porter	-	7	7
Potter	1	13	14
Printer	-	3	3
Puddler	1	13	14
Riveter	-	1	1
Sadler	-	2	2
Sawyer	-	3	3
School Master	-	1	1
Screw Maker	-	2	2
Servant	1	3	4
Shoe Maker	-	10	10
Shoe Finisher	-	4	4
Shopman	-	1	1
Silk Dyer	-	1	1
Silver Plater	-	1	1
Slater	-	1	1
Smith	-	6	6
Spinner	-	4	4
Stamper	-	1	1
Steel Roller	-	1	1
Stoker	1	4	5
Striker	-	6	6
Tailor	4	4	8
Tailor & Cutter	-	1	1
Tepinle Maker	-	1	1
Tin Maker	-	1	1
Tin Plate Maker	-	1	1
Tin Plate Worker	-	1	1
Tinner	-	1	1
Tube Drawer	-	1	1
Tube Maker	-	1	1
Turner	-	1	1
Upholsterer	-	1	1
Valet	-	1	1
Weaver	1	7	8
Whip Maker	-	1	1
White Smith	-	1	1
Wire Cleaner	1	-	1
Wire Drawer	-	1	1
Wire Worker	-	1	1
Wood Carver	-	1	1
Wood Sorter	-	1	1
Description 'Trade none'	14	9	23
Totals	**84**	**621**	**705**

Trades not known: NCOs 3 (3.5%)   Privates 21 (3.3%)   TOTAL 24 (3.3%)

YEAR AND MONTH OF ATTESTATION - 80th REGIMENT OF FOOT, 1854-1878

	JAN	FEB	MAR	APR	MAY	JUNE	JULY	AUG	SEPT	OCT	NOV	DEC	TOTAL
1854		1											1
1855													
1856													
1857									1	3			4
1858					1					1			2
1859			1	2	6	8	3		1	1			22
1860		1			1								2
1861													
1862													
1863											1		1
1864													
1865			1		1			1		2			5
1866									1				1
1867	1	5						2	1	1	1		11
1868		1			2	1	2	1			1	2	10
1869	1				1	9	1			1	1	2	16
1870	1				1			13	5	6	11	22	59
1871	17	5	1	2	2			1	4	16	7	9	64
1872	5	13	19	16	21	13				1	2		90
1873				3	4	5	1	6	17	1	1	4	42
1874	12	19	13	14				1	7	6	8	2	82
1875	5				12	16	12	1	4		2	19	71
1876	14	1	1		9	15	11	13	2	4	1		71
1877	1	1	2	10	37	13							64
1878		1				1				1			3
TOTAL	57	47	38	48	98	81	30	39	43	44	35	61	621

Total number of Private Soldiers 642
Attestation information not known 21 (3.58%)

PRIVATES

	JAN	FEB	MAR	APR	MAY	JUNE	JULY	AUG	SEPT	OCT	NOV	DEC	TOTAL
1854		1											1
1855													
1856	1												1
1857										1			1
1858							1						1
1859	1			1	3								5
1860			1										1
1861													
1862													
1863			1			1		1					3
1864					1				2	1			4
1865													
1866									1				1
1867	2												2
1868											1	1	2
1869						1	4		2		1		8
1870	2	1				1		4	1	1		5	15
1871	3	1							4	1	1		10
1872	1		1	1	5						1		9
1873		1						1	1				3
1874	2			1			1						4
1875	1	1					2					1	5
1876	1	1				1	1	2					6
1877			1	1	1								3
1878													
TOTAL	14	6	3	4	11	8	5	9	10	4	4	7	85

Total number of Non - Commissioned Officers 87
Attestation information not known 2 (2.29%)

NON-COMMISSIONED OFFICERS

YEAR AND MONTH OF ATTESTATION - 80th REGIMENT OF FOOT, 1854-1878

	JAN	FEB	MAR	APR	MAY	JUNE	JULY	AUG	SEPT	OCT	NOV	DEC	TOTAL
1854		2											2
1855													
1856	1												1
1857									1	4			5
1858					1		1			1			3
1859	1		1	3	9	8	3		1	1			27
1860		1	1		1								3
1861													
1862													
1863			1			1		1			1		4
1864					1				2	1			4
1865			1		1			1		2			5
1866								1	1				2
1867	3	5						2	1	1		1	13
1868		1			2	1	2	1			2	3	12
1869	1				2	13	1		2	1	2	2	24
1870	3	1			1	1		17	6	7	11	27	74
1871	20	6	1	2	2			1	8	17	8	9	74
1872	6	13	20	17	26	13				1	3		99
1873		1		3	4	5	1	7	18	1	1	4	45
1874	14	19	13	15			1	1	7	6	8	2	86
1875	6	1			12	16	14	1	4		2	20	76
1876	15	2	1		9	16	12	15	2	4	1		77
1877	1	1	2	11	38	14							67
1878				1		1				1			3
TOTAL	71	53	41	52	109	89	35	48	53	48	39	68	706

Total number of Non - Commissioned Officers   87

Total number of Private Soldiers   642   Attestation information not known   23 (3.15%)

Total number of men   729

RANK AND FILE

Departure of reinforcements for South Africa as shown by a contemporary Illustrated London News

The memorial to the Soldiers who died in South Africa 1878-9
Lichfield Cathedral

Epilogue: The Costs of War

The Costs of War

To be involved in a war either as aggressor or defendant, the war effort must be financed. These cost implications can be calculated and the number of casualties of the opposing forces can be measured. The one item which cannot be measured is the human suffering, of both combatants and civilians alike. Only time can tell the long term implications for both the victors and the vanquished.

Human Costs

At the beginning of the war some 17,000 men had been deployed to prepare, support and fight the Zulu Nation. By the end of the war 32,400 men had taken to the field in this 'minor' colonial skirmish. Some paid the ultimate price - killed in action; of the 32,400 Colonial and Imperial forces who fought, 1084 died. Of the natives who fought on the British side, 603 are recorded as dying, although this number is incomplete. The total number of officers, non-commissioned officers and men wounded amount to 242. The returns for natives wounded is 58, but the list is incomplete.

The 80th Regiment of Foot lost 1 officer and 69 non-commissioned officers and men. A total of 7 men from the rank and file were wounded. From the 11th January 1879 to the 15th October 1879, it is recorded that 17 officers and 330 non-commissioned officers and men died of disease, of these 17 men came from the ranks of the 80th Regiment of Foot. During the Zulu campaign a total of 99 Officers and 1286 non-commissioned officers and men were invalided out of the conflict.

Financial costs

At the onset of war against the Zulu Nation it was never envisaged by the military and political leaders of a modern army that it would suffer a major defeat during the early stages of invasion. The Zulu warriors soon proved that they would not be an easy adversary. This minor colonial war suddenly became an embarrassment to the Government at home. Reinforcements were hastily organised and transported to South Africa. The Zulu army on the 4th July 1879 were defeated at Ulundi and the Zulu King Cetchwayo finally captured on 28th August 1879. It is estimated that the cost to the Crown for waging war against the Zulu Nation was in the region of £5,230,323

For the Zulu Nation, the cost of defending its land in lives is estimated as 8,000 Zulu warriors killed and possibly 16,000 wounded. The financial implications are unknown.

Casualties of the 80th Regiment of Foot (Staffordshire Volunteers)

Isandhlwana - 22nd January 1879

Sergeant	1271	Johnson,	William.	Killed in action
Privates	1377	Chesterton,	John.	Killed in action
	1433	Holman,	Edwin.	Killed in action
	559	McDonald,	William.	Killed in action
	675	Seymour,	William.	Killed in action
	2081	Thompson,	Henry.	Killed in action
	9/60	Whitehouse	Joseph.	Killed in action

Intombi River- 12th March 1879

Captain		Moriarty,	David Barry.	Killed in action
Colour Sergeant	459	Fredericks,	Henry.	Killed in action
Lance Sergeant	1627	Sansam,	George.	Killed in action
Corporals	19/544	Johnson,	Ernest.	Killed in action
	19/733	McCoy,	John.	Killed in action
Drummer	1647	Leather,	John.	Killed in action
Privates	546	Adey,	Jonah.	Killed in action
	19/585	Anthony,	John.	Killed in action
	19/202	Banks,	Arthur.	Killed in action
	943	Banner,	John.	Killed in action
	19/745	Broughton,	George.	Killed in action

48	Brown,	James.	Killed in action
19/488	Brownson,	Henry.	Killed in action
1290	Chadwick,	John.	Killed in action
1797	Christie,	James.	Killed in action
19/1042	Day,	Alfred.	Killed in action
19/953	Dodd,	John.	Killed in action
260	Dutton,	John Henry.	Killed in action
1028	Farnell,	William.	Killed in action
222	Findley,	William.	Killed in action
19/176	Flyfield,	William.	Killed in action
1465	Fox,	William.	Killed in action
1925	Furniaux,	John.	Killed in action
19/50O	Gittins,	Edwin.	Killed in action
1697	Green,	Joseph.	Killed in action
19/536	Hadley,	George.	Killed in action
2008	Hart,	Julian.	Killed in action
19/227	Haynes,	George.	Killed in action
19/999	Hawkes,	Eli.	Killed in action
19/783	Healey,	Thomas.	Killed in action
19/1021	Hill,	Henry.	Killed in action
709	Hodges,	Thomas.	Killed in action
1499	Hughes,	John.	Killed in action
902	Ingham,	John.	Killed in action
1919	Jacobs,	Henry.	Killed in action
1865	Lafferty,	John.	Killed in action
19/996	Leese,	Ralph.	Killed in action
19/1931	Lodge,	Henry.	Killed in action
19/1378	McSherry,	Bernard.	Killed in action
19/590	Meadows,	Henry.	Killed in action
2063	Middow,	Arthur.	Killed in action
1976	Mitchell,	George.	Killed in action
2048	Moore,	Robert.	Killed in action
1032	Moran,	William.	Killed in action
1926	Night,	Henry.	Killed in action
220	Phipps,	William.	Killed in action
2085	Pritchard,	Charles.	Killed in action
1163	Pummell,	Arthur.	Killed in action
1974	Ralphs,	Frederick .	Killed in action
19/259	Robinson,	John.	Killed in action
2070	Ruffle,	Henry.	Killed in action
19/615	Sherridan,	Michael.	Killed in action
1770	Silcock,	Joseph.	Killed in action
19/510	Smith,	Henry.	Killed in action
19/587	Tibbott,	Joseph.	Killed in action
1291	Tomlinson,	Richard.	Killed in action
19/1705	Tucker,	George.	Killed in action
19/104	Tucker,	Thomas.	Killed in action
370	Vernon,	James.	Killed in action
19/716	Weaver,	Joseph.	Killed in action
1605	Woodward	Herbert.	Killed in action

Commissariat and transport staff	Conductor Whittington,Joseph.	Killed in action
Army Medical Department	Civil Surgeon Cobbin, William Ingram.	Killed in action

Kambula- 29th March 1879

Lance Sergeant	1387	Brown,	Thomas.	Severely wounded in the head

Ulundi- 4th July 1879

Sergeants	1249	O'Neill,	Thomas.	Severely wounded
	1630	Watts,	James Henry	Killed in action
Corporal	19/636	Beecroft,	Albert.	Severely wounded
Privates	1616	Duffy,	Michael.	Severely wounded
	1892	Floyd,	Joseph.	Killed in action
	1213	Lunt,	William.	Dangerously wounded
	669	Tully,	Patrick.	Dangerously wounded

Sekukuni's Kraal - 28th November 1879

Private	287	Chare,	Calib Edwin.	Slightly wounded

Other Non-commissioned Officers and Men who died in South Africa 1878/79

Sergeants	2104	Tatum,	Charles.	Died at Pretoria	05/03/79
Lance Sergeant	900	Duggan,	Myles.	Died at Mooi River	01/10/79
Lance Corporal	3642	Graham,	Ewen.	Died at Middleburg	04/01/79
Privates	16	Bond,	William.	Died at Lydenburg	29/12/78
	278	Butler,	Frederick.	Died	18/07/79
	1232	Cook,	Thomas.	Died in Transvaal	08/10/79
	1169	Corry,	John.	Died at Whistlestroom	19/09/79
	1900	Dyball,	William.	Died at Lydenburg	29/01/79
	181	Manson,	Alexander.	Died at Utrecht	10/09/79
	964	Morris,	Thomas.	Died	19/11/79
	131	Moss,	John.	Died	23/04/79
	1062	Norton,	John.	Died at Whistlestroom	16/09/79
	1240	Owens,	Richard.	Died	26/10/79
	819	Simpson,	Arthur.	Died	21/07/79
	1063	Smith,	Johnson	Died at Fort Weeber, Transvaal	10/12/79
	657	Smith,	Joseph	Died	14/10/79
	902	Upton,	Henry.	Died	22/11/79

Supplementary List of Officers, Non-commissioned Officers and Men who died 1877-1880

The following list contains the names of soldiers of the 80th Regiment of Foot who died whilst in the service of H.M.Queen Victoria. Where possible the soldier's rank has been indicated including the place and date of death where known. It should be taken that the place of death is in South Africa unless otherwise stated. Where there is a * following a surname, the name is not in any of the preceding medal lists. The names of the men listed below are not on the Memorial Shields in Lichfield Cathedral, but are recorded in the Regimental Digest of the regiment.

Lieutenant Colonel		Twenlow*	George Hamilton.	Died at King William's Town	08/11/77
Major		Rowlands*	Henry	Died at Newcastle	17/11/77
Quartermaster		Belt*	John.	Died at Mooi River	05/08/78
Sergeant	2065	Lawrence,	Robert.	Died (To Army Reserve 4/10/79)	30/10/79
Privates	704	Adams,	Robert.	Died (place not known)	14/02/80
	169	Burgwin,	Thomas.	Died at Sea	10/05/80
	1609	Burtenshaw,	Henry.	Died in South Africa	30/03/80
	1202	Dutton,	Noah.	Died at Sea	17/04/80
	1813	Garvey,	Thomas.	Died at Pinetown	19/12/79
	1777	Hall,	John.	Died in South Africa	07/03/80
	1580	Meachin,	Alfred.	Died at Pietermaritzburg	26/12/78
	486	Rohen,	Peter.	Died at Netley, England	29/03/80
	1423	Ryan,	Joseph.	Died (place and date not known)	
	1245	Tansley,	Jas. Frederick.	Died (place not known)	13/05/80
	423	Varley,	John.	Died at Pietermaritzburg	22/07/80
	1289	Weaver,	John.	Died (place not known)	26/03/80
Ranks not known	509	Burton*,	Thomas.	Died at Pietermaritzburg	28/06/78
	641	Collins*,	Hugh,	Died at Durban	03/04/77
	559	Edwards*,	James.	Died Transvaal	12/10/78
	1274	Gissio*,	Harry.	Died at Pretoria	28/09/78
	150	Hain*,	William.	Died at Pietermaritzburg	19/02/78
	277	Mollast*,	John.	Died (place not known)	01/11/77
	276	Parr*,	Joseph.	Died (place not known)	13/05/79
	1536	Taylor*,	William.	Died at Newcastle	18/08/78
	270	Weatherer*,	James.	Died at Newcastle	25/02/78
	2076	Wiltshire*,	Samuel.	Died at King William's Town	26/05/77

The Regiment's Battle Honour

For their service in South Africa, especially in the Sekukuni and Zulu War Campaigns during 1878 and 1879, the 80th Regiment of Foot (Staffordshire Volunteers) was awarded the Battle Honour, SOUTH AFRICA 1878 - 79

APPENDIX
Members of the 1st Squadron Mounted Infantry

As you have previously read, Private Samuel Wassall's deeds on January 22nd 1879 earned him the Victoria Cross. He was a member of the 1st Squadron Mounted Infantry attached to No.3 Central Column which remained at the camp at Isandhlwana on the morning of January 22nd. The Mounted Infantry at this time were made up of volunteers from various branches of Her Majesty's Imperial Forces in South Africa. The First Squadron, which Samuel was part of, consisted of twenty non-commissioned officers and men. Of those who took part in the battle at Isandhlwana, only those who had a horse had any chance of escape and survival!

80th Regiment of Foot

Sergeant	1271	W. Johnson	Killed in Action
Privates	1377	J. Chesterton	Killed in Action
	1433	E. Holman	Killed in Action
	559	W. McDonald	Killed in Action
	675	W. Seymour	Killed in Action
	919	S. Wassall	
	228	T. Westwood	
	9/60	J. Whitehouse	Killed in Action

6th Dragoon Guards

Private	J. McStravick	Killed in Action

9th Lancers

Farrier	H. Sampson

2nd Battalion 3rd Regiment of Foot

Sergeant	45/149	P. Naughton	
Privates	45/736?	E. Evans	
	45/810	J. Shaw	Killed in Action
	45/389	G.Wheatley	Killed in Action

1st Battalion 24th Regiment of Foot

Privates	194	H. Davis	
	946	E. Turner	Killed in Action
	375?	J. McCann	
	611	W. Parry	
	499?	J. Power	

1st Battalion 13th Light Infantry

Private	1985	D.Whelan

BIBLIOGRAPHY

The sources of literature used as the basis for my research. I hope that others will enjoy as much as I have reading their books. There is no doubt much more to be researched and written about the Zulu War.

Bancroft, J.W. *THE VICTORIA CROSS ROLL OF HONOUR* Aim High Productions, London 1989

Bancroft, J.W. *THE ZULU WAR, 1879 RORKE'S DRIFT* Spellmount Ltd., Speldhurst 1988

Bancroft, J.W. *THE ZULU WAR VCs* J.W. Bancroft, Manchester 1992

Barthorp, M. *THE ZULU WAR A PICTORIAL HISTORY* Blandford Press, Poole 1980

Bennett, I.H.W. *EYEWITNESS IN ZULULAND* Greenhill Books, London 1989

Clammer, D. *THE ZULU WAR* Pan Books, London 1973

Cook, H.C.B. *THE BATTLE HONOURS OF THE BRITISH AND INDIAN ARMIES 1662-1982*
Leo Cooper, London 1987
Droogleever, R.W.F. *THE ROAD TO ISANDHLWANA COLONEL ANTHONY DURNFORD IN NATAL AND ZULULAND* Greenhill Books, London 1992

Duminy, A.H.& Ballard, C.C. *THE ANGLO-ZULU WARS NEW PROSPECTIVES* University of Natal,
Pietermaritzburg S.A. 1981

Edgerton, R.B. *LIKE LIONS THEY FOUGHT THE LAST ZULU WAR* Weidenfeld and Nicholson,
London 1988
Emery, F. *THE RED SOLDIER THE ZULU WAR 1879* Hodder & Stoughton, U.K. 1977 &
Jonathan Ball Paperbacks, Johannesburg S.A. 1983

Forsyth D.R. *SOUTH AFRICAN WAR MEDAL 1877-8-9. THE MEDAL ROLL* D.R. Forsyth.

Furneaux, R. *THE ZULU WAR:ISANDHLWANA & RORKE'S DRIFT* Weidenfeld and Nicholson,
London 1963

Holme, N. *THE SILVER WREATH, BEING THE 24th REGIMENT AT ISANDHLWANA & RORKE'S DRIFT 1879* Samson Books, London 1979

Joslin, E.C. Litherland, A.R. Simkin, B.T. *BRITISH BATTLES & MEDALS* Spink & Son, London 1988

Knight,I. *BRAVE MEN'S BLOOD THE EPIC OF THE ZULU WAR 1879* Greenhill Books, London 1990

Knight, I. *"BY ORDERS OF THE GREAT WHITE QUEEN"* Greenhill Books, London 1992

Knight, I. *NOTHING REMAINS BUT TO FIGHT THE DEFENCE OF RORKE'S DRIFT,* 1879
Greenhill Books, London 1993

Knight, I. *ZULU ISANDLWANA & RORKE'S DRIFT 22-23 JANUARY 1879* Windrow & Greene,
London 1992

Knight, I. Castle, I. *THE ZULU WAR THEN AND NOW* After the Battle, London 1993

Laband, J. *FIGHT US IN THE OPEN* Shuter & Shooter (Pty) Ltd., Piertermaritzburg S.A. 1985 and 1987

Laband, J. *THE BATTLE OF ULUNDI* Shuter & Shooter (Pty) Ltd, Piertermaritzburg S.A. 1988

Laband, J.P.C. & Thompson, P.S *FIELD GUIDE TO THE WAR IN ZULULAND AND THE DEFENCE OF NATAL 1879* University of Natal, Pietermaritzburg S.A. 1987

Mitford, B. *THROUGH THE ZULU COUNTRY ITS BATTLEFIELDS AND PEOPLE*   Kegan Paul,
            Trench & Co 1883   Greenhill Books, London 1992

Morris, D.R. *THE WASHING OF SPEARS*   Abacus, London 1966

Norris-Newman, C.L. *IN ZULULAND WITH THE BRITISH THROUGHOUT THE WAR 1879*
                                        Greenhill Books, London 1988
Percival, J. *FOR VALOUR, THE VICTORIA CROSS COURAGE IN ACTION*
                                        Thomas Methven, London 1985

Roe, F.G.   *THE BRONZE CROSS*   P.R. Gawthorn, London 1945

Smail, J.L. *WITH SHIELD AND ASSEGAI*   Howard Timmins, Cape Town 1969

Smyth, J. Sir. *THE VICTORIA CROSS 1856-1964*   Frederick Muller Ltd. London, 1965

Tavender I.T. *CASUALTY ROLL FOR THE ZULU AND BASUTO WARS SOUTH AFRICA 1877-79*
                                        J.B. Howard & Son., Suffolk 1985

Vale, W.L. *HISTORY OF THE STAFFORDSHIRE REGIMENT*   Golden Polden Ltd, Aldershot 1969

War Office Intelligence Branch *NARRATIVE OF THE FIELD OPERATIONS CONNECTED WITH
            THE ZULU WAR OF 1879* London, 1881   Rep. Greenhill Books, London 1989

Young, J. *THEY FELL LIKE STONES BATTLES & CASUALTIES OF THE ZULU WAR 1879*
                                        Greenhill Books, London 1991

Osprey. Elite Series *BRITISH FORCES IN ZULULAND 1879* Osprey Publishing Ltd., London 1991

Osprey Elite Series *THE ZULUS* Osprey Publishing Ltd., London 1989

Osprey. Men at Arms Series *THE ZULU WAR*   Osprey Publishing Ltd., London 1988

Osprey. Campaign Series *ZULU WAR 1879* Osprey Publishing Ltd., London 1992

This England Books *THE REGISTER OF THE VICTORIA CROSS*   Cheltenham 1981

Zulu Study Group *THERE WILL BE AN AWFUL ROW AT HOME ABOUT THIS* , Victorian Study
        Group 1987 The Zulu War Introduction by - Morris, D.R. Edited by Knight, I.J.

Harris, B *BLACK COUNTRY V.Cs*. The Black Country Society 1985

NEWSPAPERS AND JOURNALS

COBBING KITH & KIN   Issue No. 7 August 1994
LONDON GAZETTE
THE STAFFORD KNOT (THE JOURNAL OF THE STAFFORDSHIRE REGIMENT)   Issue No. 40 April 1979
THE STAFFORD KNOT (THE JOURNAL OF THE STAFFORDSHIRE REGIMENT)   Issue No. 41 October 1979
TAMWORTH HERALD
THE ILLUSTRATED LONDON NEWS
THE NATAL MERCURY

OFFICIAL SOURCES
The Public Records Office. Kew, London.
WO 16   Series, Regimental and Corps Pay Lists
WO 76   Officers Information
W010O/47 Medal Lists